Social movements are a prominent feature of 1 tracted increasing attention from scholars in brings together a set of essays that focus on p< tion structures and strategies, and cultural frai are comparative and include studies of the for Europe, the United States, Italy, the Netherlands, and West Germany. Their authors are leaders in the development of social movement theory and the empirical study of social movements.

Comparative perspectives on social movements

Comparative perspectives on social movements

Political opportunities, mobilizing structures, and cultural framings

Edited by

DOUG McADAM
University of Arizona

JOHN D. McCARTHY
Catholic University of America

MAYER N. ZALD
University of Michigan

 **CAMBRIDGE**
UNIVERSITY PRESS

PUBLISHED BY THE PRESS SYNDICATE OF THE UNIVERSITY OF CAMBRIDGE
The Pitt Building, Trumpington Street, Cambridge CB2 1RP, United Kingdom

CAMBRIDGE UNIVERSITY PRESS
The Edinburgh Building, Cambridge CB2 2RU, United Kingdom
40 West 20th Street, New York, NY 10011-4211, USA
10 Stamford Road, Oakleigh, Melbourne 3166, Australia

First published 1996
Reprinted 1997

Printed in the United States of America

Typeset in Times

Chapter 10, by Kim Voss, includes material published in "Disposition Is Not Action: The
Rise and Demise of the Knights of Labor," *Studies in American Political Development* 6 (Fall
1992); 272–321, and in *The Making of American Exceptionalism: The Knights of Labor and
Class Formation in the Nineteenth Century* (Ithaca, N.Y.: Cornell University Press, 1993).
Used by permission.

Library of Congress Cataloging-in-Publication Data
Comparative perspectives on social movements: political
opportunities, mobilizing structures, and cultural framings / edited
by Doug McAdam, John D. McCarthy, Mayer N. Zald.
p.   cm. – (Cambridge studies in comparative politics)
Includes bibliographical references (p.   ) and index.
ISBN 0-521-48039-6 (hc). – ISBN 0-521-48516-9 (pbk.)
1. Social movements.   2. Comparative government.   I. McAdam,
Doug.   II. McCarthy, John D., 1940–   .   III. Zald, Mayer N.
HN13.C644   1996
303.48′4–dc20   95-8940
                                     CIP

A catalog record for this book is available from the British Library.

ISBN 0-521-48039-6 hardback
ISBN 0-521-48516-9 paperback

Contents

Biographical sketches of contributors

ELISABETH S. CLEMENS is Assistant Professor of Sociology at the University of Arizona. Her primary interests lie at the intersection of political and organizational analysis. She is currently finishing *The People's Lobby: Organizational Innovation and the Rise of Interest Group Politics, 1890–1920*, a study of the consequences of popular mobilization by workers, farmers, and women for state transformation.

DONATELLA DELLA PORTA is Professor of Local Politics at the Faculty of Political Science of the University of Florence. She has carried out research in Italy, France, Spain, the Federal Republic of Germany, and the United States. Her main fields include social movements, political violence, terrorism, political corruption, maladministration, public order, and the police. On these topics she has published extensively in several journals and anthologies in Italy and abroad. Among her books are *Terrorismo e violenza politico* (editor with Gianfranco Pasquino), *I terrorismi in Italia* (editor), *Il terrorismo di sinistra*, *Lo scambio occulto: Casi dio corruzione politica in Italia*, and *Social Movements and Violence*.

WILLIAM A. GAMSON is Professor of Sociology at Boston College and past President of the American Sociological Association. His most recent book, *Talking Politics*, examines how working people think and talk about political issues and the ways in which they make use of media discourse and the larger political culture it reflects. He codirects the Media Research and Action Project at Boston College, a group focused on the media and public education strategies of social change organizations.

SJOERD GOSLINGA works at the Department of Social Psychology of the Free University Amsterdam, the Netherlands. He is involved in a joint research program of the Free University and the CNV Labour Union Federation. The main topics on which he is currently working are union participation and industrial action.

BERT KLANDERMANS is Professor of Applied Social Psychology at the Free University Amsterdam, the Netherlands. His research focuses on mobilization and participation in social movements. He is currently studying the Farmer's Protest in the Netherlands and Spain, and the responses of movement and countermovement supporters to the social and political transitions in South Africa (with Johan Olivier). He is the editor of *Social Movements, Protest and Contention*, a series of books on social movements. His *Social Construction of Protest: Social Psychological Principles of Movement Participation* will soon appear. He is the editor with Craig Jenkins of *The Politics of Social Protest: Comparative Perspectives on States and Social Movements* (1995) and, with Hank Johnston, of *Social Movements and Culture* (1995).

HANSPETER KRIESI is Professor of Political Science at the University of Geneva, Switzerland. He has taught at the Faculty of Political and Social-Cultural Sciences at the University of Amsterdam and at the Sociological Institute of the University of Zurich. He has participated in a number of studies of the mobilization of social movements in Western Europe. He has also studied business interest associations, the participation of Swiss citizens in direct democratic procedures, and the structure and decision-making process of the Swiss political system. His current research interests include comparative analysis of the mobilization of new social movements in Western Europe, right-wing radicalism, and the potential for ecological behavior among Swiss citizens.

DOUG MCADAM is Professor of Sociology at the University of Arizona. He is the author of *Political Process and the Development of Black Insurgency, 1930–1970* (1982) and *Freedom Summer* (1988), as well as many articles on the dynamics of social movements. His current research interests include the role of social movements in demographic change and the globalization of social movement processes.

JOHN D. MCCARTHY is Ordinary Professor of Sociology and a Member of the Life Cycle Research Institute at the Catholic University of America, in Washington, D.C. In recent years he has studied the U.S. movement against drunken driving, and he continues his research projects on protest in Washington, D.C. (with Clark McPhail and Jackie Smith) and local U.S. poor-empowerment community organizations (with Jim Castelli).

DAVID S. MEYER is Assistant Professor of Political Science at the City University Graduate Center and the City College of New York. The author of *A Winter of Discontent: The Nuclear Freeze and American Politics* (1990) and many articles in political science and sociology journals, he is primarily interested in relations among public policy, protest, and institutional politics. His current research interests include cycles of antinuclear protest in American history and movement–countermovement interaction in abortion politics.

ANTHONY OBERSCHALL is Professor of Sociology at the University of North Carolina, Chapel Hill. Throughout his professional career, he has researched and written on social movements and collective action. He is the author of *Social Conflict and Social Movements* (1973) and *Social Movements: Ideologies, Interests, and Identities* (1993).

DIETER RUCHT is Senior Researcher at the Social Science Center, Berlin. He is the author, co-author, or editor of several books on social movements, including *Research on Social Movements: The State of the Art in Western Europe and the USA* (1991) and *Modernisierung und neue soziale Bewegungen: Deutschland, Frankreich und USA im Vergleich* (1994). Currently he is working on a study of protest events during the past four decades in (West) Germany and on a study of local movement infrastructures in Berlin and Leipzig.

SIDNEY TARROW is Maxwell M. Upson Professor of Government at Cornell University. The author and editor of many books on social movements and political parties in Italy and France, he published *Power in Movement: Social Movements, Collective Action, and Politics* (1994) in the Cambridge Studies in Comparative Politics series.

KIM VOSS is Associate Professor of Sociology at the University of California, Berkeley. She is the author of *The Making of American Exceptionalism: The Knights of Labor and Class Formation in the Nineteenth Century* (1993). Her current research compares the framing of defeats by labor activists in England and the United States.

MAYER N. ZALD is Professor of Sociology, Social Work, and Business Administration at the University of Michigan. He has published widely on complex organizations, social welfare, and political sociology. Aside from essays on social movements, he is currently engaged in studies of the intersection of sociology as science and humanities. In 1986–7 he was Vice President of the American Sociological Association. In 1994 he was elected to membership in the American Academy of Arts and Sciences.

ELENA ZDRAVOMYSLOVA is a Senior Research Fellow at the Institute of Sociology (St. Petersburg Branch) of Russia's Academy of Sciences. She is the author of *Paradigms of the Western Sociology of Social Movements* (1993, in Russian), as well as several articles on political movements and political process in contemporary Russia. Her research interests include the role of social movements in political transformation, the formation of political and national identities, and the construction of emergent political symbolism in Russia.

Preface

From the vantage point of 1995, it would be hard to convey to an outsider just how much the study of social movements has changed in the last ten years. Although the field grew apace with the political turbulence of the 1960s and 1970s, European and especially American scholars continued to work in relative ignorance of each other until well into the 1980s. Among the earliest vehicles facilitating contact between movement scholars from different countries were two conferences organized by Bert Klandermans, Hanspeter Kriesi, and Sidney Tarrow and held at Cornell University and the Free University in Amsterdam in the summers of 1985 and 1986, respectively. Stimulated by the contacts established at these two meetings, the cross-national discourse between movement scholars accelerated markedly over the next few years. Between 1986 and 1992 at least five other international gatherings of movement scholars took place. One of the most fruitful of these was held in Berlin in July 1990 under the sponsorship of the research unit on "social movements and the public" of the Wissenschaftszentrum Berlin. Under the direction of Friedhelm Neidhardt, this unit has functioned more generally as one of the central nodes in the rapidly expanding international network of movement scholars.

It was in the spirit of these international gatherings that we decided to organize the conference at which most of the essays included in this volume were first presented as papers. Under the title "Opportunities, Mobilizing Structures, and Framing Processes," the conference took place at the Life Cycle Research Institute at the Catholic University of America in Washington, D.C., in August 1992. Moreover, since that gathering, at least four other international conferences of social movement scholars have taken place, including meetings in Amsterdam and Geneva in the summer of 1995. Finally, the many sessions organized by the Working Group on Collective Behavior and Social Movements at the Thirteenth World Congress of the International Sociological Association held in Bielefeld in July 1994 afforded movement scholars from many countries yet another opportunity to meet and exchange work.

In short, the density of contact between European and American movement scholars is now so great as to make it difficult to speak of distinct American and European perspectives on social movements. The intellectual impact of this cross-fertilization has been dramatic and salutary. Two effects in particular should be noted: First, exposure to different perspectives has undercut the theoretical provincialism characteristic of most earlier work. Second, confronting cases drawn from a number of different national contexts has forced movement scholars to adopt a more comparative view of social movements. Both of these intellectual "gains" are reflected in the pieces included in this volume. To a greater or lesser extent, all of the chapters are comparative in their focus. And all of their authors speak an eclectic theoretical language born of an appreciation for the profusion of useful analytic tools that have developed from the clash of "competing" perspectives over the past ten years or so.

Rarely, in academe, does one have a chance to engage in a thorough and systematic review of empirical work and theory across a broad field of study. Our collaborative work on this volume has given us this opportunity. In particular, our decision to prepare comprehensive surveys introducing each of the three main sections of the volume required that we review the development of theory and research in regard to each of our three main concepts. Having done this, we are convinced that real progress has been made, that knowledge has indeed cumulated in the field. Anyone who doubts this assessment would do well to compare the works in the section on political opportunities – including the introduction – with the early "classic" treatments of the concept (e.g., Eisinger, 1973; McAdam, 1982; Tilly, 1978), which, by contrast, now seem highly preliminary. The same is true when one compares the classic works of Zald and Ash (1966) and McCarthy and Zald (1973, 1977) on social movement organization with the "state-of-the-art" contributions included here in the section on mobilizing structures. Perhaps only in the area of framing processes does current work – as reflected in this volume – seem only slightly more advanced than the earliest works in the area (Melucci, 1985; Snow et al., 1986). Much of this progress we attribute to the synergic effect of the expansion of cross-national discourse among movement scholars.

Still, we should not congratulate ourselves overmuch. The new comparative riches available to movement scholars are based, almost exclusively, on research rooted in core democracies and focused primarily on contemporary movements. Thus, the "international" community of movement scholars is a bit of a misnomer, dominated as it is by American and Western European scholars. If our understanding of collective action dynamics has benefited as much as we contend from comparing cases across this relatively homogeneous set of polities, imagine what we are likely to learn from broadening our perspective to include those set in very different times and places. Two distinct injunctions are implicit in this observation: First, we must seek to broaden the community of movement scholars to include those studying collective action in peripheral and semiperipheral countries and all manner of nondemocratic contexts. The chapter by Elena Zdravomyslova in this volume, comparing the development of two very different movements in Leningrad/St. Petersburg during the "protest cycle of perestroika," speaks to the scholarly riches we can expect should we act on this injunction. Second, as movement scholars, we need to be more faithful to the role of history in shaping the context within which collective action takes place. Although interest in social movements and revolutions has greatly increased among historians and historically oriented social scientists over the past twenty years, the majority of political scientists and sociologists working in the area remain only dimly aware of the relevant historical scholarship. In our view, the field has suffered from this neglect. One need only read the contributions by Elisabeth Clemens and Kim Voss in this volume to appreciate the scholarly riches to be had from combining the methods and perspectives of history with the analytic tools developed by the narrower community of movement scholars reviewed here. The challenge, then, will be to consolidate the theoretical and empirical gains of this community while expanding it to incorporate scholars studying collective action in very different times and places.

Let us close this preface on a more prosaic note by acknowledging the myriad others who have contributed in some way to the production of this volume. Our first thanks go to the authors themselves. The volume is as much theirs as it is ours. Not only were they consistently inspired in their approach to the intellectual "assignments" we gave them; they were remarkably responsible in carrying them out. The typical nightmare associated with edited collections stems from the difficulties inherent in coordinating the activities of multiple authors. In this case, we were blessed to be working with scholars who somehow managed to do the impossible, that is, produce at least three drafts of their papers while conforming closely to the requirements of the demanding production schedule we established. We remain as amazed by this outcome as we are grateful.

The strength of the individual contributions is owed, in part, to the feedback the authors received at the 1992 Catholic University conference at which the pieces were first presented. Thanks are therefore due to all those who took part in the conference. In addition to our authors, they include David Allison, Dan Cress, John Crist, Bob Edwards, Craig Jenkins, Alberto Melucci, Kelly Moore, Friedhelm Neidhardt, Ron Pagnucco, Michele Pinkow, Gretchen Rodkey, Jennifer Sell, Jackie Smith, David Snow, and Suzanne Staggenborg.

The conference, in turn, would not have been possible without the financial support and administrative assistance of a number of people. The Office of International Research of the University of Michigan, the Department of Sociology of the University of Arizona, and the Life Cycle Research Institute at the Catholic University provided small grants to the organizers for planning and carrying out the conference. As well, the Goethe Institut of Washington, D.C., the German Academic Exchange Service, and the Center on Philanthropy of Indiana University provided invaluable financial support. We thank the principals of each of these supporting institutions.

Finally, we could not have organized the conference without the help of the staff at the Life Cycle Research Institute at the Catholic University. Dorothy Kane administered the budget, handled travel and housing arrangements, and kept things running smoothly throughout the conference. In this she was aided by Zita Kelly, who got stuck with the heavy copying assignments but never complained, as well as Martin Scanlan and Daniel McGrath. Words cannot adequately convey the gratitude this dedicated staff earned from us before, during, and after the conference.

In preparing the volume for submission to Cambridge University Press, we benefited enormously from the help of a number of people. Key, in this regard, was Barbara McIntosh, who not only typed several of the chapters but also spent long hours pulling together the integrated bibliography that follows the text. In addition, several articles were subjected to thorough English-language editing in advance of submission. Dan Madaj served as our copy editor at that stage.

Finally, we would be remiss if we failed to express our deep appreciation for the help we have received from all those associated with the project at Cambridge. Our greatest debts of gratitude in this regard go to the series editor, Peter Lange, who first expressed interest in the project, and to our editor at Cambridge, Alex Holzman, who executed his many responsibilities on the project with great skill and efficiency. But we also want to thank Tom Vanderbilt for his editorial assistance on the project, Cynthia Benn for a superb job of copy editing, and the two anonymous reviewers whose early feedback on the individual articles was consistently insightful and helpful by pointing out shortcomings that needed to be redressed in the subsequent revision.

Introduction:
Opportunities, mobilizing structures, and framing processes – toward a synthetic, comparative perspective on social movements

DOUG McADAM, JOHN D. McCARTHY, and MAYER N. ZALD

In a widely read book published in 1960, the sociologist Daniel Bell proclaimed the "end of ideology." As the 1960s dawned, a good many social scientists believed we had reached a stage in the development of society where ideological conflict would gradually be replaced by a more pluralistic, pragmatic consensus. Bell and his colleagues could not have been more mistaken. In the very year Bell's book was published, black students staged sit-in demonstrations throughout the American South. In turn the sit-ins revitalized both a moribund civil rights movement and the tradition of leftist activism dormant in America since the 1930s. During the ensuing decade the country was rent by urban riots, massive antiwar demonstrations, student strikes, and political assassinations. On a global level, student movements proliferated: in France, Mexico, Italy, Germany, Spain, Japan, Pakistan, and numerous other countries. In Czechoslovakia, an effort to reform and "humanize the face of communism" was brutally suppressed by Soviet forces.

In short, the 1960s witnessed a proliferation in the very kinds of social movements and revolutions that Bell had assumed were a thing of the past. The last twenty-five years have only served to underscore the poverty of Bell's argument. If anything, social movements and revolutions have, in recent decades, emerged as a common – if not always welcome – feature of the political landscape. In the 1970s Islamic fundamentalists wrest power from the Shah of Iran. The Sandinistas depose Somoza in Nicaragua. Terrorist groups in Germany and Italy step up their attacks on military installations, politicians, and symbols of "corporate hegemony."

The 1980s were witness to more of the same. In the Philippines, the 1984 assassination of Ferdinand Marcos's longtime political rival, Benigno Aquino, sparks a popular revolt that sweeps Marcos from office. In the United States, growing fear of the nuclear threat catalyzes a nationwide Nuclear Freeze campaign. In South Africa a revitalized antiapartheid movement forces the release of its longtime leader, Nelson Mandela. The decade comes to a stunning and improbable end as, one after another, the Warsaw Pact regimes collapse under the pressure of popular revolts.

Set in motion by the turbulence of the 1960s and fueled by the myriad movements of the last quarter century, the study of social movements and revolutions has clearly emerged as one of the scholarly "growth industries" in the social sciences, in both Europe and the United States. Working from a variety of perspectives, sociologists, political scientists, and historians have produced over the past twenty years a wealth of theoretical and empirical scholarship on social movements/revolutions. It is time to take stock of this mushrooming literature. Within this profusion of work we think it is possible to discern the clear outlines of a synthetic, comparative perspective on social movements that transcends the limits of any single theoretical approach to the topic. This book rests on that perspective, even as it seeks to extend and apply it comparatively.

THE EMERGING SYNTHESIS

Increasingly one finds movement scholars from various countries and nominally representing different theoretical traditions emphasizing the importance of the same three broad sets of factors in analyzing the emergence and development of social movements/revolutions. These three factors are (1) the structure of political opportunities and constraints confronting the movement; (2) the forms of organization (informal as well as formal), available to insurgents; and (3) the collective processes of interpretation, attribution, and social construction that mediate between opportunity and action. Or perhaps it will be easier to refer to these three factors by the conventional shorthand designations of *political opportunities, mobilizing structures,* and *framing processes.*

The emerging consensus among movement scholars regarding the importance of these three factors belies the very different and oftentimes antagonistic perspectives in which they developed. We begin by discussing each factor separately, with an eye to acknowledging the divergent intellectual streams that have influenced work on each.

Political opportunities

While it is now common for movement scholars to assert the importance of the broader political system in structuring the opportunities for collective action and the extent and form of same, the theoretical influences underpinning the insight are actually fairly recent. In the United States it was the work of such *political process* theorists as Charles Tilly (1978), Doug McAdam (1982), and Sidney Tarrow (1983) that firmly established the link between institutionalized politics and social movements/revolutions. Drawing on these works, a number of European (or European trained) scholars schooled in the *new social movements* tradition brought a comparative dimension to the study of *political opportunity structures.* Among the Europeans who have explored the links between institutionalized and movement politics are Hanspeter Kriesi (1989), Herbert Kitschelt (1986), Ruud Koopmans (1992), and Jan Duyvendak (1992).

Though the work of all of these scholars betrays a common focus on the interaction of movement and institutionalized politics, this shared focus has nonetheless been motivated by a desire to answer two different research questions. Most of the early work by American scholars sought to explain the *emergence* of a particular social movement on the basis of *changes in the institutional structure or informal power relations of a given national political system.* More recently, European scholars have sought to account for *cross-national differences in the structure, extent, and success of comparable movements* on the basis of *differences in the political characteristics of the nation states in which they are embedded.* The first approach has tended to produce detailed historical case studies of single movements or protest cycles (i.e., McAdam, 1982; Costain, 1992; Tarrow, 1989a), while the second has inspired more cross-national research based on contemporaneous descriptions of the same movement in a number of different national contexts (i.e., Kriesi et al., 1992; Joppke, 1991; Ferree, 1987). In both cases, however, the researcher is guided by the same underlying conviction: that social movements and revolutions are shaped by the broader set of political constraints and opportunities unique to the national context in which they are embedded.

Mobilizing structures

If institutionalized political systems shape the prospects for collective action and the forms movements take, their influence is not independent of the various kinds of *mobilizing structures* through which groups seek to organize. By mobilizing structures we mean *those collective vehicles, informal as well as formal, through which people mobilize and engage in collective action.* This focus on the meso-level groups, organizations, and informal networks that comprise the collective building blocks of social movements and revolutions constitutes the second conceptual element in our synthesis of recent work in the field.

As was the case with the work on political opportunities, the recent spate of research and theorizing on the organizational dynamics of collective action has drawn its inspiration largely from two distinct theoretical perspectives. The most important of these has been resource mobilization theory. As formulated by its initial proponents (McCarthy and Zald, 1973, 1977), resource mobilization sought to break with grievance-based conceptions of social movements and to focus instead on *mobilization processes* and the formal organizational manifestations of these processes. For McCarthy and Zald social movements, while perhaps not synonymous with formal organizations, were nonetheless known by and became a force for social change primarily through the social movement organizations (SMOs) they spawned. In some ways, theirs was less a theory about the emergence or development of social movements than it was an attempt to describe and map a new social movement form – professional social movements – that they saw as increasingly dominant in contemporary America.

The second theoretical tradition to encourage work on the organizational dynamics of collective action has been the political process model. Indeed, one of the characteristics by which scholars in this tradition are known is their common dissent from the resource mobilization equation of social movements with formal organization. Charles Tilly and various of his colleagues (1975, 1978) laid the theoretical foundation for this second approach by documenting the critical role of various grassroots settings – work and neighborhood, in particular – in facilitating and structuring collective action. Drawing on Tilly's work, other scholars sought to apply his insights to more contemporary movements. For example, Aldon Morris (1981, 1984) and Doug McAdam (1982) analyzed the critical role played by local black institutions – principally churches and colleges – in the emergence of the American civil rights movement. Similarly, Sara Evans's (1980) research clearly located the origins of the women's liberation movement within informal friendship networks which were forged by women who were active in the civil rights movement and in the American New Left. Even the more recent tradition of network studies of movement recruitment (Gould, 1991; Kriesi, 1988; McAdam, 1986; McAdam and Paulsen, 1993; Snow, Zurcher, and Ekland-Olson, 1980) would seem to betray an underlying theoretical affinity with the political process model's emphasis on informal, grassroots mobilizing structures.

While some proponents of these approaches initially treated the two models of movement organization as mutually exclusive, over time the profusion of empirical work inspired by both has led to a growing awareness among movement scholars of the diversity of collective settings in which movements develop and organizational forms to which they give rise. So instead of debating the relative merits of these "opposing" characterizations, movement scholars have increasingly turned their attention to other research agendas concerning the organizational dynamics of social movements. Among the more interesting of these agendas are (1) comparison of the "organizational infrastructures" of countries both to understand historic patterns of mobilization better and to predict where future movements are likely to arise, (2) specification of the relationship between organizational form and type of movement, and (3) assessment of the effect of both state structures and national "organizational cultures" on the form that movements take in a given country.

Framing processes

If the combination of political opportunities and mobilizing structures affords groups a certain structural potential for action, they remain, in the absence of one other factor, insufficient to account for collective action. Mediating between opportunity, organization, and action are the shared meanings and definitions that people bring to their situation. At a minimum people need to feel both aggrieved about some aspect of their lives and optimistic that, acting collectively, they can redress the problem. Lacking either one or both of these perceptions, it is highly unlikely that people will mobilize even when afforded the opportunity to do so. Conditioning the presence or absence of these perceptions is that complex of social psychological dynamics – collective attribution, social construction – that David Snow and various of his colleagues (Snow et al., 1986; Snow and Benford, 1988) have referred to as *framing processes*. Indeed, not only did Snow coin, or more accurately, modify and apply Erving Goffman's term, to the study of social movements, but in doing so helped to crystallize and articulate a growing discontent among movement scholars over how little significance proponents of the resource mobilization perspective attached to ideas and sentiments. In reasserting their importance, Snow and his colleagues drew not only on Goffman's work, but ironically on the collective behavior tradition which resource mobilization had sought to supplant as the dominant paradigm in the field. Within that older tradition, both Smelser (1962) and Turner and Killian (1987) had assigned to ideas a prominent place in their respective theories.

But Snow was not alone in asserting the importance of the more cognitive, or ideational dimensions of collective action. Two other streams of recent work have also called for further attention to the role of ideas or culture more generally in the emergence and development of social movements and revolutions. For many of the new social movement scholars it was the centrality of their cultural elements that marked the new social movements as discontinuous with the past. Small wonder then that the work of many of the most influential new social movements theorists focused primarily on the sources and functions of meaning and identity within social movements (Brand, 1985a, 1982; Inglehart, 1979, 1977; Melucci, 1988, 1985, 1980; Touraine, 1981).

The final theoretical perspective to emphasize the importance of shared and socially constructed ideas in collective action was the political process model. Though best known for their stress on the political structuring of social movements/revolutions, such theorists as Gamson (1992a), Tarrow (1989a, 1983), and Tilly (1978) also acknowledged the critical catalytic effect of new ideas as a spur to collective action. McAdam's (1982) discussion of the necessity for "cognitive liberation" as a prerequisite for mobilization is only the most explicit acknowledgment of the importance of ideas within the political process tradition.

For all the convergence in these various theoretical perspectives little systematic work on framing processes (or the cultural dimensions of social movements) has yet been produced. To this point, the literature is long on ringing programmatic statements regarding the necessity for "bringing culture back in," but short on the kind of cumulative scholarship that we now have on the role of political opportunities or mobilizing structures in the emergence and development of movements. In part this lacunae may be a consequence of the ephemeral, amorphous nature of the subject matter. Studying political systems and various kinds of organization is inherently easier than trying to observe the social construction and dissemination of new ideas.

But it may also be that a lack of conceptual precision in defining what we mean by "framing processes" has handicapped efforts to study this important aspect of collective action. Though Snow and his colleagues meant something quite specific by their use of the term, recent writings have tended to equate the concept with any and all cultural dimensions of social movements. This usage threatens to rob the concept of its coherence and therefore its theoretical utility. In this volume we want to return to David Snow's original conception and define framing rather narrowly as referring to the *conscious strategic efforts by groups of people to fashion shared understandings of the world and of themselves that legitimate and motivate collective action.*

In undertaking this volume, we were guided by four aims. First, we wanted to abstract from the voluminous literature on social movements those three concepts that have emerged as the central analytic foci of most scholarship in the area. Second, by taking their theoretical measure we hoped to refine and sharpen our understanding of each of these concepts. We take up this second goal in the essays with which we introduce each of the book's three parts. Each essay focuses on one of the three concepts, sketching our current understanding of it, the limits of that conceptualization, and the modifications or conceptual refinements that might redress the limitations.

That leaves the third and fourth goals alluded to earlier. The third goal is to advance our understanding of the dynamic *relations* among opportunities, mobilizing structures, and framing processes. Whereas most scholarship has focused on one or another of these factors, we use this volume to sketch a broader analytic framework on social movements/revolutions that combines the insights gained from the study of all three factors. Finally, we wanted to explore the comparative uses of this emerging framework by discussing the concepts of political opportunities, mobilizing structures, and framing processes in cross-national perspective. In commissioning the chapters for this volume we sought to directly address these final two goals. Each author was asked to focus on the relationship between any two of our three concepts and, wherever possible, to do so in a way that furthered the comparative understanding of movement dynamics. But we would be remiss if we relied on the contributors alone to advance the final two goals of the volume. Accordingly, in the remaining two sections of this introductory essay, we will take up each of these topics in turn. We begin with some thoughts on the dynamic relationships among our three concepts.

LINKING OPPORTUNITIES, MOBILIZING STRUCTURES, AND FRAMING PROCESSES

Scholars have tended to study only one aspect of a movement – for example, the effect of expanding political opportunities or the organizational dynamics of collective action. The challenge, of course, is to sketch the relationships between these factors, thus yielding a fuller understanding of social movement dynamics.

The problem is there exist many relationships between our three factors. Which ones become relevant depends upon the research question of interest. We emphasize two such questions here. The first concerns the origins of social movements and revolutions; the second, the extent and form of the movement over time. In each case we are interested in understanding the factors and processes that shape the movement: its emergence on the one hand, and it ongoing development on the other.

The question of movement emergence

Understanding the mix of factors that give rise to a movement is the oldest, and arguably the most important, question in the field. Moreover, virtually all "theories" in the field are, first and foremost, theories of movement emergence. That includes the various perspectives touched on earlier. Proponents of collective behavior see strain, variably conceived, and the shared ideas it gives rise to, as the root cause of social movements. Though there is great diversity among those working in the new social movements tradition, most proponents of the perspective betray adherence to at least a broadly similar account of the movement emergence. That account highlights the role of the distinctive material and ideological contradictions in postmaterial society in helping to mobilize new political constituencies around either nonmaterial or previously private issues. Resource-mobilization theorists focus on the critical role of resources and formal organization in the rise of movements. The political process model stresses the crucial importance of expanding political opportunities as the ultimate spur to collective action.

In our view all of these theories have something to recommend them. Our starting point, however, reflects the underlying assumption of the political process model. We share with proponents of that perspective the conviction that most political movements and revolutions are set in motion by social changes that render the established political order more vulnerable or receptive to challenge. But these "political opportunities" are but a necessary prerequisite to action. In the absence of sufficient organization – whether formal or informal – such opportunities are not likely to be seized. Finally, mediating between the structural requirements of opportunity and organization are the emergent meanings and definitions – or frames – shared by the adherents of the burgeoning movement. As both collective behavior and new social movements theorists have long argued, the impetus to action is as much a cultural construction as it is a function of structural vulnerability.

Having stressed the significance of all three of our factors, it is important to add that their effects are interactive rather than independent. No matter how momentous a change appears in retrospect, it only becomes an "opportunity" when defined as such by a *group* of actors sufficiently well organized to act on this shared definition of the situation. Implicit in this description of the beginnings of collective action are two critically important interactive relationships. The first concerns the relationship between framing processes and the kinds of "objective" political changes thought to facilitate movement emergence. The point is, such changes encourage mobilization not only through the "objective" effects they have on power relations, but by setting in motion framing processes that further undermine the legitimacy of the system or its perceived mutability. So, it is pointless to ask whether Gorbachev's reforms encouraged the revolutions in Eastern Europe by changing the political structure of the former Warsaw Pact countries or by heightening people's subjective awareness of the system's illegitimacy and vulnerability. Clearly they had both effects. Gorbachev's stated unwillingness to intervene militarily in defense of the Warsaw Pact countries encouraged collective action both by objectively weakening the social control forces available to those regimes and by heightening public perception of their illegitimacy and vulnerability. Expanding political opportunities, then, derive their causal force from the interaction of those structural and perceptual changes they set in motion.

A similar reciprocal dynamic defines the relationship between organization and framing processes. Framing processes clearly encourage mobilization, as people seek to organize and act on their growing awareness of the system's illegitimacy and vulnerability. At the same time, the potential for the kind of system critical framing processes we have described here, is, we believe, conditioned by the population's access to various mobilizing structures. As Murray Edelman (1971: 32) has written, the perceptual roots of collective action are bound up with the "cuings among groups of people who jointly create the meanings they will read into current and anticipated events."

For us, the key phrase in the preceding sentence is "groups of people."

That is, framing processes are held to be both more likely and of far greater consequence under conditions of strong rather than weak organization. The latter point should be intuitively apparent. Even in the unlikely event that system-critical framings were to emerge in the context of little or no organization, the absence of any real mobilizing structure would almost surely prevent their spread to the minimum number of people required to afford a basis for collective action. More to the point, however, is the suspicion that lacking organization these framings would never emerge in the first place.

This suspicion rests, in part, on the supposition that what Ross (1977) calls the "fundamental attribution error" – that is, the tendency of people to explain their situation as a function of individual deficiencies rather than features of the system – is more likely to occur under conditions of social isolation rather than organization. Lacking the information and perspective that others afford, isolated individuals would seem especially likely to explain their troubles on the basis of personal rather than system attributions. Only "system attributions" afford the necessary rationale for movement activity. For movement analysts, then, the key question becomes, What social circumstances are productive of system critical framing processes and the system attributions they yield? Following Ferree and Miller (1977: 34) the answer would appear to be: "among homogenous people who are in intense regular contact with each other." Their description speaks to the essence of what we have called mobilizing structures.

Besides defining the broad parameters of a model of movement emergence, our three factors can also be used to shed light on a second question concerning the beginnings of collective action. This is the critically important, yet woefully neglected, question of movement form. That is, under what conditions can we expect a given type of movement (e.g., grassroots reform movement, public interest lobby, revolution) to emerge? The important implication of the question is that the various types of movements are simply different forms of collective action rather than qualitatively different phenomena requiring distinct explanatory theories. This is most germane to the study of revolutions, a form of collective action that has, in recent years, come to be studied as a phenomenon distinct from other categories of movements. We demur. Rather than assuming difference, we need to treat movement type as a variable and seek to account for variation in type on the basis of particular combinations of opportunities, mobilizing structures, and collective action frames.

Space constraints and the complexity of the issue do not permit a full-blown theory of movement type, but we can at least sketch our preliminary thinking on the topic and, in the process, illustrate the utility of our basic perspective for addressing this important question. Not surprisingly, we start by again stressing the central importance of political opportunities to an understanding of movement dynamics.

In our introduction to the "political opportunities" part of this volume, we take up an issue that has begun to be addressed by scholars in the political process and new social movements traditions. Concerned that the concept of political opportunities lacks conceptual precision, scholars such as Hanspeter Kriesi (1991) and Sidney Tarrow (1994: chap. 8) have sought to identify those specific dimensions of political systems that impact the structuring of collective action. We applaud these efforts and in the introduction to Part I offer our own schema for differentiating the relevant dimensions of "political opportunity structures." We leave the details of that scheme till then. For our present purposes, however, we need to at least list these dimensions. They are as follows:

1. The relative openness or closure of the institutionalized political system
2. The stability of that broad set of elite alignments that typically undergird a polity
3. The presence of elite allies
4. The state's capacity and propensity for repression

So, for example, scholars seeking to explain the emergence of collective action would be advised to analyze the ways in which *changes* in one (or more) of these dimensions rendered the political system more receptive or vulnerable to challenge by insurgent groups. But, apropos of our present discussion, it may be that the *form,* as much as the *timing,* of collective action is structured by the available political opportunity. That is, a change in any of the four dimensions may encourage mobilization, but the form the mobilization takes is very likely to be affected by the kind of opportunity presented.

In Chapter 5 of this volume, Elena Zdravomyslova provides two examples that nicely illustrate the argument, contrasting two movement groups that developed in Leningrad/St. Petersburg in the wake of Gorbachev's reforms. The first, the Democratic Union, was founded in 1988, largely in response to the Gorbachev-inspired thaw in public discourse and the attendant *relaxation of social control* by state authorities. In turn, in its form and practices, the Democratic Union clearly bore the imprint of these specific changes or opportunities. The group was oriented, almost exclusively, to disruptive public demonstrations aimed at exploiting and extending the state's more tolerant policy on public gatherings and political demonstrations.

In contrast, the second group Zdravomyslova analyzes, the Leningrad People's Front, emerged following passage of the Electoral Law of 1988. That law mandated popular elections to be held the following year, thus granting insurgents *new electoral access.* Consistent with the nature and "location" of the opportunity granted, the Leningrad People's Front mounted a broad-based *electoral campaign.*

In short, insurgents can be expected to mobilize in response to and in a manner consistent with the very specific changes that grant them more leverage. In the case of Zdravomyslova's two groups, insurgents were oriented to a relaxation in social control and the granting of electoral access respectively. But the same argument holds for the other two dimensions of political opportunities as well. The routine electoral transfer of institutional power from one group of incumbents to another can be expected to encourage the creation (or reactivation) of reform movements who interpret the transfer of power as granting them new elite allies. So, just as movements on the Left mobilized in the United States during the Kennedy and Johnson administrations, so too did the Reagan/Bush years see a marked increase in protest activity on the Right.

Finally, the broadest reform and revolutionary movements would seem to owe, not to the routine circulation of stable elite blocs but to those momentous, if rare, cleavages in previously stable governing alliances. So, the American civil rights movement recognized and successfully exploited the growing rift between two important partners in the New Deal Coalition: Southern Dixiecrats and Northern "labor liberals." As regards revolutions, virtually every major theorist of the form has stressed the critical importance of elite cleavages as a central impetus to mobilization (Goldstone, 1991; Skocpol, 1979).

The important implication in all this is that in both their timing and form social movements bear the imprint of the specific opportunities that give them life. But what was true of timing is no less the case with form; that mobilizing structures and framing processes mediate the effects of political opportunities. Once again, the American civil rights movement affords a nice example of these processes. The breadth and scope of the movement owed, first and foremost, to the significance of the political realignments and elite divisions that presaged it. At the same time, nothing about the type or "location" of this opportunity can account for the specific organizational form or ideological content of the movement. To understand that one must look to the particular mobilizing structures within which the movement emerged and to the framing processes that characterized the movement at the outset. Clearly these two factors are related. In the case of the civil rights movement, initial mobilization centered largely in the black church (McAdam, 1982; Morris, 1984). Given the church's institutional centrality in the early days of the struggle, it is hardly surprising that the initial "framings" coming out of the movement had a distinctly religious cast to them. On the contrary, the influence of this particular mobilizing structure was evident in any number of specific organizational features of the movement, from reliance on the mass meeting as a mobilizing device, to the disproportionate number of ministers in the ranks of early movement leaders.

Thus, type of opportunity may dictate the broad category of movement, but the formal and ideological properties of the movement are apt to be more directly influenced by the organizational forms and ideological templates available to insurgents. And these, in turn, are largely a product of the mobilizing structures in which insurgents are embedded on the eve of the movement.

The question of movement development and outcomes

Having used our three factors to analyze the timing and form of movement emergence, we turn our attention to the later stages of collective action. What can a perspective stressing the role of opportunities, mobilizing structures, and framing processes tell us about the dynamics of movement development? A great deal, we think. Indeed, we see a lot of continuity between the processes shaping movement emergence and those influencing the ongoing development and eventual decline of collective action. The similarities and differences between these two phases of collective action should become clearer as we discuss each of the three factors.

Political opportunities. Little needs to be added to our earlier discussion of this factor. Suffice it to say, the broad political environment in which the movement is embedded will continue to constitute a powerful set of constraints/opportunities affecting the latter's development. So, for example, cross-national differences in the more stable, institutional features of political systems should have significant effects on the trajectories of particular movements. For instance, the stark contrast between the American winner-take-all electoral system and West Germany's partially proportional system of representation probably accounts for the very different developmental histories of the American and West German environmental movements. While the restrictive structure of electoral politics in the United States foreclosed that as a viable developmental option for American environmentalists, the opposite was true in West Germany. Though no less "radical" than their American counterparts, the West German Greens found the ease of electoral access too alluring to pass up. As a consequence the West German – and now, German – environmental movement has long had a more electoral or institutional character than its American counterpart.

Besides helping to account for cross-national differences in the development of comparable movements, a focus on *changes* in the structure of political opportunities can contribute to our understanding of the shifting fortunes of a single movement. In accounting for the decline of the American civil rights movement one would want to mention a number of factors. But among the most important would have to be the redemocratization of voting rights in the South, the development of significant Republican strength in the region, and Nixon's recognition and exploitation of this development in his successful 1968 presidential campaign. The success of Nixon's "Southern strategy" in 1968 dealt a serious blow to the black struggle, by forcefully demonstrating the irrelevance of the "black vote" to Republican Party fortunes, thereby granting the movement little leverage over Nixon or any of his Republican successors.

So the structure of political opportunities, as defined by both the enduring and volatile features of a given political system, can be expected to continue to play a major role in shaping the ongoing fortunes of the movement. What is different from the emergent phase is the fact that, after the onset of protest activity, the broader set of environmental opportunities and constraints are no longer independent of the actions of movement groups. The structure of political opportunities is now more a product of the interaction of the movement with its environment than a simple reflection of changes occurring elsewhere. Thus to understand fully the impact of the environment on the developing movement we will need to look much more closely at the movement itself and specifically those of its features which appear to account for much of its capacity to reshape the broader political landscape.

The organizational structure of the movement

The relevant organizational question in regard to movement emergence is whether insurgents have available to them "mobilizing structures" of sufficient strength to get the movement off the ground. However, once collective action is underway, the nature of the organizational challenge confronting the movement changes significantly. It is no longer the simple availability of mobilizing structures, but the organizational profile of those groups purporting to represent the movement that becomes important. The nature of these groups is apt to change a great deal as well. While movements often develop within established institutions or informal associational networks, it is rare that they remain embedded in these *nonmovement* settings. For the movement to survive, insurgents must be able to create a more enduring organizational structure to sustain collective action. Efforts to do so usually entail the creation of the kinds of formal social movement organizations (SMOs) stressed as important by resource-mobilization theorists. Following the emergent phase of the movement, then, it is these SMOs and their efforts to shape the broader political environment which influence the overall pace and outcome of the struggle. In turn, the empirical literature would seem to suggest that the success or failure of these efforts owes primarily to some combination of three organizational factors.

Disruptive tactics. Notwithstanding the pluralist's claim that political effectiveness depends on tactical restraint and respect for "proper channels," there is increasing empirical evidence to the contrary. McAdam (1983b) found that the pace and effectiveness of civil rights protest was largely a function of the movement's ability to devise innovative and disruptive tactics that temporarily broke the stalemate between civil rights forces and their segregationist opponents. Lacking sufficient power to defeat Southern segregationists in a local confrontation, insurgents sought, through use of new and provocative tactics – the sit-ins, freedom rides, the Freedom Summer project – to induce their opponents to disrupt public order to the point where supportive federal intervention was required.

In his study of fifty-four "challenging groups," William Gamson (1990) reports evidence consistent with the single case study cited above. Gamson finds that groups which used "force and violence" against their opponents tended to be "more successful" than groups that did not. These findings are not so counterintuitive as one might think. The successful use of "proper channels" would seem to depend upon control over precisely the kinds of conventional political resources – money, votes, influence with prominent others – that movement groups tend to lack. Lacking such resources, movements may have little choice but to use their ability to disrupt public order as a negative inducement to bargaining.

Finally, in his seminal synthesis of recent movement scholarship, Tarrow (1994) argues persuasively that it is disruption or the threat of same that grants to movements their improbable effectiveness as vehicles of social change.

"Radical flank effects." Besides the narrow function of disruptive tactics, movements would, in general, appear to benefit from the presence of a "radical" wing. Or, more precisely, movements that boast a number of groups spanning a wide tactical spectrum seem to benefit from what has come to be known as the "radical flank effect" (Barkan, 1979; Haines, 1988). The term is used to describe one effect that often follows from the presence of "extremist" groups within the same movement with other more "moderate" SMOs. As Haines (1988) shows in his analysis of changes in the funding of the major civil rights organizations, such a situation is likely to redound to the benefit of the moderate SMOs. In effect, the presence of extremists encourages funding support for the moderates as a way of undercutting the influence of the radicals.

A similar dynamic may also characterize relations between the state and the movement. In the modern era, the demands of most movements are ultimately adjudicated by representatives of the state. To respond to a movement, state actors must focus on those movement leaders and organizations that seem to speak for the movement and yet who are perceived to be reliable negotiating partners. In such a situation, the presence of groups deemed extremist can actually help legitimate and strengthen the bargaining hand of more moderate SMOs. Ironically, pressure from the extremists may simultaneously push the moderates to adopt more radical positions themselves. The end result is often state support for legislative or policy changes once deemed far too radical, by both moderates and the state alike.

Goals. In their efforts to interact successfully with the broader political and organizational environment, SMOs rely heavily on their goals. That is, the reactions of other major parties to the conflict – the state, countermovement, the media, and so on – are shaped to a considerable degree by the group's stated goals. Encoded in those goals are perceived threats to the interests of some groups and opportunities for the realization of others. Thus, the mix of opposition and support enjoyed by a given SMO is conditioned by the perception of threat and opportunity embodied in the group's goals. Given this dynamic, another finding from Gamson's study of "challenging groups" makes intuitive sense. He found that groups whose goals required the "displacement" of their opponents were much less likely to be successful than those whose objectives were "non-displacing" (Gamson, 1990: 41–44).

We close our discussion of the effect of goals on movement development by noting one additional finding from Gamson's study. Besides the substance of group goals, Gamson also looked at the sheer number of objectives pursued. Specifically, he distinguished groups based on their pursuit of "single" versus "multiple" goals. At first blush, there might appear to be a virtue in the second approach, promising as it does to draw more people into the movement based on its diverse set of goals. Then too a single-issue organization that succeeds in achieving its goal faces extinction. Not so with a group pursuing many goals.

On reflection, however, it seems clear that there are a number of dangers with the multiple-goal strategy as well. The pursuit of a number of goals promises to spread thin the already precious resources and energy of the SMO. Just as dangerous is the impetus to internal dissension and factionalism that may accompany the pursuit of multiple goals. Who gets to decide which goals will be accorded top priority and what resources will be expended for which purposes? If a group settles on a single goal, it immediately eliminates potentially divisive issues such as these. Consistent with this latter view, Gamson finds single-issue groups to be successful more often than those addressing multiple goals (Gamson, 1990: 44–46).

Our point in surveying the literature on these three factors was not to get us bogged down in the empirical details of movement studies. Rather it was to underscore the central point of our discussion of movement development: *Movements may largely be born of environmental opportunities, but their fate is heavily shaped by their own actions.* Specifically, it is the formal organizations who purport to speak for the movement, who increasingly dictate the course, content, and outcomes of the struggle. In terms of our three factors, this means that both political opportunities and framing processes are more the product of organizational dynamics than they were during the emergent phase of the movement. We have already said a good bit about the role of political opportunities in the later stages of collective action. We close this discussion, then, with a few words about framing processes and their increasing "organizational" character following the emergence of the movement.

Framing processes

As with political opportunities, framing processes remain just as important to the fate of the ongoing movement as they were in shaping the emergence of collective action. Movements are no less dependent on the shared understandings of their adherents during the later stages of insurgency than they were early on. The difference is that, in the mature movement, framing processes are far more likely (1) to be shaped by conscious, strategic decisions on the part of SMOs, and (2) to be the subject of intense contestation between collective actors representing the movement, the state, and any existing countermovements. We take up each of these issues in turn.

Framing is no less a collective process during the early days of the movement than it is later on. But the collective settings within which framing takes place and the nature of the framing process are apt to be very different at the two points in time. We can expect the initial framing processes to be less consciously strategic than later efforts. In fact, at the outset, participants may not even be fully aware that they are engaged in an interpretive process of any real significance. This is certainly not the case later on as various factions and figures within the movement struggle endlessly to determine the most compelling and effective way to bring the movement's "message" to the "people."

In the absence of such a strong strategic self-consciousness, the initial framing process also has a more emergent, inchoate quality to it than do later framing efforts. Accordingly, the outcome of the process is less predictable than it is later on, when insurgents are typically acting to reaffirm or, at most, extend an existing ideological consensus. That is, later framing efforts tend to be heavily constrained by the ideas, collective identities, and worldviews adopted previously (Moore, 1993).

Finally, and most important, later framing processes tend, far more than the earlier efforts, to be the exclusive "property" of formal SMOs. Established organizations or institutions may serve as the *settings* within which initial framings get fashioned, but typically they are not produced by the recognized leadership as a part of normal organizational procedures. This tends to change during the later periods of movement development. So just as the structure of political opportunities comes, in part, to be responsive to SMO actions, so do later framing efforts come to be the product of formal organizational processes.

Besides these changes in the *internal* character of movement framing processes, the broader *environmental* context in which framing takes place differs dramatically between the early and later stages of collective action. While the political establishment is apt to be either unaware or amused and unconcerned by initial framing efforts, their reaction is expected to change if and when the movement is able to establish itself as a serious force for social change. Assuming this happens, later framing efforts can be expected to devolve into intense "framing contests" between actors representing the movement, the state, and any countermovements that may have developed. To complicate matters further, these contests will not be waged directly but, rather, will be filtered through various news media. Thus the outcome of later framing efforts will turn, not only on the substantive merits of the competing frames, but on the independence, procedures, and sympathies of the media.

To summarize, then, we see the central analytic focus of movement research shifting over the life of the movement. While environmental opportunities would seem to play the critical determinant role during the emergent phase of collective action, thereafter the movement itself comes to occupy center stage. Specifically, the extent, character, and outcomes of collective action are expected to turn, in large part, on the interaction of the movement – or, more precisely, the SMOs that purport to speak for it – with other organized parties parties to the conflict.

USING THE PERSPECTIVE COMPARATIVELY

Unlike earlier theoretical approaches to the study of social movements, the perspective outlined has emerged out of a sustained dialogue between scholars working in a wide variety of national contexts. As a result the perspective has always had an implicit comparative focus. However, we aim to make this implicit focus more explicit. To do so we will again take up each of our three central concepts, suggesting how each can be used to illuminate cross-national differences and similarities in movement dynamics.

Political opportunities

As was noted earlier, most research on political opportunities has sought to show how *changes* in some aspect of a political system created new possibilities for collective action by a given challenger or set of challengers (Costain, 1992; McAdam, 1982; Tarrow, 1989a). Thus, the concept has typically been employed in case study fashion to help explain the emergence of a particular movement or "cycle of protest." Recently, however, the concept has informed a very different, and explicitly comparative, research agenda. Instead of focusing on the role of expanding political opportunities in facilitating the emergence of a single movement, scholars have begun to compare movements cross-nationally, seeking to explain variation in their size, form of organization, and degree of success by reference to cross-national differences in the formal structures of political power.

So, for example, Myra Marx Ferree (1987) has sought to understand the different character and form of the West German and U.S. women's movements, in part, by reference to differences in institutionalized politics in the two countries. Likewise, in his comparative account of the emergence and development of the U.S. and West German antinuclear movements, Christian Joppke (1991) has attributed many of the key differences between the two movements to the very different national political contexts in which they have developed. Dieter Rucht (1990) also studied the antinuclear movement, but broadened his list of cases to include France as well as the United States and West Germany. But in doing so he again accounts for variations in "the courses, strategies, organizations, action repertoires, and outcomes of these struggles" on the basis of an interpretive scheme "which focuses on [differences in] . . . political opportunity structures." Finally, in the most ambitious research effort to date regarding the relationship between national political context and the extent and nature of collective action, Hanspeter Kriesi and several of his colleagues (Kriesi et al., 1991, 1995) have studied the rise and subsequent development of new social movements in France, Switzerland, Germany, and the Netherlands.

Mobilizing structures

A similar comparative turn can be discerned in recent work by movement scholars on the origins and effects of various mobilizing structures. Dieter Rucht, in Chapter 8 of this book, represents a prime example of this trend. Rucht seeks to describe and explain the different "social movement structures" exhibited by the so-called new social movements in France, Germany, and the United States. In an earlier article, John McCarthy (1987) compared rates of institutional affiliation cross-nationally to help explain the very different loci, form, and character of collective action in different countries. He sought, for example, to account for the religious roots and character of many American movements on the basis of significantly higher rates of church affiliation in the United States than in comparable Western democracies. Finally, Kim Voss is currently studying the historical fate of early labor movements in the United States and England to determine whether differences in their organizational forms might help to account for the demise of the American Knights of Labor and the ultimate success of its English counterparts. (See Chapter 10.)

The variety of these efforts suggests the rich potential for comparative work in this area. Taking only the three examples touched on here, researchers have sought to understand cross-national variation in (1) the likely institutional locations of mobilization, (2) the role of the political system in structuring the organizational profile of the movement, and (3) the effect of the organizational structure in facilitating or constraining movement survival.

Framing processes

Reflecting the recency of the framing concept and the somewhat underdeveloped nature of theory in this area, it is perhaps not surprising that our third concept has yet to yield much in the way of comparative research. We are convinced, however, that the potential for such research is as great with this concept as with the other two.

In the essay introducing the section on framing processes, we seek to refine our conceptual understanding of the concept by distinguishing between five related, but clearly distinct, topics. These are (1) the *cultural tool kits* (Swidler, 1986) available to would-be insurgents; (2) the *strategic framing efforts* of movement groups; (3) the *frame contests* between the movement and other collective actors – principally the state, and countermovement groups; (4) the *structure and role of the media* in mediating such contests; and (5) the *cultural impact* of the movement in modifying the available tool kit.

Besides sharpening our understanding of the basic framing concept, the preceding list is useful for the clear comparative lines of research it suggests. Indeed, all five topics lend themselves easily to cross-national research on framing dynamics. For example, as regards the first topic, one could imagine a comparative mapping of ideas and attitudes similar to McCarthy's (1987) cross-national work on "institutional affiliations." That is, instead of comparing countries in terms of their "infrastructural deficits and assets," one could seek to discern which ideational themes were especially resonant in which national contexts.

Our second topic suggests a narrower research agenda focusing on the similarities and differences in the framing strategies employed by movement groups in specified countries. Or by seeking to include as objects of study the framing efforts of the state and countermovement groups as well as the movement the researcher could well expand the empirical focus to address our third topic as well. Indeed, an ongoing collaborative research project by German and U.S. scholars is currently attempting to do just that for the American and German pro- and antiabortion movements. In a preliminary report of that research (see Gamson et al., 1993), project members seek to sketch the major "frame packages" advanced by proponents and opponents of abortion in the two countries.

Our fourth topic, the role of the media in shaping public and policymaker perception of the movement, would make for an interesting and important comparative study. To better understand the role of the media in movement dynamics one could study cross-national variation in media characteristics – for example, degree of autonomy from the state, operating procedures, editorial orientation, and so forth – and seek to link these differences to variation in movement outcomes. For example, impressionistically, at least, the failure of the Perot campaign in the 1992 presidential campaign and the success of

Berlusconi in the 1994 Italian elections would seem to stem from significant differences in the media's ability to expose crucial policy weaknesses on the part of the two candidates. In turn, this difference in outcomes would seem to owe much to variation in several key characteristics – independence and editorial orientation in particular – of the media in the two countries.

Finally, one could also make our fifth topic the object of systematic comparative research. The goal would be to assess the extent to which a given movement has managed, in a number of countries, to reshape the terms of public discourse. So, for example, one could imagine a comparative study of "the feminization of public discourse," designed to gauge the ideational impact of the women's movement in all Western industrial democracies. Or to take a much debated historical case, one could seek to determine whether "American exceptionalism" in its relative lack of class consciousness was as much the effect as the cause of a weak labor movement. That is, by assessing the shifting ideational content of public discourse throughout the West one might be able to determine whether America was always "exceptional" in its antagonism to labor, or whether class movements in other countries were more successful in encoding labor's interests into public discourse.

CONCLUSION

Reflecting the ambitious aims of this book, we have covered a lot of ground in this introductory essay. Specifically, we have tried to do four things here. First, we sought to sketch a broad analytic perspective on social movements that we see as having emerged among movement scholars over the past decade or so. This perspective stresses the determinant and interactive effects of *political opportunities, mobilizing structures,* and *framing processes* on movement dynamics. Second, we tried to identify the various intellectual influences that have contributed to our understanding of each of these three concepts. Third, we sought to infuse the perspective with a sense of dynamism by addressing two questions of long-standing interest to movement scholars and identifying the *relationships* between our three factors that we see as especially critical in shaping (1) the emergence or (2) the development or decline of collective action. Finally, we sketched what we see as the inherent comparative nature and empirical promise of the perspective.

It should be obvious how seriously we take the comparative agenda. Much of the richness of the perspective sketched here is owed to the cross-national discourse that informs it. This book is an attempt not only to synthesize the fruits of that discourse but to encourage and contribute to it as well. For only by abandoning the limits of the nationally specific case study approach to the study of social movements can we ever hope to advance our understanding of collective action.

PART I

POLITICAL OPPORTUNITIES

1

Conceptual origins, current problems, future directions

DOUG McADAM

Writing in 1970, Michael Lipsky (1970: 14) urged political analysts to direct their attention

> away from system characterizations presumably true for all times and all places. . . . We are accustomed to describing communist political systems as "experiencing a thaw" or "going through a process of retrenchment." Should it not at least be an open question as to whether the American political system experiences such stages and fluctuations? Similarly, is it not sensible to assume that the system will be more or less open to specific groups at different times and at different places?

Clearly Lipsky felt the answer to both questions was yes. He assumed that the ebb and flow of protest activity was a function of changes that left the broader political system more vulnerable or receptive to the demands of particular groups. Three years later Peter Eisinger (1973: 11) used the term "structure of political opportunities" to help account for variation in "riot behavior" in forty-three American cities. Consistent with Lipsky's view, Eisinger (1973: 25) found that "the incidence of protest is . . . related to the nature of a city's political opportunity structure," which he defined as "the degree to which groups are likely to be able to gain access to power and to manipulate the political system."

Within ten years the key premise informing the work of Lipsky and Eisinger had been appropriated as the central tenet in a new "political process" model of social movements. Proponents of the model (e.g., Jenkins and Perrow, 1977; McAdam, 1982; Tarrow, 1983; Tilly, 1978) saw the timing and fate of movements as largely dependent upon the opportunities afforded insurgents by the shifting institutional structure and ideological disposition of those in power.

Since then this central assumption and the concept of "political opportunities" has become a staple in social movement inquiry. The emergence and development of instances of collective action as diverse as the American women's movement (Costain, 1992), liberation theology (Smith, 1991), peas-

My thanks to Sidney Tarrow for his insightful comments on a draft of this chapter.

ant mobilization in Central America (Brockett, 1991), the nuclear freeze movement (Meyer, 1993a), and the Italian protest cycle (Tarrow, 1989a), have been attributed to the expansion and contraction of political opportunities. Most contemporary theories of revolution start from much the same premise, arguing that revolutions owe less to the efforts of insurgents than to the work of systemic crises which render the existing regime weak and vulnerable to challenge from virtually any quarter (i.e., Arjomand, 1988; Goldstone, 1991; Skocpol, 1979). Finally, this stress on institutionalized politics has spawned a comparative tradition among European political scientists in which variation in the "political opportunity structure" of various national states has been used to explain the fate of similar movements in a number of countries (i.e., Kriesi et al., 1992, 1995; Kitschelt, 1986; Rucht, 1990).

The concept of political opportunities has thus proven to be a welcome addition to the analytic arsenal of movement scholars. But the widespread adoption and general seductiveness of the concept carries with it its own set of dangers. As Gamson and Meyer note in their contribution to this volume (Chapter 12): "The concept of political opportunity structure is in trouble, in danger of becoming a sponge that soaks up virtually every aspect of the social movement environment – political institutions and culture, crises of various sorts, political alliances, and policy shifts. . . . Used to explain so much, it may ultimately explain nothing at all."

Mindful of the very real danger to which Gamson and Meyer refer, I hope to use this introductory essay to bring greater analytic clarity to the concept by addressing three issues that have tended to muddy the conceptual waters. These issues concern (1) "political" versus other kinds of "opportunities," (2) the dimensions that compose the "political opportunity structure," and (3) the very different dependent variables to which the concept has been applied.

Having addressed the key sources of variation in the use of the concept, I will briefly touch upon three topics that have gone largely unexamined in the work on political opportunities. These topics represent both conceptual holes in the field and exciting frontiers for future research and theory on the links between institutionalized politics and social movements. I will conclude by highlighting the ways in which the chapters in this part embody some of the more interesting directions for future research and theory on the topic of political opportunities.

THREE ISSUES IN THE STUDY OF POLITICAL OPPORTUNITIES

As with most general concepts, consensus regarding the term "political opportunity" has proven elusive. Scholars have defined or interpreted the term differently, applied it to a variety of empirical phenomena, and used it to address an equally wide range of questions in the study of social movements. This lack of consensus is clearly a problem. To the extent that the concept is defined or used in very different ways, it threatens to be of little use to anyone. In this section I want to address what I see as three key sources of variation in the present use of the term. In doing so I will also argue for those delimitations of the concept that I think are most defensible. In this way, I hope to aid the effort to achieve greater consensus among movement scholars in their understanding and use of the concept.

Differentiating political opportunities from other facilitative conditions

The earliest formulations of the concept were, without exception, quite vague. Any environmental factor that facilitated movement activity was apt to be conceptualized as a political opportunity. This conceptual plasticity has continued to afflict work in this area, threatening to rob the concept of much of its analytic power. In the words of Gamson and Meyer, the term "political opportunity" "threatens to become an all-encompassing fudge factor for all the conditions and circumstances that form the context for collective action."

Ironically, despite their articulate caution, Gamson and Meyer could well be accused of contributing to the very problem they seek to remedy. In their contribution to this book they note that "opportunity has a strong cultural component and we miss something important when we limit our attention to variance in political institutions and the relationships among political actors." Gamson and Meyer are, of course, right. One can certainly think of ways in which cultural factors or processes create opportunities for movement activity. Nor are they alone in making such an argument. Karl-Werner Brand (1990b) has sought to link the ebb and flow of movement activity in the industrialized West to cyclical shifts in the "cultural climate." Elsewhere (1994) I have identified four general types of "expanding cultural opportunities" that appear to increase the likelihood of movement activity. These four are (1) the dramatization of a glaring contradiction between a highly salient cultural value and conventional social practices, (2) "suddenly imposed grievances," (3) dramatizations of a system's vulnerability or illegitimacy, (4) the availability of an innovative "master frame" within which subsequent challengers can map their own grievances and demands.

For their part Gamson and Meyer emphasize the critical importance of the framing of political opportunity and the important role played by the media in structuring this process. Again, there is no question that they are right to stress the importance of these processes to a full understanding of movement dynamics. But, in doing so, they blur an important analytic distinction. The kinds of structural changes and power shifts that are most defensibly conceived of as *political* opportunities should not be confused with the collective processes by which these changes are interpreted and framed. While the two are closely related, they are not the same. To treat them as separate not only preserves the definitional integrity of political opportunities, but also allows us to discern two profoundly interesting empirical phenomena: those cases in which clearly favorable political shifts do *not* yield the kinds of empowering interpretations so necessary to collective action and those in which collective action develops in the absence of any significant change in the relative power position of the challenging group(s).

Another example of the confounding of political opportunities with other kinds of facilitating conditions concerns early efforts to incorporate the concept into the classic resource-mobilization perspective. Advocates of this approach argued that political opportunities were simply one of many resources whose availability generally keyed the emergence and development of social movements. This conceptualization of resources was problematic for the same reason an overly inclusive definition of political opportunities is dangerous. Defining resources as anything that facilitates mobilization robs the concept of its analytic bite. Better to define resources *and* political opportunities narrowly to determine their relative contribution to the emergence and fate of social movements.

And so I would argue more generally. We need to recognize that a number of factors and processes facilitate mobilization and resolve to try to define and operationalize them so as to maintain their analytic distinctiveness. Only by doing so can we ever hope to determine their relative importance to the emergence and development of collective action.

Specifying the dimensions of political opportunity

Even restricting ourselves to narrowly political factors, movement analysts have demonstrated a wide latitude in interpreting the concept. As Tarrow noted in 1988 (p. 430): "political opportunity may be discerned along so many directions and in so many ways that it is less a variable than a cluster of variables – some more readily observable than others."

In an effort to bring more analytic clarity to the concept, various authors have, of late, sought to specify what they see as the relevant dimensions of a given system's "structure of political opportunities." Among those who have offered such schema are Charles Brockett (1991), Kriesi et al. (1992), Dieter Rucht (Chapter 8 in this volume), and Sidney Tarrow (1994). A listing of the dimensions specified by each of these authors is reported in Table 1.1. Ignoring terminological differences, one can see that there is actually a fair amount of overlap in these four lists. Basically, all four authors have sought to distinguish the formal institutional or legal structure of a given political system from the more informal structure of power relations that characterize the system at a given point in time. The first item listed by all four authors con-

Table 1.1. *Various authors' conceptions of the dimensions of political opportunity*

Brockett[a]	Kriesi et al.[b]	Rucht	Tarrow[c]
meaningful access points	formal institutional structure	access to the party system	openness or closure of the polity
presence of allies	informal procedures in relation to a given challenge	the state's policy implementation capacity	stability of political alignments
elite fragmentation and conflict	the configuration of power as regards a given challenger	the alliance structure as regards a given challenger	presence/absence of elite allies
level of repression		the conflict structure as regards a given challenger	divisions within the elite
temporal location in cycle of protest			

[a]See Brockett, 1991: 254.
[b]See Kriesi et al., 1992: 220.
[c]See Tarrow, 1994.

cerns the former dimension, while items 2–3 for Brockett, 2–4 for Tarrow, 3–4 for Rucht, and 2–3 for Kriesi address the latter. Synthesizing across these four approaches yields the following highly consensual list of dimensions of political opportunity:

1. The relative openness or closure of the institutionalized political system
2. The stability or instability of that broad set of elite alignments that typically undergird a polity
3. The presence or absence of elite allies
4. The state's capacity and propensity for repression

The first dimension merely emphasizes the importance attributed to the formal legal and institutional structure of a given polity by all of the authors. Similarly, items 2 and 3 speak to the significance attached, by all authors, to the informal structure of power relations characteristic of a given system. The only difference between my formulation and some of the others centers on my effort to distinguish that enduring set of elite alliances (i.e., labor and the Democrats in the American context) that tend to structure political systems over time from the more ephemeral presence or absence of elite allies.

Included in the latter category would be routine administrative transfers – Laabour replacing Conservatives in England, for example – that grant greater or lesser entree to all manner of challenging groups.

The only nonconsensual dimension I have incorporated into my list is state repression. Other than Brockett, none of the other authors include this in their schema. I find this omission puzzling. There is considerable empirical evidence attesting to the significance of this factor in shaping the level and nature of movement activity. Some observers (e.g., della Porta, 1995) have speculated that state repression is really more an *expression* of the general receptivity or vulnerability of the political opportunity structure, rather than an independent dimension of the same. I am not convinced that this is the case. To view systems of repression as merely expressive of other features of a polity or as mere tools of specific political interests is to blind us to the unpredictable nature of repression and the complex social processes that structure its operation. Anyone who doubts this point would do well to reflect for a moment on the fate of the 1989 Chinese student movement. On many key dimensions of political opportunity the movement appears – even in retrospect – to have been in reasonably good shape. While the system remained formally closed to the students, they clearly were able to mobilize a number of key elite allies – most notably, the state-controlled media – during the conflict. Moreover, there were clear divisions among the ruling elite that granted an unprecedented opportunity to the students. Nonetheless, Communist Party hard-liners were still able to mobilize the social control capacity and political will necessary to thoroughly repress the movement. The fact that in seemingly similar situations (e.g., Iran in 1979) the ruling elite was not able to do what the Chinese hard-liners did suggests the merit of considering state repression as a separate, though clearly related, dimension of the structure of political opportunity.

Finally, let me offer a few comments about the two dimensions that I left off of my list. The first was Brockett's inclusion of "temporal location in the cycle of protest" as one of his five dimensions of political opportunity. I certainly concur with Brockett's judgment regarding the importance of this factor. Indeed, the relationship between political opportunities and cycles of protest is one of the three neglected topics I intend to take up at the close of this essay. However, as consequential as this factor may be in shaping the timing and fate of a movement, I fail to see what makes this a form of *political* opportunity, as opposed to a more general temporal facilitator of (or constraint on) movement activity. For this reason, I have omitted it from my list.

The second omission involved Rucht's inclusion of a system's "policy implementation capacity," which he defines as "the power of authorities to implement adopted policies, regardless of internal or external resistance." This factor bears a strong family resemblance to Kitschelt's (1986) stress on the critical importance of "the capacity of the political system to effectively meet demands." I omitted this dimension for the same reason that Brockett did in his conceptualization of political opportunity. This factor, wrote Brockett (1991: 254), "is often one of the decisive determinants of outcomes. . . . However, the determinants of outcomes of political conflict often differ from those of collective action; therefore the position taken here is that it is more useful not to conflate and confuse the two discussions."

Brockett's point is an important one. The dimensions of political opportunity vary depending on the question one is seeking to answer. This brings us to the third critical source of variation: the uses to which scholars have put the concept of political opportunity.

Specifying the relevant dependent variable

The concept of political opportunity structure has been used as a key explanatory variable in regard to two principal dependent variables: the timing of collective action and the outcomes of movement activity. Ostensibly the earliest use of the concept was in regard to the first of these questions. Seeking to understand the emergence of particular movements, proponents of the political process model sought to link the initial development of insurgency to an "expansion in political opportunities" beneficial to the challenging group (Costain, 1992; McAdam, 1982). Ironically, however, Eisinger's (1973) initial use of the concept was motivated by a desire to explain variation in riot intensity across a large sample of American cities. Thus, the recent spate of comparative works analyzing strength of movement activity across a number of national polities (e.g., Kitschelt, 1986; Kriesi et al., 1992; Rucht, 1990) is really more in keeping with Eisinger's initial use of the concept that the nominally "older" tradition of single case studies of movement emergence.

Nor is it clear that these two independent variables exhaust the range of movement phenomena that are profitably viewed as owing to the effects of political opportunities. As we suggested in the introduction to this volume, *movement form* would appear to be yet another variable that owes, in part, to differences in the nature of the opportunities that set movements in motion. If we array movements along a continuum from the narrowest of institutionalized reform efforts on the one pole to revolutions on the other, we can, I think, discern a general relationship between type or form of movement and changes in the dimensions of political opportunity specified above. Changes in the legal or institutional structure that grant more formal political access to challenging groups are apt to set in motion the narrowest and most institutionalized of reform movements. By narrow I am referring primarily to the tactics one can expect such movements to employ. To the extent that the movement has mobilized in response to specific changes in access rules, we can expect it to act primarily to exploit that new crack in the system. So, for example, Ross Perot's independent candidacy in the 1992 U.S. presidential election sought to take advantage of newly liberalized procedures and guidelines structuring the mobilization and operation of third-party campaigns.

The emergence of new allies within a previously unresponsive political system is again likely to be linked to the rise of a narrow and generally institutionalized reform movement. Most of the movements that fit the imagery of the classic resource-mobilization perspective would seem to be of this type. So the anti–drunk-driving movement, with its single-issue focus and stress on institutionalized tactics, was born of the sponsorship of the National Highway Transportation Safety Agency and other allies in the Reagan administration. Similarly, the Nixon administration helped initiate the U.S. environmental movement through its active sponsorship of the first Earth Day in 1970. And although radical environmental groups such as Earth First continue to receive a disproportionate amount of media attention, the movement as a whole continues to adhere to the generally institutionalized reform approach embodied in such "industry leaders" as Sierra Club and the Nature Conservancy.

As we move to the more radical or even revolutionary end of the movement continuum, the other two dimensions of political opportunity come increasingly into play. A significant decrease in either the will or ability to repress tends to be related to the rise of noninstitutionalized protest movements, of the sort exemplified by the chronologically first of the two movements described by Elena Zdravomyslova in Chapter 5 of this volume. The group, the Democratic Union, was founded in Leningrad/St. Petersburg in 1988, largely in response to the Gorbachev-inspired thaw in public discourse and the attendant relaxation of social control by state authorities. Note, however, that this decline in repression did not grant dissidents greater *institutionalized* access to the system. The movement thus remained amorphously radical in its aims and *noninstitutionalized* in its means.

Finally, as virtually all major theorists of revolutions have argued, the development of significant divisions among previously stable political elites is among the key precipitants of this very special and consequential form of collective action (Goldstone, 1991; Skocpol, 1979). It should be noted that the rise of broad-based political reform movements such as the American civil rights movement (McAdam, 1982) have also been attributed, in part, to the collapse of enduring elite alignments. The point is that the simple distinction between reform and revolution becomes blurred at this point. The distinction only makes sense in retrospect. Revolutions, by definition, are associated with generalized system transformations; broad reform movements are not. In other words, the distinction owes less to internal differences between the movements and more to the relative strength or weakness of the systems they seek to challenge. In their internal form most revolutions and radical reform movements look the same. They espouse a wide range of goals and use a mix of institutionalized and noninstitutionalized strategies to pursue them.

The point of this section is not to sketch a full-blown theory of the link between political opportunity and movement form, but simply to call attention to the fact that there are a variety of phenomena that movement analysts can and have sought to explain by reference to the concept of political opportunity structure. While this attests to the potential richness of the concept, it also should serve as a caution. If we are to avoid the dangers of conceptual confusion, it is critical that we be explicit about *which dependent variable* we are seeking to explain and *which dimensions* of *political* opportunity are germane to that explanation.

DIRECTIONS FOR FUTURE RESEARCH

For all the interesting work that has been done to date, there remain many new and exciting avenues of research and theory to explore in regard to the concept of political opportunities. Space constraints preclude providing anything close to a comprehensive accounting of these scholarly possibilities. Instead, I have simply identified three topics related to the concept that I think are intriguing and have yet to be studied in any serious way by movement scholars. These three topics should convey a sense of the range and diversity of possible new directions in the study of political opportunities.

Protest cycles and political opportunities

While I earlier took issue with Brockett's (1991: 254) inclusion of a movement's "temporal location in the cycle of protest" as a separate dimension of political opportunity, I nonetheless think he is right to emphasize the importance of this variable as a critical factor differentiating the developmental trajectories of movements. There is good reason to believe that the movements which help set a cycle in motion are subject to very different developmental dynamics than those which arise later in the cycle. "The first category consists of those rare, but exceedingly important, *initiator movements* that signal or otherwise set in motion an identifiable protest cycle. . . . The second and more 'populous' category of movements include those *spin-off movements* that, in varying degrees, draw their impetus and inspiration from the original initiator movement" (McAdam, 1995).

What does all of this have to do with the concept of political opportunities? In my view, everything. The appearance of a highly visible initiator movement significantly changes the dynamics of emergence for all subsequent movements. This becomes clear when we seek to account for the rise of spin-off movements on the basis of the three explanatory factors emphasized in this book. While mobilizing structures and framing processes would seem to be important in the case of all movements, "expanding political opportunities" may be less relevant to the rise of many spin-off movements. By expanding political opportunities I mean changes in either the institutional features, informal political alignments, or repressive capacity of a given political system that significantly reduce the power disparity between a given challenging group and the state. Given this definition, one would be hard pressed to document a significant expansion in political opportunities in the case of all – or even most – spin-off movements. There is one general exception to this statement. This concerns the extraordinary expansion in opportunities that accompanies *any* revolutionary cycle. In the case of revolutions, the old regime is so crippled by initiator movements – or what Tarrow (1994) calls "early risers" – as to leave it vulnerable to challenge by all manner of "latecomers."

In the case of reform cycles, however, there is no necessary increase in system vulnerability as regards all subsequent spin-off movements. Take the case of the American reform cycle of the 1960s. Much as those on the Left came to believe that the American state was on the verge of collapse in the late 1960s, a cursory look at various measures of fiscal and political stability would seem to support the opposite conclusion. The state remained strong throughout the period and generally invulnerable to most of the movements that proliferated in those years.

The gay rights movement affords a good case in point. The so-called Stonewall riot of July 1969 is typically credited with giving birth to the movement. The riot developed when patrons of the Stonewall, a gay bar in Greenwich Village, fought back following a police raid on the premises. The movement developed quickly from that point, spawning a number of gay rights groups, but by the late 1970s, it had waned as an organized phenomenon.

It is difficult to account for the rise of this movement on the basis of expanding political opportunities. One would be hard pressed to identify any specific change in the institutional features of the system that suddenly advantaged gays. Nor would it appear as if the movement benefited from any major political alignments during this era. In fact, the movement was preceded by a highly significant electoral realignment that can only be seen as disadvantageous to gays. I am referring, of course, to Richard Nixon's ascension to the White House in 1968, marking the end of a long period of liberal Democratic dominance in presidential politics. If anything, then, it would appear as if the movement arose in a context of *contracting* political opportunities.

In general, there would seem to be a certain illogic to the argument that a protest cycle improves the bargaining leverage of *all* organized contenders. On the contrary, the demands of the initiator and other early riser movements would seem to preclude much leverage for the latecomers. Certainly the history of the American protest cycle of the 1960s can be interpreted in this way, with the civil rights and other early riser movements – principally the student, antiwar, and women's movements – garnering the lion's share of attention and significant victories and the latecomers – gay rights, the American Indian movement, and so forth – never really able to generate the public attention as leverage necessary for success. I cannot be certain that my interpretation is correct. But it is at least consistent with a more general suspicion that not all spin-off movements are necessarily advantaged by their embedding in a larger reform cycle. Specifically, I think there is good reason to suspect that those movements which arise fairly late in a reform protest cycle are disadvantaged by the necessity of having to confront a state that is already preoccupied with the substantive demands and political pressures generated by the early risers.

Finally, in arguing against the idea that protest cycles invariably render the affected political system vulnerable to challenge by *all* participating movements, I have steered clear of that special category of spin-off movements for whom the opportunities argument is clearly untenable. Here I have in mind those spin-off movements that develop in countries other than that of the initiator movement. The point is, despite our descriptive language (e.g., "the Italian protest cycle of the 1960s and 70s"), protest cycles do not necessarily conform to neat national boundaries. The generalized political turbulence that marked much of Western Europe in 1847–48 is an obvious and instructive case in point. Most of the scholarly attention granted these years has been lavished on France and the Paris revolt of February 1848. But as Tarrow (1994) notes, "no less French a historian than Halevy would assert that 'the revolution of 1848 did not arise from the Parisian barricades but from the Swiss civil war.'" Preliminary findings from an ongoing study of the links between the American and German student New Left of the 1960s supports a similar conclusion. The rise of the German student movement would appear to owe as much to events in the United States as to substantive political shifts within Germany (McAdam and Rucht, 1993).

The important theoretical implication of all this is that by focusing the lion's share of empirical attention on highly visible initiator movements such as the American civil rights movement (McAdam, 1982) and the American women's movement (Costain, 1992), we may have exaggerated the role of political opportunities in the *emergence* of collective action. To better understand the role of political opportunities in movement emergence we need to look at the developmental dynamics of latecomers as well as early risers. My own suspicion is that spin-off movements owe less to expanding political opportunities than to complex diffusion processes by which the ideational, tactical, and organizational lessons of the early risers are made available to subsequent challengers. But only through systematic empirical work will we be able to test this impressionistic hunch.

The international context of political opportunities

As with so many aspects of political life, extant work on political opportunities has tended to betray a state-centered or closed-polity bias. That is, movement scholars have conceived of the structure of political opportunities almost exclusively in terms of domestic political institutions and processes. What is missed in this conceptualization is the critical role of international trends and events in shaping domestic institutions and alignments. In short, movement scholars have, to date, grossly undervalued the impact of *global* political and economic processes in structuring the *domestic* possibilities for successful collective action. Fortunately, there are signs that this neglect may be waning.

Potentially the most important work in this vein is the research of Azza Salama Layton (1995) on the international political pressures that so profoundly expanded the domestic political opportunities of the American civil rights movement. In her dissertation, Layton documents in exhaustive and convincing fashion the critically important role of emerging Cold War pressures in undermining the political calculus and alignments on which America's racial politics had been structured prior to World War II. By effectively terminating the isolationist foreign policy that had long defined America's relation with the rest of the world, World War II exposed federal officials – especially in the Executive Branch – to international political pressures and considerations that their predecessors had been spared. With the United States locked in an intense ideological struggle with the Soviet Union for influence among the emerging Third World nations, American racism took on international significance as an effective propaganda weapon of the Soviets. Motivated by a desire to defuse this weapon, a succession of Cold War presidents – principally Truman, Eisenhower, and Kennedy – were moved to embrace civil rights policies unimaginable prior to the war. Similarly, officials in the State and Justice departments were prodded into action as never before. In the postwar years it became common for officials from either or both agencies to appear before congressional committees or to file legal briefs in connection with Supreme Court cases pressing for changes in federal civil rights policy. Translated into the language of political opportunities, these and many other actions documented by Layton granted civil rights forces new "elite allies," and new "legal/institutional openings," while simultaneously undermining the enduring set of "elite alignments" on which the segregationist status quo had previously been structured.[1]

Nor is Layton alone in pursuing this line of inquiry. In his analysis of the emergence in the mid-1970s of the broad-based protest movement against a Taiwanese state dominated by aging, mainland Chinese, Wang (1989) also grants considerable importance to shifting international conditions. Specifically, Wang argues that President Nixon's historic visit to China in 1969 and the eventual integration of the People's Republic into the international community seriously undermined the ideological and institutional basis of mainland Chinese rule in Taiwan. Rooted in claims that they were the true voice of the Chinese people and heirs to an imminent return to mainland authority, the aging Taiwanese elite were hard pressed to retain their dominance in the face of shifting international realities. The effect of these shifts was to grant the burgeoning protest movement new elite allies, both domestically and internationally, and to create new institutional openings as segments of Taiwanese society began successfully to challenge the legal basis of the mainland Chinese dominance of domestic politics.

Other examples of movements set in motion or otherwise critically affected by the decisive effect of international pressures or events come to mind readily. The rise and ultimate triumph of the Sandinistas in Nicaragua would certainly seem to owe, in part, to a significant decline in the repressive capacity of the previous regime under Anastacio Somoza. In turn, this decline was occasioned by the sudden withdrawal of U.S. military and other foreign aid to the Somoza regime under the terms of President Carter's human rights initiative in foreign policy. In similar fashion, Gorbachev's stated unwillingness to intervene militarily in the domestic affairs of the Warsaw Pact nations critically weakened the repressive capacity of those regimes, thus helping to usher in the string of revolutions that dismantled the Soviet bloc in 1989–91.

I will close with a more contemporary example. From the beginning of European integration, fears that distinctive regions or regional subgroups would be sacrificed in the drive to continental union prompted European Community/European Union (EC/EU) planners to privilege the regions in their deliberations and in the design of EC/EU institutions (Marks and McAdam, 1993). So, for example, a consultative Committee of the Regions was established to ensure a voice for the regions in EC/EU deliberations. More important, the European Community saw fit to establish a Regional Fund to disperse monies in support of various regional projects. By organizing regional interests into the institutional structure of the embryonic EC, Community planners significantly expanded the domestic opportunities for regional ethnic mobilization. Any number of movements, from the Basque and Catalan separatists in Spain to the Welsh nationalists in the United Kingdom have benefited from this expansion in political opportunities induced by the EC/EU.

Political opportunity structure as a dependent variable

Finally, as Gamson and Meyer remind us in Chapter 12, "Opportunities open the way for political action, but movements also make opportunities." Though indisputably true, Gamson and Meyer's observation is not widely reflected in the extant literature.[2] While lavishing attention on the impact of political opportunities on the timing, form, and consequences of social movements, movement scholars have spent comparatively little time and energy systematically studying the role that movements have played in reshaping the institutional structure and political alignments of a given polity. Given that most movement scholars would probably say they study movements because they view them as a powerful force for change in society, our collective failure to undertake any serious accounting of the effect of past movements on the various dimensions of political opportunities is as puzzling as it is lamentable. Hopefully this will change. The potential value of such studies is exemplified by the handful of first-rate works that exist on the topic.

Among the best is James Button's (1989) systematic assessment of the impact of the civil rights movement on the political structure of six Southern communities. Button's findings show clearly that the movement has dramatically expanded political opportunities on all of the dimensions noted above. The movement has created any number of new legal and institutional openings in the structure of Southern politics. Chief among these, as Button shows, is unprecedented electoral access and a consequent rise in the number of black elected officials. One side benefit of this electoral access has been a marked decline in the routine use of violence against blacks in the South. Electoral access has eliminated the political impunity that made the routine use of violence on the part of Southern officials possible. Finally, the redemocratization of voting rights in the South and the institutional gains achieved by blacks have served to destroy the old political alignments – nationally no less than regionally – on which the segregationist status quo was structured.

In her recent comparative study of "protest policing" in Germany and Italy during the 1960s, 1970s, and 1980s, Donatella della Porta (1995) shows clearly that the new social movements have had similar effects on police practices in the two countries. Since the 1960s there has been a generalized routinization and professionalization of protest policing by law enforcement officials in both Germany and Italy as well as the passage of legislation in both countries clarifying and expanding the rights of citizens to legitimate dissent. The net effect has been an overall decline in the repressive capacity of both states as regards social movements.

The first two examples concern changes in dimensions of political opportunity that were sought by at least some segments of the movement. At least as interesting are those unintended modifications of the political opportunity structure that result from movement efforts. Scholars of the American women's movement such as Ann Costain (1992) and Jo Freeman (1973) have long acknowledged the importance of one such unintended consequence to the development of the women's movement. I am referring to the inclusion of women in the list of targeted groups covered by the provisions of Title VII of the Civil Rights Act of 1964. Clearly a product of the civil rights struggle, the Act nonetheless created new legal and institutional openings for other "minority" groups, including women.

A less known, but perhaps more consequential example of an unintended movement-initiated change in the structure of political opportunities concerns the role of the civil rights movement in undermining the electoral alignments that had served as the basis of liberal Democratic control of the White House since 1932. By redemocratizing voting rights in the South, the movement not only expanded electoral access for blacks, but also destroyed the monopoly that Dixiecrats had enjoyed in Southern politics. As a consequence viable Republican parties were reborn in every state in the region. By pairing this newfound electoral strength with the votes of their traditional strongholds (namely the West and the Midwest), the Republicans were able not only to undermine the New Deal coalition, but to fashion an electoral coalition of their own that has dominated presidential politics since 1968. From the perspective of social movements, the practical effect of this transfer of electoral power has been to foreclose institutional options for progressive movements while opening up new channels of access for the kinds of conservative groups long associated with the "Reagan Revolution."

These last two examples capture what I think is the typically fluid, reciprocal, unpredictable, and crucially important relationship of social movements to structures of political opportunity. Those structures simultaneously constrain and facilitate collective action by a wide range of challenging groups. Those who temporarily benefit from the structure are apt to act aggressively to take full advantage of the opportunities accorded them. In doing so, they are likely to effect legislative or other forms of change that serve to restructure – in both intended and unintended ways – the legal and institutional or the relational basis of the political system or both. Thus transformed, the structure of political opportunities acts back to once again confront the population of challenging groups with new constraints and possibilities for action.

SITUATING THE CHAPTERS IN THIS PART

Having sketched a few of the more promising new directions in the study of political opportunities, I am now in a position to discuss the ways in which the following four chapters extend, enhance, or clarify our understanding of the role of political opportunities in movement dynamics.

Over the past decade or so Sidney Tarrow has done as much as anyone to advance our understanding of the dynamic relationship that exists between institutionalized political systems and social movements. He continues his seminal theoretical work in Chapter 2 of this book. He begins by sketching a novel typology to distinguish the various approaches to the study of political

opportunity structure. The key distinction he discerns in the literature is between "proximate" and "state-centered" perspectives on political opportunities. Those who adhere to the former approach tend to study particular policy
or group-specific changes that facilitate collective action. State-centered
scholars, on the other hand, tend to be more concerned with the ways in
which the overall institutional design of a political system (e.g., weak state
versus strong state, centralized versus decentralized, etc.) shapes the possibilities for and forms of collective action.

Tarrow then distinguishes what he terms "cross-sectional statism" from
a more "dynamic" statist approach to the study of social movements and
revolutions. He goes on to critique many aspects of the former perspective
while highlighting the virtues of the latter. Specifically, Tarrow continues to
advocate for a dynamic and reciprocal view of the relationship of states to
social movements. Not only are we able to make sense of movements only by
understanding the *changing* institutional and relational features of a given
system, but the converse is true as well. Systems of institutionalized politics
can only be understood in relation to the movement (and other dynamic
political) processes that shape them over time. In espousing this view, Tarrow
is implicitly urging movement scholars to treat features of the political opportunity structure as dependent as well as independent variables. By re-
acting to shifts in the broader institutional environment movements become
significant change agents in their own right, not only modifying the immediate prospects for action, but potentially remaking features of the system as
well.

Donatella della Porta's chapter, "Social Movements and the State:
Thoughts on the Policing of Protest," is arguably the most thoughtful theoretical treatment of repression since Tilly's 1978 discussion of this critically
important but often neglected dimension of political opportunity. Della Porta's piece is also important for being, to my knowledge, the only comparative
study of the "policing of protest" published to date.

For those with an interest in political opportunities, della Porta's chapter
is important for two additional reasons. First, in her theoretical discussion,
she raises the provocative issue of whether repression should be considered a
barometer rather than a distinct dimension of the political opportunity structure. Consistent with a number of other authors, I continue to subscribe to
the latter point of view. But della Porta makes a compelling case for treating
protest policing as more a reflection of the overall opportunity structure than
an independent phenomenon in its own right. Whether one agrees with her
position or not, consideration of the question should ultimately help to clarify the dimensions of political opportunity. Finally, della Porta's chapter is
unique for a second reason. As noted previously, her essay and the larger
project from which it is drawn represent one of the few empirical attempts to
treat political opportunity as a dependent as well as an independent variable.

That is, della Porta, while clearly seeing repression as an important determinant of the extent and form of collective action, also understands that the reverse is true as well. She shows clearly that police practices in both Germany and Italy were themselves shaped over time by the interaction of movement groups with both state and law enforcement officials.

Anthony Oberschall's "Opportunities and Framing in the Eastern European Revolts of 1989" (Chapter 4) is groundbreaking in several ways. First, it represents one of the very first attempts to bring recent theoretical advances in the study of social movements to bear on the revolutions in Eastern Europe. As such, his is an interesting test of the applicability of models of social movements developed largely in the context of Western democracies to the rise of protest elsewhere. Though far from definitive, Oberschall's analysis suggests the comparative promise of several of the key conceptual tools developed in the West over the last ten to fifteen years.

But Oberschall's piece also points up some of the limits of recent scholarship as well. In particular, he demonstrates convincingly the need to take account of international trends and events in understanding shifts in the political opportunity structure of national polities. As he argues, states are embedded in "both a *domestic* and an *international* political environment." And in the case of the Eastern European revolts, the critical expansion in political opportunities would appear to have occurred internationally rather than domestically.

Chapter 5, by Elena Zdravomyslova, offers an interesting contrast to Oberschall's. Both represent efforts to apply the conceptual fruits of recent movement scholarship to an understanding of the sudden and unexpected development of collective action in the former Communist states. And, like Oberschall's, Zdravomyslova's work suggests that these Western conceptual imports hold up reasonably well when applied to movements born elsewhere and under very different political circumstances. In particular, both authors stress the importance of the reciprocal influence of expanding opportunities and framing processes to an understanding of the movements they study.

There are significant differences between the two pieces as well. Whereas Oberschall focuses on the revolutions in four former Soviet satellites – Hungary, Poland, Czechoslovakia, and East Germany – Zdravomyslova analyzes the development of popular protest within the former Soviet Union. And whereas Oberschall focuses on the revolutions at the most macro level, Zdravomyslova offers a detailed portrait of two local protest movements in St. Petersburg. The result is a rich, meso-level analysis as intrinsically interesting as it is theoretically important. The theoretical significance of Zdravomyslova's analysis stems from her use of the concept of political opportunity to explain yet another aspect of a social movement: namely the *form* of collective action. Each of the movements in St. Petersburg sought to exploit a different dimension of political opportunity – relaxed social control in one instance and an electoral opening in another – with the form of their efforts tailored to the differences in the kind of opportunities to which they were attuned. This is important stuff. Just as Oberschall calls our attention to the broad international dimension of political opportunities, Zdravomyslova reminds us that opportunities are also highly specific and localized. Movements may seek to exploit the former, but they must do so by adapting most immediately to the latter.

2

States and opportunities:
The political structuring of social movements

SIDNEY TARROW

In a 1991 article, John McCarthy, David Britt, and Mark Wolfson begin with an assertion that is often acknowledged in the social movement field but seldom receives the attention it deserves. They write:

> When people come together to pursue collective action in the context of the modern state they enter a complex and multifaceted social, political and economic environment. The elements of the environment have manifold direct and indirect consequences for people's common decisions about how to define their social change goals and how to organize and proceed in pursuing those goals. (1991: 46)

Their observation reflects the findings of a loose archipelago of writings that has developed since the early 1970s around the theme of "political opportunity structure." In his introduction to this part, Doug McAdam points out that, rather than focus on some supposedly universal cause of collective action, writers in this tradition examine political structures as incentives to the formation of social movements. But there are two major ways of specifying political structures in relation to collective action: as cross-sectional and static structures of opportunity and as intrasystemic and dynamic ones. This essay briefly discusses both but explores in much greater depth why – in my view – "dynamic" opportunities appear to impinge more directly on the decision-making of social movements and permit them to create their own opportunities.

A TYPOLOGY OF OPPORTUNITY STRUCTURES

As in any developing paradigm, there is a healthy and many-sided debate about how to conceptualize political opportunity structure. Some researchers

Parts of this essay first appeared in my *Power in Movement* (1994), and were also published in the *Kölner Zeitschrift für Soziologie und Sozialpsychologie* (1991b). I am particularly grateful to Friedhelm Neidhardt and Dieter Rucht for their thoughtful comments on that paper. The current, much expanded version was written as part of an Interpretive Research grant from the National Endowment for the Humanities and has benefited greatly from the comments of Dona-

	Scope	
	Proximate	*Statist*
Cross-		
Sectional	Policy-	State
	Specific	Variations
Specification		
Dynamic	Group	State
	Change	Change

Figure 2.1. A typology of opportunity structures.

have focused on large-scale structures, others on ones that are proximate to particular actors; some analyze cross-sectional variations in political opportunity, while others look at how changes in political conflict and alliances trigger, channel, and demobilize social movements. What has emerged is an implicit typology of approaches to political opportunity structure (Figure 2.1).

Proximate opportunity structure

Let us survey these types of approach briefly before turning to the major argument of this chapter. Scholars of what I will call "proximate opportunity structure" focus on the signals that groups receive from their immediate policy environment or from changes in their resources or capacities. Not inevitably, but understandably, much of the research in this tradition is infranational and – as it happens – comes from the United States. Within it, there are two main subtypes of research:

Policy-specific opportunities. The focus of most "policy-specific" approaches to opportunity structure is on how the policy and institutional environment channels collective action around particular issues and with what consequences. McCarthy and his collaborators work in this tradition when they focus on how concrete institutions and political processes, like the federal tax code, postal regulations, and state and local fundraising and demonstration

tella della Porta, Craig Jenkins, Hanspeter Kriesi, Doug McAdam, David Meyer, Dieter Rucht, and Charles Tilly.

regulations and their enforcement shape the collective action decisions of contemporary American movements (1991 and in this volume). Peter Eisinger does the same when he analyzes how different municipal institutional settings affected urban protest in the 1960s (1973). Amenta and Zylan do the same when they compare the opportunity structures of different American states (1991).

Group-specific opportunities. In contrast to the policy-specific environment that the various authors cited stress, several scholars have focused on the opportunity structure of specific *groups* and how these change over time. For example, after a long period during which American labor faced legal obstacles to organizing workers, the passage of the Wagner Act in the 1930s facilitated American labor's organizing capability, giving it a new resource to use vis-à-vis business, while the passage of the Taft-Hartley Act removed a good deal of this advantage after the war. As long as friendly administrative judges were appointed, the National Labor Relations Board (NLRB) favored organized labor, an advantage that disappeared as the courts shifted to an antilabor stance in the 1980s (Goldfield, 1982).

Changes in a group's position in society affect its opportunities for collective action as well. For example, in their study of the civil rights movement, Piven and Cloward argue that African Americans benefited from the postwar rural-to-urban migration patterns that removed them from the worst abuses of Jim Crow, as well as from the realignment of party politics that followed the breakup of the Solid South (1979: chap. 4). Conversely, groups which sprouted from the civil rights movement – like the National Welfare Rights Organization – suffered from constricting opportunities in the political environment of the late 1960s. The changing policy environment affected these groups both positively and negatively.

State-centered opportunity structure

The approaches to opportunity structure just described have one major commonality: They are couched at the subnational or group level. What of studies of comparative social movements? What kind of analytical leverage does political opportunity structure afford them? A promising approach to understanding how political institutions and processes structure collective action derives from the "statist" paradigm that became popular in American political science in the 1970s and 1980s.[1] Two complementary approaches, often conflated but actually quite distinct, offer themselves.

Cross-sectional statism. As it developed in the 1970s and 1980s, the statist paradigm was a reaction against earlier approaches in which the state was merely the crossroads of the parallelogram of group forces. Its advocates saw the state as "an autonomous, irreducible set of institutions" (Bright and Harding 1984: 3) which shaped political conflict in the interest of its own survival and aggrandizement. More recently, this has been giving way to a more nuanced view of the state as "the arena of routinized political competition in which class, status, and political conflicts . . . are played out" (3–4).

Although he eschews the "statist" label, cross-national statism lies at the heart of Herbert Kitschelt's (1986) comparison of the institutional setting of ecological movements in four countries.[2] In these states, whose open and closed "input" structures intersect with high and low capacity to implement policies, the strategies of movements are affected by their institutional policy environments in a variety of ways. For example, Kitschelt argues that the "open" Swedish system, with its high policy capacity, facilitates collective action to the point that ecological movements operate largely within institutional channels; in contrast, with regard to the "closed" French system, the ecological movement, according to Kitschelt, lacks institutional receptivity and, as a result, uses confrontational strategies (71). The overall structure of the state channels political conflict in determinant ways.[3]

Kitschelt employs cross-national statism to examine a host of documents on the antinuclear movement in four countries, but Hanspeter Kriesi and his collaborators in a collective work frame a massive primary data collection on new social movements in four countries: France, West Germany, the Netherlands, and Switzerland in the late 1970s and 1980s (1995: chaps. 1, 2). In contrast to much of the work on "new" social movements, which was either generic or simply imposed one national model on all of Europe, their achievement is to pinpoint the specificities of different national opportunity structures with a common data base.

Dynamic statism. While Kitschelt and others focus on cross-national variations in opportunity structure, other writers have focused on how states change and on how these changes produce – or reduce – political opportunities. This perspective is reflected in the work of Tilly and others, who argue that – in Bright and Harding's words – "statemaking does not end once stately institutions emerge, but is continuous. . . . [C]ontentious processes both define the state vis-à-vis other social and economic institutions *and continually remake the state itself*" (1984: 4; emphasis added).

This is in many ways the boldest thesis of the four, for its proponents argue that *entire political systems undergo changes which modify the environment of social actors sufficiently to influence the initiation, forms, and outcomes of collective action.* Tilly's work on the effects of the ends of war on domestic conflict (1992) is a recent example. When armed forces are demobilized and domestic energies are released at the same time as the international power balance shifts, opportunities open for domestic social actors across the social spectrum. A related approach can be found in Vallely's work on the first and second reconstructions in American history (1993a,b), where he uses changes in state structure and capacity to interpret the failure of the first and the success of the second in empowering African Americans politically. The boldest approach is that of Kriesi and his collaborators (1995), who examine the effects of changing alliance structures (chap. 3), protest waves (chap. 5), and diffusion (chap. 8), all of which reflect the changing opportunity structure of whole systems.

In this essay, I examine the statist perspective on the political opportunity structure of social movements in both its cross-national and its dynamic specifications. I argue that while the former allows us to link the political opportunities of social movements to a national grid of institutional regularities, the comparisons that follow from it pose a number of problems: from underspecifying subnational and subgroup variations in movement opportunities to underplaying the dynamic of protest cycles to excluding transnational influences on social movement activity. In contrast, what I call "dynamic statism" allows us to specify political opportunity for different actors and sectors, to track its changes over time, and to place the analysis of social movements in their increasingly transnational setting.

Before examining the contributions of cross-sectional and dynamic statism, I will first return to the source of both versions of the statist persuasion – who of course was Alexis de Tocqueville – and to the effects of state centralization on the structure and strategy of social movements. I will argue that the great French theorist misspecified the effects of what was a *secular* process of state-building into one of *nation-specific* centralization, thereby laying the groundwork for both a "France is different" dogmatism and the cross-national approach to state influences on collective action. Neither one captures how much contentious processes are part of state-building and help to remake continually the state itself.

THE STATIST PERSUASION

Comparing states as the major framework of collective action has a long and noble history. Although we often think of Weber as the major theorist of the state (Bright and Harding 1984: 2), the first modern observer to make explicit the linkage between states and social movements was Alexis de Tocqueville. But Tocqueville's work also shows that deriving the character of collective action from a state structure has pitfalls even for the eighteenth century. The problem is not that states do not matter but that the behaviors he traced to particular national institutions actually were emerging aspects of collective action throughout the West, and not specific properties of the French or American state.

Tocqueville on states and collective action

States are so central a focus of the mobilization of opinion today that we often forget that this was not always the case, and neglect to trace how it occurred. Tocqueville provided a first response. He argued that centralized states (read: France), aggrandize themselves by weakening and coopting the intermediate corporate bodies in civil society. The result is that *the stronger the state, the weaker its encouragement of institutional participation and the greater the incentive to confrontation and violence when collective action does break out.* Tocqueville's language as he makes this claim is worth quoting in detail, for it has influenced much of recent thinking about the influence of the state's strength on collective action:

It was no easy task [in the French Revolution] bringing together fellow citizens who had lived for many centuries aloof from, or even hostile to, each other and teaching them to co-operate in the management of their own affairs. It had been far easier to estrange them than it now was to reunite them, and in so doing France gave the world a memorable example. Yet, when sixty years ago [in 1789] the various classes which under the old order had been isolated units in the social system came once again in touch, it was on their sore spots that they made contact *and their first gesture was to fly at each other's throats.* (1955: 107; emphasis added)

In contrast, in weak states (read: the United States) strong civil societies were free to develop moderate and widespread forms of participation, allowing liberal democracy to flourish and resist the kind of violent confrontations Tocqueville decried in the French Revolution. When collective action does develop, it is around the corporate bodies and voluntary associations whose established positions and real power enables them to gain advantages within the institutional framework of the state. Tocqueville's vision of France and America provides a convenient starting point for us to attack the problem of how states structure social movements.

French centralization. Tocqueville began by asking why the French Revolution should have broken out in France – where the peasantry was far removed from feudalism – and not in more backward countries of Europe (1955: x). His answer was that it was because state aggrandizement had stripped the French nobility of its positive functions, reducing it to a parasitic weight on the peasantry, and had turned municipal office into a state-dependent sinecure. Because it was denuded of intermediate tissue of autonomous corporate bodies, French society became an aggregate of "self-seekers practicing a narrow individualism and caring nothing for the public good" (1955: xiii). The result was jealous egalitarianism, sporadic and uncontrolled mobilization, and ultimately, the Revolution: "a grim, terrific force of nature, a newfangled monster, red of tooth and claw" (3).

American exceptionalism. In both state and society, Jacksonian America showed Tocqueville a mirror image of the strong state and the weak society he abhorred in his native land. What he so admired in his travels through the United States was that no centralized state had emerged to constrain a vigorous associational development and a flourishing civil politics. To be sure, because of its lack of a feudal past, America never possessed the particular corporate bodies whose passage he regretted in France. But it had a functional equivalent in the churches, interest groups, and local governments which provided Americans with self-help and with a set of buffers against an overweening state (Tocqueville 1954: chap. 16). With its weak state and its flourishing associations, America had a good chance to avoid the explosions of egalitarian democracy of 1789 and 1848, and, as a result, had a protection against the despotism that followed them in 1800 and 1851.

Comparing France and America. But we now know that Tocqueville's image of a France bereft of association exaggerated the subtraction of associational fiber from French society on the eve of the Revolution, while his picture of Jacksonian America glossed over the relations among association, state-building, and collective action in that country. For one thing, the bucolic picture he drew of Jacksonian America left the volatile relationship between association and mobilization in the shadows. For another, Tocqueville mistook the non-European character of the early American state for the absence of a state *tout court*.

Although the nineteenth-century American state was not a centralized European state, neither was it a *non*-state. The Federalists had constructed what was for the late eighteenth century an extremely effective state for their purposes – fiscal consolidation, diplomatic maneuver and westward expansion (Bright 1984: 121–22). As Charles Bright observes, "the periods of greatest paralysis in federal policy corresponded with the periods when party mobilization was the fullest and the margins of electoral victory the slimmest" (136). The state that Tocqueville found in his travels was weak, but this was no characterological trait: The American state had been weakened, not by Americans' inherent love of freedom or by grassroots pluralism, but by a political stalemate between two expanding, sectionally based socioeconomic systems (121, 134).

What of collective action? The center of gravity of American social movements was still local in 1832. But regional and national movements rapidly developed a capacity for collective action in a rough dialectic with the national struggle for power. It was while Tocqueville was passing through an apparently serene American landscape that a torrential movement of evangelical protestantism "burned over" the towns and cities of the Northeast (Cross 1950), laying the groundwork for movements for temperance, abolitionism, and, indirectly, for the first true feminist movement in the modern world. As for sectionalism, it began by paralyzing the development of national policy and ended in the most cataclysmic episode of collective action in the nation's history – one that would remake the state into a modern Leviathan (Bensel 1991).

State-building and collective action

What was Tocqueville's problem? Like many modern statists, he focused on French state centralization and on its putative effects on collective action. The French Revolution was the major watershed around which his theories turned. Both before and after it, he saw a strong state throttling associational life and lending a normally choked-up, but episodically explosive character to collective action. But even before the Revolution – and in countries that were more pacified and less statist than France – the national state was gaining unprecedented power to structure the relations between citizens and other citizens and between them and the state. Expanding states made war and needed roads and postal networks, armies and munitions factories to do so (Brewer 1989). To finance these improvements, states could no longer rely on a surplus extracted from the peasantry, but depended on the growth of industry and commerce, which in turn required that law and order be maintained, food supplied, associations licensed, and a citizenry develop the skills necessary to turn the wheels of industry (Tarrow 1994: chap. 4).

These efforts were not intended to support social mobilization: quite the reverse. But they provided expanded means of communication through which opinion could be mobilized, created a class of men experienced in public affairs and led to increased financial exactions on citizens who were not always disposed to pay. In addition, states that took on the responsibility for maintaining order had to regulate the relations between groups, and this meant creating a legal framework for association as well as providing more subtle mechanisms for social control than the truncheons of the army or the police.

Not only that: By producing policies intended for large populations and by standardizing the procedures that citizens used in their relations with authorities, states provided centralized targets for mobilization and broader cognitive frameworks in which challenging groups could compare their situations to more favored constituencies and find allies with similar interests. As Raymond Grew writes;

All states, as if by irresistible mandate, encouraged easier nationwide communication and a minimal universal education. . . . No state, having once permitted a formal, written constitution, subsequently managed for long without one. . . . Once citizenship became a formal matter of birth or oaths registered by the state, it remained so even though specific criteria could be altered. (1984: 94)

States made war and collected taxes; war and taxes required the infrastructure of a consolidated state; social movements emerged from the conflicts and opportunity structures surrounding the process of state consolidation. In states as different as liberal constitutional Britain, absolutist France, and colonial America, the policies attending state consolidation became major arenas of contention and for the construction of national social movements.[4] In France, even before the Revolution, efforts to assure provisioning of grain led to coalitions of resistance to state policy between local officials, growers, and consumers (Kaplan 1984). In colonial America, the attempts of the British to increase taxes created the framework in which a national network of corresponding committees were created (Maier 1972). And in Britain, the Revolutionary War period saw the first national movement associations to organize outside the sphere of religion (Christie 1982; Drescher 1987).

Like state-building in general, each new policy initiative produced new channels of communication, more organized networks of citizens, and more unified cognitive frameworks around which insurgents could mount claims and organize. The consolidated national state increasingly became the target, the fulcrum, and the umbrella for collective action. The national social movement – a sustained, conflictual interaction between organized groups and authorities – became the major expression of citizen opposition.[5]

If social movements were developing a similar vitality and organizational basis in countries as different as Britain, France, and the United States, it could not have been national specificities in state structure that produced the outcomes Tocqueville found in France. In all three countries, it was the processes surrounding state-*building* that produced the major thresholds in social movement emergence and development. The appearance of what Tilly calls the "consolidated state" all over the West produced the social movement, and this was as true in colonial and Revolutionary America as it was in mercantile and parliamentary England or centralized and cosmopolitan France.[6]

But these observations suggest that while Tocqueville's claim regarding the role of state centralization in fomenting the French Revolution was excessive, his emphasis on state-building as the source of movement opportunities was right on target. The lesson is that the dynamic of changes in state-related opportunity structure may be a more fruitful way for present and future scholars of social movements to proceed than by looking only at static cross-sectional variations in state structure. Let us examine both these approaches in a more contemporary light.

NATIONAL STATES, MULTILEVEL MOVEMENTS

Since the eighteenth century, social movements have increasingly directed their activities at the national state, so it was logical that differences in the institutional structures of different states would be seen to structure social movements. Thus, the centralized French state produced movements whose center of gravity rose to the national level, while the federal American state produced movements that were more often couched at the state and local levels. The relatively permissive British state encouraged the use of the mass petition and the open-air demonstration while the repressive Russian state induced opponents to go underground and turn to clandestine organization and the use of terror.

Images of social movements to some extent reflected these differences. Thus, the semiauthoritarian Prussian state influenced the rise of a social democratic movement that was characterized as a "state within a state" while the anarchist or anarchosyndicalist movements of southern Europe were seen as backward correlatives of the not very modern Italian and Spanish states. The French labor movement embraced an associational "vocabulary" that reflected the *loi le Chapelier*,[7] while American movements developed a vocabulary of "rights" that reflected the importance of the law in American institutions and practice.

These cross-national variations in state structure provide scholars with a useful grid for the interpretation and prediction of national variations in the emergence and structuring of social movements. But four fundamental problems dog the cross-sectional statist perspective: first, as Bright and Harding point out, "contentious processes both define the state vis-à-vis other social and economic institutions and continually remake the state itself" (1984: 4). The obvious inference is that, unless social movements obediently mimic the state structures around them, the trajectories of state-building cannot be predicted from formal structure alone. Second, although they are influenced by institutions, social movements are not *themselves* institutions, and as a result, they are less easily interpreted or predicted in the light of institutional structures than, for example, interest groups or parties. Third, the opportunity structures of different movements in the same country cannot be expected to be any more similar than the life chances of the various social actors who constitute them. And, fourth, in a world of movement as global as ours has become, it seems unlikely that different forms and strategies of social movements can be confined to single types of states.

Movements appear at the subnational and subgroup level, they rise and fall and change their shapes rapidly during cycles of protest, and they are profoundly influenced by trends that transcend national boundaries. These three dimensions of movement dynamics – infranational variations, cycles of protest, and transnational collective action – can be briefly illustrated.

Infranational movement variations

If social movements simply reflect national institutional contexts, there would be much less *infra*national variation in movements than we actually see, both between movement sectors and within them. Consider the variety of types of mobilizing structures that we find between the prolife and prochoice sectors in the United States. In the latter, according to McCarthy (1987), a sophisticated leadership and an affluent constituency developed an action repertoire that was centered around direct-mail campaigns by formal movement organizations that channeled financial contributions into publicity, education, and lobbying of Congress. The prolife movement, based on a largely parish-based organization, led a lower-middle-class constituency into direct action campaigns and door-to-door canvassing. Both were equally at home in the "open" political opportunity structure of American public life.

Now consider the variations that are possible within the *same* movement – for example, the "new" environmental movement. Although "emphasis is usually placed on their loose, heterogeneous, decentralized structure," "there is no clear evidence that such structures are always present," writes one of the movement's foremost European interpreters (Rucht 1989a: 63). In Germany, where the state is federal, there is a great variety of forms, extending from "patterns of conventional interest associations and foundations through unconventional associations based on autonomous membership groups and informal networks with specific interests," all the way to the Green Party (73). Perhaps Germany's relatively open political opportunity structure (65–6) helps to explain the movement's heterogeneity, but if so, why did Rucht find the environmental movement equally heterogeneous in countries as diverse as France and Italy?[8]

Although some national opportunity structures are clearly more "open" than others, state elites are far from neutral between different social actors and movements. Compare the ease with which the nineteenth-century temperance movement was free to operate in the United States with the repression that the labor movement suffered in the same period. The middle-class Protestant women who militated in the former were certainly more cordially received by state elites than the lower-class, immigrant masses that worked the mines and mills of industrializing America. Or compare the warm reception of the Catholic workers' movements by European states in the early part of this century to the repression suffered by Socialist-led movements in the same times and places. National opportunity structures may be the basic grids within which movements operate, but the grid is seldom neutral between social actors.

Cycles of protest

Political institutions, parties, and interest groups are relatively easy to compare cross-nationally, because they change slowly, produce records, and have institutional obligations. But the comparative analysis of social movements produces many more problems, which in part explains its rarity in the social movement literature (Tarrow 1991a). Not least among these problems is the fact that, as McAdam points out in his introduction to this part, movements seem to go through rapid phases. Thus, comparing even similar movements in different phases of their life cycles can produce a distorted picture (Tsebelis and Sprague 1989).

For example, consider the comparative study of revolution: From the start, many students took from the French Revolution an image of fanaticism, bloodshed, and internecine strife that was not typical of all of its many phases. Conversely, American views of the revolt of the American colonies pass swiftly over the many incidents of bullying, hazing, and outright expulsions of loyalists that marked its early phases (Maier 1972: chap. 2).

Even movements that are much less earth-shattering than revolutions go through distinct phases, or cycles.[9] For example, focusing on the violent clash with the French army when antinuclear protesters marched on Malville in 1977 produces an image of French movements that ignores the nonconfrontational nature of most other phases of the movement (Rucht 1990: 207–8). Comparing movements across countries can only produce valid comparisons within the framework of these infranational cyclical dynamics.[10]

Transnational movements

From their inception in the eighteenth century, organized social movements have been rapidly diffused across national boundaries: by print media, which carried word of successful revolts to the far corners of the world (Anderson 1991); by immigrants like Tom Paine, who brought the resentment of a disappointed British customs official to the more congenial environment of Philadelphia; and by transnational actors like sailors, who worked in "transatlantic circuits of commodity exchange and capital accumulation" (Linebaugh and Rediker 1990).

Not only individual agents of movement, but entire social movements have been diffused across national boundaries and states. The antislavery movement, which had its origins in Britain, made progress by diffusion – through newspapers, agents, and missionaries, and eventually through British policy itself (Drescher 1991; Rice 1982). Later in the century, social democracy diffused the German model of a centralized social democratic labor party. Although its lineaments were only vaguely realized in Italy, Spain, and France, in the Netherlands, Scandinavia, and Austria, more or less accurate copies of the SPD model were established – not because these countries had opportunity structures similar to Germany's but through transnational contacts between Socialist organizers and the legitimacy of the model.

In our era, we see not only a rapid diffusion of models of collective action from one country to another, but a great deal of cross-border collaboration in collective action campaigns – as in the European peace and environmental movements of the 1980s (Rucht 1990). In other cases, movements are organized transnationally – as in the case of Greenpeace. In an age of satellite communication, global television, and the fax machine, even movements that are independent of one another have almost instant access to information about what other movements are doing (Rosenau 1990). In the case of the democratization movements of 1989, we saw a transnational movement which employed similar strategies and rhetoric and in which the latecomers learned from their predecessors.

Foreign policy involvements also influenced the opportunities of domestic movements. As McAdam points out in his introduction to this part, three Cold War presidents – Truman, Eisenhower, and Kennedy – were influenced by America's international claim to be the home of freedom, to advance the goals of civil rights at home. In Western Europe, it was the movement against the Vietnam War that prepared a generation of New Left activists for domestic dissent. More recently, foreign policy involvements favored various factions in the Yugoslav ethnic war, for example, when Germany encouraged rival nationalisms by its premature recognition of the Croatian Republic.

If it was once sufficient to interpret or predict social movements around the shape of the national state, it is less and less possible to do so today. Because of multiple levels and sectors of movement mobilization, their changing shape in different phases of protest cycles, and their increasingly transnational links, national regularities in state structure must be seen as no more than the initial grid within which movements emerge and operate. To understand how they make their decisions, we must begin with an account of their specific goals and constituencies, the phase of the cycle in which they emerge, and their connection to transnational repertoires of organization, strategy, and collective action.

STATES AND SHIFTING OPPORTUNITIES

State-building was a secular trend that proceeded inexorably through the eighteenth and into the nineteenth and twentieth centuries. But movement mobilization did not "rise" inexorably or in linear fashion; rather, it fluctuated broadly, both between social sectors and over time, in widespread strike waves and cycles of protest. The increasing frequency in parliamentary targets that Tilly found in England in the years from 1758 to 1834, and the inflection in collective action from 1789 to 1807 that he uncovered (1993a), suggests why: Changes in political opportunity affected the likelihood that mass mobilization would be repressed or might succeed and this affected people's collective judgment about whether to protest or not.

In Britain and elsewhere, once it developed, the social movement did not go from success to success like Marx's image of the bourgeois revolution.[11] Instead, movements rose and fell, retreated and revived according to the political conditions of the moment. But what kinds of struggle and which aspects of political opportunity are most likely to provide opportunities for social movement mobilizers? Unless we can specify these better, as McAdam argues, the concept of political opportunity may remain a grab bag of ad hoc residual categories, adduced whenever "deeper" structural factors cannot be identified. I will argue, instead, that mobilization into social movements varies as opportunities for collective action open and close, allies appear and disappear, political alignments shift, and elites divide and cohere.

Elements of opportunity

By political opportunity structure, I refer to *consistent – but not necessarily formal, permanent, or national – signals to social or political actors which either encourage or discourage them to use their internal resources to form social movements.* My concept of political opportunity emphasizes not only formal structures like state institutions, but the conflict and alliance structures which provide resources and oppose constraints external to the group (Kriesi 1991; Kriesi and Giugni 1990; Kriesi et al. 1995). Unlike money or power, this opens the possibility that even weak and disorganized challengers can take advantage of opportunities created by others to organize against powerful opponents. Conversely, as opportunities narrow, even the strong grow weak and movements are forced to change their forms of action and their strategies. The most salient kinds of signals are four: the opening up of access to power, shifting alignments, the availability of influential allies, and cleavages within and among elites.

The opening up of political access. Rational people do not often attack well-fortified opponents when they lack the opportunity to do so. But are people with *full* political access any more likely to do so? Does the presence of conventional opportunities for participation encourage unconventional protest or does this lead to compliance and consensus? Political scientist Peter Eisinger argues that the relationship between protest and political opportunity is neither negative nor positive but curvilinear: Neither full access nor its absence encourages the greatest amount of protest. Eisinger (1973: 15) writes that protest is most likely "in systems characterized by a mix of open and closed factors."

The idea that partially opened access to participation encourages protest was supported by the movements for liberation and democratization in the former Soviet Union and Eastern Europe in the late 1980s. As perestroika and glasnost opened new opportunities for political action, as political scientist Mark Beissinger found (1991), protest movements developed that could both take advantage of these new opportunities and go beyond them. Although Beissinger found that *violent* protest was *not* closely connected with opening opportunity structure, nonviolent protests were clearly related to opportunity, a finding that dovetails perfectly with Eisinger's.

Unstable alignments. A second aspect of opportunity structure is the instability of changing political alignments, as indicated in liberal democracies by electoral instability. The changing fortunes of government and opposition parties, especially when signaling the possibility of new coalitions emerging, encourage insurgents to try to exercise marginal power and may induce elites to seek support from outside the polity.

In the United States in both the 1930s and 1960s, as Piven and Cloward found, changes in parties' electoral strength encouraged organized labor, the unemployed, African Americans, and other groups and led to changes in the parties' strategies for bringing unrepresented social groups into the electoral arena. Most dramatically, this produced the labor insurgency and unemployed workers' movements of the 1930s and the civil rights movements of the 1960s.

But it is not only electoral instability that encourages collective action, as the record of peasant uprisings in undemocratic systems shows. Peasants exhibit at least one "rational" uniformity: They have the good sense to rebel against authorities only when windows of opportunity appear in the walls of their subordination. This is what historian Eric Hobsbawm found when he looked into the history of Peruvian land occupations. The peasants' land grievances were age-old, dating back to barely remembered land usurpations after the Spanish occupation. But Hobsbawm finds that their decisions to take collective action against landlords co-occurred with struggles for power in the capital between elites who, exceptionally, sought support from subaltern classes. The same was true of the southern Italian peasants who seized parts of the *latifondi* during the 1848 revolution. Their land hunger and resentment at landlord abuses were age-old; but it was only as liberals and radicals destabilized the political system with urban insurrections that they invaded large landholdings in Calabria (Hobsbawm 1974; Soldani 1973).

Influential allies. A third aspect of political opportunity structure is the appearance of influential allies, which both William Gamson (1990) and Craig Jenkins and Charles Perrow (1977) found to be crucial in their research on American farmworkers. Allies can act as a friend in court, as guarantors against brutal repression, or as acceptable negotiators on behalf of constituencies which – if left a free hand – might be far more difficult for authorities to deal with.

Jenkins and Perrow's (1977) paired comparison of the success or failure of American farmworker groups in the 1940s and 1960s provides a good measure of the importance of allies to collective action. Comparing the farmworker movements of the two periods, they found that the biggest advantage of the latter lay in the presence of three external constituencies: the urban liberals who boycotted lettuce and grapes to support the United Farm Workers' (UFW's) attempts to gain legitimation, the organized labor coalition that supported it in the California legislature, and a new generation of sympathetic administrators in the U.S. Department of Agriculture.

The existence of influential allies took on particular importance in stimulating protest in state socialist regimes in the 1970s and 1980s – for example, in the role that the Catholic Church played in Poland or that of the Protestant Church in East Germany – where formal opportunities for participation were severely constrained. The example can be extended territorially outside the state: Gorbachev's warning to East European Communist elites that the Red Army could no longer be counted on to defend their regimes was taken as a signal to organize by insurgent groups in these countries.

Dividing elites. Conflicts within and among elites are a fourth factor encouraging unrepresented groups to engage in collective action. Divisions among elites not only provide incentives for resource-poor groups to take the risks of collective action; they also encourage portions of the elite to seize the role of "tribune of the people" in order to increase their own political influence. Comparing different recent cycles of protest shows how intraelite conflicts affect the incidence and extension of protest. In Italy, a key determinant of the length of the wave of collective action in the 1960s was the tendency of the Socialist party to pose as the people's tribune inside the government (Tarrow 1989a: chap. 2). In France, in contrast, where the election of June 1968 produced a consolidation of Gaullist power, the movement collapsed much faster. Divisions between elites often have the effect of widening the circle of conflict to groups outside the political system and giving them marginal power, while a unified elite leaves less opening for the exercise of such marginal power.

Short-term and long-term changes in opportunity

Although Tocqueville is often accounted the father of political opportunity structure theory (Eisinger 1973), he was actually more interested in portraying the long-term shift in power from the nobility to the crown – and from the provinces to Paris – under the Old Regime than in the changes in political opportunity that were actually occurring in the 1780s. As a result, he failed to observe that it was the aristocratic *revival* of the 1770s and 1780s and the opportunities for collective action created by the fragmented and financially strapped French state that launched the Revolution.

Far from destroying everything in its path, the French state had never overcome the resistance of the nobility, the parliaments, and the municipal officeholders to its need for cash and was unable to stop the growth of an educated and assertive Third Estate and of an enlightened public opinion.[12] The result was that the short-term decision to open the system to broader participation in July 1788 unleashed a wave of debate, association, and collective action (Lefebvre 1947; Schama 1989: Part One).

During the two years following the calling of the Assembly of Notables, networks of friends and acquaintances became political, a public relations campaign was launched, and public assemblies were called throughout the country to discuss people's grievances and elect delegates to the forthcoming Estates General. The birth of the movement that was to result in a wholesale national revolution was encouraged by the Crown's short-term attempt to solve its financial problems and create a counterweight to the recalcitrant *parlements.*

This is not to say that there are no significant long-term shifts in political opportunity structure and that they make no difference to the incidence and effectiveness of social movements. States change, sometimes profoundly, and these changes produce both opportunities and constraints for social movements. For example, Vallely's study of the impact of the two Reconstructions on Southern politics points to two fundamental changes in the American political system as probable causes of the success of the second one: "(1) the structure of the party system and (2) the extent to which the central government controlled coercion within American national territory" (1993a: 41). Where occupying federal troops could not effect the permanent enfranchisement of African Americans in the South after 1865, by 1965, the national state had developed to such a degree that the federal courts became the guarantors of black voting rights and the National Guard their enforcers. And where the parties historically magnified white supremacist influence after the Civil War, by the 1960s, "inclusionists" outweighed "exclusionists" in the American party system.

However, what strikes the observer from closer up is how often short-term changes in opportunity affect the propensity of social actors to engage in confrontational collective action. For example, looking back at the 1930s, while workers in Britain languished through most of the Great Depression, and German workers were brutally repressed by national socialism, French and American workers reacted to the crisis with unprecedented levels of collective action and by developing a new type of movement – the factory occupation. What was the reason for these cross-national differences?

The reason why there were strike waves in France and the United States and not in Germany or Britain in the 1930s was not that economic distress was greater in France or America but because of the changes in political opportunities that were offered workers in the two former countries: First, with the election of reform administrations in Paris and Washington, opportunities for access were opened up that were not available in either Britain or Germany. Second, major electoral realignments were apparent in both countries in both a shift to the left and in the formation of new governing coalitions. Third, the Popular Front in France and the New Deal in the

United States offered organized labor influential allies within the state who were willing to innovate in political economic relationships and were unwilling to support the suppression of strikes.

It was the political opportunities opened up by the Popular Front and the New Deal that explained the surge of labor insurgency in France and the United States in a poor labor market. We cannot easily explain these similarities through the nature of the French and the American state, for in both strong-state France and weak-state America, workers responded similarly to similar configurations of strain and opportunity. The obvious conclusion is that we need to interpret political opportunity along axes more varied and "conjunctural" than long-term state continuities or in political opportunity in general. This is true if for no other reason than that the movements which profit from short-term openings in opportunities frequently lose out when these opportunities disappear or when other actors – better placed to exploit them – enter the arena. Social movements not only seize opportunities; they make them, both for themselves and for others who may not share their interests or values.

MAKING OPPORTUNITIES

Unlike conventional forms of participation, collective action has the unusual property that it can demonstrate to others the possibilities of collective action and offer even resource-poor groups opportunities that are not predictable from their structural position. This occurs when bold new movements make claims on elites that parallel the grievances of those with less daring and less initiative. Moreover, collective action exposes opponents' points of weakness that may not be evident until they are first challenged. It also reveals unsuspected or formerly passive allies both within and outside the system. And, finally, it can pry open institutional barriers through which new demands can pour. Once collective action is launched in part of a system, on behalf of one type of goal, and by a particular group, the encounter between that group and its antagonists provides models of collective action that produce opportunities for others. These can be seen in four general ways.

Expanding the group's own opportunities. A group can experience changes in its opportunity structure as a function of its own actions. For example, protesting groups can increase their opportunities by expanding the repertoire of collective action into new forms. Although, as Tilly writes, people normally use forms of collective action that are culturally known to them (1978, 1995), they sometimes innovate, as in the invention of the mass demonstration in early-nineteenth-century England (Tilly 1993a), or of the sit-in by the U.S. civil rights movement (McAdam 1982). Each new form of collective action finds authorities unprepared, and while they are preparing a response, the protesting group can plan an escalation of their forms of collective action (McAdam 1983b), creating new opportunities and reaching new publics.

Expanding opportunities for others. One of the most remarkable characteristics of collective action is that it expands the opportunities of other challenging groups. Protesting groups put issues on the agenda with which others identify, and demonstrate the utility of collective action that others copy or innovate upon. For example, the American protest movements of the early 1960s – especially the civil rights movement – placed new frames of meaning on the agenda, particularly the extension of the traditional notion of "rights," that other groups could reshape around their own grievances. Although frame extension can occur gradually and in a diffuse manner through the media, educational institutions, and epistemic communities, collective action embodies new claims in dramatic ways that make them visible and available to others in the society.

The leaders of the civil rights movement also experimented with new forms of action – notably nonviolence and the sit-in – that levered open the borders of the traditional repertoire of collective action for others to enter. The sit-ins invented by American college students in the early 1960s were perhaps the most remarkable contemporary example of a new or expanded form of collective action. Its use expanded well beyond its originators to cognate and unrelated groups – even extending to those with different interests and values and to the student movement in Western Europe (McAdam and Rucht 1992; Tarrow 1989a: chap. 6).

These opportunities not only affect a movement's "alliance system"; they also affect what Hanspeter Kriesi calls its "conflict system" (1991) – and often negatively. A movement that offends influential groups can trigger a countermovement. Movements that employ violence, or can be depicted as if they did, allow repression to be employed against them. Movements that make extreme forms of policy demand can be outmaneuvered by groups that pose the same claim in more acceptable form. Movements not only create opportunities for themselves and their allies; they also create opportunities for opponents and elites.

Creating opportunities for opponents. Protesting groups can unwittingly create political opportunities for their opponents – for example, when a movement threatens another group in a general context of mobilization, leading it to take collective action against the first group; or when the gains made by the first group produce costs, or the impression of costs, to the second (Meyer and Staggenborg 1994). The current competitive ethnic mobilization in the former USSR and Yugoslavia are classical examples of this phenomenon. On the one hand, such countermobilization may lead to a sequence of concessions on the part of elites that satisfies competing claims; on the other, it can fuel a destructive spiral of violence such as occurred in Italy in the 1970s (della Porta and Tarrow 1986).

Making opportunities for elites. Finally protesting groups create political opportunities for groups and elites within the system in a negative sense, when their actions provide the grounds for repression; and in a positive sense, when opportunistic political elites seize the opportunity created by challengers to proclaim themselves as tribunes of the people. In fact, the analysis of real-life situations of protest and reform shows that protesters on their own seldom have the clout to affect the policy priorities of elites. This is both because their protests take an expressive and nonreformist form and because elites are unlikely to be persuaded to make policy changes that are not in their interest by challengers outside the system.

Reform is most likely to result when challengers from outside the polity provide a political incentive for minority elites within it to achieve their own policy goals. Reform often results less from the direct demands of individual protest movements than from a subjective or objective coalition between reformers within the polity and challengers who initiate collective action from outside it. It follows that reformist policies seldom correspond to the claims of the protesting groups; indeed, reforms triggered by their efforts sometimes provide benefits to groups other than themselves, which goes a long way to explaining the radicalization that is often typical of such groups after the reformist response to their claims.

Political elites are most likely to behave in a reformist way when there are political advantages to be gained from it. Political opportunism is not a monopoly of either Left or Right, parties of movement or parties of conservation. Thus the (conservative) Eisenhower administration responded in essentially the same way as the (liberal) Kennedy administration to the challenge of the civil rights movement – for the simple reason that both were suffering electoral challenges in the South (Piven and Cloward 1979: chap. 4). Similarly, the (conservative) Gaullist government responded to the revolt of May 1968 with a sweeping reform of higher education, in the face of its conservative factions' opposition to compromise with the students (Tarrow 1992b).

When are parties and interest groups most likely to take advantage of the opportunities created by social movements? They appear to do so mainly when a system is challenged fundamentally by a range of social movements, and not when individual movement organizations mount challenges which are easily repressed or isolated. That is to say, reformist outcomes are most likely when civil society produces generalized opportunities to confront elites and authorities with collective action. Since this occurs more easily than the creation of wholly new state institutions, changing opportunities within states are more important to emerging movements than static differences between states.

CONCLUSIONS

Underlying the rise of new social movements is a system of socioeconomic cleavages, individual motivations, and group and organizational capacities. But the history of collective action varies with too much volatility for such slowly evolving structural and motivational factors to explain it fully. This is no more than saying that we cannot hope to understand the dynamics and the impact of movements by "placing" them in a static grid of cleavages, conflicts, and state institutions; we must watch them as a moving target, much as we study ordinary politics. What I have called "dynamic statism" is one way of doing this.

Movements arise as the result of new or expanded opportunities; they signal the vulnerability of the state to collective action, thereby opening up opportunities for others; the process leads to state responses which, in one way or another, produce a new opportunity structure. This picture is complicated further by the possibly transnational nature of the contemporary social movement, which both crosses national boundaries and transcends state structures. The social movement has been transnational since the Atlantic Revolution of the eighteenth century. Whether the increasingly global economy, and the supranational institutions that have been developing around it over the past few decades, has so thoroughly escaped the national state as to create transnational movements is a question students of political opportunity structure will have to face.

3

Social movements and the state: Thoughts on the policing of protest

DONATELLA DELLA PORTA

The relation between social movements and the state is a crucial theme for the understanding of collective action. Long neglected, it acquired a new relevance with the development of the "political process" approach to social movements (Tilly 1978; McAdam 1982). Within this approach, the "political opportunity structure" (POS) (Eisinger 1973; McAdam 1982; Tarrow 1983) is the most inclusive concept we have for dealing with the external, political conditions for protest. In this chapter, while referring to political opportunities for social movements in Italy and the Federal Republic of Germany after World War II, I focus on protest policing as one single variable. I consider protest policing an important barometer of the political opportunities available for social movements, and suggest it has an important effect on action repertoires. Looking at the evolution of policing styles and protest forms of action, I stress the importance of framing processes.

I discuss some advantages of a research on protest policing and summarize the relevant information on the evolution of protest policing in Italy and Germany, comparing the historical evolution of policing styles in the two countries. After this description, I develop a model for the study of causes and consequences of protest policing, and propose some hypotheses on the political opportunities and constraints on protest policing, looking at the more stable political opportunities, the more volatile configuration of power, and police preferences, as well as the potential effects of policing strategies.

PROTEST POLICING AS A BAROMETER OF POLITICAL OPPORTUNITIES: AN INTRODUCTION

I define one specific aspect of state response to protest, the policing of protest, as "the police handling of protest events" – a more neutral description for what protestors usually refer to as "repression" and the state as "law and order." Although the variable "repression" is included in several explanatory models on insurgencies and revolutions, protest policing has received very little attention in the research on contemporary social movements in both Western democracies and in studies on police. Charles Tilly's influential theoretical work mentioned the relevance of governmental repression for social movements (Tilly 1978: esp. 101–6), but studies on the relationship between police and protest are still rare. Moreover, in the vast literature on the police, police behavior during protest activities is dealt with only in terms of the extreme case of riot control. To my knowledge, neither political theorists nor law experts have considered how protest affects the understanding of democracy and citizens' rights. I hope to fill this gap, but also to indicate possible solutions for problems related to the research on political opportunities.

Protest policing, political opportunities, and cultural understanding

Focusing on an in-depth analysis of *one single variable* can be a promising alternative to the dangerous trend of increasing the number of variables in the definition of the POS. In his introduction to this part of the volume, McAdam expresses concern for the lack of consensus regarding the relevant dimensions of the POS. I believe this lack of consensus resulted in an accelerating growth in the number of dimensions considered part of the POS. While the first studies in the 1980s on political opportunities focused on a few variables,[1] several scholars have referred to the concept of political opportunity structure in a number of case studies and cross-national comparisons, often adding new variables to the original set (in particular, Brand 1985b; Kitschelt 1986; Rucht 1989b; Kriesi 1991). These theoretical efforts have enlarged the explanatory capacity of the concept but reduced its specificity. The result is a complex but nonparsimonious model. Especially in cross-national comparative studies, it is almost impossible to handle such a high number of variables and assess their explanatory power properly. Focusing on an in-depth analysis of a single contextual variable would allow, instead, a better understanding of the interactions between social movements and their environment.

A second advantage of research on protest policing is that it addresses a variable which has *a most direct impact on social movements*. This helps address additional problems related to the study of the POS. The distance between the variables indicated as part of the political structure and the assumed effect on social movements is sometimes so great that it is difficult to show the logical connections between the values of the independent variable and the (presumed) effects on the movements. As Koopmans (1990b) observed, movements do not react to abstract categories (such as electoral volatility) but to a limited set of their derivates – so far, that has not been properly singled out. I suggest that protest policing is indeed one of these "derivates" of political opportunities that have a direct impact on social movements.

Indeed, protest policing is a barometer of the available POS. As part of the state response to social movements, it should be very sensitive to the relevant opportunities and constraints, and therefore represent a general expression of the state's degree of openness or receptivity. By studying protest policing, we can better understand the effect of the numerous indicators of the POS. Not only is protest policing a barometer because it is sensitive to political opportunities, but my research on radical groups in Italy and Germany indicated that movement activists consider protest policing as one of the best and most "visible" indicators of institutional attitudes to protest (della Porta 1992b).

Even if protest policing is not the only state response to protest, I assume it has a relevant effect on social movements, and, in particular, on *movements' behavior*.[2] By focusing on a single characteristic of social movements I hope to overcome another problem of POS studies, the lack of clarity about the *explanandum*. The available POS has been investigated in order to explain a growing number of dependent variables, ranging from movement mobilization capabilities (Eisinger 1973) to movement effects (Tarrow 1983) to movement dynamics (Kitschelt 1986) to movement strategies (Kriesi 1991). I assume that protest policing is the single variable that has a most direct effect on a specific characteristic of collective action: protest behavior. Referring to the distinction McAdam makes in his introduction, I am not concerned here with the emergence or strength of the movements, but with their form and development. In particular, I assume that protest and police tactics (as described by McAdam 1983b) adapt to each other through a process of reciprocal influence, involving innovation and adaptation.

A last choice in my research was to consider not only actual protest policing, but also the *cultural understanding* influencing both police strategies and their consequences. As Gamson and Meyer notice in Chapter 12, looking up structural opportunities can be misleading if the cognitive processes that intervene between structure and action are not taken into account. Although empirical research on the perceptions of all components of the POS would be very difficult to carry out, I believe that the study of framing processes on protest policing is not only feasible but necessary and promising. First of all, protest policing has an important effect on the activists' understanding of available political opportunities. Second even a first look at the effects of protest policing shows that they are "mediated" by cultural variables. McAdam, McCarthy, and Zald suggest in their introduction to this book, that frames are lenses for perceiving the political opportunities. More specifically about repression, Tilly has stressed the need to "distinguish between the volume and type of repressive activity, on the one hand, and its *symbolic significance,* on the other hand" (1978: 104; emphasis added). Third, the political discourse on protest policing is especially important for various political and social actors. When "how to police protest" becomes a relevant policy choice about which several actors contend, the very framing of the issue is the subject of bitter disputes. As Zald notes in Chapter 11, the different actors engage in competitive processes in different arenas in order to spread their frames. This is especially true for the discourse on public order. Unlike most other crimes, "disturbing the public peace" (and political crimes in general) have only a very vague jurisprudential definition (e.g., see Roach and Thomanek 1985). Whether a protest action is defined as a citizen right or a "disturbance of the public order" has a vital effect on the legitimation of the different actors. The question of what does and does not constitute a legitimate form of protest in a democracy is a "hot" topic endlessly debated by protestors and police, parties and policymakers, media and experts. Radical protest and tough police intervention trigger what Zald here refers to as "cultural contradictions": that is, moments in which two or more cultural themes that are potentially contradictory are brought into active contradiction. During the peak of collective mobilization, protestor rights and police rights are a controversial topic polarizing allies and opponents of the social movements. Fourth, while the single issues and claims change in the various protest cycles, the policing of protest is an always present "meta"-issue. Studying the evolution of frames on protest policing allows us to analyze cultural changes over a long time span.

The styles of protest policing

In presenting some questions and hypotheses referring to the policing of protest in Italy and Germany, as well as more generally in contemporary Western democracies, the first task is to describe the techniques police used and use to control protest. For this description we need a classification that goes beyond an oversimplified categorization of policing styles as either "tough repressive" or "tolerant control."

Two approaches to classify the forms and nature of state control have already appeared in the social movement literature. Gary Marx (1979) distinguished repressive actions according to their specific aims: the creation of an unfavorable public image, disinformation, restricting a movement's resources and limiting its facilities, derecruitment of activists, destroying leaders, fueling internal conflicts, encouraging conflicts between groups, and sabotaging particular actions. Charles Tilly's typology (1978) does not deal with repressive actions per se but more generally with political regimes, which he classifies according to the degree of repression and "facilitation" they manifest toward various collective actors and actions. This approach yields four types of political regimes: repressive regimes, which repress many groups and actions while facilitating few of either; totalitarian regimes, which repress fewer groups and facilitate a wide range of actions, even to the point of making them compulsory; tolerant regimes, which accept a wide range of actions, but reduce the power of the stronger groups; and weak regimes, which have a wide range of tolerance and little repression or facilitation.

For my purposes, Gary Marx's list of repressive forms appeared too phenomenological for an attempt to trace evolutionary trends, and Tilly's typology of political regimes was too general for a comparison of Western democracies. While acknowledging that several institutions and political actors do "respond" to protest, I wanted to concentrate on one single actor: the police. I therefore formulated some new classifications, including the following dimensions: (1) "repressive" versus "tolerant," according to the range of prohibited behaviors; (2) "selective" versus "diffuse," according to the range of groups subject to repression; (3) "preventive" versus "reactive," according to the timing of police intervention; (4) "hard" versus "soft," according to the degree of force involved; (5) "dirty" versus "lawful," according to the degree to which respect for legal and democratic procedures is emphasized.

On some methodologic choices and the status of this essay

My research on protest policing in Italy and West Germany after World War II combined historical and cross-national comparison. An historical approach would help analyze the complex process of "institutionalization" of protest repertoires. The cross-national comparison is particularly important since past research has indicated the existence of distinct national strategies of conflict resolution while simultaneously the growing cross-national flow of information (between governments and between movement activists) allows us to assume an international convergence of techniques and frames for protest policing.

The following discussion presents some first thoughts from an empirical research on protest policing in the two countries. Although based mainly on a qualitative analysis of secondary sources, the ongoing research project includes a series of case studies of police handling of violent demonstrations.[3] On critical events and time-limited campaigns relevant to protest policing, I am collecting information based on newspaper reports, debates on public order laws in parliament, and publications printed in both movement and police presses.[4] Although the results of this part of the project are not yet complete (and therefore are not systematically analyzed here), several remarks come from the case studies. In this sense, my hypotheses are intermediate between the more general thought on which research proposals are normally based and the systematically "controlled" results of an empirical, qualitative research based on case studies.

THE POLICING OF PROTEST IN ITALY

In Italy, the style of protest policing has changed dramatically over the last four decades, as can be seen by observing developments in five different periods roughly coinciding with (1) the repressive 1950s, (2) the years of Center-

Left governments in the 1960s, (3) the years characterized by the "strategy of tension" (first half of the 1970s), (4) the "emergency period" (second half of the 1970s), and (5) the moderate 1980s.

The repressive 1950s

Throughout the 1950s, the protest policing was characterized by a hard repression of several political groups and forms of collective action.[5] One of the few books on the Italian police notes that "the primary means of keeping public order was the use of firearms by policemen against protestors, strikers, peasants who occupied land, etc." (Canosa 1976: 181). The fact that almost 100 demonstrators died in the 1940s and 1950s when police charged go-ins and sit-ins using firearms is a grim testament to the truth of this statement.[6] The laws on public order as well as some organizational changes in the police forces favored this hard and diffuse style of protest policing. As for the legislative asset, the body of law regulating public security (which was a legacy of the fascist regime[7]) gave large power to the police. Moreover, in 1948, a new law allowed for the immediate arrest of protesters who blocked traffic, and the "Regulations on the Territorial and Garrison Service" gave the police greater latitude in using firearms against protest gatherings whenever the officer leading a police intervention thought there was a "threat to public order." The "Regulations" stated that: "Fire should be addressed directly against those who look most dangerous, who incited others to violence, against the leaders of the demonstrators" (in *Vie Nuove* 1969: 14).[8] Organizationally, a hard and diffuse repression was facilitated by the purging of police forces of left-wingers and former partisans, and the establishment of their direct dependency on the national executive branch. As members of a militarized body, policemen were not allowed to form or join a trade union. They received no special training in crime control and had poor equipment. Training was primarily physical, military, and oriented to repressing mass disorder.

The style of policing reflected more general characteristics of the party system and the political culture. The first postwar governments in Italy based their plans for political and economic reconstruction on low wages and the exclusion of the working class from power, with the consequent repression of the trade unions and the Communist Party (the PCI). The governments considered preserving public order the police's primary task. In Parliament, the Left often called for reforms to reduce such police power as the *fermo di polizia* (the right to keep "suspect" or "dangerous" people under arrest without permitting them access to a judge or a lawyer). Public opinion and the press were internally divided along the traditional Left-Right cleavage. In a polarized political system, the Right considered most protesters to be Communists and puppets of Moscow, and the Left denounced police misconduct (especially against former partisans) as systematic persecution of the political opposition.

The contradictions of the Center-Left

If a repressive policing of protests prevailed throughout the 1950s, by the time the student movement developed the climate was quite different. In the '60s, protest policing became less repressive and softer: From 1963 to 1967 not a single demonstrator was killed. Police handling of student protest, however, was quite contradictory, mixing tolerance and hard tactics. In general, during the early years of the student movement, the police took a much "softer" approach to the control of protest than it had in the past when confronting other social groups. The police often tolerated spontaneous protest marches and the occupation of public buildings, and did not resort to firearms to disperse demonstrators. At times of particular tension, however, the more traditional forms of protest control resurfaced (see Canosa 1976: chap. 4). At the end of the 1960s, when protest exploded, the police again abandoned restraint – in 1968, three people were killed during marches organized by trade unions; another three were killed in demonstrations in 1969.

The contradictions in protest policing reflected those in the political system. In 1962, a Center-Left government had been formed, joining the Socialist Party (PSI) with the Christian Democracy (DC) and a few minor parties. The reformist Center-Left governments took a more liberal position toward civil and political rights than their Centrist predecessors, and oversaw a series of new laws.[9] Student protest, however, polarized the political spectrum and public opinion. The Left – including the PCI, the PSI, the trade unions, and the left-wing press – openly supported the students, often accusing the police of brutality. While the DC was internally divided, right-wing pressure groups, including elements in the press, called for the use of "hard-line" tactics against the lazy and/or "red" students. At the same time, the Socialists proposed a radical reform, including the disarmament of the police, and even a few Christian Democrats criticized the hard line chosen by their party. Beyond "visible politics," right-wing forces acted underground, planning coups d'état and using the secret services to blackmail the Left.[10]

A "strategy of tension"

In the early 1970s, the state responded to the radicalized left-wing movements with a use of police force that on several occasions reverted to the most brutal traditions of the 1950s. Protest policing continued to mix more tolerant tactics – which produced a well-developed system of bargaining between police leadership and movement leadership – with an increasing use of hard repression. Although the police did not use firearms, the tactics for control of mass demonstrations encouraged escalation, especially when large police squads charged the demonstrators with jeeps and tear gas (Canosa 1976: 274–85). The list of protesters who lost their lives during police charges at public demonstrations grew in the early 1970s. Between 1970 and 1975, policeman killed seven people – protesters and passers-by – during police intervention at political gatherings (ibid.). In these incidents, the victims did not fall under police fire as in the 1950s but were beaten to death with clubs, crushed under police jeeps, or hit by tear gas candles.

The shift in protest policing corresponded to a change in the party system. The crisis of the Center-Left governments strengthened the hard-liners' position. At the beginning of the 1970s, a more conservative coalition had replaced the previous one. Although there was some reform, it was widely believed in the Left that several of those in power were ready to use any means to block political changes. The repression was perceived as directed in general against the Left, so the Old Left and the trade unions sided with the social movements in denouncing state repression and fascist aggression. Public opinion was increasingly polarized, and the political discourse increasingly inflamed. Confronted with a strong and violent radical Right and a radicalized New Left, the more conservative political forces demanded a policy of law and order to contain the "opposite extremisms." And the new Center-Right coalition used right-wing terrorism and a wave of organized and petty crime as a rationale to pass new, restrictive laws on public order (Pasquino 1990).[11] The relations between protesters and the police only worsened with time. While the fights between the movements' militants and neofascists triggered the escalation of political conflicts (della Porta 1991), widespread rumors of complicity between police officials and right-wing militants undermined the confidence of the left-wing public in the state. Claims that the secret service protected the radical Right were particularly frequent in the period of the *stragismo* – the "strategy" of massacres perpetrated by right-wing terrorism.[12] The strategy to control protest came to be widely known as the "strategy of tension" – the government's covert manipulation of the radical political groups to incite outbursts so as to induce public opinion to favor authoritarian policies.

The "years of emergency"

The strategy of protest policing changed again the mid-1970s, when it was characterized by the harsh repression of increasingly violent movement groups. With the decline of mobilization, the "dirty" tactics were partially abandoned.[13] Right-wing radicals lost their institutional protection: For a few years they fell into an organizational crisis, emerging after 1977 with a strategy of attacking the state and engaging in daily brutal – sometimes deadly – fights with the radical Left. In the radicalized climate of the terrorist emergency, police forces intervened to break up the often violent marches. As the first information I collected from the press on some protest campaigns in the spring of 1977 indicated, police tactics seemed inappropriate to control most of the violence that flared in demonstrations. First of all, the police resorted to firearms to cope with radical activists armed with revolvers. Second, the police would charge an entire march, hitting peaceful demonstrators as well as militant ones. Third, often armed undercover agents were also present and, according to press reports, on a few occasions they fired against the protestors. Fourth, the police intervened in large units and tried to overcome with numbers their deficiencies in armaments and technical expertise. To discourage attempts to defy the frequent prohibitions against public gatherings, the police and the army joined together in military occupation of some Italian cities.

The hard line on protest policing, as well as its larger selectivity, reflected some political characteristics of the period. Protest policing represented the institutional and symbolic effects of the most dramatic wave of terrorist attacks. Terrorism and street crime shocked the public, and only small minorities criticized the institutional and police strategies for dealing with violent protest. During these "years of emergency," public order policies and internal security policies were in fact intertwined (della Porta 1992b). If this climate pushed for hard policing, the PCI's "historic compromise" – its proposal for cooperation between "Catholic and Communist masses" – and its 1978 and 1979 support of the Christian Democrat–led national governments probably reduced the influence of the more conservative forces on the government. In their search for legitimation, the Communists gave up their position as defenders of citizens' rights, so that choices of hard repression found little challenge. While increasing conflicts among the ruling parties and parliamentary instability worsened the government's capacity for implementing a coherent policy,[14] the fight against terrorism became a unifying aim. Identified as "terrorists" or "sympathizers for terrorism," the radical activists became scapegoats. Both the government and the parliamentarian opposition defined most protest as dangerous "disorder." The emergency laws,[15] designed to fight terrorism, constrained protest as well, in so far as they could be (and were) used against the radical wings of the movements.[16] Although the government of national unity was a sign of a depolarization in the political system, for social movement activists Italy was recast in the image of an authoritarian state by the emergency legislation as well as the frequent death of demonstrators by police charges. Consequently, the period 1977–79 came to be known as the "years of lead" – gray, heavy, and toxic.

The "national reconciliation"

The style of protest policing changed in the 1980s so dramatically that it seems inexplicable until one realizes how profoundly terrorism had shocked both the movement organizations and state apparati. The disbanding of the radical groups made hard repressive measures superfluous. The decline of terrorism brought calls for a "national reconciliation," including a revision of the emergency legislation.[17] The implementation of long-overdue police reform contributed to a change in practice on the part of the police and to their understanding of the external reality.[18] These changes were manifested in a more tolerant attitude toward the peace movement in the decade's beginning, and the other movements later on. In the 1980s, the policing of protest thus became extremely "soft" and very selective. When the tiny groups of surviving radical *Autonomi* tried to disrupt the large marches of the peace movement, police intervention was usually aimed to keep the "troublemakers" under control while the nonviolent movement organizations informally collaborated with the police in order to avoid escalations. The policing of acts of civil disobedience also became more tolerant. In only a few cases did "hard" police repression escalate the conflict (for instance, when police charged peace movement demonstrators staging sit-ins at a Sicilian nuclear missile base site in Comiso). Institutional reactions against the nonviolent techniques of some movement organizations primarily involved the judiciary. But when the nonviolent activists on trial for breach of peace criticized the judicial system, it was not to decry repressiveness but to complain that the judges were too inclined to "bargaining."[19]

Also in this period, protest policing reflected some characteristics of the political system. At the beginning of the 1980s, the first governments with non-Christian Democratic prime ministers in the republic's history signaled willingness to change, and the governmental parties insisted on a new image of "efficacy." In the same period, the PCI, once again in the opposition, became more receptive to protest activities. To stop a steady electoral decline and reach a broader range of voters, the party tried to shed its image as "the working-class party" and presented itself as a "point of reference for the progressive forces in the society." The Twentieth Congress of the PCI in February 1991 thus became the First Congress of the Democratic Party of the Left, at which the party declared itself open to "all the leftist, progressive, alternative, environmental forces." The issues championed by the new movements – in particular, peace and ecology – did not polarize the press. Movement speakers were given space to present their opinions, and the movements' action repertoires, now emphasizing nonviolence, were rarely criticized. The political discourse on law and order and internal security became quite moderate and pragmatic, even during the campaigns on such symbolic topics as amnesty for former terrorists.

THE POLICING OF PROTEST IN GERMANY

In Germany as in Italy, the policing of protest underwent a variety of changes in the past four decades. We can observe some parallels and some differences with concurrent conditions in Italy. I divide the forty years into five main periods: (1) the conservatism of the Adenauer era (the 1950s and early 1960s); (2) the contradictions of the Grand Coalition (the late 1960s); (3) the reformism of Chancellor Willy Brandt (beginning of the 1970s); (4) a partial conservative rollback under Chancellor Helmut Schmidt (the 1970s); and (5) the larger tolerance but also the few escalations of the 1980s.

The conservatism of the Adenauer era

Compared to the Italian case, protest policing in Germany in the 1950s was generally more selective and (relatively) less hard. The police handling of protest was characterized by a frequent but not brutal use of force to implement the prohibitions against public marches.[20] According to recent research, before the student movement emerged the German police had "an image of any gathering of people as potentially destructive, an irrational 'formation of a mob,' from which a danger to the state order could rapidly develop. The orientation to such an understanding of demonstration kept the executive and the judiciary loyal to a predemocratic equipment of control by the state and the police" (Busch et al. 1988: 319). Any potential threat to public order – including disruption of traffic – tended to be considered as sufficient rationale to prohibit public demonstrations. Although in the early 1950s the police charged marches against rearmament and on labor issues, killing two protestors (on May 11, 1952, and May 1, 1953), they rarely used force in the handling of later industrial conflicts. In these years, state control of protest relied instead on a frequent intervention of the judiciary[21] and the outlawing of neo-Nazi groups and the Communist Party.

The state strategies were influenced by some internal and international political features. Inside the Federal Republic, the relative strength of the trade unions in the factories and of the Social Democrats (SPD) in some states dissuaded the conservatives in the federal government from making greater use of police force. The attempt by the police to regain legitimacy among the population in the new democracy was probably another check on hard-line intervention, as was the fear that claims of police brutality could stir up bitter memories of the Weimar Republic and the Nazi regime. But the very existence of the German Democratic Republic and the division of Berlin provided a rationale for a judiciary repression of the opposition, including the outlawing of the Communist Party in 1956.

The Grand Coalition

At the time the student movement evolved, protest policing included a mixture of "hard" and "soft" tactics, which was particularly visible in the long protest campaign in Berlin. In the beginning, student protest was tolerated, but the claim of "disturbing the pedestrian traffic" sometimes produced police charges on student marches in the city center, in line with the tradition of the previous period. Altogether, the police tended to avoid physical repression, and were criticized for it in the right-wing press until the state government (and SPD's mayor) pressured the police to intervene more forcefully. The conflict escalated on June 2, 1967, when a policeman killed a student, Benno Ohnesorg, during a protest against the visit to Berlin of the Shah of Iran. According to several reports *(Kursbuch* 1968; Sack 1984), police strategy triggered an escalation of the conflict. In what was called "an exercise for an emergency," the Berlin police resorted to the tactic known as the "sausage": pushing a crowd of demonstrators on its flank so that the protesters were forced to move to a place where the police could charge them.

The protest policing of the student movement reflected and simultaneously contributed to the changes in the German party system and public opinion in the second half of the 1960s. When the student movement emerged, the SPD had joined the conservative CDU-CSU in a government called the Grand Coalition. Part of the federal government for the first time after World War II, the SPD, pushed both by its coalition partners and its search for legitimation, took a fairly negative attitude toward the student movement. Because of their general mistrust of disorder, the majority of the Old Left did not trust the students and opposed their strategy of "restricted rule-breaking." Generally, the political elites in power felt seriously challenged by the radical stance of the protest, while – partly as a result of the CDU-CSU coalition with the Social Democrats – the radical Right simultaneously won more votes. The conservative press (and especially the *Bild,* the scandal-mongering daily with a large Berlin circulation) launched campaigns against students whom they labeled as "puppets of the Communist regimes," "infiltrated by East-German secret service," and "violent anarchists." Particularly in the peculiar position of West Berlin, the student activists experienced a pogromlike climate, a violent rejection by part of the population. At the same time, however, the students gained sympathy and sparked the formation of civil rights coalitions that also included members of the Old Left. When the police and the students confronted each other, both the press and public opinion split on opposite judgments. The liberal press criticized police intervention, singling out some episodes of police brutality as a sign that German society was not yet fully democratized. So the shock of the death of Benno Ohnesorg led the Social Democratic mayor of Berlin to resign, and intensified the internal conflicts of the SPD. Even among police, there was growing criticism of the more repressive politics of the previous years and demands for greater democracy. One of the most long-lasting results of the late 1960s was that "the ways of reciprocal behaviors of the state powers and the protestors became a theme of great relevance in the public discussion: The marches and their control by the police became a political issue" (Busch et al. 1988: 318).

The reformist years

The policing of protest changed radically at the beginning of the 1970s, becoming extremely tolerant and soft. As Busch and his colleagues (1988: 320) observed, "In the administration of justice the opinion tended to prevail that demonstrations should not only be tolerated, but that, as active citizen rights, they must take priority over concerns about executive order. The intervention of the police – until now oriented to fight violent troublemakers with closed units – had to be rethought according to the 'principle of the flexible reaction' and through an intervention suitable to the specific situation, designed to avoid the escalation of conflict and violence." New police strategies developed with the precise aim of avoiding escalation. For example, the Berlin police created a *Diskussionkommando,* composed of small groups of policemen, in uniform but without arms, who spoke with activists during demonstrations, trying to convince them to avoid violence (Hübner 1979: 212). In Munich, the police leadership – after the new model elaborated by the "study-group for politological research on communication" – sent policemen in uniform to "discuss" with the demonstrators and "convince" them to avoid illegal actions (Malpricht 1984: 83–85). An effect of the choice of "softer" police tactics was no deaths occurring during political marches throughout the entire decade.

The tolerant turn in protest policing coincided with a change in government which was itself partly a result of the student movement. In 1969 the SPD-CDU coalition broke up, replaced by a Social Democratic coalition with the liberal FDP. The shift produced a much more open attitude toward protest. Adopting the slogan "to dare more democracy," Brandt's government introduced reformist politics, meeting the demands for a more liberal understanding of the right to demonstrate.[22] One of the first, highly symbolic actions of the Social Democratic-Liberal coalition was to grant amnesty to those involved in the student unrests. Then, on May 22, 1970, criminal law was liberalized to allow the right to demonstrate, and the *Landfriedensbruchparagraph,* the law regulating the crime of "breach of peace," was abolished. The terrorist actions of 1972 and CDU-CSU's aggressive electoral campaign in the same year marked the beginning of another shift: a partial reversal of the recently liberalized protest rights. In response to the accusation of being unfit to contain the "radical extremists," the SPD-FDP government issued the *Radikalenerlass* (January 1972), which was designated to concretize and unify the various procedures developed by the different states to block civil service access to individuals with "anticonstitutional" attitudes. The *Radikalenerlass* thus increased the control over those who applied for civil service positions. Although actual exclusions were rare,[23] the symbolic effect was quite strong, and many saw Germany again as an authoritarian state. Moreover, police interventions to arrest terrorists often did result in casualties, and thus criticism (see Böll et al. 1976). In the movements in particular, criticism of the state's authoritarianism intensified when the imprisoned terrorists staged hunger strikes to call attention to their harsh living conditions – particularly the high-security units and isolation – which many defined as inhuman.

Conservative rollback?

Although the more tolerant attitudes toward protest that had evolved in the early 1970s (and had almost completely eliminated violence from the political conflicts) did not entirely disappear, the mid-1970s represented a new turning point. Especially in the handling of the antinuclear protest, which often involved the occupation of sites where nuclear plants had to be built, the police deviated from the more tolerant behavior of previous years. On many occasions the police strategy was based on large preventive interventions and (tendentially) selective use of physical force against the more militant wing of the movements (Busch et al. 1988: 328–41). Usually, the police forces' first move was to make the nuclear sites difficult to penetrate from outside – installing water cannon and building high protective walls, for instance. They then prohibited marches and imposed restrictions on the routes the marches could follow and the clothes demonstrators could wear, guided by the principles of extensive control and preventive action.[24] But the lessons of the 1960s were not completely forgotten; in order to avoid escalation, prohibitions were often not enforced. Moreover, the police avoided frontal attacks on demonstrations, and tried to develop techniques for a focused repression of the more violent groups. Even in instances where police did use physical force, particularly in fights with the more radical wing of the antinuclear movement, nobody was killed (Busch et al. 1988: 341–2). All things considered, the tactics the police used in the 1970s were much more selective and much less "escalating" compared to those used in the 1960s. In comparison with the larger tolerance of the early 1970s, however, they became clearly harder and more repressive.

A more repressive handling of the protest reflected the changes produced in the political system when the economic crisis of the early 1970s undermined the reformist attitudes of the government. In fact, after Chancellor Brandt was forced to resign because of a scandal involving an East German spy, the reelected SPD-FDP federal coalition – now led by Helmut Schmidt – revised its slogans and programs, concentrating on the defense of the welfare state and abandoning its more ambitious reform projects. In the second half of the 1970s, only a minority within the Social Democratic Party cooperated (although with some friction) with movement organizations on issues of nuclear energy, ecology, women's liberation, and disarmament. Faced with two waves of terrorist attacks, in Germany as well as Italy, protestors were often assimilated with dangerous criminals. On the other side, a radicalization of frames affected also the movement activists. Even relatively "soft" police intervention had a negative symbolic effect, for the political discourse had changed since the sixties. The more aggressive handling of protest, together with changes in legislation concerning civil rights,[25] fostered the image of an authoritarian state in the minds of movement activists. A massive number of house searches and the erection of street barricades to capture fugitive terrorists intensified the liberal citizens' sense that civil and political rights were threatened. Among movement activists, the impression of increasing authoritarianism – even a renazification of the German state – was also reinforced by the isolation of terrorists in prison, the government's hard line toward those terrorists who undertook hunger strikes (two of whom eventually died), and the suicide in prison of four members of the terrorist Rote Armee Fraktion (RAF). Terrorism and antiterrorism had therefore the effect of polarizing the political culture and, then, "dramatizing" the frames used by authorities and movement activists to evaluate the presumed dangers of protest and repression respectively.

Bargaining and escalation in the 1980s

At the beginning of the '80s, protest policing changed again, and the peace movement met with less resistance than the antinuclear movement had in the 1970s. Protest policing became more selective, with a large tolerance for nonviolent repertoires and a stricter control of the radical wing of social movements. Although terrorism continued to be an issue, the "years of lead" were over. My studies of police intervention in Berlin in the 1980s seem to indicate that the police looked for tactics that could avoid escalation, and that peacekeeping now clearly took priority over law enforcement. The police experimented with new tactics oriented mainly at isolating the violent wing of a demonstration rather than attacking nonviolent as well as violent protestors, and containing rather than charging potentially dangerous demonstrators (using police barriers or military isolation of areas where radicals held their meetings). These new tactics evolved partly from technical changes within the police forces, specifically the reorganization of the units specialized in maintaining public order into smaller and more mobile subunits, and the introduction of new and more sophisticated equipment, such as protective helmets, fireproof clothes, armored trucks, and CN and CS gas. At the same time, they reflected also some cultural changes in the police itself. First of all, the frames of demonstrators as "puppets of the Communist regimes" had been substituted by frames of violent individuals as psychologically weak individuals (della Porta 1994). Second, the police seemed to increasingly take into account the reactions of public opinion and the media. More than once, police leaders asked the political forces to provide a political response to social protest. But despite social learning about how to avoid escalation, conflicts did escalate on some occasions: during the occupation of houses in Berlin at the beginning of the 1980s; during the long campaign against the expansion of the Frankfurt airport; in the protest against the proposed nuclear plant in Wackersdorf; and during the meeting of the World Bank Fund and the visit of President Reagan in Berlin in the late 1980s.[26] The more violent confrontations evolved especially during symbolically important events, when police forces from the most disparate German states converged on Berlin, Frankfurt, and Wackersdorf to keep law and order while the *Autonomen* called for national "happenings." Even if the police perfected techniques for isolating troublemakers, the dynamics of the physical confrontation often escalated into spirals of violence in which peaceful demonstrators or standers-by became involved. In these cases, police handling of protest was often perceived by the more moderate wing of the movements as repressive, hard, and diffuse. A massive deployment of police forces for preventive control of peaceful protest campaigns as well as a large number of charges against civil disobedience sometimes spoiled the tolerant climate of the 1980s.[27]

Once again, we can observe that styles of protest policing reflected political circumstances. The 1980s began with the crisis in the SPD-FDP federal government and the return of the CDU to government. But this did not harden police handling of protest, as one might have expected. The CDU reassured its more right-wing supporters with symbolic law-and-order campaigns. In 1985, for example, the national parliament passed a *Vermummungsverbot* prohibiting demonstrators from disguising themselves when taking part in public marches – a law specifically directed against "Black Block" militants who attended demonstrations dressed in black clothes with balaclava helmets covering their faces. But essentially the CDU-FDP government maintained a tolerant attitude toward protest. With the decline of terrorism and the end of the economic recession of the 1970s, political conflicts deescalated. Although a new antiterrorist law was passed in 1986 (following two assassinations by the RAF), in 1987 the Federal Office for the Defense of the Constitution unofficially offered to "help" those who abandoned the terrorist organization; in 1989 a new law on internal security reduced the penalties for terrorists who confessed; and in 1992 the Federal Minister of Justice, Klaus Kinkel, offered to free terrorists who were ill or imprisoned for a long time in exchange for an RAF declaration of a "suspension" of its armed attacks. A liberal understanding of demonstration rights prevailed also in public opinion. But public tolerance for hard-line police approaches grew when demonstrators themselves resorted to even the "lightest" form of violence.

COMPARING STYLES OF PROTEST POLICING

I have described the evolution of protest policing in the two countries. As mentioned, the available information is not sufficient for an accurate state-

Table 3.1. *Protest policing in Italy and Germany, 1950–1990*

Italy		Germany	
Phase	Characteristics	Phase	Characteristics
The "repressive" 1950s	Repressive Diffuse Reactive Hard Legal	Adenauer's era	Repressive Selective Reactive (Relatively) hard Legal
The Center-Left governments	(More) tolerant Diffuse Reactive Soft(er) (Mainly) legal	The Grand Coalition	(Relatively) repressive Selective Reactive (Relatively) hard Legal
The strategy of tension	Repressive Diffuse Reactive Hard "Dirty"	The Brandt government	Tolerant Selective Preventive Soft Legal
The emergency years	Repressive (More) selective Reactive Hard (Mainly) legal	The Schmidt government	(More) repressive Selective Preventive Soft (occasionally hard) Legal
The 1980s	(Very) tolerant Selective (More) preventive Soft Legal	The 1980s	(More) tolerant Selective Preventive Soft Legal

ment of the various characteristics of the single periods. With the limited aim of developing some hypotheses, I shall try to sketch a provisional comparison of both historical and cross-national similarities and differences. For Table 3.1 I used the five classifications of protest policing styles to summarize the information provided.

Comparing the two countries, in Italy several forms of protest were repressed for a longer time. This was particularly true in the early 1970s; in the 1980s, Italy had a more visible break with the previous "hard" style of protest policing than did Germany. Consistently in all periods, the police handling of protest seems to have been more selective in Germany than in Italy. Since the beginning, German police tended to intervene only very sporadically in the industrial conflicts, and repression focused especially on small political groups. In Italy, especially in the 1950s and early 1970s, there was a "hard" police handling of larger groups, including the trade unions and the Communist Party. Moreover, the search for techniques of handling protest that could selectively address the violent groups developed earlier in Germany than in Italy. Only in the 1980s did Italian police start to focus repression on the violent groups – an attempt the German police had already started in the previous decade. While in Italy protest policing tended to involve a higher degree of force (at least until the 1980s), in Germany protest policing was characterized by a greater dependence on intelligence (collection of information, etc.). We also observed that the Left often accused Italian police forces of resorting to "dirty" tactics, such as large and unconstrained use of *agents provocateurs,* the protection of neofascists, and a direct involvement of the secret services in massacres and plotting coups d'état. Similar claims have been much less frequent in Germany, where the police seemed more constrained by a formal respect of the *Rechtsstaat.* For this reason, we can also infer that the German judiciary played a more important role than the Italian in the control of social movements.

In both countries, during the decades from 1950 to 1990, protest control evolved toward more flexible forms based on a more liberal understanding of demonstration rights. And in both countries, public order policies became more tolerant, more selective, more oriented toward prevention, more respectful of democratic procedures, and "softer." This evolution was hardly linear ("relapses" occurred in both countries when political conflicts escalated into violent forms). Over time, cross-national differences seem to diminish, probably because of international cooperation and cross-national flows of information involving both movement organizations and law enforcers.

PROTEST POLICING: AN ANALYTIC MODEL

The comparison of protest policing styles in Italy and Germany raises at least two very different questions. If we look at protest policing as a barometer of the POS, we should ask which of the political opportunities seem to have influenced the observed cross-national differences and historical changes in protest policing. If we look at protest policing as an intermediate level between political structures and social movements, we should ask which are the effects of the different policing styles on protest repertoires. Figure 3.1 provides an outline of the different analytical levels that appear to be relevant for an analysis of protest policing.

A first analytical level refers to the stable opportunities in which a certain style of policing develops – that is, what Gamson and Meyer define in this volume as "some aspects of opportunities [that] are deeply embedded in political institutions and culture." First of all, I argue that *institutional features –*

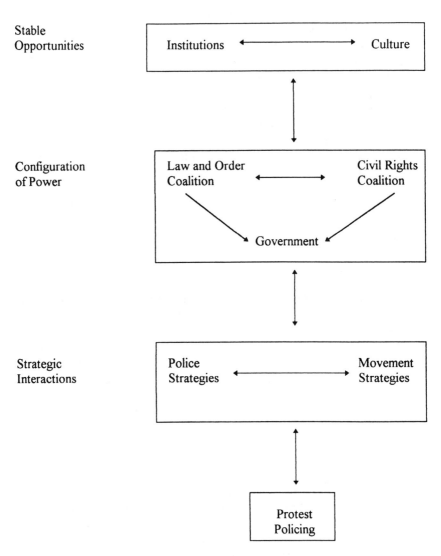

Figure 3.1. A model for analysis of protest policing.

police organization, the nature of the judiciary, law codes, constitutional rights, and so forth – play an extremely important role in defining the opportunities, and the constraints on, protest policing. To use McAdam's distinction in his Part I introduction, we can say institutional or legal structure sets the conditions for the actual strategies of protest policing. And, following Brand (1985b), Kitschelt (1986), and Kriesi (1991), we can assume that some aspects of the *political culture,* particularly those referring to conceptions of the state and citizens' rights, also have important effects.

In addition to the relatively stable context, policing styles depend on a second (more "volatile") analytical level: the shifting results of the interactions of different actors. Various collective actors put forward their interests or opinions, forming what Kriesi (1989b) refers to as configuration of power, and McAdam as *informal alliance structure* (in Chapter 1, the introduction to this book's Part I). First of all, social movements intervene on citizens' rights and police tasks – they organize protest actions to denounce police brutality and they ask for more democracy. As McAdam noted, this means that social movements influence their environment, and the various characteristics of the POS. But social movements are not the only collective actors to take positions on protest policing. Political parties, interest groups, trade unions, and voluntary associations conflict or cooperate with them on how to police protest. Like-minded actors on each side of the issue form coalitions upholding, on the one hand, "law and order," and on the other, "civil rights" (see level 2 in Figure 3.1).

The actual protest policing as well as protest strategies are then influenced by the interactions *between protesters and the police* (the third level in Figure 3.1). Protesters and the police, social movements and the state, influence each other in the strategic choices they make, in a process involving innovation and adaptation on both sides. As McAdam, McCarthy, and Zald put it in their introduction to this book, if we look at the development of social movements, we have to take into account that political opportunities result from the interactions between the movements and their environment.

STABLE OPPORTUNITIES AND PROTEST POLICING

In this and in next two sections, I shall put forward some hypotheses on all the mentioned analytic levels, starting with the stable opportunities. In his distinction of an "input" and an "output" structure, Herbert Kitschelt (1986: 61–64) emphasizes the relevance of *constitutional features.* Looking at a less formalized but still "stable" political opportunity, Kriesi applied to social movements the concept of national strategies of conflict resolution, elaborated in the analysis of the industrial conflicts.[28] He notes, "National strategies set the informal and formal rules of the game for the conflict" (1989b: 295).[29]

A historical and cross-national comparative perspective seems to indicate that protest policing is indeed "constrained" by some long-lasting institutional characteristics. As for constitutional features, the German case seems to indicate that a formally open political system sometimes favors social movements, but sometimes their opponents instead. As for the effects of federalism and decentralization of power, local governments often implemented a different police style than that defended by the federal government – sometimes softer and sometimes harder repression. For example, in the policing of the antinuclear movement, the CDU state governments often adopted confrontational politics jeopardizing the SPD-FDP coalition's negotiation attempts in the federal government. After a few minor incidents in 1975, the conflict escalated in Brokdorf in 1976, in northern and traditionally Christian Democratic Schleswig-Holstein, when the movement organizations (*Burgerinitiativen*) threatened to occupy the site of a projected nuclear plant if the authorities began building without waiting for the administrative court decision. As it happened, the SPD-FDP federal government – supportive of the nuclear projects – hoped to negotiate with the *Burgerinitiativen,* but the state governments called for a resolute intervention against the "small active minority" infiltrated by "extremists" (Busch et al. 1988: 321–32). Similarly, strong judiciary power sometimes improved but sometimes worsened protest opportunities. Especially in the 1980s, in several trials for breach of the peace, the defendants were acquitted and police accusations rejected, and on occasion administrative courts refused police prohibitions against public demonstrations. But in some cases, the courts used a principle of indirect responsibilities, ordering the convenors or leaders of some protest event to pay for the damages produced by others during public marches that turned violent.

Of course, other laws besides constitutional codes influence protest policing. In particular, our description suggests that *the legislation on public order and demonstrations, police rights, and citizen rights* affects the choice of protest policing.[30] For example, militarization of the police appears conducive to a "hard" strategy of repression (as in the Italian case, until the eighties), whereas professionalization and access to technical means encourage the use of more sophisticated forms of control, which in turn reduce the necessity of resorting to force (as in the German case). The degree to which the judiciary can control police behaviors also helps determine the forms protest policing will take. In Germany, for instance, the possibility of protestors appealing to the Administrative Court to reverse police decisions prohibiting demonstrations was a deescalating factor.

Traditions are embedded not only in laws but also in the political culture. As Zald mentions in Chapter 11, his introduction to Part III of this book, the movements as well as their adversaries draw their frames on a cultural stock that defines, among other things, how to protest and how to control protest. Protest policing seems to be particularly sensitive to *cultural understanding of civil rights and police power.*[31] A brief look at the national political culture of each country provides some illustration. The "dirty repression" that often characterized the reactions of the Italian state – contributing to the escalation of the political conflict and the growth of terrorism – was consistent with a mentality geared to conspiracies, to the idea of a Machiavellian "state of the Prince." In Germany, the constant references by both protestors and the state to the *Rechtsstaat* suggest why, unlike in Italy, even the "hard" strategies of police control of protest remained within the limits set by law. These different "master frames" of the role of the state had an important effect, since they were internalized by the police as well as the general public. Accordingly, Italians and Germans generally had very different ideas about the proper roles and responsibilities of the police. As Peter Katzenstein observed in his study on security policy, in Germany "the normative order in which the police operates is shaped by a German tradition that grants the state the position of a prepolitically accepted, rather than a politically contested, order. . . . The West German police thus views itself as a part of a normative order that accepts the rule of the law." (1990: 1). At the same time, the constitutional definition of the German democracy as a "militant democracy" – a democracy that can suspend some civil rights in order to save democracy itself (Finn 1991) – justified the legal prosecution of several forms of protest and the frequent call for outlawing one or another of the movement organizations. The Italian police, in contrast, since the creation of the Italian state had been accustomed to seeing itself as the *longa manus* of the executive power, and thus put preservation of law and order before the control of crime. This tradition continued to play a role after World War II: "The refusal of DC ministers in 1949 to demilitarize the police reflected the view that the major function of the police was that of internal security of the state – the preservation of public order – rather than the prevention and investigation of crime and in these latter fields the police corps (Corpo delle guardie di pubblica sicurezza) has remained underdeveloped, lacking both expertise and equipment" (Furlong 1981: 81).

In summary, institutions and political culture produce a *quite stable set of opportunities and constraints* on protest policing. Looking at single movements, it is probably true that this set of opportunities and constraints can be considered "stable." To use Kriesi's terms, our description suggests that historical traditions, or "national strategies," do indeed influence protest policing. First, both in Italy and Germany the institutional and emotional legacy from prewar fascist regimes was reflected in *the lack of fully developed democratic cultures.* The state's lack of confidence in democratic protest combined with the protestors' lack of confidence in the democratic state institutions often resulted in escalations. Thus, protest was perceived by the institutions as a threat to democracy, and state reactions were perceived by the movement activists as a sign of fascism. Second, the strategies adopted after World War II to deal with the labor movement produced norms and institutions that affected the way future social movements were handled. Probably more than any other factor, Germany's adoption of a neocorporatist model of industrial relations in the immediate postwar period was responsible for the state's relatively tolerant attitudes toward the social movements. In Italy, meanwhile, the fact that class conflict was not institutionalized in any way explains both the development of a large system of alliances between the Old Left and the movements, and the harsh repression they encountered in the 1950s and again in the first half of the 1970s. Third, both in Italy and Germany, the traditional techniques of the 1950s often reemerged during times of crisis in the 1960s, 1970s, and 1980s. As movement organizations (McCarthy notices in this volume) adopt mobilizing forms that are known to them from direct experience, also the police forces use the forms of disorder control with which they have more experience.

Looking over several decades, we could observe that the legacy of the past does not last forever – even the most stable conditions do change. If national strategies are reproduced by socialization processes, traumatic events can produce or accelerate learning processes which eventually institutionalize protest tactics, with the consequences of a "soft" police handling of protest. As Tarrow shows in Chapter 2, history offers several examples of these gradual processes of institutionalization of emerging protest repertoires. When movements first mobilize, the institutional actors deny legitimacy to the new protest tactics and attack them as antidemocratic or criminal. In the short term, a polarization in the political spectrum follows; in the long term, new forms of collective action become part of the accepted repertoires. From an historical perspective, this means that social movements do influence even the more stable institutions and deep-rooted political cultures.

CONFIGURATION OF POWER AND PROTEST POLICING

Stable institutional and cultural opportunities and constraints influenced the evolution of protest policing along the four decades. Besides the stable context, however, protest policing resulted from the interactions of various actors and the resulting "configuration of power." Following some recent studies of the POS (in particular, Kriesi 1990, and della Porta and Rucht 1991), I particularly believe that the position of the Left has an important effect on protest policing. In this part, I shall put forward some ideas on the preferences and attitudes of left-wing parties (and governments) on protest policing.

Protest policing and interest intermediation

Many political actors influence protest policing. Political parties, interest groups, and movement organizations express their preferences, addressing either their constituency, the public, or the policymakers directly. Often they use the mass media to voice their assertions: The protestors and their allies launch campaigns to denounce "brutal" repression and defend civil rights; the conservative groups push for law and order. The effects of these campaigns on protest policing could be various. On the one hand, the very fact that internal security policies are publicly discussed is a sign of a larger, democratic tolerance. On the other hand, hard-line policies are often implemented in response to pressure exerted by law-and-order coalitions.[32] Two questions should be addressed: What strategies did the two coalitions – the civil rights' defenders and the law-and-order proponents – adopt in the two countries? What factors determined the temporary victory of one coalition or the other?

In my research, I have tried to answer these questions by systemically analyzing public statements in the mass media and in parliament. Though preliminary, my research results suggest some hypotheses about the actors' strategies for influencing policy choices and their public discourse on protest and the police, revealing some historical trends and cross-national differences.

First, both in Italy and in Germany, *the position of the Old Left was particularly relevant for the vicissitudes of the civil rights coalition.* The power of the civil rights coalition increased greatly when the Old Left joined it; conversely, it shrank dramatically when the Old Left responded instead to law-and-order discourses. In the latter case, the hard line of protest policing tended to prevail, as happened in both countries in the second half of the 1970s. The mere presence of the Old Left, however, did not guarantee that the civil rights coalition would gain influence over actual policing. If the Old Left was in a marginal position in the party system (as was the case in both countries in the 1950s and in Italy until the 1980s), the "hard line" tended to prevail. When the Left was gaining power but was not yet in government, "dirty" forms of protest policing could predominate, as occurred in Italy in the early 1970s.

Second, in both countries, *law-and-order coalitions gained favor at times when national political discourse was polarized.* When the conflict between social movements and the state was presented as a zero-sum game (often by both sides), public opinion tended to side with the state. But when political discourse became less polarized, and fear about the loss of law and order diminished, the demonstrators were gradually granted more rights. Criticism of policing strategies gained a larger audience and greater influence when framed in terms of improving an existing democracy rather than in terms of exposing signs of fascist conspiracies. In the early 1970s in Germany and in both countries in the 1980s, for instance, police tactics changed from one protest event to another, in response to previous criticisms in a larger and more "moderate" public opinion.

Third, I observed that the *"civil rights" coalition gradually grew over time, while the law-and-order coalition shrank.* In both countries, not only was there a consistent increase in the number of collective actors who felt they had a right to intervene on the policing issue, but more and more "neutral" actors – such as members of professional associations – came to criticize the police hard line while movement organizations specialized (as McCarthy observed here also for the United States) in legal defense and litigation.

A fourth and last observation can be briefly made: *The configuration of power between law-and-order and civil rights coalitions was influenced by the very forms of protest.* We observed in our account that radicalizations in protest forms brought new supporters to the law-and-order coalitions. In the second half of the 1970s in both countries, the law-and-order coalitions gained sympathizers even in the Old Left during terrorist campaigns. The German experience indicates that the civil rights coalition weakened even when only a tiny minority of the movements chose violence. Conversely, the larger tolerance toward protest in the 1980s could very well be a consequence of the moderation of protest tactics. This indicates that the presence of a radical flank not always has the positive effects mentioned also by McAdam, McCarthy, and Zald in their introduction: in several occasions, violence is very likely to alienate the public support and isolate social movements.

Protest policing and governments

Shifts in the policing of protest – or techniques of repression – have often been traced to changes in the makeup of the government. In his model of the determinants of repression in the United States, Goldstein (1978) considered the ideological position of the president as the most important variable. Funk's (1990) study of internal security in Germany, however, suggested that the main parties do *not* differ much from one another in their position on internal security policy.

The previous description of our two national cases seems to indicate that the policing of protest was an issue on which parties polarized along the traditional Left-Right cleavage. Left-wing parties, with vivid memories of state repression of the labor and socialist movements, tended to rally in favor of civil liberties; conservative parties, fearful of losing votes to parties further to their right, often advocated law and order. In general, protest policing was "softer" and more tolerant when the Left was in government, whereas conservative governments were inclined to use "harder" tactics. In Italy, for example, the Center-Left governments broke the tradition of allowing the police to shoot at demonstrators; in Germany, the first SPD-FDP governments developed a more tolerant style of protest policing, and also liberalized laws concerning public marches and citizens' rights.

But it would be inaccurate to state that left-wing governments are *always* more tolerant of protest than conservative governments. Protest policing is, in fact, a tricky issue for left-wing governments. Left-wing governments often had to face difficult campaigns of law and order launched by the conservative opposition (as happened under Chancellor Brandt). Especially when the Left felt a need to legitimate itself as "fit-to-govern," it had to make concessions to the hard-line proponents of law and order. This compromised not only inevitably disappointed social movement activists (usually to the advantage of the most radical wings); it also elicited internal criticism in the Old Left (usually from the trade-unionists). The experiences of the antinuclear campaign under Chancellor Schmidt in Germany and of the "government of national unity" in Italy clearly illustrate these dynamics. In Germany, the massive police intervention in the antinuclear conflict coincided with a conservative rollback of the SPD-FDP federal government led by Helmut Schmidt. In the second half of the 1970s in Italy, the PCI – while supporting the national government "from outside" – ceased calling for a softer strategy toward radical protest, thus losing several sympathetic supporters among movement activists. In both cases, the presence of violent, even terrorist, left-wing groups clearly helped embarrass the Left.

Just as left-wing governments are not automatically lenient toward protest, conservatives in power do not always implement repressive policies. The German CDU, back in power in the 1980s, did not seem interested in an escalation of the political conflicts. The shift in the state government from the Left to the Right amid the turmoil of the Berliner squatters' movement, for instance, did not interrupt negotiations for a political solution, even though some incidents escalated into violence simply because the squatters anticipated a harder reaction by the conservative government (*Cilip* 1981). Similarly, in Italy, when the PCI returned to a position of "full opposition" and the politics of a "national front to fight an emergency situation" was superseded, a more repressive strategy of protest policing did *not* ensue.

PROTEST POLICING AND THE POLICE

Protest policing is not only a consequence of stable opportunities and the configuration of power. To understand the choices of one style or another, we have also to consider the role of the bureaucracy that has to implement policy choices: the police. Research on the police usually emphasizes that they have a certain degree of discretion in the implementation of political decisions. Thus it seems important to examine how the police arrive at preferences either for carrying out or for resisting policies that might lead to escalation.

One hypothesis about police behavior holds that organizational *internal dynamics can sway the police to support the hard line in the control of protest.* That is, preferences for strict control of protest could develop from a particular socialization and training of police agents, as well as from a kind of internal dynamics within the repressive apparati. For instance, Gary Marx observes that agencies that deal with intelligence gathering and the prevention of crime or subversion have an inherent tendency to expand: "[Their] role can be defined in such a way as to create an appetite that can never be satiated" (1979: 112). Referring to the control of protest in the United States in the 1960s and the 1970s, he adds, "Factors that explain the origin of a phenomenon may not necessarily explain its continuance. Thus the origin of government programs for social movement intervention generally lies in events that most members of a society would define as a crisis or a serious threat. However, the programs can take on a life of their own as vested interests develop around them, and new latent goals may emerge. Rather than social control as repression, deterrence, or punishment, it can become a vehicle for career advancement and organizational perpetuation and growth. The management and even creation of deviance, rather than its elimination, can become central" (1979: 114). Control agencies would consequently produce political deviants. Indeed, internal dynamics such as those Marx describes might partly account for the "deviations" of the secret services that appeared so often in Italy, as well as for the "hard" intervention of "special squads" in both countries.

An additional hypothesis is that *the organizational characteristics of the police can lead to escalation during their interactions with demonstrators.* As Monjardet observes (1990: 217 ff.), there are at least three main mechanisms in police intervention that favor escalation: the dialectic of centralization and autonomy in police units, the difficulties of coordinating the different groups, and uncertainty about the aims of the intervention. Although a police force may have well-developed techniques for controlling large masses, it may be ill prepared to isolate and control small groups operating within larger crowds (Monjardet 1990: 233). Also, some much criticized "hard" interventions of the police in our two countries, which eventually led to escalations, happened during peaceful mass demonstrations "infiltrated" by small radical groups, when the handling of law and order required a difficult equilibrium between control of the radicals and respect of the rights of the moderates. Moreover, especially in Germany in the 1980s, claims of police brutality often followed the authorities' decisions to deploy units from different states to police some protest events. In these cases, lack of coordination and a poor knowledge of the territory may have helped the conflict escalations, even when a strategy of deescalation had been planned by the police leadership.[33]

Although some conditions can bring the police to escalative tactics, our narratives seemed to indicate that escalation usually followed political choices for a confrontational handling of protest. Often the police criticized repressive choices, inviting politicians to give "political responses" to protest. This was particularly visible in Germany. In Berlin, during the student movement of the 1960s, as well as during the squatter movement of the 1980s, the police leadership intervened in the political arena and in the media and stressed that protest requires a political rather than a police response (Sack 1984). In these instances, the main concern of the police was losing legitimation and popular support. The Italian police also showed signs of dissatisfaction with the deployment of massive police force at political gatherings, although their discontent was at first mainly related to their working conditions (for instance, their long hours; see letters of policemen, collected by Fedeli 1981). Only in the 1970s, with the emergence of the police movement for demilitarization, did a concern for public legitimation also emerge among the Italian police (see autobiographies collected by Medici 1979). It therefore seems that the police tended to resist being involved in "hard" repression, especially when they feared a liberal public opinion would accuse them of partisan attitudes.

ESCALATION AND DEESCALATION:
THE CONSEQUENCES OF PROTEST POLICING

We can turn now to the effects of protest policing on social movements, and in particular on protest tactics. The social science literature provides several hypotheses. Some scholars have stated that a reduction in repression facilitates the development of social movements. According to Skocpol (1979), social revolutions are triggered by political crises, which weaken the political control and the state's capacity for repression. McAdam (1982) also indicated that diminishing repression was a facilitating factor, specifically for the civil rights movement. Moreover, a higher degree of repression was often associated with radical behavior on the part of the challengers. Goldstein concluded his comparative analysis on political repression in nineteenth-century Europe by observing that "those countries that were consistently the most repressive, brutal, and obstinate in dealing with the consequences of modernization and developing working-class dissidence reaped the harvest by producing oppositions that were just as rigid, brutal, and obstinate" (Goldstein 1983: 340). Kitschelt (1985: 302–3) hypothesized that an illiberal political culture will push movements to adopt antagonistic and confrontational positions.

Other scholars have reported less clear-cut outcomes. In a review of studies of the American protest movements in the 1960s and 1970s, Wilson (1976) observed that the empirical results are somewhat contradictory, indicating at some times a radicalization of those groups exposed to police violence, at other times their retreat from unconventional actions. To explain such differences, he suggested we take into account such variables as the level of repression, the degree of commitment to the protest issue, and the degree of popular support for both elites and challengers. Similarly, contradictory findings can be integrated into a more coherent explanation if one assumes a curvilinear relationship between the challengers' violence and the repressiveness of authorities (see Neidhardt 1989).[34]

A few hypotheses can be drawn from the description of the German and Italian cases, which come into focus if we relate the evolution of protest policing as reported above with the evolution of social movement repertoires as described in other studies (for instance, see della Porta and Rucht 1991). It seems that a *more tolerant, selective, and softer police behavior favors protest.* Especially in Italy, the protest first emerged when more tolerant policing developed. In both countries, the state reacted to protest with a (transitory) increase in repression. The harder repression of the mid-1970s coincided with the "return to the private sphere" – or a political demobilization – in social movements. In the 1980s, when a tolerant police handling of protest developed, mobilization grew again in both countries.

A second hypothesis is that *more repressive, diffuse, and hard techniques of policing tend to, at the same time, discourage the mass and peaceful protest while fueling the more radical fringe.* In Italy, for instance, radicalization processes in the movements coincided with a period of harder repression when the police again killed demonstrators at public marches. Moreover, the belief that the institutions were involved in a "dirty war" worsened the relationships between movement activists and state representatives. Conversely, the relative absence of radical strategies in Germany during the first half of the 1970s reflected the reformist attitude of the social-liberal government and a tolerant, selective and "soft" protest policing. In both countries, the highest levels of repression coincided with a shrinking of the more politically oriented wing of the movements, a decline that indirectly helped the most radical behavior to prevail – as was particularly the case in Italy in the 1970s. The lower degree of violence during protest events in the 1980s corresponded instead to an increasing tolerance for different forms of protest.

A last question refers to the *reciprocal adaptation of police and protestors' tactics.* We had previously observed that hard police tactics "coincided" with hard protest tactics. We also suggested that harder police tactics produced harder protest forms, to a certain extent. It should be added that the relationship between protesters and police does not have a unique causal determination – we observed that protest tactics influenced the police tactics through interactive processes. For instance, the escalation of the antinuclear protest in Germany involved the ritualization of the conflicts between an increasingly militant wing of activists and an increasingly aggressive police. On one side of the conflict, a militant group began to organize, appearing at all the various protest events and pushing for direct confrontation; on the other side, the state police, bolstered by police units from different states, used massive intervention.[35] A similar ritualization of physical confrontations (on a larger scale) involved the Italian police and protestors all through the 1970s. These interactive processes have to be taken into account to explain the dynamics of escalation.

A SUMMARY

In this essay, I have focused on protest policing – an important barometer of the political opportunities available for social movements. My ongoing cross-country and historical comparative project on protest policing in Italy and Germany after World War II provided some illustrations for several hypotheses on the characteristics, origins, and consequences of protest policing.

Searching for a satisfactory description of different strategies of protest policing, I first distinguished the selectivity of intervention, referring to both the forms of collective action and the type of collective actors. I also considered the amount of force used, the timing of police intervention, and the emphasis on the "respect for lawful procedures" as opposed to tolerance for "dirty tricks." I used these classifications of police styles for a description of protest policing in the two countries over the past forty years. I observed that police control has generally followed a trend toward more tolerant, selective, soft, preventive, and legal measures; but I also cautioned not to overlook important cross-national differences and reversals in the general trend.

In order to explain protest policing, I then tried to single out which of the variables mentioned in the studies on political opportunities have a more direct impact on the police handling of protest, starting with the more stable institutional and cultural environment. In considering the role of institutions, I indicated the relevance of legislation on public order and demonstrations, police rights, and citizen rights. Apropos of the political culture, I emphasized the presence of different frames and political discourses referring to the state, civil rights, and police power. I observed that although the national strategies of Italy and Germany tended to survive, they underwent quite dramatic changes through the period we are analyzing.

To understand the evolution of protest policing, I looked at a second set of political opportunities: the (more volatile) configuration of power. Looking at the actors of interest intermediation – political parties, pressure groups, and movement organizations – I concluded that protest policing and tactics are particularly sensitive to the interactions of two opposing coalitions: civil rights, and law and order. Analyzing the interaction of the two coalitions, I observed that (1) the position of the Old Left had a pronounced effect on the strength of the civil rights coalition; (2) the law-and-order coalition gained strength and influence when the political discourse was most polarized; (3) the civil rights coalition gradually expanded while the law-and-order coalition shrank; and (4) the configuration of power between the civil rights and law-and-order coalition was influenced by protest tactics. Looking at the attitudes of different parties in government, I suggested that, as expected, the Left generally tended to take a more tolerant attitude toward protest than did the Right. But protest policing proved a delicate matter for leftist governments, for they were often pressured toward a hard-line policy by law-and-order campaigns. In time, however, Left and Right moved closer together on this issue: in the 1980s, even conservative governments had become more tolerant of protest, probably reflecting a more tolerant public attitude.

Eventually, protest policing is influenced by the preference of the bureaucracy that implements policy choices: the police. Although internal dynamics sometimes pushed the police to adopt a hard line, the fear of losing public support often brought the police to oppose using hard, repressive tactics during protest events.

After looking at the causes of protest policing, I also proposed some hypotheses on its consequences on social movement repertoires. I suggested that in general a tolerant and soft style of policing favors the diffusion of protest. A repressive and hard policing of protest results in a shrinking of mass movements but a radicalization of smaller protest groups. Whereas preventive, selective, and legal protest policing isolates the more violent wings of social movements and helps the integration of the more moderate ones, reactive, diffuse, and "dirty" techniques alienate the more moderate wings from the state. Protest and police repertoires evolve through processes of reciprocal adaptation and innovation.

4

Opportunities and framing in the Eastern European revolts of 1989

ANTHONY OBERSCHALL

The idea that the force of truth, the power of a truthful word, the strength of a free spirit, conscience and responsibility not armed with machine guns . . . might actually change something was quite beyond the horizon of [a Marxist philosopher's] understanding. . . . Communism was overthrown by life, by thought, by human dignity. Our recent history has confirmed that.

Vaclav Havel (1992)

INTRODUCTION

The year 1989, like 1848 and 1968, was a vintage year for students of collective action and social movements. One after another, like dominos, and quite unexpectedly, seemingly powerful Communist regimes were challenged and toppled in Eastern Europe by an opposition that grew within days into huge mass movements of the citizenry that demanded free elections and democracy and, except in Romania, achieved their goals without violence. Together with equally momentous events in the Soviet Union in the past few years, the 1989 revolutions spelled the end of the Cold War and started the spread of democracy beyond Western Europe. Somewhat reminiscent of 1848, when the liberal revolutions against authoritarian monarchies got confounded with nationalism, the weakening of the Soviet empire, the last colonial empire of the twentieth century, stimulated nationalist movements that led to civil war and strife in parts of the former Soviet Union and Yugoslavia. But elsewhere, the new democracies are striking root despite enormous economic problems and the pains of changing from socialism to capitalist market economies.

Do the revolutions of 1989 have lessons for social movement analysts? Can we comprehend them in a satisfactory manner with the concepts, variables, and models that have become our tools? Over the last thirty years, despite differences in emphasis, social movement theorists have come to share a common language and models for movement analysis: grievances, issue framing, participation, mobilization, collective action repertoires, diffusion, political opportunity, social control. In this chapter, I will concentrate on framing, mobilization, and opportunity, and on four countries: Poland, Hungary, East Germany, and Czechoslovakia. I will argue that opposition in Eastern Europe was driven by international as well as domestic political opportunity. There was diffusion of opposition frames, popular protest, and regime response across borders. I maintain that the legitimacy of the state, that is, the citizens' moral approval of the state's authority, is an important dimension of opportunity. Loss of legitimacy puts a regime at a disadvantage in the contest for framing issues in a crisis, leads to a rapid erosion of the regime's authority, and weakens the loyalty of the social control agents. Moral force was an effective weapon when challengers faced an opponent lacking legitimacy. I will also describe the creation of novel collective action repertoires and examine the interplay between social movement organizations (SMOs) and mass demonstrations in mobilization.

POLITICAL OPPORTUNITY

In the analysis of social movements, four dimensions can be usefully distinguished (Oberschall, 1993): (1) discontents and grievances; (2) ideas and beliefs about justice and injustice, right and wrong, and more comprehensive ideologies through which discontents and issues are framed, and institutions and leaders evaluated and criticized; (3) the capacity to act collectively, or mobilization of a challenger; and (4) political opportunity.

The four dimensions are necessary but not sufficient causes of the emergence and growth of social movements. In the 1980s, a reservoir of popular discontent existed everywhere in Eastern Europe due to the systemic crisis of socialism and the persistent decline in living standards (Bunce, 1990). Loss or lack of legitimacy opened a democracy frame for the opposition that prevailed over the "reformed communism" alternative. Capacity to mobilize is low in a Communist party-state. In 1989 dissidents and citizenry compensated mobilization deficits by exploiting an increasingly favorable political opportunity environment.

Political opportunity was central in the 1989 democracy movements (McAdam, 1982; Tilly, 1978). For a state or regime target, as occurred in the 1989 democracy movements, it is well worth spelling out what political opportunity concretely means. A state has both a *domestic* and an *international* political environment. For East European regimes, the international environment was the Warsaw Pact, the dominant part of the Soviet Union in it, and the close links of their Communist parties in which again the Soviet Union and its leaders overshadowed all others.

Most important was the "Gorbachev" factor. Observers (Tarrow, 1991d; Bunce, 1990) have underscored the thaw in the Cold War and the signals Gorbachev was sending about welcome reforms in Eastern Europe and non-

Table 4.1. *Political opportunity*

Arena	Institutional structure		Short-term events
Domestic	party-state (−)* lack of legitimacy (+)	divided elite (+)	failed reforms (+) erosion of authority (+) reform among allies (+)
International	regime alliance system (−)	Gorbachev factor (+)	opposition success among allies (+)

(*) sign shows direction of opportunity for challengers in 1989.

intervention in internal affairs, although it should be remembered that Gorbachev's position in the Soviet Union was by no means fully secure. Nor had the limits of the Soviet hands-off policy been tested: Would it extend the non-Communist governments, to withdrawal from the Warsaw Pact? Nevertheless, in 1989, there was a favorable international environment for opposition in Eastern Europe, and far more favorable than in the past.

The domestic or internal aspect of political opportunity was the Communist party-state, and the monopoly of power of the Communist Party. It closed off conventional political avenues for political power by non-Communists. Both the alliance system and the party-state were stable, *institutional* structures of exercising power. Nevertheless, a constitutional arrangement, even when backed by state force, is vulnerable to overturn when it lacks moral authority, that is, legitimacy (Weber, 1958). The conformity of those excluded from the polity, indeed the compliance of the state apparatus to regime elites will in that case result from expediency and coercion alone. If the stability of a regime becomes uncertain in a challenge, expediency dictates siding with the winner. Lack of regime legitimacy is an opportunity for opponents.

There are also *short-term,* volatile aspects of governance and thus also of political opportunity for regime opponents. In the domestic arena, a divided elite, a failed reform, the erosion of authority of the regime over its state bureaucracy, open opportunities for a challenge. In the international arena, political liberalization among allies can set the terms of new debate and contention, create expectations of reform, and provide models that were unthinkable earlier. The success of opposition in an allied neighbor state can trigger widespread unrest.

By way of summary, the most salient political opportunity structures and events in the 1989 democracy movements against Communist regimes are shown in Table 4.1. The contest between challenger and regime occurs in an international as well as domestic arena, and political events in a system of similar states impact domestic goals and expectations of all political actors in the opposition as well as the regime. The importance of influences and diffusion across state borders in an alliance system cannot be overrated in the 1989 revolutions. Sequence, timing, and type of political events in allied states shifted the locus of opportunity from the domestic to the international arena for prodemocracy challengers in the fall and winter of 1989–90.

I describe below how the Polish opposition acted on its own for a decade in an unfavorable international opportunity milieu. It took ten years of massive opposition by Solidarity, and massive repression and containment by the Polish party-state, before the regime acknowledged that a national disaster stemming from flawed and failed reforms would be averted only by yielding the party-state monopoly of political power. This opening then, the climax of over a decade of bitter opposition and resistance by Solidarity, was the key opportunity in the electoral and parliamentary demise of the communists. Quite telling for an opportunity-centered view of social movements, by far the most powerful and mobilized anti-Communist challenger achieved the most limited immediate gains of the four countries under review because of uncertain international opportunity.

In contrast, Hungary in the late 1980s had but a frail anti-Communist opposition. The party-state nevertheless wanted to forestall a Polish stalemate by power sharing with non-Communists. The Communist elite divided between conservatives and reformers, and the ensuing erratic reformism made for the rapid erosion of power of the party-state.

East Germany was a strong, unified party-state in mid-1989 and had no domestic opposition to speak of. Alone among Communist states in Europe it was in an anomalous vulnerable position because of the division of Germany into two states. Though recognized in international treaties, the division was experienced as artificial by many who resented the barriers to movement and interaction imposed by the East German regime. The Hungarian reform Communists' decision to open their East-West border in the summer of 1989 rather than abide by Warsaw Pact agreements on sealed borders precipitated the exit crisis and the massive demonstrations for political and human rights reforms, and shortly for German reunification.

Finally, the Czechoslovak party-state unraveled in one month though it had successfully suppressed the heroic yet futile protests of dissidents for a decade. By November 1989 the people there had watched the East German exodus and the next-door toppling of an equally powerful party-state by mass protests. When a precipitating incident occurred in Prague, hundreds of thousands demanded the end of Communist rule, and were successful in short order. Thus, in the two states where the regime was united and the capacity to mobilize an opposition low, volatile changes in the international arena created an opportune environment that made up for opposition weakness on crucial dimensions. Still, why did these regimes surrender so rapidly, and why did peaceful demonstrators prevail over armed police and security forces?

LEGITIMACY

The second dimension of social movement analysis concerns the ideas and beliefs about right and wrong, justice and injustice, and more systematic ideologies composed of cognitive images and moral evaluations, with which people interpret and frame their discontents, evaluate their circumstances, define public issues, and demand public action. Framing and interpretation are a social process for articulating a variety of private beliefs and preferences into shared meanings and values for joint action (Snow et al., 1986). In a democratic society, opinion leaders, the news media, and interest groups articulate meaningful symbols and action programs on public issues (Gamson and Modigliani, 1989). Without free media and an opposition, the definition and framing of public issues in communist states took a different route. In East Germany, the people themselves in massive demonstrations came to frame the issue at contention between themselves and the regime from an initial freedom to travel and the reform of socialism to "*We* are the people!," and later to "We are *one* people!" and "free elections." These last three frames challenged the legitimacy of the party-state's claim to represent the people and even more fundamentally the existence of a separate socialist East German state. In Czechoslovakia, the human rights activists and dissidents in Civic Forum used the popular indignation against police violence and calls for resignation of those responsible to demand free elections and democracy, and not simply to redress specific wrongs. Together, Civic Forum and the people challenged the legitimacy of the Communist party-state itself and defied the authorities until the regime collapsed. Even more astonishing, in both countries, the Communists made no attempt to contest the opposition's framing of the issues and to defend the values and principles they had once claimed as their own. According to George Kennan (1990), already before the 1989 crisis, neither the people nor the Communists believed in communism:

> The officials of the regimes, not believing a word of it [the Communist ideology] said what they thought necessary for them to say. The people, also not believing a word of it, said the things they thought the regime wanted to hear. And the regime, knowing that they were pretending, pretended to be satisfied.

Communist discourse and frame had become empty rhetoric. When a regime lacks or loses legitimacy, the challenger's discourse and frame prevail.

What is legitimacy? In a fundamental sense, legitimacy explains why people conform and obey the state's authority. In addition to fear, apathy, habit, and expediency or interest, which are the external sources of compliance, Max Weber (1958) maintained that compliance also rested on an inner source or justification: the belief or conviction that authority is morally right. Unlike the popularity of political leaders and their policies, which waxes and wanes depending on performance, legitimacy confers on the authorities a reserve of compliance and restraint even when their effectiveness for delivering the material welfare, public order, and international respect expected of a contemporary state declines. When the government is low on effectiveness, the incumbents will be voted out of office or replaced in some other fashion. But when the state itself lacks legitimacy, ineffective performance will threaten the political institutions of the state itself, not merely the incumbents (Lipset, 1963). A regime that lacks both legitimacy and effectiveness is skating on very thin ice. Since it is ineffective, it cannot expect compliance based on expediency or interest, or only from a limited number of incumbents and privileged clients. Bereft of legitimacy, the regime must then survive on fear and the threat of force.[1]

Communist states based their legitimacy on two values: the fulfillment of egalitarian values and a just society under socialism, and the promise of material plenty. In the fifties and sixties, when the Communist regimes were still young, it was possible to believe that communist values were being approached. Later, in the seventies and eighties, with corruption rampant and the cadre privilege system firmly entrenched, with economic reforms stalled and political reforms defeated, it was disingenuous to expect it.

Communist states were vulnerable on national sovereignty. Communism was an international movement, and Marxism-Leninism a universal ideology that condemned nationalism. East European communism was dominated by Soviet communism. The East European states had been created by Soviet force, and had been propped up by the Soviet armies, in Hungary in 1956, in East Germany in 1953, in Poland in 1956, and in Czechoslovakia in 1968. To many, communism was a mask for the extension of the Soviet empire into their own country. It was an alien illegitimate authority.

A second weakness of the party-state's legitimacy was the lack of freedom, in government, in intellectual and cultural life, and in information and the mass media. Communism was a political system that enshrined the monopoly power of the party in the constitution itself. It was fundamentally different from a democratic state.

East European Communist regimes achieved some legitimacy. Communist consolidation could not have been accomplished without dedicated and volunteer work by party cadres and members who were committed to building the future society and not just lining their own pockets. Eventually dedication and enthusiasm wore off, careerism and privilege became the main motivation, and party work and ideology became ritualized, void of meaning (Przeworski, 1991).

By the 1980s, even some regime leaders did not believe in the legitimacy of the Communist state. In the 1989 crisis, there were massive resignations from the Communist parties. One cannot help but contrast the silence of the Communist leaders in 1989 with the mammoth counterdemonstration in Paris in 1968 in response to President de Gaulle's call to defend the Republic in a great speech after a month of nationwide student unrest and strikes when it seemed that another French Republic would be overthrown (Oberschall, 1993). Citizens' actions are proof of loss of legitimacy: Everywhere in 1989 they demanded the abolition of the privileged constitutional position of the Communist Party; they stripped Communist symbols and names from public life and places; they turned out by the tens and hundreds of thousands in prodemocracy demonstrations; and they soundly trounced the Communists in the first free elections.

Without legitimacy and without effectiveness, these regimes could no longer rely on interest and on moral approval for compliance. The citizens conformed from habit, apathy, and fear. When fear vanished and opportunity presented itself, the opposition would strike at the very foundations of these states.

LACK OF LEGITIMACY: FRAMING AND COLLECTIVE IDENTITY

Modes of framing and framing techniques have gotten more attention than explaining which of several competing frames wins out in public discourse (Snow et al., 1986). To be sure, the idea of narrative fidelity is promising. In framing theory, the source or agent of framing has been SMOs or activists, or the mass media interacting with interest groups and experts (Gamson and Modigliani, 1989). But these do not exhaust the possibilities. In East Germany, it is the participants in demonstrations who initiated and provided the interpretative frame, and they prevailed both against the regime and against the antiregime dissidents. That frame was "free elections" and "democracy." It diffused rapidly by way of the mass media to other countries where demonstrators started with those demands right off the bat. The media did not create the frame: They were a vehicle for communicating it. It was embedded in the popular culture which viewed Western European political institutions as the antithesis of the Communist party-state. According to Ash (1990),

the truly remarkable thing is . . . the degree of instant consensus . . . [T]ake a more or less representative sample of politically aware persons. Stir under pressure for two days. And what do you get? The same fundamental Western European model: parliamentary democracy, the rule of law, market economy.

The Eastern European regimes had for forty years propagandized the party-state and socialism in education, in cultural life, in the mass media. By 1989, it had long been empty rhetoric and meaningless symbolism. Loss of legitimacy had discredited the regime's discourse.

The lack of a credible Communist frame in the confrontations enabled the rapid formation of a collective identity among hundreds of thousands of hitherto apolitical citizens. In the Leipzig Monday evening marches, the shared identity of "We are the people" is constructed against "Them, the Communists" during the demonstrations. Elsewhere, in Czechoslovakia, that identity is created overnight, and symbolized by the ringing of keys in unison, meaning "The time has come for you the communists to resign; your time is up." When the Communist rulers' claim of representing the people exclusively is denied, not just questioned – that is, when the regime's legitimacy is denied – public discourse compels the recognition of other groups and institutions as legitimate representatives of the people and the nation. In the absence of any other representation, that could only be the people themselves. The "we-they" dichotomy was embedded in the very fabric of the Communist party-state. And because "we" are from all classes, ages, regions, and religions, that "we" is indeed "the people." The proof was the thousands of demonstrators from all walks of life. Despite years of apathy and atomization, bereft of a civic culture, a collective identity formed in the streets and squares.

LACK OF LEGITIMACY: EROSION OF AUTHORITY

In a democratic state, governance incorporates external and internal checks. Opposition parties, the news media, the judiciary, independent public and private bodies – all limit the government's authority. Although a totalitarian regime's power is not so limited and divided, its effectiveness depends on controls in all institutions and at several levels of hierarchy to back it up across the board: officials who declare a gathering or organization illegal; police who arrest and disperse dissidents; judges who sentence them; censors who ban their publications; newsmen who ignore their demands and use party labels to discredit them. And as a complementary phenomenon, people in public life and cultural gatekeepers, from television producers and playwrights to news reporters and university professors, exercise self-censorship because they fear the regime and do not want to jeopardize their privileges.

Despite such formidable social control, the erosion of authority in these regimes was rapid. Lack of legitimacy weakened the mutually supporting controls of the party-state. When a state has legitimacy, its agents enforce laws, follow administrative rules, and comply with executive orders not only because they might be disciplined if they didn't, but because it is morally right to do so. If the state is illegitimate, its agents conform to regime leaders from expediency and fear, just as the population does. In a crisis, when the regime weakens and the opposition might emerge the winner, the agents of the state lose fear of their superiors and expediency dictates that they build some credit with the opposition. There is no moral check for doing otherwise.

Communications specialists and cultural gatekeepers start reporting news about previous nonpersons, criticize the government, and ask hitherto forbidden questions. Censors pass material they would have banned earlier. Judges become lenient in sentencing. The police no longer rough up demonstrators and fail to make arrests. Newscasters discover that dissent makes great news. Corruption is exposed once more. Such permissive controls embolden previously fearful and silent individuals and groups to speak out, and dissidents get coverage and an audience. Party groups that used to intimidate government agencies and the news media find themselves under fire. Thus a crescendo of criticism and opposition spread in all institutions. And the party-state was powerless to stop it without Soviet backing. As the authority of the state eroded, the people poured into the streets and became participant citizens.

The transition to democracy in a small town near Budapest has been particularly well described (Mihály, 1991). Emboldened by the new law permitting civic associations, some residents formed a municipal beautification association. At first they busied themselves with parks and historic restorations. As they gained adherents and the national political climate became more permissive, they took on the local Communist mafia which had entrenched itself for decades in local government, the party branch, the state farm, and other organizations. The mafia had run the town in a secretive fashion. Public offices, land, municipal services, housing, money, jobs were swapped and circulated among insiders at public expense. The association managed to stop toxic chemical dumping into a local stream, reclaim an office building and land from the Mafia for the town, reroute a major highway project, and block an ill-conceived shopping center that was a giveaway to Austrian investors and profited mafia members at the town's expense. In all this power struggle between association and Communists, the courts, commissions, advisory boards, ministry experts, and others who for decades had automatically approved what the Communists wanted, now became responsive to inquiries, objections, petitions, and demands of the association. Thus many decisions were reversed, and new standards of openness, honesty, legality, and information access incorporated into local government. Public life was made democratic. In the local government elections of 1990 members of the association got elected to a majority of the council seats and terminated Communist rule.

MORAL FORCE

In the 1989 democracy movements, the challengers did not seize television and radio stations, telephone exchanges, airports, government buildings, party headquarters, nor did they try to capture Communist leaders or disrupt the daily routines of work and government business. They did not try to persuade the police and the army to defect; at most they tried to shame the riot police and security forces who were facing them. The Czechoslovak strike was a symbolic demonstration of nationwide support for the opposition activists and not a coercive move for disrupting the economy. Instead the challengers acted with the moral conviction that they were in the right for demanding free elections, democracy, and the resignation of the hardline communist leaders. They were in the right because they were "The People."

But how could the challengers get that message across to their fellow citizens, and just as important, to the Communist leaders, cadres, and security forces? They had no weapons, no organizations, no printing presses, no television at the start. Instead, huge crowds marched and demonstrated in squares and along avenues, making demands and supporting opposition leaders. They conveyed their moral message through numbers, persistence, and totally public, nonviolent and nonthreatening collective actions. By massing day after day, in growing numbers, in historic places, they seemed to be saying: "We are not going to engage in violent insurrection, seize the government, and hunt down the Communist leaders who have tormented us all these years. We don't have to do that because we are the people, and we're in the right. We are going to come back day after day until you have resigned and we have free elections. You can't arrest us all, and bully us into compliance. You can't govern without us, and we won't quit until our demands are met." This, in short, was a display of moral force against a foe that held all the cards but one: It had organization, a police and an army, and the mass media, but it lacked moral authority for governance.

Dissidents had confronted the party-state with moral principle, as in Czechoslovakia ever since the founding of Charter 77. Though they were few, they set a precedent. For the democracy demonstrators in 1989, a moral identity was forged during the confrontations themselves. Strangers sharing the same convictions in the face of a common danger provided each other courage, solidarity, and commitment for standing their ground before the police and security forces. Moral force aims at bystanders as well as opponents. In the civil rights movement, moral force and nonviolence worked when much of the American public became the movement's conscience constituency and carried political clout with the Congress and the president. In Eastern Europe, the bystanders that moral force influenced were the hitherto apathetic, timid, and atomized mass of citizenry who came alive and joined the challengers – indeed, became the challenger.[2]

Nonetheless, regimes in great danger of being toppled will pay a high price. Poland had been under military rule for six years. In East Germany and Czechoslovakia, the regimes had repressed dissidents earlier when they had been few. In East Germany, party chief Honecker wanted repression to stop the Monday night marches in Leipzig, but his orders were not executed (Krenz, 1990: 134–36). For the rank-and-file police facing nonviolent marchers and demonstrators day after day, policing had become troubling and even repugnant. Regime leaders became uncertain about the reliability of their social control agents, and the grassroots party members deserted them at the crucial hour.

MOBILIZATION

In the four country studies below, I describe in some detail mobilization of the democracy movements and their confrontations with the Communist regimes. In all four, the capacity to mobilize an opposition was limited. Still, in all four, and especially in East Germany and Czechoslovakia, crowds and mass demonstrations played a dramatic and leading role that dwarfed leaders and SMOs (Oliver, 1989). How was this possible?

It is not surprising that SMOs cannot form openly in a Communist country. In Tilly's view (1978), "catness" (categoriness) and "netness" (networkness) in a population facilitate mobilization, but a Communist society lacks both. The citizens lead an atomized private life, and there is no civil society. It had been dismantled when the Communists abolished or took over all voluntary associations, cultural groups, scientific bodies, publishing organs, social welfare agencies, educational institutions, youth organizations (Hankiss, 1990). The suddenness of the 1989 opposition movements precludes the organization resources stressed by Zald and McCarthy (1987b), and block recruitment of viable communities and associations (Oberschall, 1973) does not operate when there are no blocks to recruit.

All these theories have room for the formation of groups of dissidents. According to Gerlach and Hine (1970), movements grow from loosely connected, leaderless small groups based on interpersonal bonds. In Eastern Europe as well, small circles of dissidents could lead restricted lives, somewhat freer when a regime loosened social control, and harassed and persecuted when hard-liners cracked down. Even when a regime was permissive, dissidents spent much effort helping each other survive, pay legal costs, keep up the spirit of those imprisoned and their families, raise money for those out of work. There was neither the opportunity nor the capacity for building an SMO. To keep member name and addresses would be sheer folly. Regular meetings would be infiltrated by police informers. Phones were bugged, and mail was opened. Printing and reproduction equipment was easily seized. Occasionally dissidents had access to some resources as when a circle formed in a scientific or cultural institute, and they could use copiers and other facilities. The churches might provide some resources, as in Poland and East Germany, but these were meager. The condemnation of the regime for human rights violations by Western governments and human rights monitors (Helsinki Watch, Amnesty International) when dissidents were imprisoned and harassed helped reduce the severity of sanctions. But all of these did not overcome the difficulties of forming an SMO and the even more formidable problem of recruiting and activating a large following.

The theoretical issue is how spontaneous mass demonstrations developed and how dissidents joined them to form an opposition movement. When leaders and SMOs emerge on the back of mass demonstrations, as they did in East Germany and Czechoslovakia, the accent shifts from SMOs to the diffusion of a protest culture and a collective action repertoire (Tilly, 1978), from organization variables to loosely structured collective action, shared symbols and collective identity (Oberschall, 1993).[3] That is a useful way of thinking about mobilization in the democracy movements of Eastern Europe. I turn to how this happened in the four countries, in the context of growing opportunity and the erosion of regime authority.

POLAND

In Poland, opposition to the Communists was long-standing, vocal, and organized. It had confronted the Communist party-state in 1980–81 when Solidarity was formed. The economic crisis of socialism forced the regime to raise prices, which workers and miners resisted by going on strike. Helped and advised by intellectuals, the workers in 1980–81 created independent trade unions that enabled them to coordinate strikes beyond individual factories and workplaces and to bargain collectively with the state, and not only with particular management teams. Such a massive workers' opposition was a striking failure of the Communist Party, which claimed to be the vanguard of the working class.

Polish workers in the 1970s and 1980s created a collective action repertoire and protest culture of sit-down strikes and mine occupations led by strike committees. Factory gates were decorated with flowers, the Black Madonna, the Polish crowned white eagle, the cross. These symbols hark back to earlier national movements in the eighteenth and nineteenth centuries, and were blended with the Solidarnosc logo suggesting a militant marching column against the red and white colors of the Polish flag (Laba, 1991: 133). Protest rituals included huge monuments to fellow workers killed in strikes that were dedicated in Gdansk and Gdynia before hundreds of thousands, and the pilgrimage to the shrine of the Black Madonna which Lech Walesa undertook at the conclusion of the August 1980 strikes. These symbols and rituals of Polish workers' social identity were a negation of the Communist symbolism and ritual, the red flag, the hammer and sickle, the red star, the May Day parade, the Stakhanovite worker, which expressed the international character of the working class and its subservience to the Communist Party and to the Soviet Union.

Opposition to the party-state had a mass base that gave it the power to disrupt the economy. It also had the support of the Catholic Church (Ziolkowski, 1990). The strikes in 1988 were set off by the steepest price hikes since 1982. Opposition mobilization followed the precedent of 1980–81 (Ost, 1990). The difference was that the regime imposed martial law at the end of 1981, broke the sit-down factory occupations with troops and police, banned Solidarity, and arrested or interned most of its leaders, whereas in the perestroika era of 1988, with reform Communists in charge and the economy even more hopelessly in crisis, the regime took a chance on limited political power sharing. For its part, because of limited political opportunity, Solidarity agreed to power sharing as the junior partner. Poland was surrounded by what looked like solid Communist states. The Polish regime had withstood several massive challenges. There was no precedent for power sharing in a Communist regime. As it turned out, the Party and Solidarity both badly miscalculated the political temper of the Polish voters.

The overriding issue for Poles in the late 1980s was the ailing economy. There were daily irritations and worries about getting food and other necessities of life; people waited in long lines; the currency was worthless; the inflation so high that as soon as people were paid, they left their workplaces to look for essentials to buy. The Communist Party itself became divided between a conservative and a reform faction. The reformers knew that some compromise was necessary with Solidarity, the Catholic Church, and the people. The entire nation had to be enlisted for solving the economic crisis (Weschler, 1989). Political reforms were to be bargaining chips so long as Solidarity would share the burden of imposing work discipline and industrial peace during the coming painful restructuring of the economy. As regime and Solidarity were edging closer to formal talks in 1987 and 1988, another strike wave erupted from the grass roots and speeded the process.

The regime suppressed the April-May strikes with a mixture of coercion and conciliation, but in August, the month of anniversaries for the opposition in Poland, a second, more powerful strike wave was unleashed in accord with the Polish workers' protest culture. It started on August 14 in Gdansk on the eighth anniversary of the outbreak of the 1980 unrest. In short order, miners in Silesia struck for higher pay, better working conditions, and the legalization of Solidarity. Then dockworkers and transport employees struck in Szezecin, then more miners, the Lenin steel workers, the Ursus tractor workers, then the Lenin shipyard in Gdansk, all demanding the legalization of Solidarity on top of other demands. All had been hot spots of strikes and worker protests for more than a decade.

Though the regime response was tough and the strikes weakened, the regime had to admit that it couldn't restore industrial peace without its arch enemy Solidarity. On August 31, the eighth anniversary of the 1980 accords, accompanied by a bishop, Lech Walesa joined an emergency meeting with Interior Minister Kiszczak, who proposed roundtable negotiations on all issues, including the legalization of Solidarity. In the following months, a complex deal for legalizing Solidarity and limited power sharing was agreed on. Solidarity took a great risk in agreeing to elections. The Communists had all the resources of a forty-year incumbent, whereas the opposition had no funds, phones, offices, printing presses, or copiers. Walesa was quoted as saying, "None of us want these elections . . . they are the terrible price we have to pay in order to get our union back" (Weschler, 1989). Nevertheless the worker-intellectual alliance that was the hallmark of Solidarity quickly created thousands of citizen committees which ran the campaigns of the non-Communist candidates. The citizens' committees became the political arm of the broadbased opposition movement of the past two decades.

In the June 1989 elections, the citizen committee slate triumphed beyond anyone's wildest expectations.[4] The election results undermined the assumption shared by all, including Solidarity, that the Communists and their allies would remain in power. In a telling instance of the Communists' erosion of authority in Eastern Europe, Lech Walesa cut a deal with the former popular front allies of the Communists, the Peasant Party and the Democratic Party, who switched their support to a Solidarity government under Prime Minister Mazowiecki. It became the first elected non-Communist government in Eastern Europe, indeed the first ever in a Communist country. The Sejm changed the country's name to Polish Republic (dropping the Communist "People's"). It repealed the constitutional provision on the leading role of the Communist Party in Poland. The Party itself swiftly collapsed. In its last congress in January 1990, it changed its name to the Social Democratic Party. This was going to be the Party's fate in Hungary, East Germany, and Czechoslovakia as well, sooner than anyone expected.

HUNGARY

Like Poland, Hungary was trapped in the socialist economic crisis. Unlike Poland, there was no strong Catholic Church standing up to the Communists, and more important, no tradition of militant opposition like Solidarity. The 1956 revolution had been a national revolt against the Communists and the Soviets. After it was repressed, except for a small number of intellectual dissidents who were fired from their jobs and marginalized, no opposition existed. After the mid-1960s, the Kadar regime bought the compliance of the people with a policy of economic reform and with economic opportunities for small entrepreneurs in the second economy, which were unique for Eastern Europe at the time. It was "goulash communism."

By the 1970s, goulash communism had cooled. State enterprises lacked incentives for efficiency, profitability, and technological innovation. By the 1980s, many economists, planners, and other intellectuals and even some Communist cadres came around to believing that there was no magic third way between socialism and capitalism. The issue of private property and privatization of state enterprises would have to be faced squarely. As in Poland and increasingly in the Soviet Union, reform Communists knew that restructuring the nation's economy necessitated hardship and would increase discontent. Restructuring wouldn't work without cooperation from the people. Its price would have to be political liberalization, even political power sharing with non-Communists (Bruszt and Stark, 1992). At all costs, the regime wanted to avoid the Polish confrontations and stalemate of the 1980s. The compromise strategy was a gamble. No Communist state had a proven blueprint for economic and political restructuring. In the Soviet Union, Gorbachev himself was zigzagging to an uncertain future. The Poles in 1988 were bogged down in massive strikes and growing civil strife.

As in the Soviet Union, the Hungarian reform Communists had to prevail against the conservatives or hard-liners, and limit public support for an emerging opposition. Divisions in the Party ran deep between May 1988 when the aging Party boss Kadar was ousted and April 1989 when the reform Communists gained a majority on the Central Committee. Although the reform communists prevailed against their own hard-liners, they succumbed to their non-Communist challengers. Opposition in Hungary didn't entail massive strikes as in Poland, nor massive popular demonstrations as in East Germany and Czechoslovakia. Still in 1988 to 1990, there were repeated patriotic anti-Communist demonstrations organized by the emerging opposition, the Hungarian Democratic Forum, FIDESZ (an independent youth group), Greens, the Free Democrats, revived political parties of the pre-Communist era, and others.

Without grassroots organization and access to the news media, the opposition groups could do this only by appealing to a shared culture of national symbols that the Communists had tried to suppress in the last forty years: the March 15 anniversary of the patriotic revolution of 1848, Hungary's traditional national day, which the Communists had replaced with May Day; and October 23, the start of the 1956 revolution, which the Communists had condemned as a counterrevolution. The dissidents also demanded the reburial of Imre Nagy, the leader of the 1956 revolution, who was convicted and shot. Though Nagy had been a Communist, his leadership in 1956 was viewed as a patriotic anti-Soviet and anti-Communist action by the public. Thus June 16, the anniversary of Nagy's execution, became another focal date of popular protests.[5] Dissident groups were also able to mobilize a groundswell of dissatisfaction over the half-completed Danube dam. First raised as an issue by small groups of Greens who opposed the environmental harm of the undertaking, construction of the dam acquired a wider significance because it symbolized the uneconomic, mammoth projects of the regime at the expense of the national welfare.

Popular mobilization by the anti-Communists exposed the regime's lack of legitimacy. Ten thousand people marched on 15 March 1988 to commemorate the 1848 revolution. Fifty thousand demonstrated against Romanian oppression of Hungarian ethnics in Transylvania on 27 June. Thirty thousand protested the Danube dam on 12 September, and more in October. A petition of over one hundred thousand signatures to halt dam construction was presented to parliament, followed by an even larger petition for a referendum on the dam. In October 1988, protests marked the 1956 anniversary and called for a rehabilitation of Nagy. A quarter of a million people participated at the 16 June 1989 state funeral for Nagy's reburial in Heroes' Square. Seventy-five thousand marked the anniversary of the 1956 revolution on 23 October. In the crucial year and a half from the beginning of 1988, such demonstrations made the opposition visible, discredited the Communists, emboldened mass media independence, and made the social control agents cautious and permissive.

Communist power eroded rapidly in 1988 and 1989 when Party divisions ran deep. The news media led the way. Already in February 1988 the journalists' union campaigned for an end to censorship. By the spring of 1989, according to Ash (1990), "radio and TV were in the vanguard of emancipation . . . there was a riotous competition to publish everything and anything." On May Day 1989, the league of independent trade unions – a rival of the Communist trade unions – organized a larger rally and got equal time on TV with the government-sponsored official celebrations. Thus the opposition was making up a visibility and organization deficit and reaching out to the public.

Hungarians witnessed a most peculiar event in 1988 and 1989. A ruling Communist Party repudiated its historic legacy and ideology, legalized the political opposition, agreed to compete with it in free elections and pledged to abide by the results. It expected to do well, and early public opinion polls confirmed that it would. It possessed tremendous resources and nationwide organization, and was now led by leaders who were reformers. Yet it suffered a humiliating defeat, capturing only 9 percent of the vote, and with some of its leading members defeated by unknowns. The hard-line Communists polled even less, with just under 4 percent. How can this be explained?

The erosion of authority that led to liberalization in all institutions penetrated the Party organization itself (Hankiss, 1990). With the handwriting on the wall, Party cadres converted their increasingly shaky political power into economic positions while the going was good. It was possible to do so under the privatization legislation, and with very little accountability and obstacles from the finance ministry and other public bodies. Lack of accountability led to massive corruption, and this the voters took to be yet another indication that communism, reformed or otherwise, was rotten at the core. Correspondingly, the cadres who chose economic bailout, and there were many who did quite successfully, lost interest in the fate of the Party, and were not available for political and electoral work. As a matter of fact, many such people wanted to distance themselves from their Communist pasts.

In conclusion several points emerge in this analysis of the Hungarian democratic transition. The Communists divided, which was a favorable political opportunity for the opposition. Also, the Communists jettisoned their ideology, the socialism frame, their past. That weakened them. They were telling the public that the past forty years had been a mistake, and that they were to blame. Meanwhile the opposition moved in to fill the ideological vacuum with national and patriotic symbols, a democracy frame, and with moving the country "back to Europe," which is where the people thought they should be. Poland proved it was possible. Opposition mobilization became easier as the erosion of the party-state accelerated from within. In the end the Communists had nothing to offer to the voters and the nation that the other parties could not provide better.[6]

EAST GERMANY

In the East German revolution, with little or no leadership from intellectuals and dissidents, the people created two complementary and effective collective action repertoires – the mass invasion of embassies abroad and the mass march in their cities. In a short two months, the protesters reframed the issue from the right to travel abroad and other limited freedoms to challenging the very legitimacy of the Communist party-state by demanding German reunification, whereas the intellectuals and the churches sought a reformed, socialist East Germany. Meanwhile the SED and the Stasi, the most powerful Communist Party and social control apparatus in Eastern Europe, yielded to the moral force of persistent, massive, nonviolent demonstrations. The confrontations between people and regime in East Germany triggered diffusion of democracy demonstrations in Czechoslovakia and the Balkans.

The repressive East German regime didn't tolerate mere passive conformity. It demanded that citizens spy, inform on, and denounce their fellows. The malaise in East Germany was known as "wall sickness" (Reich, 1990). It was a unique situation of a people literally walled in by the iron curtain and the Berlin wall. Many tried escape or sought legal emigration to West Germany despite high risk, sanctions, and marginalization by the regime. Naimark (1992) has shown that since World War II there had been a huge, half million, legal and illegal flow of East Germans to the West. After the 1975 Helsinki accords provided for the right to emigrate, thousands applied for exit even though applicants were harassed by the authorities, lost their jobs, and jeopardized their children's higher education. Marginalized and with little to lose, these applicants for emigration gathered at some churches for fellowship, and created centers for a nonconforming subculture. Thus already prior to 1989, strong demand for exit existed. The leadership turned down reforms such as Gorbachev was undertaking in the Soviet Union and maintained that such "experiments" were irrelevant to East Germany's advanced stage of socialism. Many East Germans had given up waiting for internal reforms and renewal. They wanted out.

Such was the context of the 1989 summer-fall mass exodus from East Germany which started the chain of events leading to the 1989 revolution.[7] East German containment depended on the cooperation of other Communist regimes, but in 1989 Hungary was heading to reform communism and had a greater stake courting favor with the West than in backing up the hard-line regime in East Germany. In May the Hungarians started to dismantle the border fortifications with Austria. It was a unique opportunity for East German exiters to converge on Hungary for the summer holidays and attempt to flee to the West. In July and August, this was not yet a sure thing. Although the Hungarian border guards did not shoot people crossing the border illegally, neither did they simply let them walk across. Those caught were sent back to Budapest for repatriation. Many refused to leave. A growing number of East Germans, running out of money, camped out in tent colonies, subway stations, and public parks. Becoming more desperate, some decided to invade the West German embassy, and shortly hundreds followed, in Budapest itself, in Prague, in Warsaw, in the West German mission in Berlin. This was a new repertoire of collective action. Previously, in Eastern Europe, only a single or small number of political dissidents sought refuge in a Western embassy, and when that occurred, guards would surround an embassy. When hundreds, and eventually thousands, of ordinary citizens invaded embassy grounds with their families, they precipitated a food crisis, a public health crisis, and an international political crisis in the full glare of the international news media. The Red Cross was called in for humanitarian reasons. The governments were loath to arrest refugees, women, and children, and pressured the East German regime into negotiating a solution. In the end the East German government agreed to evacuate them to West Germany by special trains passing through East Germany. The evacuations reduced the cost of exit and precipitated an even greater wave of embassy invasions. Meanwhile the Hungarian government repudiated its bilateral treaty with East Germany on September 11, and announced it would no longer require a valid visa for East Germans crossing into Austria. When the East German government stopped issuing visas for Hungary, the exiters invaded the West German embassy in Prague, creating a crisis there.

The massive exodus was a tangible indication of popular discontent and the regime's lack of legitimacy. It provided an opportunity for protest by those who wanted domestic reforms because they intended to stay. Exit and voice were thus fatefully linked. Dissidents and intellectuals were emboldened to seek a dialogue with Communist leaders and demand democratic reforms and a more humane socialism to stem the flow of emigrants. But the citizenry created its own protest culture with mass marches and demonstrations in which they forged a collective identity as "We the People" and used nonviolence as a moral weapon. The key events occurred in Leipzig.

Leipzig was the second-largest city in East Germany. In the historic center since 1982, every Monday evening at 5 P.M., the Nikolai church held a peace prayer service (Grabner, 1990). The ministers at the Nikolai church had provided a meeting place and discussion forum for nonconformist youth who were given a role in organizing the service.[8] By appropriate choice of Bible reading and sermon, veiled criticism of the regime could be expressed in religious language.

Table 4.2 provides an overview of the protests and demonstrations in Leipzig and the authorities' social control measures.[9] Several patterns can be noted. First, the protests were small scale before the exit crisis erupted in full force during the summer recess in July-August. Second, the social control measures were costly to participants but not enough to suppress them. The protests lasted only a few minutes, or were squelched at the start, or even successfully banned, as on May 4. Participants numbered in the low hundreds at most, and crowd size did not increase in the spring. When there were no arrests, it was because of the presence of Western news media (March 13, July 7–9). Nonconformists used such presence to good tactical advantage. It was the only political opportunity they had at this time.

The exodus during summer and fall sharply raised the political opportunity for opposition compared to the spring. Despite heavy security measures in September at the Nikolai church peace prayer services and many arrests and beatings, the protests locked in on the Monday evening peace prayer service cycle. Church attendance increased as did the number of protesters outside the church. Exit petitioners and nonconformist youth were joined by ordinary folk, and the numbers rose from hundreds to a few thousand, and in October from a few thousand to hundreds of thousands. The demonstrators created a repertoire of collective action with the mass march from the Nikolai church along major streets to the huge Karl Marx square, allowing tens of thousands to join. Without leadership and organization, thousands of marchers expressed demands with singing, chanting, banners, and posters as they forged a collective identity. Several innovations were important in the surge of popular protest. On September 18, there was a new chant: "We want to remain," meaning We want reforms because we don't intend to leave the country like the exiters. Monday evening at the Nikolai church started attracting protesters beyond the small group of exit petitioners and nonconformists in the spring. On September 25, the crowd, spontaneously, for the first time marched out of the church square to the city center. The police were unprepared to bar their way. The protesters were searching for a shared identity and purpose. Some sang the "Internationale," some "We Shall Over-

Table 4.2. *Leipzig protests and demonstrations, 1989*

Date	Occasion/venue	Number of participants	Social control/ outcome	Opportunity/ innovation
January 15	Karl Liebknecht and Rosa Luxemburg Anniv.	150–200	53 arrests; 11 arrests before march	
March 13	Nikolai church prayer service, silent march	300	12 arrests– dispersed after 300 meters	Leipzig fair; Western news media in city
May 4	World environment day	none	police ban march	
May 7	Election fraud protest	250	72–100 arrests	
May 8	From this date police presence outside Nikolai church at peace prayer services.			
July 12	Nikolai church	100	25 arrests	
July 7–9	Evangelical church day	100	no arrests	Western media in city
Summer recess of Nikolai services				
September 4	Nikolai church peace prayer service resumes	1,000 outside church	many	Exit: "We want to get out"
September 11	Nikolai church	1,300 in church, many outside	104 arrests, many fined	Leipzig fair; Western news media in city
September 18	Nikolai church	2,500 in church, many outside	242 arrested	Voice: "We want to remain"
September 25	Nikolai, first march to city center	3,000 in church, many outside, 3,500 march	6 arrested, one fined	march from church to city center

Table 4.2 *(cont.)*

Date	Occasion/venue	Number of participants	Social control/ outcome	Opportunity/ innovation
October 2	Nikolai, march to center	10,000–25,000 marchers	20 arrests	collective identity: "We are the people"; collective action repertoire complete
October 7	40th anniversary celebration	10,000	?	
October 9	Nikolai, march to center	70,000	no arrests; proclamation of Leipzig Six, police withdraw	
October 16 and every Monday until Christmas	Nikolai, march to center	110,000 to 450,000	"no force" order	Demands for German reunification grow: "nationalism" joins "democracy"

come"; others called out, "Liberty, Equality, Fraternity!" The next Monday, October 2, they found both identity and purpose with "We are the people" and a mass march. By reclaiming "the people" for themselves and denying it to the regime, which had used it ubiquitously (as in "people's" democracy, "people's" police, "people's" newspaper), they challenged the regime's right to govern. The Monday night marches had become collective bargaining with the regime for reforms, for democracy, and shortly, for German reunification. Excluded from the ballot box, the people voted with their feet and voices.

Why was social control ineffective in the fall of 1989? The authorities grasped the spontaneous, unorganized character of the opposition, yet were at a loss for countermeasures. Had there been organizers, the Stasi would have detected and arrested them. In the mass media, the authorities blamed West German agents and local "rowdies," but they knew otherwise. On August 31, the Stasi chief in Leipzig gave the following report to a gathering of the Stasi high command:

We make the following assessment: the peace prayer meetings don't need to be organized any longer. For months they have become a traditional meeting place of the exiters. No flysheets are needed, nor any other kind of activity. People gather completely on their own. The peace prayers proceed relatively harmlessly inside the church . . . there is no incitement on the part of church officials. There are a lot of expectations. We too expect a lot of curious people to attend to find out what goes on in the city. The situation is complex, but I believe we're on top of it. (Mitter and Wolle, 1990: 128)

The analysis was accurate; the conclusion, mistaken.

The erosion of authority spread within the regime itself, and accelerated throughout the country in October, November, and December. The Leipzig party had mobilized its "fighting groups," the Communist workplace militia, for backing up the police and Stasi along the anticipated march route on October 2. One group leader recalls how his men were told to defend the city against "rowdies" and troublemakers. Instead they witnessed a peaceful throng of their fellow citizens and neighbors carrying candles. The next day they read in the "people's" newspaper how the fighting groups had saved Leipzig. In disgust, the group voted to ignore mobilization orders henceforth (Sievers, 1990). Eyewitnesses throughout the country observed the unsettling and demoralizing impact on police of orders to block, charge, and arrest nonviolent demonstrators who shouted "join us," "fathers against sons," "shame," and in the case of one Berlin woman, "I could be your grandmother, and you stand there with your truncheon" (Reich, 1990: 86–87). In Leipzig, a shielded policeman pleaded with a woman, "Leave us alone, we just want to go home" (Sievers, 1990: 72). Moral force confronted physical force, and moral force was prevailing.

Regime leaders became hesitant to order the use of force to disperse large crowds. The turning point came the following Monday on October 9.

The first October week was the most violent in the 1989 revolution in East Germany. In Leipzig, fear of repression spread. On the nights of October 3 and 4, when the special trains of exiters passed through Dresden to West Germany, there were violent clashes at the train stations between protesters and security forces. The celebrations of the fortieth anniversary of East Germany were followed by bloody clashes between protesters and police in many cities, including Leipzig. There were rumors of a "Chinese solution," army movements and troop deployment, of blood being stored for emergency use. Nevertheless, on Monday, the Nikolai church was already full at 2 P.M. Four other churches were open for peace prayer services and were also full. Seventy thousand people assembled at and near the Nikolai church for the protest march. To the great relief of all, at the eleventh hour, a proclamation calling for a peaceful dialogue between citizens and regime signed by three local Party leaders, a minister, the head of the Leipzig symphony orchestra, and an entertainer was read at the churches and played on the city loudspeakers and radio. The proclamation of the Leipzig Six was widely interpreted as a guarantee of nonviolence by the authorities. An immense march spread from the Nikolai church through the boulevards surrounding the inner city. The police withdrew. The slogans now heard were "We are the people" together with "No violence" and "We remain here." People referred to the nonviolent evening of October 9 as the "Miracle of Leipzig."

It had been a close call. Party chief Honecker wanted a crackdown, by force if needed. Mielke, the Stasi chief, ordered all officers to be on call and armed. (Mitter and Wolle, 1990: 201). Party headquarters in Berlin ordered that "hostile actions must be suffocated at the core," and that "organizers of counterrevolutionary action must be isolated," a euphemism for detention. Krenz, the Party chief in charge of security, knew that repression wouldn't work. A Leipzig public opinion researcher informed him that even among Party members there was a majority favoring political reforms and Honecker's resignation (Krenz, 1990: 134–8). Krenz tried to contravene Honecker's orders. In the event, the Leipzig police chief made the final decision: When Mielke ordered on the telephone to disperse the marchers, the police chief refused because the crowds were far too large (Wimmer et al., 1990). On October 9, the regime's innermost circle of leaders divided on repression versus conciliation.

Although a battle had been won, the war was not yet over. The people of Leipzig possessed a viable protest routine, a collective identity, and a common issue with which they relentlessly pressured the regime in the coming weeks. The marches were spreading to other cities. The sayings and slogans, often in rhyme, on posters and banners became political satire and folk wit all over East Germany and an instant barometer of public reaction to momentous political events that were accelerating. In short order, Party boss Honecker resigned, the border and the Berlin wall were opened, the hated Stasi disbanded, and free elections scheduled.

Leipzig was not the only arena of confrontation between the people and the regime. Opposition groups of writers, professionals, and intellectuals surfaced in September and October. They used the exit crisis and popular unrest to wrest concessions from the regime for a democratic, socialist East Germany with a human face. New Forum, founded by thirty people on September 9, called for dialogue between the regime and the people and for a renewal of socialism. Democracy Now and Democratic Renewal were formed also at this time. On September 24, eighty reform groups met and made New Forum their umbrella association. These groups were several steps behind the political mood and demands of the marchers. Pastor Eppelman, a founding member of Democratic Renewal, called for the preservation of what is positive in socialism. The writer Christa Wolf, a leading intellectual, told a huge crowd in Berlin, "Imagine there is socialism and no one emigrates." Leading opposition leaders signed a declaration "for our country," which meant a reformed socialist alternative to the Federal Republic. But events had over-taken them. The population clamored for reunification and against socialist experiments at their expense. Even though the opposition intellectuals were given a polite hearing at the mammoth assemblies of the democracy march-ers, they failed to lead the popular movement.

CZECHOSLOVAKIA (CSSR)

The "velvet" revolution was more sudden and rapid than its counterpart in East Germany. Dissidents had created a culture of protest using national symbols, anniversary dates, and historic sites: October 28, the founding of the Republic; August 21, the invasion of the Soviet army in 1968; January 15, the immolation of Jan Palach in 1969 protesting Soviet occupation; and Wenceslas Square in the center of Prague and also the symbolic heart of the country's history. When dissidents were arrested for demanding human rights, tried, and convicted, others would mount further protests or start a petition for the detainees' release, which would lead to further arrests and convictions in a continuing cycle of challenges and repression. As in other East European countries, most people had withdrawn into private life. The dissidents lacked a mass base and the citizenry was apathetic. All this changed dramatically in the fall of 1991 with the success of the democracy demonstrations in East Germany. If the Germans had done it, why not the Czechs and Slovaks? Opportunity in the international arena had turned pos-itive.

As in East Germany, the regime had resisted economic reforms and politi-cal liberalization in the wake of Gorbachev's perestroika and glasnost. Hard-liners had been in power for twenty years, ever since the Soviet and Warsaw Pact armies invaded to defeat Dubček's "socialism with a human face." Many of the victims of 1968 had been reform communists. "Normalization" under Husak (still in power in 1989) meant half a million party members purged. Eight hundred thousand people lost their jobs. The repression was especially hard on writers, artists, intellectuals, "the cream of the nation." Many emi-grated or were expelled (Urban, 1990: 108). Those who didn't were harassed, together with their families. Thousands were forced to work as unskilled la-borers. The Communists humiliated people by pressuring them to denounce their friends or lose positions, careers, and schooling opportunities for their children. Some of those who refused, and there were many, formed a subcul-ture of dissent in Prague.

From the mid-1970s on, the subculture grew slowly. Alienated youth joined the old-timers. Drama and readings were performed in apartments. Novels and essays were circulated in *samizdat*. Banned rock and roll bands per-formed in village barns. As in the other East European countries, youth es-caped with Western rock and pop music. The 1975 Helsinki accords, which

Czechoslovakia signed, gave dissidents a boost. They formed the human rights association Charter 77 in defense of the freedoms in the Helsinki accords. The signatories were beaten, imprisoned, and fired from their jobs.

Gorbachev's reforms after 1987 put the regime into a dilemma because it had for so long faithfully followed the Soviet communist lead. The government started playing it both ways, with an eye on Gorbachev. It repressed dissidents, but punishment became milder (Laber, 1989). Loosened social control emboldened new opposition youth groups – the "Independent Peace Association," "Unijazz," the "John Lennon Peace Club," "Democratic Initiative." A Communist reform group, Obruda, surfaced. Dissidents developed ties with Poles and Hungarians, who were further along on the road to pluralism. Petition campaigns got more signatures as people became less afraid to sign. One of the largest demanding democratization obtained 40,000 signatures in 1989. In these petition campaigns, dissidents and their supporters got to know each other (Judt, 1992: 97). The tempo and scale of opposition increased in 1988 and 1989. A member of Helsinki Watch wrote after a visit, "The lid is being slowly lifted by the remarkable spirit of people who are willing to risk prison to put the regime on the defensive" (Laber, 1989).

Why did the democracy movement not start before the autumn of 1989? If one examines antiregime demonstrations in Prague in 1989, shown in Figure 4.1, one notes a peak that occurred in a week of unusually intense and repeated protests starting on January 15, 1989, the twentieth anniversary of Jan Palach's immolation, yet no massive popular support built up as it would in November. On January 15, five thousand people in Wenceslas Square were dispersed by police and the People's Militia, who used dogs, teargas, and water cannon and made ninety-one arrests. A smaller number continued to protest on January 16 and 17. On January 18, five thousand again gathered in the square shouting "freedom," "Where is Havel?" (he had been arrested on January 16), and "We want to live like humans." On January 19, riot police charged thousands of mostly youthful demonstrators, beating, injuring and arresting some. On January 20, demonstrators again gathered near the square. The next day, police prevented a mass pilgrimage to the grave of Jan Palach in a nearby city and arrested many. On January 22, police barricades blocked a march by dissidents to Prague castle, the president's residence. Then the protests stopped. The masses did not join.

The January protests could well have precipitated a much larger opposition movement, but international opportunity was not yet favorable. Poland did not have its Solidarity government; in Hungary the reform Communists were still battling the hard-liners; in East Germany the Honecker government seemed like the rock of Gibraltar. Eleven months later, by November 17, Poland had its Solidarity government, the first non-Communist government freely elected in a Communist country, and massive demonstrations by hundreds of thousands in East Germany had ousted Honecker, had forced the

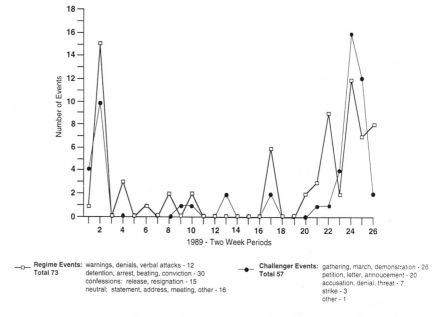

Figure 4.1. 1989 protests in Czechoslovakia.

opening of the East German border and breached the Berlin wall. The East German regime was on the run, making more and more concessions, and Gorbachev was keeping his hands off. East Germany became the model.

In September, the invasion of the West German embassy in Prague by hundreds of East Germans made a profound impression (Urban, 1990: 115). In October, the East German party boss Honecker, who symbolized the same hard line as President Husak and Party chief Jakes did, was forced to resign. An atmosphere of expectation was building up in Prague, yet no one knew who would ignite the tinder, or when (Urban, 1990: 116). As it happened, two small demonstrations occurred on November 15 and led to clashes with plainclothesmen. Then on the seventeenth, students at Charles University marched in commemoration of the fiftieth anniversary of the crushing of the Czech student movement by the Nazis. During the march, with many bystanders joining, the anti-Nazi theme changed to demands for freedom. Security police surrounded demonstrators in the center of Prague and severely beat them. Rumors of several deaths spread and inflamed public opinion. The students started an occupation of the university and called for punishment of those responsible for the violence and for a general strike in the entire country on November 27. Drama students had close links with actors and theater people, and persuaded them to join the strike. Prague actors had links with the provincial theater, which they activated. Overnight the entire

Czech theater was on strike. It was important because the arts had always carried great moral authority in the country (Urban, 1990: 116). Theaters gave dissidents a meeting place and a forum for addressing the public, which welcomed political debate instead of watching a drama, as had happened at the start of the Prague Spring in 1968. Students meanwhile spread the strike call to other universities and high schools. On November 20, some four hundred dissidents assembled at a Prague theater and founded Civic Forum as the alliance of some forty opposition groups, including some popular front parties, like the Socialist Party, which broke with the Communists. The erosion of authority started. The "Forum" concept was modeled on the East German New Forum and the Hungarian Democratic Forum.

Meanwhile, on November 18 and 19, thousands of youths milled about Wenceslas Square waiving flags and shouting slogans. Then on Monday, November 20, two days after the acts of police brutality and alleged deaths, two hundred thousand people converged on the square after work and protested police violence. They shouted and chanted "freedom," "resignation," and "now's the time." The crowds came back the next three days, and grew to an estimated 350,000 by November 23. Havel and other dissidents had addressed the demonstrators for the first time on November 21 from the balcony of a Socialist publishing house located in the square. Dubček, the hero of 1968 who hadn't been heard from in the past twenty years, joined Havel in addressing the demonstrators on November 23. In his speech, Dubček tried to frame the demands against the regime as "socialism with a human face," the goal of 1968. It did not work in 1989, as it had not worked in East Germany, Poland, or Hungary. "Free elections" is what the Prague crowds chanted, and they organized a general strike for November 27 to back its demands with muscle (Ash, 1990). Civic Forum and the people wanted free elections and democracy.

Civic Forum gained in stature and legitimacy as the voice of the people when the crowds in Prague came back day after day after day, listened to and roared approval of its speakers who voiced demands and reported back on how the negotiations with the regime were faring. Crowds responded to Forum speakers by chanting names and repeating the speakers' demands in unison – for example, "Havel, Dubček," and "freedom" and at the end of a speech, "the people down in the square make the most extraordinary spontaneous gesture. They all take their keys out of their pockets and shake them, all three hundred thousand key rings, producing a sound like massed Chinese bells" (Ash, 1990).

This simple gesture signified the unity of the people, their support for Civic Forum, and the nonviolent moral force they stood for.

In the CSSR, the crowd response to the violence by police on November 17 was on such a huge scale – two hundred thousand on the first day of demonstrations, and more on subsequent days – that police alone could not stop them. Yet the failure of repression by a hard-line Communist regime that had not hesitated to do so earlier bears scrutiny. Although the top leaders have not yet commented in print or in interviews about their decisions in the crisis, Czechs believe that regime leaders appealed for help to Soviet leaders but were turned down and cautioned against the use of the military. Hasty meetings of Communist Party branches were called throughout the country, but the rank and file deserted the leadership. They too wanted reforms in the Party and the state. The People's Militia refused the call to defend the regime and to "restore order." Party leaders became demoralized.[10]

Throughout the six-week revolution, Civic Forum managed to get across to the regime the message of itself as a nonviolent moral force, and conveyed it just as successfully to its enthusiastic supporters. According to a Civic Forum activist (Urban, 1990: 119):

We (at Civic Forum) knew perfectly well that a few dozen riot police could have taken us in five minutes: we were not barricaded in (at the Magic Lantern). But from the first moment, we wanted to be aggressively non-violent in our stance – to make a power out of our lack of weapons. It worked, even during mass demonstrations when a quarter of a million people were in the streets . . . there were no stones thrown. It was magic in our street.

The crucial event in the challenge to the Communists was the November 27 general strike. It was an "identification" move for demonstrating Civic Forum's following not just among students, artists, intellectuals, and the Prague middle class, but in the entire country and across all social classes (Oberschall, 1993). It was quite a risk to take for Prague was not the rest of the country, and even in Prague Civic Forum was uncertain of industrial working-class support. In the event, the strike was a huge success, everywhere in the country. Thousands of strike committees had formed in workplaces and turned out millions of people.

The regime itself at first gave as little as possible, and stalled. The Politbureau and Central Committee resigned, but the replacements were hard-liners. Angered by these tactics, the crowds came back, day after day, in sleet and snow, and backed Civic Forum's demand for a broad coalition government, for free elections, freedom of assembly and of the press, the release of political prisoners, the disbanding of the people's militia, the removal of Marxism-Leninism in education and culture, the repeal of the constitutional provision for the leading role of the Communist Party, in short the end of Communist monopoly in the institutions and governance of the country and its replacement with democracy. In five short weeks, by December 31, Civic Forum and the protest crowds had got all their demands.

CONCLUSION

A comparison of the January 1989 protests in Prague with the November demonstrations, and of the spring Leipzig protests with the fall opposition campaign dramatically demonstrates the importance of political opportunity in an overall explanation of collective action. What else was the missing ingredient which in those two cities kept the lid on protests to a few hundred dissidents in early 1989, and yet only a few short months later precipitated massive participation by citizens, from all walks of life? Of the four dimensions of opposition movement emergence, grievances, ideology, capacity to organize, and political opportunity, the first three were set already in late 1988 and early 1989, and probably even earlier. Dissatisfaction with economic performance and political liberties was not new. A nationalist and democratic ideological alternative to Marxism and socialism was not novel. On capacity to organize, the party-state had been quite successfully blocking dissident mobilization for years. Even some aspects of political opportunity, shown in Table 4.1, were constant in early and late 1989: lack of legitimacy and the Gorbachev factor. What changed suddenly and favorably for popular opposition were short-term and international aspects of political opportunity: the democratic opposition's success in other Eastern European party-states, the cracks in the Communist states' alliance system. The Polish regime allowed free elections which exposed the tenuous popular appeal of communism, and the reform Communists in Hungary broke the solidarity of Communist regimes by permitting the exodus of East Germans in the summer of 1989. The success of the popular movement in East Germany convinced Czechs and Slovaks that they too were capable of a successful, peaceful revolution against communism.

The Polish and Hungarian events of the late 1980s also underscore the importance of political opportunity. In these two countries, opportunity was endogenously created by the regimes themselves, based on miscalculation, to be sure. These were classic examples of erratic reformism (Oberschall, 1973). When provided with the opportunity to organize a democratic movement, Solidarity in Poland and the fledgling Hungarian opposition groups capitalized on the lack of regime legitimacy, and filled the ideological vacuum with a nationalist and democratic frame that had immense appeal. Without Soviet military might to shore it up, the authority of party-states eroded. Poland and Hungary then made a new, favorable opportunity milieu elsewhere in Eastern Europe. Without design and coordination the opposition movements diffused, and were successful.

5

Opportunities and framing in the transition to democracy: The case of Russia

ELENA ZDRAVOMYSLOVA

Until recently, Russian sociologists couldn't study social movements in their own country because there weren't any. Today, with the explosion of collective actions in the former Soviet Union, researchers are trying to develop genuine approaches to them. Cultural and political conduciveness, opportunities, and resources are very specific to the Russian transition to democracy, and this will influence proposed explanatory models. I believe the Russian case will produce its own social movement paradigms of development and research. Meanwhile, it is important to test Western research approaches on the post-Soviet case. Such a test will define the boundaries of Western models and focus the specificities of Russian social movements.

The so-called political process approach – with its emphasis on political opportunities and protest cycles and their influence on the genesis, dynamics, and success of collective actions – could be useful in understanding the social movements during the perestroika years. Yet the emergent paradigm on social construction of reality – including problems of movement ideologies, framing, meaning construction, and competition over symbolism (S. Hunt and R. Benford, 1992) – seems particularly relevant to social movements in the former USSR because of the importance of struggle over symbols during the dissolution of monopolistic Communist ideology.

I would like to use "political cycle" to denote the period of perestroika in the USSR (1985–91) that included a cycle of reforms and a cycle of protest. A protest cycle started in the political thaw provided by initial Gorbachev reforms, when opportunities for collective action appeared. I intend to show how political opportunities, expanding and shifting their locus in the course of the political cycle, encouraged different preferences in framing and corresponding symbolism of democratic social movements (SM).

In the cycle's ascending phase, reforms shaped limited opportunities for protest: partly open political discourse on Russian-Soviet history, and organizational building of "informal" organizations. During the course of the cycle, political opportunities expanded and shifted locus. With these new openings, collective actions technology was developed and taught, protests expanded and became common throughout the USSR, and – no less importantly – interpretative master-frames were generated (Snow and Benford, 1988), forming official political symbolism in Russia following democratic victory in August 1991. Reciprocal SMs' framing influenced the expanding of political opportunities.

Among the agents of democratic symbolic framing were two different types of social movement organizations (SMOs) – radical and moderate. Radical SMOs, the first to enter a protest cycle, were very successful in constructing an identity frame. New authorities later adopted its symbolism. But the disruptive tactics and relevant strategy-frames of radical SMOs were not efficient for action mobilization. On the other hand, symbolic framing of the reformist SMOs was appropriate to electoral mobilization at the peak of the protest cycle, and thus aided the democratic success in 1990 elections.

PERESTROIKA AS A POLITICAL CYCLE

The political cycle (A. Hirschman, 1982; K. Pekonen, 1986) of perestroika included a cycle of reforms and a cycle of protest (S. Tarrow, 1991c), which emerged as suspended reactions to political innovations. Gorbachev announced the strategy of perestroika at the Plenum of the CPSU in April 1985, proclaiming the beginning of glasnost reforms and democratization, and thus opening opportunities for public discourse and organizational development. The protest cycle started a year later (April 1986, the first rallies in Moscow and St. Petersburg) – it takes time for people to realize new opportunities for political action. Specific political movements of perestroika were embedded in the cycles of protest. Perestroika ended with the attempted counterreformist coup d'état in August 1991.

I distinguish three periods of the perestroika cycle, corresponding to the range and locus of the challengers' political opportunities. The boundaries are marked by political events, adopted judicial acts, and SM developments.

During the initial phase (April 1985 to January 1989), opportunities for open political discourse and organizational building of informal groups first appeared, after decades of Communist monopoly. Once reforms started, there was only a short delay until the start of a protest cycle. The initial phase of protest was marked by the appearance of the first political independent groups in Moscow, Leningrad, and other large cities. These groups grew daily in number and membership, and became ideologically identified. By the beginning of the electoral campaign in 1989, there were thousands of initiative political groups in Russia. Additionally, during this period the first collective actions took place (all-city disputes and meetings, rallies, and manifestations), starting the process of mobilization. Expanding political opportunities were reified in the alternative framing which, in its turn, influenced the course of reforms.

The second phase began with the election campaign of the First Congress of People's Deputies of the USSR in 1989 and included the Second Congress (election to the Russian and local Soviets) in 1990. This period is characterized by emergent electoral opportunities that made action mobilization possible for SMs. The protest cycle was at its peak, marked by mass character, frequency, and spreading of collective actions.

The third, descending phase of the cycle includes the removal of the sixth article of the Constitution ensuring the monopoly of the Soviet Communist Party (Third Congress of People's Deputies, March 1990), the preparation of the new Union Treaty between republics, and referenda on the Unity of the sovereignty of Russia (March 1991), and elections for Russian president (May 1991). This phase is marked by the institutionalization of democratic social movements and the corresponding decline of protest actions by democratic forces. The democratic electoral victory and seizure of power in Russian central cities stimulated counterreformist mobilization, but the attempted coup in August 1991 was ultimately without popular support. Legal opportunities for the establishment of political parties and the institutionalization of social movements of different ideological trends first formed in the USSR.

The political cycle of perestroika turned into a soft revolution, leading to Russian political modernization. This became obvious after the failure of the coup, the following disintegration of the USSR, and the beginning of radical economic reforms in November 1991.

THE FUNCTIONS OF SYMBOLISM IN SMS DURING THE POLITICAL CYCLE

Among the resources of SMs provided by political reforms, I believe alternative frames and relevant symbolism were the most crucial for consensus and action mobilization (Klandermans, 1984). Their role in Russian democratic mobilization is determined by the features of (1) contested official Communist ideology and (2) so-called folk ideology. The characteristic traits of dominant Communist ideology during seventy years of the Soviet regime were: "intolerance towards other ideologies, its obligatory and compulsory character for the population, its principal orientation on the future, but not on the assimilation of the past."[1] This ideology is hierarchically constructed, has a militant spirit, and depends on continued reproduction of a defined combat task for its adherents. Though the Communist symbols and clichés became void of meaning and did not find popular response before perestroika (see Obershall, 1992), certain aspects of Communist ideology (for instance, rhetoric of justice, equality, broadly exploited appeal to the enemy-image, ritualization of public life) are deeply rooted in mass consciousness. To delegitimate the official ideology, democratic SMs had to develop alternative symbolism which was aggressive in style and confrontational in content.

Opportunities for public discourse encouraged the contesting of the symbolic framing developed by the democratic movement.

Three dimensions of SM framing can be distinguished (Neidhardt, 1992): identity, issue, and strategy subframes. These subframes were also deliberately developed by the democratic SM in Russia. Their functions are relevant to the core framing tasks (diagnostic, prognostic, and motivational) as formulated in Western frame theory (Snow and Benford, 1988). I believe there is a fourth function of Russian democratic movement framing during the perestroika cycle – the creation of new official political symbolism. Every frame is shaped by key symbols. Symbolism developed by SMs condense the meaning of frames.

The symbolic framing helped the development consensus and action mobilization among SM participants. Symbols serve as a basis of group consciousness, solidarity, and a sense of belonging. On the other hand, symbols appeared to be powerful resources that promoted participation in collective actions.

During the ascending phase of the protest cycle, democratic SMs were anxious about ideological issues, because of certain constraints in protest opportunities (limited to contesting discourse) and the urgent task of constructing a collective identity in the democratic movement. Democratic SMs were looking for appropriate values and beliefs that could cement collective identity. Thus, symbols of identification – reflecting the image of "we," determined by an understanding and assessment of the past, present, and future of Russia – came forward in SM activities.

Negative integration was the base for construction of collective identity in the democratic movement, as illustrated by key symbols like (1) the names of SMOs; (2) the dominant enemy-image used in ideological clichés of Stalinists, Communists, Marxists; and (3) disruptive collective actions that could not promote mass mobilization.

The strategy-framing was rather diverse in democratic SMOs, being predetermined by opportunities provided by protest cycle phases. Radical SMO strategy-framing was confrontational and moderate – oriented to certain compromises with authorities, which was presupposed in their identity-frames. Issue-framing of a democratic SM can be symbols developed by SMOs in pursuit of mass support during elections which corresponded to the protest cycle peak.

The fourth function of democratic symbolic framing – institutionalization of symbolism that previously was used by radical democratic SMOs – became evident after the democratic victory in August 1991.

This ideal-typical classification of the changing priority of framing in different periods of the political cycle should not prevent us from realizing that political symbols can perform many functions simultaneously. Thus, the enemy image can be used both in identity-framing and strategy-framing.

However, the relative importance of these functions changes in the course of the political cycle as a response to expanding political opportunities. In the first period of perestroika (1985–89), the identity-framing was more essential, because (1) the locus of opportunities was concentrated in the public discourse sphere revising Russian-Soviet history, and the mobilization for action was still not politically feasible; and (2) SM was in its initial stage of development. In the second period, issue framing came forward, due to (1) expanded opportunities connected with forthcoming elections, and (2) a certain maturity, revealed in movement goal instrumentality. Thus, political changes developed by SMOs caused the differences in strategies.

During perestroika, different SMOs had priorities in the development of different symbolic frames. One group demonstrated radical flank effects. Radical SMOs were the first to enter the protest cycle, and were very effective in identity framing; their symbolism determined the depth of possible confrontation with the dominant ideology for all the groups entering the cycle later. It was the symbolism of radical groups that was adopted by the new regime after the coup attempt.

On the other hand, the confrontational strategy-framing and issue-framing of radical democrats were not effective during the electoral mobilization of 1989–90. At the peak of the political cycle, the symbolism developed by moderate democrats of reformist orientation proved to be the most fruitful in providing mass support. The very fact that groups of differing degrees of confrontation coexisted in one SM's industry promoted the democratic movement's victorious outcome. I shall now consider symbolic framings in the cases of two democratic SMOs: the Democratic Union and the Leningrad People's Front.

SYMBOLIC FRAMING OF THE DEMOCRATIC UNION

There were political opportunities in the ascending phase of the political cycle. Several events and newly adopted laws influenced SMs during the first period (reforms of glasnost and democratization): regulation of voluntary associations and the Nineteenth Party conference (1988); the law on councils of workers' collectives and Supreme Soviet decrees on rallies, manifestations, and demonstrations (1989); and the laws on elections and industrial conflicts (1989). Political opportunities in this period generally opened political discourse on the history of the country and saw the emergence of social movement organizations and the first sporadic collective actions. There were, however, no opportunities as yet for vocal political opposition by challenging groups. In this initial stage, identity-framing of the democratic movement was crucial. It is not surprising that consciousness-raising groups, and philosophical and historical clubs, searching for adequate symbols in world and Russian history to identify themselves with were overrepresented among new initiative groups.

In the identity-framing of the democratic SM in Russia, the key role was played by the "Democratic Union" (DU), a radical democratic organization. The DU defined itself as an all-union political party during its founding congress (May 8–9, 1988). It had branches in more than 30 USSR cities, and a large membership – in Leningrad alone, 120 people were in the local branch. Members were representative of marginal intelligentsia – the majority worked on low-status jobs and had been imprisoned on several occasions for political reasons.

In its confrontational stance toward the CPSU, the DU declared its orientation toward radical change of the regime by nonviolent means, focusing on the tasks of building the state of law and civil society.

During the first period of the protest cycle, any issue picked up by an SMO served a symbolic function. Thus, a movement organization itself served as a symbol of vocal opposition; the attempts to give an SMO legal status by registration became a symbol of the state of law and political pluralism in the Soviet Union; the illegal collective actions symbolized the very existence and mass support of the movement and its readiness not to compromise with the authorities; the signs, pins, and uniforms of SMOs symbolized their separation from the free-riding masses and Communists; and the political language of their slogans symbolized their confrontation with official ideology and authority, and of identification with certain sets of values.

In this period, rallies and manifestations were rather infrequent and did not have a mass character. According to sociological studies and opinion polls, SMOs were comparatively small, and the population did not show any definite attitudes toward them and was not ready to offer them much support.[2]

Thus, the priority of the identity-framing can be explained by the specific locus of political opportunities, which helped awake civic consciousness but not to the point where mass mobilization was possible under the radical anti-socialist slogan.

Let us consider several groups of symbols developed in the identity-frame of the DU.

The name of an SMO as a symbol

The DU identified itself as a "political party, opposite to the totalitarian system of the USSR." Under the conditions of a single-party system legitimized in the Soviet Union Constitution, the very fact of naming an SMO a "party" symbolized new political opportunities for the establishment of a multiparty system, and the destruction of the political and ideological monopoly of the CPSU. At the same time, this self-definition symbolized possibilities for vocal, ideological, and political confrontation. In reality, neither the CPSU nor the DU were political parties.

The symbolism of the DU's identity-framing and issue-framing was inherited from the Western rhetoric of the Cold War. Its theoretical base was the American political science conception of totalitarianism. Accordingly, when revising the history of the USSR, the DU declared the Soviet regime totalitarian and unreformable on principle, and called the date of the October Revolution (October 26, 1917) a day of national tragedy.

The DU inverted the typical images of official Communist ideology – Paradise/Hell, heroes/villains. Radical SMOs adopted the symbol of the desirable future from Western democracy in a very unspecified way – the vague idea of civil society and law-ruled state, based on economic, political, and ideological pluralism. It was the DU that substituted the slogans of "true" pluralism, democracy, glasnost, and state of law for the slogans of the party-state's reformist branch – socialist democracy, socialist pluralism, socialist democratization, and glasnost.

In its program, the DU declared "negative opposition" to be its main task. Thus, the DU distanced itself from the Communist reformers who launched the cycle of reforms – "A person, rejecting the system has to say 'no' to the system." Even the rhetoric of the slogans was based on the grammatical construction of negation: "No," "Done with," and so forth. The DU emphasized that "perestroika actually means the rejection of perestroika, which goal is impossible to achieve without a radical perestroika in ideology."[3]

Constructing collective identity onto negative integration implies the use of the enemy-image. The enemy image was an effective instrument for identification, not only because of the militant Communist ideology's monopoly but also because the deep-rooted confrontational worldview of the Soviet-Russian people, who were used to ideologically constructed enemy-images under both tsarism and communism. One of the movement's participants depicted mass consciousness of *Homo sovieticus:* "The intellect is dispersing, crushed in skirmishes and internecine warfare, in confrontation of the representatives of the irreconcilable camps, in the reproduction and multiplication of the enemy-image. As long as our consciousness keeps regenerating the enemy-image bolshevism is invincible."[4]

It is not by chance that the enemy-image was also used for electoral mobilization at the peak of the political cycle, as frame resonance connecting the ideology of the democratic movement with widespread stereotypes present in mass consciousness and folk ideology (Benford and Snow, 1988). However, different symbols of the enemy were used in the identity-framing and issue-framing. For the DU, the main enemy was the CPSU, including the reformist branch headed by Gorbachev (Yeltsin never had any charisma for them; Lenin was seen as the main historical culprit). The DU's ideological leaders formulated their antireformist argument in this way: "Is there much consolation in the fact that only sixty years were a mistake, but not all seventy? And if we look for the roots of Brezhnev's stagnation in the command-administrative system, established by Stalin, why don't we look for the roots of Stalinism in the shot of the *Aurora* that was made in 1917?"[5]

What was radical about the DU was the depth of its confrontation with the regime, and its conviction was that the system was unreformable and perestroika impossible. The main indicator of the depth of political confrontation was the hostility of the DU toward Gorbachev and the CPSU, and the nomenklatura and the persistent enemy image of Communism and Leninism. The slogans of the DU included: "Shame for the bloody flag of the CPSU," "Down with the autocracy of the CPSU," "Pluralism – yes, totalitarianism – no," "Lenin – executioner #1."[6] The strategy-frame of the DU was disruptive, and the illegal rally was the main form of collective action. This radical confrontational symbolism, as well as Westernized rhetoric, was ineffective in electoral mobilization, and the DU couldn't expect mass support during the elections of 1989–90.

Symbolism in the strategy-framing of the Democratic Union

In the DU program confrontational tactics (illegal rallies and demonstrations, civil disobedience, and the active boycott of elections) were declared the only ones possible.[7] The DU called for boycotting forthcoming elections. In strategy-framing, the SMO distinguished two phases of the electoral process: the preelection period and elections per se. In the preelection period, the DU actively participated in meetings and rallies to propagandize the DU's values and goals, and to explain to the population the real goals of party-state officials.

> The main goal of participation in the electoral campaign is not victory in the elections but the dissemination of the main tasks and ideas of the DU among tens of thousands of people. . . . Not adapting to the voters, not weakening the principles of the party program but addressing attention to these principles, using a shock therapy effect, and reveal to the people the true reasons of the catastrophic situation in the country and ways to overcome it, proposed by our party. In this connection an invaluable role is played not only by propaganda and agitation of the members of the DU but the reaction of the nomenklatura. The actions of authorities toward radical democrats could influence the attitudes of the voters.[8]

This radical confrontational strategy-framing drew attention to the DU but could not provide mass mobilization.

The most popular form of collective action was the illegal rally, which became an aspect of the DU's strategy-framing. An illegal rally symbolized vocal opposition and a plurality of opinions in Soviet society, which actually did not exist. With the help of rallies and collective gatherings, social movements obtained legitimacy in society, and therefore protest actions also had a substantial, reciprocal effect on political opportunities.

The first rallies in St. Petersburg took place in the spring of 1986 and had been organized by democratic SMOs. The DU was the most active in collective actions. In Leningrad, in the year from its foundation to the beginning of the first electoral campaign (spring 1988–spring 1989), 125 rallies were organized by the DU. It used every occasion to hold a rally: state holidays, significant dates in the human rights movement, foreign and domestic policy events, new laws adopted by authorities, and so forth. Banned by the authorities, rallies helped create a collective identity in the democratic movement – both as rebels against and victims of the regime.

The legal regulation of collective actions (as one of the dimensions of political opportunities) was constantly changing during the political cycle. Before 1988 there was no legal regulation of protest actions on the state level. In St. Petersburg, local rules regulating collective gatherings were in force since August 1987. According to them, a group of ten or more people had to appeal to authorities for permission to hold a rally or a demonstration ten days in advance.

The usual pattern of a DU rally went as follows: The group notified the authorities that it intended to hold a rally in the center of the city. If the authorities decided to permit the gathering, they changed the place of the supposed-to-be rally to the outskirts of the city. The SMO regularly disagreed with this resolution, and the rally would automatically acquire an illegal status. Under the pretext of local regulations violation, the authorities would try to break up the rally by force. Participants would be arrested and sometimes beaten, and subjected to large fines. The demonstrators were ready for such actions and would sometimes provoke them, and prepared for violence by the authorities by wearing special protective clothes.

The symbolic and instrumental value of the rallies grew with attempts to ban them, and depended highly on the location of the gathering (center of city or outskirts). Democratic protesters always insisted on holding rallies in the city center, for obvious reasons: gathering in the center is not only the most effective for mobilizing attention and participation, but also in provoking reaction from the authorities. Local authorities resisted these tactics by forcing the democrats to hold their rallies on the outskirts of town.

Partly as a result of collective actions, political opportunities changed. In 1988 the laws regulating rallies, demonstrations, and elections were adopted. It was an obvious, substantive effect of SM activities. Afterwards, collective gatherings lost part of their symbolic significance and became more issue-oriented and instrumental.

After the failure of the nomenklatura candidates in the elections of March 1989 in the big cities, the DU split on the questions of strategy-framing. Demands "to participate in elections and to hold a dialogue with the CPSU as a parliamentary opposition" were made. The majority in the DU understood that tactics were their weak spot, because "confrontation with the system not only has no perspective, but is also dangerous for the participants" and that confrontation prevented the DU from expanding its social base. Thus, a significant number of DU followers argued that "those members of the party, who are oriented on real politics (not on theory-building, but . . . on real participation in the redistribution of power in the country) will detach themselves from the DU."[9] These party members criticized not only the DU's strategy-frame but also its major focus on identity-framing and on theoretical clarification and ideology. Thus, they claimed that "in most parts of the DU program the exposure of the regime prevails above the positive tasks which are ill-defined. . . . A sheet of paper, even if it has a 'minus' sign printed on it, is only a piece of paper, but not a qualitatively new way of governing."[10] "We are so much absorbed by symbolism that . . . we are not only ahead of the CPSU in this respect, but also ahead of our heavy-metalists. The only thing left is to carry portraits on the rallies."[11] This controversial argument shows that at the peak of the political cycle, when electoral opportunities appeared, the radical confrontational symbolism was pushed to the background. Its place was taken by symbolism, and used by moderate democrats in democratic SDMOs such as the Leningrad People's Front (LPF).

SYMBOLIC FRAMING OF THE LENINGRAD PEOPLE'S FRONT

In the second phase of the political cycle (the peak of the protest cycle), political opportunities were determined by assigned elections on the alternative base that had to take place in 1989, 1990, and the two Congresses of People's Deputies of the USSR. In the First Congress (June 1988), a radical democratic faction of deputies was formed (Interregional Deputy's Group, headed by A. Sakharov, Yu. Afanasiev, and others). The Second Congress (December 1989) adopted important documents concerning national elections – a decree on the political and legal revaluation of the Soviet-German pact of 1939, on the events in Tbilisi in April 1989, and on the invasion in Afghanistan. The institute of presidential power was established.

This period corresponds to the peak of the protest cycle, when collective actions were mass, frequent, and widespread. Democratic SMOs consolidated and united in the face of elections. The polarization of SMs developed, and national-patriotic SM and Communist countermovement opposed democrats. This growth of the SM sector was caused by the shifting locus of political opportunities connected with electoral mobilization. The Electoral Law of 1988, in spite of all its controversies and shortcomings, gave the citizenry a chance to express political preferences about the alternative base in legally permissible form. Rallies, meetings, and demonstrations in support of candidates were allowed. Elections created a demand for symbolic framing, very different from the one that prevailed in the previous period. Symbols of identity-framing, strategy-framing, and issue-framing served as a means of action mobilization through electoral support. The strategy of mobilization included the elaboration of frame-alignment technologies that connected democrats' programs with folk ideology (Snow et al., 1986). The symbols of the moderate SMOs were less numerous, less expressive, and less confrontational than those of the DU.

The most massive moderate democratic SMO in Leningrad was the

Leningrad People's Front (LPF). It held its founding congress in June 1989 between two elections, which provided political opportunities and triggered a framing trend oriented to mass electoral support. The main goal of LPF, as defined in the opening declaration, was "the consolidation of the democratic public and preparation for local and Russian elections." Six thousand SMO members were registered at the first congress. The idea to set up the LPF as a mass organization of unified democratic forces appeared in spring 1989 but could not be put into practice until a year later. The delay can be interpreted as a significant indicator of the gradually changing opportunities for organizational building and mass mobilization. During the intervening year, the initiators worked hard to get popular support. The initiators were liberal SMOs including intellectual clubs like "Perestroika," "For the People's Front," "Club of Friends of the Journal *Ogonoek*,"[12] and some others. Fifty-three democratic groups in the city supported organization of the Front. The club name "Perestroika," one of the predecessors of the Front, symbolizes its common stance with the part of the elite that launched reforms. The majority of LPF members were representatives of the Soviet intelligentsia, with high education (some with doctoral degrees) and successful careers.

The founding congress of LPF declared its intention to act within the framework of the legal rights guaranteed by the Soviet Constitution and Criminal Code, on the basis of common goals shared by all democratic forces in the country. Thus, the LPF was a moderate democratic SMO that was "a priori oriented on compromise with the authorities, and on the possibility of democratization of existing institutions, not on their destruction."[13]

The name of a SMO as a symbol

The words "Leningrad People's Front" have certain connotations for people in Russia and Leningrad (St. Petersburg). The noun "front" is associated in Russian with a combative and offensive task, and with confrontation and the consolidation of forces. The mobilizing mythos of the term is obvious, representing an appeal for unifying all forces against the nomenklatura, the common enemy. Another connotation derives from the role of antifascist resistance fronts of World War II. Thus, the use of the word "front" in the SMO name made clear that the organization was "created for the struggle of democracy against the administrative system and having a tendency to form a positive program . . ." The word "front" was previously used to name organizations representing national-liberation movements in Soviet republics (like the People's Fronts in the Baltic republics, in Armenia, and in Georgia). This is why "LPF" reflects the regionalization of the political process, connected with the different velocity of political change and different urgent social problems in the regions.[14]

Symbolism of identity-frame of the LPF

In their texts, moderate democrats avoided Cold War images of Soviet history. Their main political orientation was support for and acceleration of the reforms from above. The majority of moderate democrats hailed perestroika as a return to "genuine" socialism. The term "socialism" had not yet disappeared from the political language of moderate democrats. For example, one of the most radical leaders of the movement wrote:

> We are certain that the socialist idea is to be preserved as a leading idea, but not in the Bolshevik revolutionary sense. We have to consider the socialist idea in a broad sense, beginning from the doctrine of Jesus Christ about brotherhood and justice, through the torments of Lenin before his death, when he tried to find the way out of the crisis, and up to the contemporary social-democratic studies."[15]

Although the LPF rejected a vast period of Soviet history labeled "the command-administrative system," it did not reject the Communist system as a whole. Reformist ideological symbolism appeared to be an important mobilization resource in the second period of the political cycle, namely, during elections.

The enemy image was also employed in LPF's rhetoric, for it proved to be effective not only in consensus mobilization but also in action mobilization. It was in the Leningrad election campaign of 1989 that democrats learned what sort of enemy image had to be used in frame-alignment strategy. The common adversary – which consolidated and unified such so-called democratic forces as SMOs, establishment forces, and the public at large – appeared to be not a Bolshevik or Marxist, but a representative of the nomenklatura.

The simplified image of the unified enemy – the nomenklatura – was rooted in the undifferentiated horizontal social stratification of the Soviet society, with the basic line of division between the masses (population) deprived of all rights and the powerful elites (nomenklatura). This mode of social stratification was the main reason for the successful exploitation of the nomenklatura's enemy-image as a resource for electoral mobilization.[16]

A generalized symbol such as "Stalinist" was one of the enemy-images of this period that served best for consensus and action mobilization, and was broadly used in public discourse. This symbol implied a revision of Soviet history, dividing it into two unequal parts: before Stalin's seizure of power, and after. The declared goal of the moderate democrats was to overcome Stalinism and to return to Leninist socialist principles. Moderate democrats contrasted Lenin, as a symbol of being right in principle, with Stalin, as a symbol of being wrong. In one of the posters printed in the newspaper *Nabat* ("Alarm bell"), it was written: "Lenin – is a person who wanted good but didn't have time to put his intentions in practice."[17] Already in the first period of the political cycle, Bukharin, Trotsky, and other "old Bolsheviks" from Lenin's circle reentered political discourse as leaders of anti-Stalinist resistance. In the second phase, during elections, the main slogan of the LPF was "All power to the Soviets," which also testified to its reform orientation, since Stalin was considered the first to transfer power from the Soviets to the CPSU.

Strategy and issue frames of the LPF

In contrast to the negative opposition of the DU, the LPF proclaimed "constructive opposition." This SMO used legally permissible forms of collective actions: permitted rallies, discussions on the city level, mass media, meeting with Party officials and local administration, and, most importantly, participation in elections. LPF had access to official newspapers (*Smena*), and local TV and radio broadcasting. The tactics of the moderate democrats were more instrumental than symbolic, since it was oriented toward the achievement of concrete goals (like victory in elections), promoting particular reform, banning the construction of a dam across the Finnish Gulf, and so on.

Thus, issue-framing was much more elaborate in LPF than in DU. During elections, LPF picked up problems, themes, and symbols that resonated with the citizenry (Snow and Benford, 1988). The folk ideology of the Soviet people in general and of Leningraders in particular had (and still has) several important features – it is pierced by the enemy-image, and it personifies the enemy as a representative of the party-apparatus. This ideology presupposed the sanctification of dissident-martyrs of the regime (such as Andrei Sakharov) and those political leaders who suffered regime persecution, while at the same time remaining a part of the nomenklatura (such as Boris Yeltsin and Nikolaj Ivanov). Fourth, this local folk ideology is based on the myth of Leningraders' historical and cultural identification with cultural autonomy, Western orientation, and the city's martyr aura during the Soviet period. All these specific features were taken into account in the frame alignment strategies of LPF.

With the increasing polarization of social movements during the second phase of the cycle, all SMs operated with similar symbols, slogans, and labels, looking for popular support. Thus, they developed competitive framing by applying different meanings to the same symbols. For example, both democratic and conservative SMs blamed the "mafia" for the food shortages in the city, but the motives and concrete images of mafiosi were different with these contesting SMs. While moderate democrats identified "mafia" with party apparatus, the Communists reserved the same term for the new entrepreneurs and cooperatives. The third social movement – the national patriots – asserted that the "mafia" were Zionists who were "the real power in Leningrad." Elections proved that the LPF's framing had won this competition.

During the preelection, the LPF framing switched to ideological issues previously underrepresented: the problem of Russian nationalism and patriotism, and religious problems. This emphasis was caused not only by the desire to build an ideological bridge to potential supporters, but also reinforced the polarization inside the social movement industry and the competition with national patriots advancing the question of Russian national consciousness within the framework of Russian imperial chauvinism. The democrats realized during the elections that they could not leave national-patriotic symbolism and rhetorics to conservative forces. Thus, the LPF attempted to construct contesting means of democratic Russian nationalism in the mode of frame competition. SMOs supporting the LPF (the Christian Democratic Union, Leningrad branch; the Society of Christian Enlightenment, SMO "Free Russia") began publishing an independent newspaper, *Nabat,* as a "mouthpiece of the healthy national consciousness of Russians." Moderate democrats started to work out patriotic and religious rhetoric on the eve of elections to Russian and local Soviets. *Nabat*'s motto was a line from poet A. Pushkin, himself a national symbol of Russian culture – "Russia will awake from the dream." Appealing to readers in the paper's first issue, the authors proclaimed, "Today the national idea in Russia, its symbolism and sacred things are thoughtlessly given to 'Pamyat'[18] which perverts it into pure fascism. The Bell[19] has to call for a free and democratic Russia."[20] Moderate democrats considered the revival, on healthy, nonchauvinistic grounds, of Russian national consciousness to be one of their more urgent tasks. They formulated the motto of Russian democratic nationalism: "For the freedom of the Fatherland and the revival of Russian identity." The sovereignty of Russia was seen as one of the main goals of democratic nationalism.

The LPF also tried to adopt some Christian symbols, and reconsidered in its framing the controversial relationship of Orthodoxy to democratic values. The LPF assumed that Communist ideology had been replaced by the propagation of Orthodoxy and Christian values as a moral base for the ideas of liberalism, human rights, the legal state, formal consensus, and other achievements of democracy."[21] After reviving and legitimizing Christian values, the LPF began to emphasize the role of religion in "fostering Love to Motherland, Morality, and Democracy."

Another theme that emerged in the LPF's preelectoral issue-framing was the demand for nonviolent means of conflict resolution. The effectiveness of peaceful conflict-resolution propaganda was provoked by recent involvements of Soviet troops in Nagornyi-Karabakh, Lithuania, and Tbilisi. As one LPF leader put it: "If the population boycotts elections, the nomenklatura will come to power, provoke national elections and civil war will start in Russia. Boycotting elections is insane. Everyone who doesn't want an allunion massacre and tanks in the streets of Moscow, Leningrad, Sverdlovsk, and Vorkuta has to come to the polls."[22]

Appealing to the local identity of Leningraders was a very effective issue-framing element in the LPF's electoral program. The democratic press published letters that testified to frame-resonance. One respondent wrote: "I joined LPF because I sincerely believe that being a member of LPF I will be able to help the revival of my city, improve the life of simple residents that suffer from need, absence of rights, and absence of culture."[23]

All of these components of frame-alignment strategies – employing enemy symbols, national and local identity symbols, Orthodox symbolism – helped democrats mobilize the citizenry during the elections. In Leningrad, democrats received about 70 percent of the seats to local Soviets (1990). Consequently, the democratic movement became institutionalized and the protest cycle came to an end.

During the third period of the political cycle (spring 1990–August 1991), the city's official symbolism was becoming similar to the DU's radical symbolism. These changes in the institutional symbolism, from reformist to radical democracy, are illustrated in the renaming of the city – as a result of the June 1990 referendum, the decision was made to "rebaptize" the city and return its original name (St. Petersburg). This renaming was a symbol of a new renaissance in the history of St. Petersburg, its independence from the Soviet Union, of the revival of its cultural identity and its identification with radical democrats (such as the DU), who were the first to demand the return of the city's original name.

The local elections in March 1990 marked the end of the protest cycle in Leningrad, while in Russia as a whole, the cycle came to an end only after the unsuccessful coup of August 1991. In Russia, it was a period with opportunities opening up for the establishment of a multiparty system. The institutionalization of democratic symbolism in Russia went on constantly during the political cycle, but it was only in the aftermath of the coup that the symbols used in radical democrat framing became the symbols of the regime. This adoption of radical symbolism is one effect of SM institutionalism. It can also be interpreted as a vivid symbol of political revolution in Russia as well as abroad. Alternative symbolism and the rhetorics of new authorities were made possible by the radical change in political opportunities that was caused by the defeat of the conservatives in the coup d'état and following symbolic banning of the CPSU and the dismantling of the USSR.

CONCLUSION

Analysis of the symbolic framing of the DU and the LDF in Russia during perestroika shows that the changing political opportunities in the course of the political cycle determined the content and priority in framing. Symbolism developed by SMOs is one of the most vivid elements of framing. In Russia, in the cycle of perestroika we see the classic case of expanding political opportunities triggering organizational development of different SMOs and their framing.

The phases of political (and relevant protest) cycle correspond to shifts in the locus and range of political opportunities. In the first period opportunities were provided for open political discourse and initiatives, and thus symbolic framing served mainly as a means for identification of the democratic SM. The constraints on protest opportunities explain why only radical SMOs were active in their collective actions. The second period featured electoral opportunities triggering a particular trend in organizational mobilization as well as in corresponding framing. The symbolism of reformist democratic SMOs worked as a resource for electoral mobilization. The fact that the cycle ended with the adoption by the authorities of the radical movement's symbolism is vivid proof of the democratic movement's institutionalization and, in my opinion, reveals the revolutionary character of the political cycle.

Thus, the framing and corresponding symbolism of the democratic SM were formatted by changing political opportunities that featured specific tasks of the democratic SM. The task of identification was gradually replaced by the task of electoral mobilization.

PART II
MOBILIZING STRUCTURES

6

Constraints and opportunities in adopting, adapting, and inventing

JOHN D. McCARTHY

Scholars of social movements have come to a quite broad consensus about the importance of *mobilizing structures* for understanding the trajectory of particular social movements and broader social movement cycles.[1] The choices that activists make about how to more or less formally pursue change have consequences for their ability to raise material resources and mobilize dissident efforts, as well as for society-wide legitimacy – all of which can directly affect the chances that their common efforts will succeed.

But these same scholars have just begun to account for the comparative historical variation in those structures across societies, across movements, and through time. As they make progress in doing so, we will be better able to generate perspectives that account for how mobilizing structural forms emerge and evolve; how they are chosen, combined, and adapted by social movement activists; and how they differentially affect particular movements as well as movement cycle trajectories. The concepts of *political opportunity* and *strategic framing* are, I believe, particularly useful in illuminating these processes.

By mobilizing structures I mean those agreed upon ways of engaging in collective action which include particular "tactical repertoires," particular "social movement organizational" forms, and "modular social movement repertoires." I also mean to include the range of everyday life micromobilization structural social locations that are not aimed primarily at movement mobilization, but where mobilization may be generated: these include family units,[2] friendship networks, voluntary associations, work units, and elements of the state structure itself.[3] The encompassing scope of the mobilizing structures concept usefully aggregates all of these many varieties of enabling institutional configurations, allowing us to address their routine dynamics as well as their common reciprocal interrelationships with both political opportunity structures and framing processes. With it, one imagines that typical structural configurations of SMOs, civil associations, work and family interpersonal networks, and tactical repertoires exist which can be used to characterize particular historical social movements. In doing so one seeks to make general Charles Tilly's (1985) approach to characterizing "the social movement" by its typical social location and associated strategic and tactical approaches. I must not minimize the empirical difficulties in producing credible aggregate accounts of movement *mobilizing structural configurations,* but fruitful comparative analyses of the role of varying political opportunity structures and differential strategic framing approaching in the dynamics of social movements across nations and time demand, I will argue, that we succeed in doing so.

ENUMERATING THE RANGE AND VARIETY
OF MOBILIZING STRUCTURES[4]

Our most careful taxonomers of mobilizing structures have continued to caution that we describe them before we attempt to assess their causes and consequences.[5] Their caution stems from the widespread proclivity among scholars of social movements to develop elaborate explanations for the emergence of social movement forms without very clearly bounding the forms empirically or conceptually. But lately we have together, if somewhat haphazardly, made great strides in describing their range and variety. The labor-intensive inductive work entailed in depicting the vast empirical range of mobilizing structures in their historical and geographical varieties has been proceeding apace, even if, in general, *we* do tend to take conceptual and operational shortcuts as we cut to the chase in trying to explain variation in the causes and consequences of mobilizing structures.

We have a few coordinates for mapping the civil institutional turf, but they tend to be crude and elusive ones. Let me begin by outlining, briefly, what I see as the mapping task. I start by situating a few of the widely used cornerstones along with some not so well-known ones.

At the least formally organized end of the map are "families" and "networks of friends." It is upon these most basic structures of everyday life that much local dissent is built. Kinship and friendship networks have been shown to be central to understanding movement recruitment (Snow, Zurcher, and Eklund-Olson, 1980) as well as the formation of emergent local movement groups (McCarthy and Wolfson, 1988). And while scholars have recognized the importance of kinship and friendship structures for mobilization, they have rarely attempted to characterize standard movement profiles of these variable structural features of social structure. There is great potential utility in drawing upon the work of the theorists and demographers of local community networks (e.g., Granovetter, 1973; Wellman and Berkowitz, 1988; Fisher et al., 1977) for characterizing and comparatively situating these most basic features of mobilized movements. That potential can be seen in Gould's (1991) account of the centrality of informal network structures to understanding the mobilization of the 1871 Paris Commune. And while there is a strong comparative tradition of scholarship that links such variation (e.g., "clique isolation," etc.) to the variable likelihood of collective action (e.g., Gans, 1962; Putnam, 1992), its insights have rarely been applied to comparative *movement* analysis.

The role of informal structures of everyday life have been widely linked with movement mobilization. These include "communities of memory" (networks of demobilized activists) (Woliver, 1993), "subcultures of dissent" (Obserschall's term in this volume), "protest infrastructures," a bastardization of Gamson and Schmeidler's term (1984), and McAdam's widely adopted phrase, "micromobilization contexts" (McAdam, 1988b; McAdam, McCarthy, and Zald, 1988) that suggests a wide variety of social sites within people's daily rounds where informal and less formal ties between people can serve as solidarity and communication facilitating structures when and if they choose to go into dissent together. It is widely believed that these social infrastructures are important (witness the variety of terms we have coined to refer to them), but we have not mapped them very systematically. Tilly (1978) has conceived the dimension of "netness" to describe movement constituencies by the denseness of their social relations that are created by these many institutional ties.

Closer to the less organized quadrant are informal networks created primarily as mobilizing structures. Recent research along these lines compares the "suffragette" periods of the women's movement in the United States with the more recent equity feminist period (e.g., Rosenthal et al., 1985). Steven Buechler has elaborated the idea of a social movement community through his study of that contrast. He says,

The social movement community (SMC) . . . is a parallel to an SMO in that both concepts refer to groups that identify their goals with the preferences of a social movement and attempt to implement those goals. Whereas the SMO does so by recourse to formal, complex organizational structures, however, the SMC does so through informal networks of politicized individuals with fluid boundaries, flexible leadership structures, and malleable divisions of labor. With the addition of this concept, SMIs may now be defined as consisting of all the SMOs and SMCs that are actively seeking to implement the preference structures of a given SM. (Buechler, 1990: 42)

As well there is a class of mobilizing structures that are hybrids in that they are more organized, but they exist within existing organizations/institutions. Prayer groups, caucuses, study groups, sports teams, commissions – these more formally organized subgroups can also be the building blocks during protest campaigns. There exists great variation across time and place in the extent of these forms, constraints upon their existence, and their mandate (e.g., originating in preferences of organizational members or created by organizational authority).

Another common form is the free-standing protest campaign committee that links networks, organizations, and caucuses together in order to coordinate events and efforts. They are not unlike issue specific lobbying committees that bring together diverse groups for temporary legislative campaigns. And there are the more enduring coalition structures that connect diverse SMOs with one another, other community groups and diffuse networks of supporters that Suzanne Staggenborg (1991) and Robert Kleidman (1993) have brought to our attention recently. More encompassing structures may emerge which link SMOs from several collateral movements, "movement families" (della Porta and Rucht, 1991), together.

There are diverse more formally organized groups serving as movement-dedicated mobilizing structures that we have typically clustered under the social movement organization (SMO) label, but that demonstrate wide variation in institutional form. There is the "independent local" volunteer-based group emblematic of our image of the "grassroots" group (Lofland, 1985), which probably is the most typical local structural form. There are even, in the United States, local, independent professional SMOs, known as Public Interest Research Groups (PIRGs), modeled after national professional SMOs (McCarthy and Zald, 1973). But many local groups are tied to national structures – some federated into coalitions, many others branches of strong, centralized national structures. Also there are national professional SMOs that depend on a direct mail membership with very weak ties to them. And there are many mixed forms such as Common Cause and the National Abortion Rights Action League (NARAL), in the United States, that include a large direct mail membership, vigorous locals, and a large national professionalized office. International groups such as Amnesty International and Greenpeace are proliferating even more complex multitiered SMO structures (Smith, Pagnucco, and Romeril, 1994).

And there are plenty of other movement-initiated mobilizing structures that are not membership groups such as "movement halfway houses" in Aldon Morris's (1984) phrase as well as the class of movement mentoring groups that are created to provide technical advice, resources, and encouragement to groups within specific movements, movement industries, and/or movement families (Edwards and McCarthy, 1992). A common mobilizing structural form of this type in contemporary U.S. movements is the legal defense/litigation professional organization – it looks almost like a movement law firm.

I have belabored the range of building blocks of mobilizing structural forms for an uncomplicated reason – we need to describe this variation in extensive and systematic detail so that we can abstract its important dimensions, in order to describe *typical submovement, movement, movement industry, and movement family historical and national profiles of mobilizing structures.* Developing such profiles allows comparative analysis of how movements are differentially nested in the daily lives of those who make

Table 6.1. *Dimensions of movement-mobilizing structures*

	Nonmovement	Movement
Informal	Friendship networks	Activist networks
	Neighborhoods	Affinity groups
	Work networks	Memory communities
Formal	Churches	SMOs
	Unions	Protest committees
	Professional associations	Movement schools

them, and how the structures of those typical lives articulate with distinctive repertoires of collective action.

Aggregating empirical patterns of mobilizing structures into coherent mobilizing structural configurations has no simple methodological solutions but we surely want to argue for doing it more systematically than we have so far. As we try to do so, we can begin to capture more global dimensions of their aggregate and synthetic character. Following past thinking about SMOs (e.g., Gamson, 1990), I have, in my discussion thus far, implicitly contrasted the structures arrayed here with one another primarily by their degree of organizational formalization and centralization as well as their formal dedication to social change goals. Table 6.1 summarizes the elements of my presentation.

I do not mean to imply that I believe these are necessarily the most important dimensions along which mobilizing structures may vary, but once such configurations have been comparatively described, their aggregate degree and variation in centralization, formalization, and movement dedication can be estimated. So, too, can their articulation. Friedhelm Neidhardt (1992a) has suggested that the coherence of mobilizing structural configuration – the coordination between the various separate mobilizing structures that make up a functioning movement – is a key aspect. Movements surely do vary from one another and over time on such a dimension. As well, the level of contention among elements of mobilizing structural configurations can vary dramatically, often orthogonally with the level of coherence. Other dimensions that come immediately to mind are the range and diversity of structures (isomorphism) that make up a movement. Some have very narrow ranges, while others include a diverse combination of structures.

COMPARING MOBILIZING STRUCTURAL CONFIGURATIONS

The obvious purpose of conflating diverse mobilizing structures into describable mobilizing structural configurations is to link them both empirically and diachronically with variable political opportunity structures and patterns of strategic framing. The distinctively European project aimed at bounding and describing the "new social movements" represents an effort to develop a mobilizing structural configuration profile, linking, as it typically does, the daily lives, social structural location and preferred mobilizing organizational forms of activists (see Edwards, 1994a for a synthetic review). The appropriate unit of analysis for such comparisons may vary, however, usefully between particular movement segments and national movement sectors, including the intervening levels of movements, movement industries, and movement families.

Comparing such configurations among segments within a movement can raise productive puzzles. Compare the contemporary American antitoxics movements with the more widely known national environmental movement groups. It is very rich in local independent groups and local networks of activists who are typically neighbors in areas high in toxic pollution. But this aggregate of groups shows almost no national-level organizational structure. On the other hand, the better-known national SMOs are highly professionalized national offices, many of which develop local chapter structures that draw members, less obviously directly affected by environmental pollution, from broader geographic areas. These two segments display many contrasts similar to those noted for the early period of the recent U.S. women's movement (Freeman, 1975). What elements are central to a general account of variations such as these among social movement segments, as well as that which exists across historical time and space?

Comparing movements with one another highlights other contrasting features. Take for instance the fact that the U.S. civil rights movement, the women's movement, the environmental movement, and the peace movement each have shown a similar wide diversity of mobilizing organizational forms, including national professionalized groups, grassroots local groups, mentoring organizations, but the peace movement exhibits an important difference. All of the others have elaborated a number of SMOs that specialize in legal strategies and tactics – movement law firms – but the peace movement has not spawned one.[6] The widespread account for the lack of litigious formal structures in their movement among peace activists is a variant of political opportunity structure – the inability of individuals and groups to gain legal standing that would allow using the courts to attempt to constrain the U.S. government's use of violence abroad.

The chapters by Hanspeter Kriesi and Dieter Rucht in this part each convincingly illustrates the possibilities of the approach I have outlined by characterizing aspects of the mobilizing structural configuration of several movements across several European nations. Kriesi in "The Organizational Structure of New Social Movements in Relation to Their Political Context" uses evidence gathered upon 144 SMOs from the peace, ecology, Solidarity, gay and autonomous movements in the Netherlands, Germany, France, and Switzerland in order to describe formally organized structural configurations as well as their protest repertoires. He finds major variation in the level of mobilization, great diversity in the dominant organizational form, significant variation in level of outside subsidy, and major differences in alliance structures between SMOs and political parties, unions, churches, and authorities across the four nations and between the five movements.

Rucht's empirical agenda, in "The Impact of National Contexts on Social Movement Structures," is quite similar to Kriesi's although he focuses a bit more heavily upon the level of mobilization, nesting it within what he calls the "movement structure," a concept very close to our mobilizing structural configuration. He uses a far broader array of secondary evidence in order to characterize the mobilizing structural configurations of the ecology and the women's movements in France, Germany, and the United States. He finds the level of mobilization higher in each nation for the environmental movement, and the women's movement, in general, to be more decentralized. There are important cross-national between-movement differences in SMO demography – for instance, France's national umbrella environmental group knits together strong regional associations, while in West Germany Greenpeace and the "World Wide Fund for Nature" are "among the strongest [national chapters] in the world." In both of these chapters, the author aims to characterize national movement configurations as the first step to explaining the variation between them.

ACCOUNTING FOR VARIATION IN MOBILIZING STRUCTURAL CONFIGURATIONS

In any concrete social setting, a range of mobilizing structural elements are more or less available to activists as they attempt to create new movements or nurture and direct ongoing ones. More embedded social processes spawn and alter the many concrete social patterns that constitute the range of mobilizing structural forms which are available to activists at any point in time, but they can invent new ones as well as radically alter and creatively combine available ones as they try to achieve their collective purposes. More or less coherent packages of mobilizing structures typically emerge during broader historical eras, cultural zones, and shorter movement cycles. But activists must choose among their constituent elements, and the choices they make have consequences for both the intensity and shape of collective mobilization as well as in expanding or constraining the range of potential outcomes it can produce.

Adopting, adapting, and inventing: The process

The structures of everyday life may ultimately be changed by collective action, but in the short run they are relatively fixed, and serve as the relational underpinning for most collective action. The portions of mobilizing structural repertoires where the most creative effort occurs is in putting those structures to new or newly recombined uses and in building new mobilizing structures out of them.[7] Collective actors, probably most often, adopt mobilizing structural forms that are known to them from direct experience. Saul Alinsky's oft noted advice to organizers to avoid tactics "outside the experience of your people" (1972: 127) suggests a logic internal to groups for such routine adoption of familiar forms. External factors that shape the rate at which routine forms are adopted and abandoned are responsible, in part, for particular structural configurations. But also, it is the innovations, including the less fundamental adaptations of known forms as well as the more radical breaks represented by the invention of totally new forms, that may significantly alter mobilizing structural configurations over time. Scholars have devoted increasing attention to unpacking these institutional processes for understanding changing protest forms (i.e., Tilly, Sewell, Tarrow). But few have devoted attention to the role of similar processes for understanding shifting configurations of more formalized organizational structures, other than chronicling such changes (e.g., McCarthy and Zald, 1973).

The chapters by Elisabeth Clemens and Kim Voss in this part are important exceptions, however. Each uses rich historical evidence to focus expressly upon the adoption and adaptation of more formalized mobilizing structural forms by wage workers for waging collective action. Drawing heavily upon the new institutional perspective (Powell and Dimaggio, 1991), Clemens, in "Organizational Form as Frame," develops a theoretical perspective for understanding how workers adopted and adapted three specific organizational forms as they struggled to find one that would offer them more success in challenging owners. The fraternal model was borrowed from the Masons, and the military model, dependent upon common military experience among workers, was exemplified in Coxey's Army. Neither of these forms, according to Clemens, articulated well with political structures. Neither did the early American Federation of Labor (A. F. of L.) union model, which resisted adopting coherent umbrella structures with authority over diverse craft unions and common labor bargaining and political tactics. "Duncanism," which embodied these additional structural features, emerged in a number of local areas.

Voss in "The Collapse of a Social Movement," describes the adoption of a specific mobilizing structural form in great historical detail. The Noble and Holy Order of the Knights of Labor "cobbled together," as Voss characterizes it, a new organizational structure called a "local assembly" which in its mature form was geographically inclusive and surrounded by a "dense network of alternative institutions and practices, including local assemblies, boycotts, reading rooms, bands, parades, lecture circuits, sporting clubs, cooperatives, and labor practices." Peaking during the 1880s, the Knights became the largest U.S. labor organization of the nineteenth century, successfully creating a structural form that contrasted sharply with the traditional craft union form. The chapter aims to account for the puzzlingly rapid demise of the Knights in the face of the widespread popularity indicated by the enthusiastic adoption of the newly created form.

The role of framing

In effectively choosing mobilizing structures, activists must successfully frame them as usable and appropriate to the social change tasks to which they will be put. The targets of these framings are both internal – adherents and activists of the movement itself – as well as external, including bystanders, opponents, and authorities. The choices of mobilizing structures within SMOs as well as within broader movements resembles an ongoing framing contest as to their appropriateness in achieving social change outcomes. But movement actors are not the only participants in framing contests. Opponents and elites may devote great effort to directly constraining their use or indirectly doing so by delegitimizing mobilizing structures.

Both Clemens and Voss, in Chapters 9 and 10, describe how the adoption of mobilizing structures by groups depended upon the efforts of movement leaders to fashion cultural connections between the forms and widely embraced preexisting cultural elements. This is most obvious for the fraternal and military forms with which Clemens is concerned, but such a tie was equally central for the local assembly form of the Knights which was based upon "Republicanism," which "was a common interpretive frame in the nineteenth century: Groups and individuals of quite different persuasions claimed its mantle."

The strategic framing that made adoption of the forms possible, however, typically required frame amplification and bridging (Snow et al., 1980) on the part of movement leaders. So, for instance, the various units of Coxey's Army more resembled militias as they bridged their "petition in boots" military identity with other common images of movement such as raft flotillas and barnstorming baseball teams as they worked their way to Washington, D.C.

And, successful framing of the appropriateness of mobilizing structures rarely proceeded without conflict. Both movement factions as well as bystanders and opponents sometimes contested the framing of forms: or even relied upon them as justifications for stronger repression. Clemens notes that the military imagery that so usefully served to mobilize Coxey's Army also provided more latitude to authorities for violent repression in confronting it. Voss's description of the "framing of defeat" for the Knights of Labor and its consequences for subsequent patterns of adoption and adaption of mobilizing structure represents an important insight that highlights the importance of past experience upon the invention and adoption of mobilizing structural forms. Memories of past struggles, as well as the conservative mobilizing structural choices by leaders who aim to work within the experience of their people, may severely constrain the range of possible choices of form.

The role of political opportunity

More stable elements of political opportunity are central in shaping the available range of mobilizing structures in the longer run. And, more volatile elements of political opportunity are probably more important in understanding the shorter run choices among those available structures that activists make. And, particular mobilizing structures will be more or less useful for taking advantage of any existing political opportunity. The chapters by Kriesi, Voss, and Clemens, in this part, each invoke elements of the political opportunity structure in order to make sense of the diverse mobilizing structural configurational patterns each has described.

Kriesi (in Chapter 7) identifies a more stable element of POS as the "general political context" which incorporates the strength of the state and its typical degree of incorporating response to challenges. He finds variation in political context to be important in accounting for variation across the four nations in general level of mobilization as well as what he calls internal structuration, akin to our notion of mobilizing structural configuration. He conceives a more volatile element of POS as the "configuration of power," by which he means the articulation between political parties and challengers in general, and left parties and new social movement groups in particular. Among other patterns he finds these national configurations important in understanding what he calls external structuration of certain movements with other potential institutional allies, especially religious groups.

Rucht employs the idea of "context structure" which conflates national cultural, social, and political contexts, although he pays most attention to political context characterized by dimensions quite similar to those utilized by Kriesi. His chapter, 8, develops evidence that generally is consistent with his most general hypothesis "that the overall movement structure is stronger: (1) the more open the access to the decision-making system, (2) the lower the policy implementation capacity, (3) the stronger the alliance structure, (4) the weaker the conflict structure, and (5) the more consonant the value structure."

Finally Voss, in Chapter 10, isolates an important element of the political opportunity structure as she develops a general account of the rapid demise of the Knights of Labor. That was the neutrality of the U.S. state in major labor disputes, which is seen as partially responsible for encouraging the development of distinctively American employers' associations. In the local case study of Newark she implicates that level of employer mobilization as crucial to understanding the decline of the Knights.

CONCLUSION

I have sketched in this introduction to Part II a broad empirical and theoretical agenda that is consistent with our more general statement in the introduction to the volume but that places the primary focus on mobilizing structures. Each of the four chapters that follow takes a major stride in pushing that agenda forward, in great part because their authors have been important in helping us conceive the agenda in the first place. The two pairs of chapters offer a strong contrast in focusing primarily upon either the evolution of mobilizing structural configurations within nations or on static cross-national comparisons of configurations.

Elisabeth Clemens and Kim Voss provide us more insight into the effects of political opportunity and strategic framing upon the longer term processes of adoption and change in mobilizing structures since they each work with historical evidence over decades. This longer perspective also allows them more leverage for understanding strategic framing processes. Social scientists capable of mining historical evidence have much more to tell us about these mechanisms.

Hanspeter Kriesi and Dieter Rucht proceed undaunted by the difficulties in attempting to describe mobilizing structural configurations across many movements across several nations so that they may confront their central concern with the role of political opportunity structure in shaping them. Their chapters are two significant attempts to describe much more systematically the mobilizing structural configurations of the "new social movements." Their difficulties in doing so will provide important direction to others who wish to pursue this important research agenda.

Our commitment to aggregating mobilizing structures of all kinds into movement, sector, and national profiles is motivated fundamentally by a commitment to comparative historical analysis of mobilizing structures. Researchers of specific SMOs, movements, and national sectors may reasonably argue that such conflation oversimplifies the rich detail of these structures, and it does. But serious efforts at generalizing are necessary before solid comparative historical research that combines the strengths of the two approaches seen in the following chapters on movement mobilization can progress.

7

The organizational structure of new social movements in a political context

HANSPETER KRIESI

ORGANIZATIONAL DEVELOPMENT OF SOCIAL MOVEMENTS

Organizational infrastructure of social movements

Social movement organizations (SMOs) constitute crucial building blocks of the mobilizing structures of a social movement. But, as John McCarthy has pointed out in his introduction to Part II, they are by no means the only components of a movement's mobilizing structures. Other elements of these structures include kinship and friendship networks, informal networks among activists, movement communities, as well as a host of more formal organizations which contribute to the movement's cause without being directly engaged in the process of mobilization for collective action. In conceptualizing the more formal side of the mobilizing structure of a given movement, I would like to suggest that we distinguish between at least four types of formal organizations: SMOs, "supportive organizations," "movement associations," and "parties and interest groups." *SMOs* are distinguished from the other types of formal organizations by two criteria: (1) they mobilize their constituency for collective action, and (2) they do so with a political goal, that is, to obtain some collective good (avoid some collective ill) from authorities. By contrast, *supportive organizations* are service organizations such as friendly media, churches, restaurants, print shops, or educational institutions, which contribute to the social organization of the constituency of a given movement without directly taking part in the mobilization for collective action.[1] "Supportive organizations" may work on behalf of the movement, their personnel may sympathize with the movement, but their participation in the movement's mobilization for action is at best indirect or accidental. *Movement associations* are self-help organizations, voluntary as-

I thank Veit Bader, Marco Giugni, John D. McCarthy, and Charles Tilly for their detailed comments on earlier versions of this chapter.

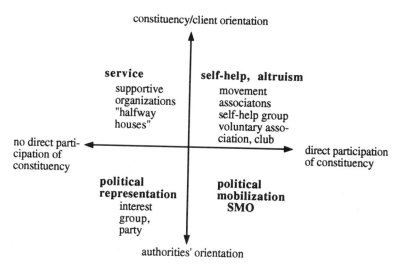

Figure 7.1. Typology of movement-related organizations.

sociations, or clubs created by the movement itself in order to cater to some daily needs of its members.[2] The mutual benefit societies of the labor movement provide a typical example.[3] Just as SMOs, "movement associations" contribute to the mobilization of a movement's constituency, but they do so in an exclusively constituency- or client-oriented way. That is, they contribute to the process of "consensus mobilization" (Klandermans 1988) or to the "creation of commitment" (Gamson 1975), but they do not directly contribute to the "action mobilization" or the "activation of commitment" for a political goal.[4] Finally, SMOs are also to be distinguished from *parties and interest groups*. While they pursue political goals just as do SMOs, parties and interest groups do not normally depend on the direct participation of their constituents for attaining these goals. They are specialized in political representation. They have sufficient amounts of resources – in particular, institutionalized access, authority, and expertise – which means that they normally do not have to have recourse to the mobilization of their constituents. While parties and interest groups also mobilize their constituencies from time to time, this is not essential to their activities, which are typically carried out by an elite. Moreover, this mobilization usually takes place within established routines. Figure 7.1 summarizes these distinctions in a schematic way.[5] All SMOs of a given social movement form its *SMO-infrastructure* (SMI). The SMO-infrastructures of all the social movements in a given polity, in turn, constitute the *social movement sector* (SMS). The SMIs of a movement family, such as the new social movements (NSMs), represent a subsector of the

SMS.[6] Given that SMOs constitute only part of the mobilizing structures of a given movement, the SMS can also be considered to be a subset of the mobilizing structures of all the movements in a society.

Parameters of organizational development

The notion of "organizational development" refers to all levels of the organizational structure, to SMOs, SMIs, subsectors of the SMOs, and the whole SMS. It has a large number of aspects. I propose four sets of parameters for its analysis:[7] parameters capturing organizational growth and decline, internal organizational structuration, external organizational structuration, and goal orientations and action repertoires. First, *organizational growth and decline* refers to the changing size of the SMI – the number of SMOs in the SMI and the amount of resources available to the various SMOs. In the initial phases of a movement, the only resources available tend to be the "active commitment, courage and imagination" of the movement's activists and adherents (Koopmans 1992). In their early phases, the organizational networks of social movements tend to be weak and informally structured. Resources from conscience constituents and supportive elites are not easily forthcoming. Movements have to attract public attention to their cause, they have to create their constituency and elite patronage on their own, either by explicit consensus mobilization (Klandermans 1988), or as a by-product of their action mobilization (McAdam 1982: 125; Jenkins and Eckert 1986). Typically, SMOs develop only in the course of the mobilization process of a social movement. The flow of resources into the organizational network of a given movement is a function of the stage reached by the series of action campaigns constituting it. A well-resourced SMI is one of the results of consensus and action mobilization of a newly developing social movement rather than its origin. The resource flow, in turn, constitutes a crucial determinant for the other aspects of the organizational development.

Internal structuration of SMOs is an immediate consequence of the resource flow. This second set of parameters refers to processes of formalization, professionalization, internal differentiation and integration. Formalization means the development of formal membership criteria, the introduction of formal statutes and established procedures, the creation of a formal leadership and office structure. Professionalization means the management by paid staff members who make careers out of movement work.[8] Internal differentiation concerns the functional division of labor (task-structure) and the territorial decentralization (territorial subunits). The integration of the differentiated functional and territorial subunits is achieved by horizontal coordinating mechanisms, and by centralization of decisions. Oligarchization – the concentration of power in the hands of a minority of the SMO members – is the most well known "integrative mechanism" of SMOs. As

SMOs grow, that is, as the amount of their resources increases, their internal structuration will become more elaborate with respect to all of these dimensions. The process of internal structuration is virtually inevitable, if the SMO is to have success in the long run. The German Greens, not an SMO but a party close to the NSMs, provide ample evidence of the inevitability of this process. Their internal structural deficits imposed important restrictions on their possible political success (Raschke 1991; Kleinert 1991). Internal structuration also contributes to the stabilization of an SMO in periods of organizational decline. McCarthy and Zald (1977) suggest that older, established SMOs are more likely than newer ones to persist throughout the cycle of organizational growth and decline. In a similar vein, Staggenborg (1988) argues that formalized SMOs are able to maintain themselves – and the movement – over a longer period of time than informal ones. This is particularly important in periods of demobilization, when movement issues are less pressing. Formal SMOs may perform important maintenance functions after the victory or demise of informal ones (Jenkins and Eckert, 1986: 827). Finally, as Staggenborg points out, formal SMOs which maintain themselves in periods of demobilization are also prepared to take advantage of new political opportunities which may arise at some point. Centralization contributes to stability of an SMO, too. Thus, Taylor (1989) shows that in a period of decline of the American women's movement, the major SMO of the movement functioned almost entirely on the national level with a federated structure in which local and state chapters had little autonomy. Centralization ensures a relatively advanced level of specialized skills among core activists.

External structuration refers to the integration of an SMO in its organizational environment. There are at least three dimensions to be taken into consideration in this regard: the SMO's relation with its constituency, its allies, and the authorities. By definition, an SMO is highly dependent on its constituency, since its main activity consists in mobilizing its constituency for collective action. Still, the dependency on the constituency can be of varying degrees. By providing selective incentives to its constituency, an SMO may be less dependent on fluctuating individual commitments. By appealing to conscience constituents, by providing services to the general public or acquiring public subsidies, the SMO may broaden its resource base. Diversification of the resource base generally decreases dependency on a single supportive group. This not only applies to the constituency, but also to allies and authorities. SMOs develop in close interaction with their allies and the authorities which they challenge. Support from a powerful ally is ambivalent from the point of view of the development of an SMO: On the one hand, such an ally may provide important resources; on the other hand, it may also reduce the autonomy of the SMO and threaten its stability in the long run. Similarly, the establishment of a working relationship with the authorities also has ambivalent implications for the development of the SMO: On the one hand, public recognition, access to decision-making procedures and public subsidies may provide crucial resources and represent important successes for the SMO; on the other hand, the integration into established systems of interest intermediation may impose limits on the mobilization capacity of the SMO and alienate important parts of its constituency, with the consequence of weakening it in the long run.

Finally, a fourth set of parameters of organizational development concerns an SMO's *goal orientations and action repertoires*. According to the well-known Weber-Michels model, SMOs typically undergo three types of changes as they age: oligarchization, goal transformation, and a shift to organizational maintenance. In this model, goal transformation inevitably takes the direction of greater conservatism – the accommodation of the SMO's goals to the dominant societal consensus. Organizational maintenance is a special form of goal transformation in which the primary activity of the SMO becomes the maintenance of membership, funds, and other requirements of organizational existence. In the process, the action repertoire of the SMO is also expected to be modified. It is expected to become more moderate, more conventional, more institutionalized. Zald and Ash (1966) have taken issue with this model, maintaining that this type of transformation is not inevitable, but that it depends on certain conditions. In a similar vein, I would like to suggest that there are at least four possible transformations of an SMO which correspond to the four types of movement-related organizations distinguished in Figure 7.1: An SMO can become more like a party or an interest group; it can take on characteristics of a supportive service organization; it can develop in the direction of a self-help group, a voluntary association or a club; or it can radicalize, that is, become an ever more exclusive organization for the mobilization for collective action. Figure 7.2 presents the different variants using the same format as the previous one.

Institutionalization implies a whole set of transformations in the course of which an SMO becomes more like a party or an interest group. This set includes the stabilization of an SMO's resource flow, the development of its internal structure, the moderation of its goals, the conventionalization of its action repertoire, and its integration into established systems of interest intermediation. *Commercialization* is the transformation in the direction of a service organization. Along this route, an SMO puts an increasing emphasis on the provision of paid services to the members of its constituency. Many SMOs use, of course, "selective incentives" to mobilize their constituencies for collective action. According to Olson's (1965) theory of collective action, there is actually no other way to get collective action going – except maybe coercion. But usually, for an SMO the provision of "selective incentives" is not an end in itself. To the extent that it becomes an end in itself, the SMO has turned into a service organization or a business enterprise. *Involution* is the path that leads to an exclusive emphasis on "social incentives," which

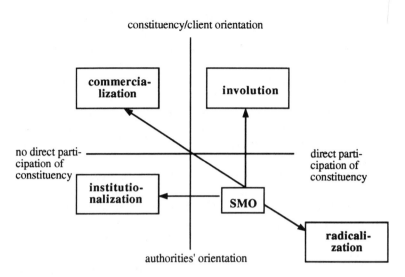

Figure 7.2. Typology of transformations of goal orientations and action repertoires of SMOs.

may stem from the solidary services to the constituency or from the social activities with the other activists of the organization. In the first variant, the SMO becomes a self-help group or a voluntary association, depending on whether the beneficiaries are identical with its constituency or not. In the second variant, it becomes a club. *Radicalization,* finally, is the path to reinvigorated mobilization. Classic discussions of the subject such as the one of Zald and Ash (1966) have focused on a juxtaposition of radicalization and institutionalization, but have not taken into consideration the other two possibilities.

Determinants of organizational development

The organizational development is a function of factors both internal and external to the SMS. With respect to internal factors we may distinguish between the internal organizational dynamics and the type of the movement in question. With respect to external factors, there are general economic and cultural preconditions as well as political ones. Here, I shall focus on the impact of the political context on the organizational development, but I do not assume that the other aspects are unimportant, nor shall I neglect them in the subsequent analysis.[9] As far as *internal organizational dynamics* are concerned, I have already pointed out that the internal structuration may contribute to an SMO's stabilization over time. The internal structuration may also affect the strategic and tactical choices of SMOs (Staggenborg

1988). For example, formalized and professionalized SMOs tend to engage in institutionalized tactics and typically do not initiate disruptive direct-action tactics. They prefer institutionalized tactics, because they are more compatible with a formalized structure and with the schedules of professionals. Moreover, the internal structuration also contributes to the integration into established systems of interest-intermediation: SMOs with formalized and professionalized structures tend to have easier access to public authorities, because government bureaucracies prefer to deal with organizations with working procedures similar to their own.[10]

The *type of movement* is quite crucial for the development of its organizational infrastructure. Movements differ especially with respect to the composition of their respective constituency, their goal orientation, and their action repertoire. We shall deal here only with the so-called new social movements (NSMs), a set of movements that have mobilized since the early seventies in Western Europe. Instead of entering a theoretical discussion of what constitutes a "new social movement," I shall simply give a list of the major examples of NSMs: the ecology movement and its antinuclear branch; the solidarity movement with its branches for humanitarian aid, political refugees, political prisoners, human rights, and antiracism; the peace movement, the women's movement, and the urban autonomous movement. While it can be argued that these movements all share a common core constituency (Kriesi 1989a), it is useful to distinguish between three types of NSMs in the present context (Koopmans 1990b): instrumental, subcultural, and countercultural movements. *Instrumental* movements seek to obtain specific collective goods or to prevent specific collective "bads." They are not much concerned with the collective identity of their constituency. Typical examples are the peace movement, the ecology movement, and the solidarity movement. By contrast, *subcultural* movements, such as the gay movement or (parts of) the women's movement, aim at the (re)production of a collective identity that is primarily constituted in within-group interaction, but which depends on authority-oriented action as well. *Countercultural* movements, such as the urban autonomous movement, are also identity-oriented, but they constitute their identity mainly in conflictual interaction with authorities or third parties.

The differences in the general orientation of the three types of movements tend to affect their organizational development in significant ways. The level and type of resources of an SMI is likely to be a function of the movement's general orientation. Thus, SMOs of instrumental NSMs are typically inclusive: They try to mobilize as large a part of the population as possible to obtain their issue-specific goal. For this reason alone, they can be expected to accumulate more members and more financial resources than the identity-oriented movements. Identity is tied to certain specific characteristics of the constituency, which implies exclusivity and a more circumscribed membership. On the other hand, exclusive, identity-oriented SMIs are likely to succeed in mobilizing a more intensive commitment from their constituency. This provides them with an alternative to internal structuration for their stabilization in the long run. Thus, Kanter's (1972) research on American communes concludes that groups characterized by high commitment are more likely to retain participants and to endure. Commitment is especially important for holding an SMO alive between stages of mass mobilization (Taylor 1989). This line of argument suggests the SMIs of sub- and countercultural movements to be particularly resistant to their movement's decline. Within the category of instrumental movements, the institutionalization of the resource flow seems to be especially problematic for all the movements which are highly issue-specific as well as for movements that focus on international issues. The more a movement focuses exclusively on a single issue, the more it becomes dependent on the issue-attention cycle. For international issues, in particular, this cycle seems to be typically quite short. Moreover, international issues tend to be highly polarized in party-political terms, which introduces an additional unpredictable element (see below). Given these considerations, the peace movement and the solidarity movement should generally have greater difficulties in stabilizing their resource base than the ecology movement. Except for its antinuclear branch, which is also rather issue-specific, the latter is confronted with a highly differentiated, complex and national problem-structure. Finally, the type of movement may also be expected to have an effect on the pattern of transformation followed by the SMI: Instrumental movements are most likely to institutionalize, subcultural movements are likely to follow the paths of involution or commercialization, whereas countercultural movements typically radicalize.

In addition to the factors internal to the SMS, external factors also determine its development. The *economic* development of a country determines the level of resources generally available for the sector. According to the argument of McCarthy and Zald (1977), an expanding supply of resources in a society will incite political entrepreneurs to found new professional SMOs, which will compete for these resources and contribute to the organizational development of the movement. *Cultural* factors may also play a role. Such factors as the Anglo-Saxon political culture or a strong Protestant heritage have, for example, been invoked to explain the differences that exist with regard to the participation in "voluntary associations" of different countries (see Curtis, Grabb, and Baer 1992).[11] In the present essay, I shall above all be interested in the way *political* factors contribute to the organizational development of NSMs. In order to study their impact, I shall rely on the conceptualization of the political opportunity structure (POS), which I have developed previously (Kriesi 1991) and which we have already applied to the comparative analysis of the level of mobilization (Kriesi et al. 1992). As in that previous analysis, I shall use the same four countries – France, Germany, the

Netherlands, and Switzerland – to illustrate and test my propositions. If political factors are not likely to have a direct impact on the internal structuration of an SMI, they seem to be particularly relevant for the determination of the level and type of resources available to an SMI, for its external structuration as well as for the general patterns of its transformation in the course of its organizational development.

THE POLITICAL CONTEXT
AND ORGANIZATIONAL DEVELOPMENT

The POS can be decomposed into three broad sets of properties: the formal institutional structure of a political system, its informal procedures and prevailing strategies with regard to challengers, and the configuration of power relevant for the confrontation with the challengers. The first two sets provide the general static setting for the organizational development, and they constrain the relevant configuration of power. The formal institutional structure determines the overall strength of the state. The latter may change over time, as a result of electoral changes, strategic decisions, or the dynamic of the interactions between challengers and authorities.

The general political context

On the basis of the first two sets, I have distinguished between four types of general settings, each of which corresponds to one of the four countries mentioned above. Figure 7.3 presents the four types. The combination of a strong state and an exclusive dominant strategy defines a situation of *selective exclusion* of challengers. In such a situation, the challenger can neither count on formal nor on informal access to the political system. Because of its strength, the state can often choose merely to ignore challengers; if it does react, however, it will most likely confront the challenger with repression. Moreover, since the state is strong, the challenger is unlikely to have some veto power. But, depending on the composition of government, he may obtain some substantive concessions. Thus, a government controlled by the Left may use the state's capacity to act for concessions on behalf of the challenging NSMs.[12] This type is represented by France. At the opposite end of "selective exclusion," we find the case of *full procedural integration,* which is characterized by the combination of a weak state with an inclusive dominant strategy. In such a situation, repression is comparatively weak and the challenger's access to the system is formally as well as informally facilitated. Given the weakness of the system, the challenger cannot count on important substantive concessions, but he may be able to block decisions by exercising a veto. This type is represented by Switzerland. The direct democratic institutions as well as the federalist structure of Switzerland provide for a large

Dominant strategy	Formal institutional structure	
	Weak state	Strong state
exclusive	**"formalistic inclusion"** - formal, but no informal facilitation of access; strong repression - possibility of veto, but no substantive concessions **(Germany)**	**"selective exclusion"** - neither formal nor informal facilitation of access; strong repression - neither possibility of veto, sub-stantive concessions, depend-ing on configuration of power **(France)**
inclusive	**"full procedural integration"** - formal and informal facilitation of access; weak repression - possibility of veto, but no substantive concessions **(Switzerland)**	**"informal cooptation"** - no formal, but informal facilitation of access; weak repression - no possibility of veto, but substantive concessions **(Netherlands)**

Figure 7.3. The general settings for the approach of members towards challengers.

number of formal access points for challengers. The traditionally integrative strategy enhances the general effect of the formal structure. Germany represents one of the two intermediate types, the one of *formalistic inclusion.* In this situation, the challenger can count on formal, but not on informal facilitation of access. There is a possibility of veto, but no concessions can be expected. The federal structure of the German Republic allows for a multiplication of points of access. Moreover, the strong position of the German judiciary provides the challengers with another set of independent access points. However, the repressive legacy of the system implies that those who articulate themselves outside of the formally available channels will be confronted with strong repression. The second intermediary case, the one of *informal coopta-tion,* is represented by the Netherlands. In such a setting, challengers do not have a lot of formal access, but they can count on informal facilitation. Since the Dutch state is also quite strong, it is able to make considerable substantive concessions, and it can prevent challengers from exerting a veto.

As Tocqueville has already observed, a strong state goes together with a weak society and vice versa. The lack of decentralized access to the state discourages self-organization at the local grassroots level. Similarly, a repressive dominant strategy serves to discourage self-organization. In the tradition of the French revolution, the French state in particular has long resisted the formation of associations of any kind. Thus, the organizational development of most associations in France has traditionally been less solid than in many other countries. The comparative weakness of the French trade unions illustrates this point (Rosanvallon 1988; Visser 1987), as does the comparative weakness of French voluntary associations in general (Curtis et al. 1992). Tilly, Tilly, and Tilly (1975: 43) have argued that this weakness of French organizations may be more apparent than real. They point out that, in France, associations often form as offshoots of organizations already in existence – the Catholic Church, the Communist Party, and so on; and though coherent and active, many do not acquire formal, legal existence. Moreover, the state's active resistance to formally constituted associations may have reinforced the tendency to form such groups in the shadows. But, informal structures and dependency on external support are no signs of organizational development. In fact, the arguments of the Tillys indicate an additional mechanism that serves to weaken the French organizational structure, to which I shall return below.

By contrast, Switzerland's weak state corresponds to a highly organized society. The self-organization of society has gone very far in this country, the central state having traditionally intervened only as a last resort. According to the principle of subsidiarity, societal problems are first tackled by private self-organization, then by the local or regional branches of the state. Only if these subsidiary instances are no longer able to deal with a given problem, it is up to the central state to find a solution. At first sight, the Netherlands' strong, centralized state is not as propitious to organizational development as the weak Swiss federal state. However, with respect to the stimulation of society's self-organization, Dutch pillarization has long served as a functional equivalent to Swiss federalism (Kriesi 1990). Pillarization implied the construction of parallel organizational infrastructures in different walks of social life; that is, it constituted a very strong stimulus to societal self-organization. If both federalism and pillarization stimulate self-organization, they have, however, quite different implications for organizational structuration: Federalism is a state structure that stimulates the self-organization of society but that also implies that the development of the societal organizations is, as long as possible, left to their own devices. By contrast, pillarization is a societal structure that, while having traditionally stimulated self-organization, always coexisted with a centralized, strong state, that has facilitated this self-organization, following its strategy of "informal co-optation." Such facilitation includes public recognition, consultation, and even subsidization. We would, therefore, expect the Dutch SMIs to be at least as well developed as the Swiss ones, but possibly even more than the latter. According to the comparative study of Curtis et al. (1992), the Dutch have, indeed, a very high level of membership in voluntary associations. Excluding church and union memberships, their level turns out to the highest one of all the countries compared.[13] Although Switzerland has not been included in this study, comparable figures are available from a study on Swiss values (Melich 1992). It turns out that the Swiss level of membership in voluntary associations is exactly as high as the one in the Netherlands if we exclude both church and union memberships (which both are comparatively weak in this country).[14]

Germany, finally, presents an intermediary case. The openness of the weak state stimulates societal self-organization, but the repressive legacy and the traditional distance between the state and German society suggest that, with respect to the public sphere, this self-organization is less developed than in the two smaller countries. Sontheimer (1989: 111) argues that Germany is characterized by a well-organized private sphere, which is, however, not sufficiently integrated into the structure of the public space. Private and public spheres are not automatically complementary in this country. Thus, Almond and Verba (1963) had found a rather high level of membership in voluntary associations for Germany, but the percentage of *active* membership was as low as in Italy or Mexico. They interpreted this result as an indication that while the political structures in Germany were well developed, they did not (yet) play a significant role in the lives of the citizens. Since the early sixties, the attitude of the citizens toward their state has improved and political participation has substantially increased. Germany has become a "normal" Western democracy (Rudzio 1987; Koopmans 1992). According to the data of Curtis et al. (1992), German membership in voluntary associations, excluding church and unions, is slightly above the average of the countries compared. It is certainly higher than in France, but lower than in the Netherlands and Switzerland.

The configuration of power

With respect to the configuration of power in the party system of relevance for NSMs, I have maintained that particular attention should be paid to the configuration of power on the Left (Kriesi 1991). The supporters of NSMs have typically been recruited from the political Left. Only more recently, the parties of the Right have made attempts – especially in the area of environmental politics – to take up some of the demands on the agenda of the NSMs. To the extent that they become more open to NSMs' demands, we would expect the configuration of power of the parties on the Right to become more relevant, too. Two aspects of the configuration on the Left are of particular importance: whether or not the Left is divided between a major Communist current and a Social Democratic/Socialist one, and whether or not the Left participates in government. Among our four countries, France is the only one with a split Left. This has implied a strong polarization within the Left as well as between the Left as a whole and the Right. Under conditions of a split Left, both major currents within the Left try to instrumentalize the NSMs for their own purposes: first, to gain ascendancy on the Left and then to win the electoral competition with the Right. From the point of view of the organizational development of a movement's infrastructure, all party political instrumentalization is likely to have a destabilizing effect. The SMI becomes dependent on the vicissitudes of party politics. If the terms of party competition change, the Left is likely to abandon its support for the SMI in question. This has happened in France, when the Left came to power in 1981 (Duyvendak 1992). The implications for the overall resource levels of the SMIs of the NSMs can be expected to have been very serious, given that these movements have become highly dependent on the support by the Left. Moreover, the Communists' strategy with respect to NSMs has particularly negative implications for the development of an SMI: while the Social Democrats tend to ally themselves more loosely to already existing SMOs in a given movement, the Communists tend to create their own SMOs in order to dominate the SMI of the movement in question (see Garner and Zald 1987: 313f.). The presence of SMOs colonized by the Communist Party is bound to introduce competitive tensions within the SMI, since not all SMOs are likely to associate themselves with the Communist cause, and most are unlikely to accept the Communists' claim to leadership. We should add that the Communists' strategy to control SMIs has not touched all NSMs to the same extent. It has been especially virulent in the case of instrumental NSMs related to international issues that concern the competition between the former Communist regimes and the West, that is, in the case of the peace movement and the solidarity movement. The ecology movement, by contrast, has been much less affected by this strategy. Ceteris paribus, we, therefore, expect that the French peace and solidarity movements have particularly weak SMIs.

Party political instrumentalization of NSMs with all its negative consequences for the stabilization of the SMIs is less conspicuous in the other three countries. But the Left in other countries has not been free of attempts to instrumentalize certain movements for its own purposes: Thus, the Dutch Social Democrats have been very supportive of the peace movement's campaign against cruise missiles. After it had turned out that this support did not pay off in electoral terms, the Social Democrats abandoned the movement after their defeat in the 1986 elections, contributing to its decline (van Praag, Jr. 1992). This is an example of the atypical case of a Social Democratic Party in the opposition that withdraws from supporting an NSM. By moving closer to the center, the Dutch Social Democrats hoped to become a viable coalition partner again for the governing Christian Democrats. There is also an example of the unlikely case of a Socialist government supporting the mobilization of a new movement: The French socialists in government lent a helping hand to SOS racism, thus reinvigorating the French solidarity movement beyond what I have just expected. The Socialists' support of this particular movement was part of their strategy against the extreme Right in France, which proved to be increasingly menacing in electoral terms (Duyvendak 1992). These two examples serve to relativize the general notion that the Left in government will not facilitate the mobilization of NSMs, while it will do so when in government.

DATA

In a research project on the development of NSMs in Western Europe during the eighties, systematic information has been gathered on the organizational development of five NSMs in the four countries introduced above.[15] The five NSMs studied include the three most important instrumental movements – the peace, ecology, and solidarity movements, a subcultural movement – the gay movement, and a countercultural movement – the urban autonomous movement. At the outset, we decided to study in detail at least the five most important SMOs of each movement. For various reasons, the number of SMOs finally studied is more variable than we had originally planned. In some cases, we have information on less than five SMOs, mainly because of problems of access (especially in the case of the urban autonomous movement), but also because there simply were not enough SMOs of some importance (in the cases of the gay movements in Germany and Switzerland). For some instrumental movements, considerably more than five SMOs have been studied, mainly for reasons linked to the respective country studies. This uneven character of the data base obviously poses a problem of comparability. At various points, I shall, therefore, analyze subsamples of organizations which are more comparable than the sample as a whole in order to check for the latter's representativeness. Table 7.1 gives a summary view of the set of organizations included in the study.

   The data were collected on the basis of documentary materials and of personal, highly structured interviews with representatives of the SMOs. They include information about all aspects of the organizational development that have been discussed. Most of the data concern the situation in 1988–89. For some aspects, we have obtained rough indicators of time trends during the eighties. In some instances, we have been able to obtain yearly figures for membership and financial resources concerning the period from 1975 to 1989. Unfortunately, the quality of the data is rather low. There are many missing values, and many rough estimates based on informed judgment by the interviewers or interpolations by the author. SMOs typically do not busy themselves with keeping detailed records of their own development. Moreover, to the extent that such records exist somewhere, the present-day staff

Table 7.1. *Data base*

Movement	Country				
	Netherlands	Germany	France	Switzerland	All
Peace movement	2	4	5	6	17
Ecology movement	10	11	4	10	35
Solidarity movement	7	8	8	13	36
Gay movement	4	3	7	3	17
Autonomous movement	1	2	1	5	9
Total	24	28	25	37	114

has often not been able or willing to unearth them and to make them available for research. Given the limited number of cases and the low level of measurement, the subsequent analysis will typically be quite simple.

Before turning to the presentation of some results with respect to each one of the four sets of parameters of organizational development, I would like to draw the reader's attention to one more limitation of this dataset: Data on the most important SMOs of a social movement give only a partial idea of the extent and the character of its organizational development. In fact, these SMOs constitute only the tip of a movement's organizational iceberg. Moreover, this tip is likely to represent the SMI's most developed part. The following analyses shall, therefore, without any doubt overestimate the extent of the organizational development of the organizational infrastructure of the NSMs as a whole. There is one exception to this limitation: With respect to the transformation of the movements' action repertoires some additional data are available. Following the lead of others (Kriesi et al. 1981; McAdam 1983b; Tarrow 1989a; Tilly et al. 1975), we have collected systematic data on protest events by analyzing the Monday editions of one major newspaper in each country for the period 1975–1989. For each event, we have coded a limited number of facts, among which the the identities of up to three (if any) SMOs that were associated with it. These data provide an opportunity to compare the development of the action repertoires of the various movements and of different parts of their organizational infrastructures in the four countries.

ORGANIZATIONAL GROWTH AND DECLINE

The two indicators for the level of resources to be used here are membership size and amount of financial resources in 1988–89. The most important SMOs of a movement typically include those most richly endowed with re-

Table 7.2. *Membership of four international SMOs in 1989 by country (in thousands)*

	Country			
SMO	NL	G	F	CH
Greenpeace	640	600	5	24
WWF	100	75	–[a]	130
Amnesty International	120	23	21	47
Terre des Hommes	66	40	28	30
Total (absolute)	926	738	54	231
Total (per million inhabitants)	62	12	1	36

[a]No information.

sources, although this has not been the only criterion for their selection. Some SMOs may be important for their mobilization capacity, even if they do not have many members or much financial resources at their disposal. The German BBU (Federal League of Citizen Initiatives for Environmental Protection), for example, is a peak association of the ecology movement with no direct membership and only a small amount of resources, but with an impressive mobilization capacity and an important impact on public opinion during most of the period studied (Rucht 1989a: 73). I shall use three types of comparisons with respect to resource levels: (1) the comparison of four international SMOs with chapters in all four countries, (2) the comparison of the four largest SMOs per movement in each of the four countries, and (3) the comparison of our whole sample of SMOs across the four countries and the five movements. The four counties are, of course, of widely different size, with the German and French populations being about four times as large as that of the Netherlands and about ten times as large as that of Switzerland. To take these differences into account, I present not only absolute figures but also corresponding relative figures per 1 million inhabitants.

Table 7.2 presents the first comparison for size of membership. The four SMOs compared include Greenpeace and the World Wildlife Fund (WWF) from the ecology movement, and Amnesty International and Terre des Hommes from the solidarity movement. The results are quite clear: In absolute and in relative terms, these organizations are strongest in the Netherlands, followed by Germany (in absolute terms) and Switzerland (in relative terms), while their French counterparts are much weaker. The exceptional size of the Dutch and German branches of Greenpeace are particularly noticeable. Their weight will make itself felt in all the following analyses. If we take the four largest SMOs per movement and compare across countries, these first

results are largely confirmed.[16] Table 7.3 shows the French SMOs again to be
by far the weakest. The Swiss SMOs now appear to be about as strong as the
Dutch, if the different sizes of the countries are taken into account. In absolute terms, the Dutch SMOs can count on the largest membership, although
the country is much smaller than Germany or France. Taking into account
the size of the countries, German SMOs take an intermediary position. In
addition, Table 7.3 indicates systematic differences between the membership
levels of the various movements, which are largely independent of the country under study. In line with our expectations, instrumental movements typically have more members than the subcultural movement.[17] Moreover,
among the former, the ecology movement has by far the largest number of
members, and the peace movement by far the least. The only exception from
this general pattern turns out to be France. In France, the four largest SMOs
of the solidarity movement have more members than their counterparts in
the ecology movement. The explanation rests with the fact that in France, as
we have seen, the solidarity movement has received strong support from the
Socialist government, whereas the same government has not been supportive
at all with regard to the ecology movement. As a matter of fact, the French
Socialist government has launched an outright attack on Greenpeace: With
its consent, the French secret service bombed the *Rainbow Warrior* in
New Zealand in 1985, killing one man. Greenpeace France suffered much
from this blow, losing both members and financial support in its aftermath.
The results for financial resources (not shown here) largely parallel those
for membership, since, as we shall see below, membership contributions are
generally the most important source of income of the SMOs. In particular,
the analysis of the financial resources again reveals the striking weakness of
the French ecology movement. As a matter of fact, roughly 80 percent of
the financial resources of the French NSM subsector are in the hands
of the SMOs of the solidarity movement.

   Our data allow a more detailed analysis of membership growth of the ecology movement in the three countries, where this movement has come to dominate the NSM subsector. Figure 7.4 shows how the three (or four) largest
SMOs of the movement have developed in the period 1975–1989. Overall, all
three SMIs have grown impressively during this period. Analyzing the pattern of growth in more detail, we notice that traditional *conservationist*
SMOs – such as the German association for bird protection (DBV) or the
Dutch association for the protection of nature (*natuurmonumenten*) – which
had been founded long before the rise of NSMs, grow very slowly or have
an essentially stable membership. Somewhat older *environmentalist* SMOs –
such as the WWF in Switzerland – which adopt a pragmatic attitude toward
the preservation and improvement of the human environment, no longer
grow very much either. In fact, the rapid growth of these SMIs in the eighties
is primarily due to the spectacular growth of newly created environmentalist
or *ecologist* SMOs – such as the Swiss transport association (VCS) and,

Table 7.3. *Membership of the four largest SMOs in 1989 per movement and country*[a]

	Country			
SMO	NL	G	F	CH
(in thousands)				
Ecology movement	1,026 (4)	1,024 (4)	12 (3)	373 (4)
Solidarity movement	165 (3)	113 (4)	77 (4)	93 (4)
Peace movement	–[b]	25 (3)	31 (4)	16 (4)
Gay movement	24 (3)	19 (3)	35 (4)	1 (3)
Total (absolute)	1,215 (10)	1,181 (14)	155 (15)	483 (15)
Total (per million inhabitants)	81	19	3	74
(in %)				
Ecology movement	84	86	8	77
Solidarity movement	14	10	50	19
Peace movement	–[b]	2	20	3
Gay movement	2	2	23	0
Total	100%	100%	100%	100%

[a]In parentheses: number of cases.
[b]No information.

above all, Greenpeace.[18] The Swiss pattern proves to be particularly interesting, since it implies a diversification of the SMI to a new policy area – transport policy – which is accompanied by an increase in the division of labor and horizontal coordination among the SMOs in the sector. Thus, the newly founded VCS concentrates on transport issues, while the Swiss energy foundation focuses on energy policy, the small Swiss association for the protection of the environment on questions such as air pollution, and the WWF as well as the large, traditional Swiss federation for the protection of nature deal in the first place with the conservation of the environment. In comparison to the Swiss pattern, the development of the German and Dutch SMIs appear to be more fragile, given the competitive attitude Greenpeace has adopted with regard to the other SMOs in the field.

As I have argued here, early in the mobilization process of a social movement, its SMOs cannot yet count on a stable resource flow. Instead, they depend on ad hoc commitments of activists. To the extent that they survive the vicissitudes of the early phases of the mobilization process and that they are able to establish a certain reputation for themselves, SMOs are likely to acquire a stable membership and a continuous financial resource flow. In other words, we expect that the amount of resources of a given SMO is not

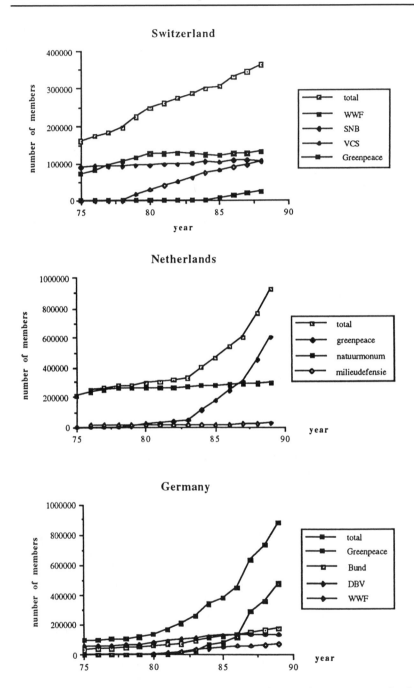

Figure 7.4. Membership growth of major SMOs of the ecology movement in three countries.

only a function of the political context and the type of SMI it is operating in, but also a function of its *age*. For a test of this hypothesis, I distinguish very roughly between SMOs founded before 1965 – that is, before the first mobilizations of the NSMs took – and those that have been founded later on. As the discussion of the patterns of growth of the ecology movement have already indicated, we have included SMOs of the movements in question that had been created long before the so-called NSMs were first mobilized. The fact that these SMOs had already been established when the NSMs first appeared does not exclude them from being part of the SMIs of the respective movements. As a matter of fact, many of the classic SMOs have been reinvigorated by the new waves of mobilization, they have transformed their goals and action repertoires in accordance with these NSMs, and they have integrated themselves into the SMIs of these movements. Independently of the political context of the specific SMI, these classic SMOs can be expected to have more members and more financial resources than the SMOs that have been founded by the NSMs themselves.

Table 7.4 shows that, in general, this is, indeed, the case. On the average, classic SMOs have more members and more financial resources than the more recently founded SMOs. But there is one exception to this generalization, which is so important that it reverses the relationship in one of our four countries, that is, in Germany. The exception concerns Greenpeace. If we include Greenpeace in the analysis, the more recently founded SMOs in Germany turn out to be more resourceful than the classic ones. If we exclude Greenpeace from the analysis, Germany joins the general pattern. Germany is special in that the enormous mobilization by Greenpeace far exceeds anything that has previously been known in this country. In a sense, this exceptional situation confirms our general discussion of the German political context. As I have argued, political participation has traditionally been low, which would explain the relatively low level of membership of the classic SMOs. With the rise in the level of political involvement, especially in the younger generations, it is the newcomers to the political scene who have been likely to profit the most. From this perspective, it is also quite telling that the resource level of the classic German SMOs is close to the French one, which is extraordinarily low compared to the corresponding levels in the Netherlands and Switzerland. By contrast, the resource level of the more recent German SMOs more closely resembles the corresponding levels in the smaller European countries. This result is in line with the general idea of Germany becoming a "normal" democracy.

INTERNAL STRUCTURATION

While the political context has been shown to have a strong influence on the resource level of the SMIs of NSMs, with respect to the internal structuration

Table 7.4. *Average resource levels by date of foundation and country[a]*

SMO	Before 1965	After 1965 (including Greenpeace)	After 1965 (without Greenpeace)	Total[b]
		Date of foundation		
Average membership (in thousands) per million inhabitants				
NL	5,710 (4)	3,530 (17)	1,080 (16)	3,940 (21)
G	790 (6)	1,140 (13)	411 (12)	1,020 (19)
F	250 (7)	80 (17)	80 (16)	130 (24)
CH	6,310 (6)	1,680 (26)	1,600 (25)	2,550 (32)
Total	2,920 (23)	1,640 (73)	920 (69)	1,950 (96)
Average financial resources (in thousand dollars) per million inhabitants				
NL	928 (2)	142 (11)	105 (12)	252 (13)
G	56 (7)	60 (20)	31 (19)	58 (27)
F	16 (6)	8 (15)	8 (14)	10 (21)
CH	827 (6)	89 (22)	69 (21)	246 (28)
Total	348 (21)	70 (68)	50 (64)	132 (89)

[a]Number of cases between parentheses.
[b]Corresponds to the respective columns in the previous table.

of the SMOs it is likely to be only of indirect significance. As suggested above, we expect the internal structuration to be mainly driven by the level of available resources and by the age of the SMO. The older and the more resourceful an SMO, the more likely it is to formalize, professionalize, and to differentiate its internal structure. Indirectly, by facilitating or constraining the amount of resources available to an SMO, the political context may contribute to the level of its internal structuration. As a first approximation, however, we may assume the internal structuration to result from internal organizational dynamics.

I have two indicators of internal structuration at my disposal, one for an SMO's degree of formalization and one for its degree of professionalization. *Formalization* is operationalized by a scale which takes into account whether an SMO has a legal status, whether it has a formal membership criterion (possibly based on financial obligations of one kind or another), whether it has institutionalized formal functions, and, if so, whether it has differentiated only the most basic functions (president, secretary, and treasurer) or also some more specialized ones. The resulting scale has a maximum value of 5. Only a small minority of the SMOs we studied have a structure which is not formalized at all. More than half of them (57%) score on four or all five points considered. In other words: The overall level of formalization reached by the SMOs in our sample is quite considerable. It is a far cry from the decentralized, segmented, and informal organizational networks which have been said to be typical of NSMs. One should, of course, immediately add that our sample is not representative of the SMOs of the movements in question, since we have only considered the most important SMOs in each movement. Nevertheless, the relatively high level of formalization of these SMOs indicates that, at their center, the organizational networks of the NSMs have undergone substantial structural change by the end of the 1980s.

Professionalization is simply measured by the number of paid personnel. Admittedly, this gives us only an approximation of the actual level of professionalization, since not all the paid personnel are of a professionalized type. On the average, the SMOs in our sample have a paid staff of fourteen persons. The mean does not take into account large differences which exist in this respect: Roughly one-fourth of the SMOs do not have any paid staff at all, and about one-half do not have more than four paid staff members. On the other hand, about 10 percent of the SMOs have fifty paid staff members or more.

Formalization and professionalization are positively correlated, as are both of these indicators with the resource level and the age of an SMO. Table 7.5 presents these correlations (excluding Greenpeace). Independently of type of movement and country, the two parameters of internal structuration are a positive function of an SMO's age and resources, as we have expected.[19] But how are they precisely related to age and resources? We already know that resources are a positive function of age and I have already mentioned that financial resources are a direct function of a membership. In addition, it can be shown that the degree of formalization is a direct function of age and of the size of membership, but not of the level of financial resources. It is the complexity involved with large numbers of members which exerts pressure for formalization. Formalization, in turn, can be shown to be a first step in the direction of professionalization. Moreover, the greater the number of members and the larger the amount of financial resources available, the greater the need for professionalization, but also the more important the means allowing for this step to take place.[20] Given that, in absolute terms, they have a larger number of members and greater financial resources than their French and Swiss counterparts, the German and Dutch SMOs are more professionalized. The average number of persons employed varies between 23.5 and 18.2 for Germany and the Netherlands, on the one hand, and 9.2 and 8.6 for France and Switzerland, on the other hand. One may wonder why the Swiss SMOs are no more professionalized than the French, since they have considerably more resources at their disposal. The answer may again have to do with the peculiar political context of Switzerland: The fact

Table 7.5. *Bivariate correlations between characteristics of organizational*
*structure (*n = *72; without Greenpeace)*

	1	2	3	4	5
1 age	–				
2 membership	.42	–			
3 financial resources	.33	.78	–		
4 formalization	.35	.39	.29	–	
5 professionalization	.32	.68	.64	.42	–

that the whole Swiss political system is still today functioning on a militia basis – another example of the pervasive applicability of the subsidiarity principle in this country – may account for the relative lack of professionalization of Swiss SMOs. Still, it should be noted that not all Swiss movements are unprofessional: The Swiss ecology movement turns out to be highly professionalized. In all the countries, the differences between the degree of professionalization of the various movements generally correspond to their levels of resources. Thus the ecology and solidarity movements are generally the most professionalized, while the urban autonomous movement and the peace movement are least professionalized.

EXTERNAL STRUCTURATION

Contrary to the internal structuration, the external structuration is, of course, a direct function of the political context. I have two indicators at hand for the analysis of this aspect of the organizational development of SMOs: the party preference of its membership base, and its alliances with partners outside of the subsector of the NSMs. With respect to the *party preferences* of the membership base, we find that virtually all the SMOs in all four countries have a membership preferring parties on the political Left. However, in addition to partisans of left-wing parties, some SMOs also recruit sympathizers of parties on the political Right. It comes as no surprise that, on the one hand, these SMOs are most numerous in Switzerland, where 43 percent of the SMOs also recruit sympathizers of the Right, and that, on the other hand, there exists not a single SMO recruiting sympathizers of the Right in France. The strong party-political polarization forces all the participants in French politics to take sides (Duyvendak 1992), while the less conspicuous character of the opposition between Left and Right in Switzerland allows for crossing the fault lines. Germany and the Netherlands lie between the extremes with 32 percent and 14 percent SMOs respectively that also recruit partisans from the Right.

Table 7.6. *Allies outside of the subsector of the NSMs: percentages of SMOs maintaining a given type of alliance*

Type of alliance	Country			
	NL	G	F	CH
All movements				
Left parties as a whole	38%	67%	68%	52%
Social Democrats	25	*67*	21	24
Communists	6	15	21	14
New Left/Greens	25	26	*53*	*48*
Unions	25	37	37	48
Churches	25	33	5	38
Authorities	*44*	4	0	5
n	(16)	(27)	(19)	(21)

In three of the four countries, a majority of the SMOs are also *allied* to parties on the Left, as is shown by Table 7.6.[21] Only two SMOs in our sample seem to be allied to a party on the Right – one in the Netherlands and one in Switzerland. Although SMOs of NSMs generally tend to have alliances with parties of the Left, there are some differences between the countries with respect to the most preferred alliance partner among the parties of the Left: While, in Germany, at the end of the 1980s the SPD was clearly the most likely alliance partner of the SMOs in our sample, in France and in Switzerland our SMOs preferred alliances with the Greens or with one of the small parties of the New or "Second" Left, which were founded in the aftermath of the students' movements of the late 1960s and have always been close to the cause of NSMs. The Dutch case is ambiguous in this regard. The Communists are a nonnegligible partner of these SMOs, but nowhere do they constitute their preferred ally, not even in France. It is tempting to interpret the differences between Germany, on the one hand, and Switzerland and France, on the other, by the fact that in Germany, the SPD has been out of government since the early 1980s, whereas the PS has been the governing party in France during most of the 1980s and, in Switzerland, it has participated in the governing coalition ever since 1959. While the SPD looked for a closer relationship with the NSMs in the course of the 1980s, chose a candidate for the chancellorship whose position was rather close to that of the supporters of NSMs, and allied itself with the Greens on the level of several Länder, the French PS has largely abandoned the NSMs' cause; Duyvendak (1992) even speaks of betrayal.

Table 7.6 also contains some information with respect to three other possible alliance partners: the unions, the churches, and the authorities. With respect to *unions,* I have argued in a previous paper (Kriesi 1991) that highly encompassing, corporatist union systems – such as the German one – are not very likely to facilitate the mobilization of NSMs. In addition, I have suggested that in union systems which are fragmented along party lines and dominated by a Communist controlled federation – such as the French system, there is a chance that a minoritarian union might appeal to segments of the new middle class which tend to be neglected by the dominant federation. The CFDT in France provides an illustrative example. Finally, I have suggested that union systems – such as the Dutch and the Swiss systems, which are fragmented along religious lines, but integrated into policy networks and pacified, provide the most favorable context from the point of view of NSMs. Not only has the class struggle been pacified in these countries, but the fragmentation of the union system makes for competition among unions, from which NSMs stand to profit. The present results do not allow any confirmation of these hypotheses, since there are no significant differences in the extent of support received by the NSM subsectors in the four countries. In all four cases, union support is substantial. A more detailed analysis shows that union support in all four countries primarily goes to SMOs of the peace and the solidarity movement, that is, to the two movements that have typically been most politicized by the Left: 38 percent of the SMOs of the peace movement and 61 percent of those of the solidarity movement have been supported by unions. Germany is the only country where also some SMOs of the ecology movement receive union support.

The peace movement and the solidarity movement are also the only ones that receive *church* support in all countries except France: overall, 25 percent of the SMOs of the peace movement and 49 percent of those of the solidarity movement have received support from churches. It is, of course, well known that churches are involved in these two movements. But it comes as a surprise to me that churches in France do not seem to share this involvement. The question is, whether this apparent absence of the churches from the two French movements is also a consequence of the strong politicization of these two movements in terms of the polarization between Left and Right.

Finally, the Netherlands turn out to be exceptional with respect to the large share of their SMOs which count the *authorities* among their allies. Almost half of the Dutch SMOs of our sample seem to be allied to some authorities, while there are no such ties in France and only one case each in the two other countries. If we analyze in more detail, we note that it is above all in the Dutch ecology movement, where these ties are frequent: All of the SMOs of this movement maintain alliances with authorities! This is the result, on the one hand, of the "new realism" adopted by the Dutch ecology movement in the course of the eighties (Cramer 1989), but, on the other hand, it also reflects the strategy of "informal cooptation" so typical for the Dutch authorities.

The *diversification of alliance relationships* may prove to be crucial for an SMO. This point is illustrated by a Swiss organization of the solidarity movement that mobilized for the solidarity with immigrant laborers in Switzerland (Cattacin and Passy 1992). It received substantial financial support from the major union of construction workers, a larger majority of whose members are immigrants from Southern Europe. The SMO defended the cause of the union in the delicate political issue of the statute for seasonal workers, allowing the union to keep a low profile without losing face. When this issue lost its political explosiveness, the union also lost interest in the SMO and stopped its support, which left the SMO with insufficient resources for survival. The number of external allies may serve as a rough indicator of an SMO's diversification of its external relations.[22] According to this indicator, the Swiss SMOs generally have a more diversified network of alliances than the SMOs in the other countries. Controlling for the impact of the political context, SMOs from instrumental movements have more diversified networks than the sub- and countercultural ones, with the networks of the SMOs from the peace and solidarity movements being most diversified.

TRANSFORMATION OF GOALS AND ACTION REPERTOIRES

Goal transformation is difficult to capture by the kind of structural data I have at my disposal. However, indirectly, by analyzing the sources of revenue of an SMO, it is possible to get some limited idea of the direction of goal transformation. We have asked questions about the shares of an organization's revenue coming from membership contributions, public subsidies, allies and other sources. The lower the share of membership contributions to an organization's budget, the more autonomous it is with respect to its members and the greater the likelihood that goals which are not of immediate concern to its members are playing an important role in the considerations of the organization's dominant coalition. The overall distribution of an SMO's revenue over the four sources of income gives an idea of the degree to which its resource base is diversified and of its degree of autonomy with respect to any specific type of environment. The share of public subsidies in particular not only indicates the extent to which an SMO is integrated into established systems of interest intermediation, but also serves as an indicator of a certain pragmatism in terms of its goal orientation.[23]

As is shown by Table 7.7, there are important country-specific differences with regard to the *sources of revenue*. Swiss SMOs turn out to be more dependent on their membership than the SMOs in the other three countries.[24] This means that the Swiss subsector which has the most diversified network of alliances is at the same time the one most reliant on its own devices – a result

Table 7.7. *Sources of revenue of SMOs (average shares of total revenue)*

	Membership	Subsidies	Allies	Other sources	(*n*)
Country					
NL	55%	22%	7%	16%	(16)
G	60	16	14	9	(23)
F	61	9	8	22	(25)
CH[a]	81	5	1	13	(12)
Movement[b]					
Ecology	55	23	5	17	(22)
Solidarity	56	12	16	16	(18)
Peace	68	2	21	9	(9)
Gay	60	14	4	22	(13)
Autonomous	94	5	0	0	(2)
Grand mean	63%	13%	8%	16%	(78)

[a]Information on some SMOs of the solidarity movement only.
[b]Excluding the Swiss SMOs.

which perfectly reflects the specificity of the Swiss political context: It is a context which allows for extensive consultation and political concertation, but which also puts a prime on self-reliance and self-organization following the principle of subsidiarity (see Kriesi 1980). The Dutch context, by contrast, not only favors mutual concertation, but it tends to lend a helping hand as well. The ecology, solidarity, and the gay movements all receive important subsidies in the Netherlands. This difference is illustrated by the sources of income of the Dutch Nicaragua Committee and the corresponding Swiss Committee for Central America: while the former is 60 percent subsidized by public authorities, the latter depends 90 percent on its membership and 10 percent on "other" sources. Pursuing this example one step further, we may note that the French Nicaragua Committee gets 50 percent of its revenue from its membership and 50 percent from "other sources" – "other sources" which are generally more important in France than elsewhere – compensating for the lack of membership and government support in this country. Public subsidies are most prominent for the ecology movement and the gay movement, which have received such support not only in the Netherlands, but also in the other countries. Thus 45 percent of the budget of the German BBU – the peak association of the citizens' action groups for environmental protection – is covered by public subsidies, as are roughly one-third of the budgets of the French Amis de la Terre and of the FFSPN – the French professional peak association for environmental protection. If, in Switzerland, public support is still not forthcoming for the ecology movement, it has become important with respect to the gay movement in this country, too, as a consequence of the AIDS crisis. Everywhere, the governments are now collaborating with the subcultural SMOs that serve as intermediaries with respect to a population at risk to which the authorities have little access otherwise. The AIDS crisis provides an example of "suddenly imposed grievances" which restructure the external relations of an SMI and transform its goal orientations in a dramatic fashion, irrespective of the political context.

Financial support from allies is most likely for SMOs of the peace movement (in France), and for those of the solidarity movement (in the Netherlands and Germany). In France, the major SMOs of the peace movement are either allied to the Communist Party – such as the Mouvement de la Paix and the Appel des Cent, or to the New Left (the "Second Left") – such as CODENE (the committee for nuclear disarmament in Europe). They receive between 40 percent and 50 percent of their revenue from these allies. Needless to say that such support comes with strings attached. It illustrates once again the general point made about the politicization of the French peace movement in particular.

Turning now to the *transformation of the action repertoires,* we should first note that there are country-specific differences of action repertoires which correspond to what we would have expected on the basis of the differences in the political contexts (Kriesi et al. 1992): The French movements tend to be most radical; that is, they use unconventional and even violent forms of action more frequently than the movements in the other countries. The Swiss movements tend to be most moderate, given their frequent use of conventional channels of articulation of protest, while, overall, the action repertoires of Dutch and German movements tend to be of an intermediary degree of radicality.[25] In addition to these systematic overall differences, we also find important differences with respect to the transformation of the action repertoires over time which are related to differences in the corresponding political contexts. I would like to illustrate this point by studying more closely the development of the action repertoire of the *ecology movement* in particular. Figure 7.5 presents the development of the yearly percentages of unconventional events, smoothed over adjacent periods of three years for the ecology movement in each one of the four countries.[26] For France, we note that the percentage of unconventional events increases during the period 1975–1989. This indicates that the French ecology movement, which was already the most radical at the beginning of the period, radicalized even more throughout the 1980s. This development is in stark contrast with the strongly increasing conventionalization of the Dutch and the German branches. At the end

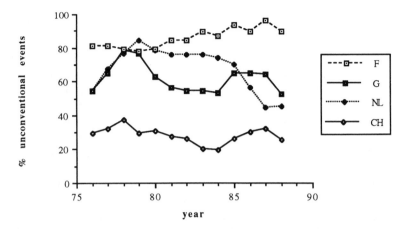

Figure 7.5. Development of the action repertoire of the ecology movement in the four countries.

of the 1970s, the action repertoires of both the German and the Dutch movements were about as radical as that of their French colleagues as a result of their radicalization in the course of the conflict about nuclear energy. Since the early 1980s, however, the repertoires of the German and Dutch movements have become more conventional, developing in the direction of the very conventional Swiss movement. These differences reflect the inverse changes in the configuration of power in France and Germany: Although the ecology movement lost its strongest ally, when the PS came to power in France in 1981, it gained an ally in Germany with the SPD losing power in 1982. In the case of the Netherlands, the conventionalization rather reflects the "new realism" of the ecology movement which came to dominate it after the defeat of its antinuclear energy branch in the early 1980s. However, not all the new social movements in a given country follow the same pattern of transformation of their action repertoire. There are differences in this respect between the various movements within a given country, which can, at least in part, be explained by movement-specific differences in political opportunities within one and the same country. This is illustrated by a comparison of the French ecology and solidarity movements (Figure 7.6). While the French ecology movement radicalized in the eighties, the French solidarity movement, which was also quite radical at the beginning of the eighties, deradicalized as it received increasing support from the governing PS.

It is possible to refine the analysis of the transformation of the action repertoire of the ecology movement somewhat further by looking more specifically at the organizations responsible for the various types of protest events. Even if not all events of a given movement are produced by its own SMOs, the general trend of the action repertoire of the movement as a whole is likely

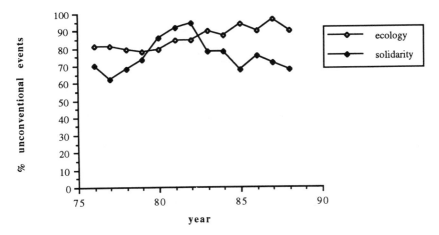

Figure 7.6. Development of the action repertoire of the French ecology and solidarity movements.

to bear the marks of the development of its organizational base, and, in turn, is bound to have repercussions on it.[27] For this analysis, I introduce a distinction between the most important, relatively professional SMOs – that is, between the most developed part of the SMI of the ecology movement and organizationally less developed, more informal citizens' action groups.[28] Given the assumption that the large professional SMOs typically have a more moderate action repertoire than the latter groups, the development of the action repertoire of a given movement may be the result of a transformation of the action repertoire of each one of the two types of organizations or of a shift of the initiative from the one type to the other. Figure 7.7 allows a separation of these two effects for three of the four countries under study.[29] It shows the development of the total number of events and of the number of unconventional events for both professional SMOs and citizens' action groups for Switzerland, Germany, and the Netherlands. In other words, it not only shows trends (as the previous two figures) but it also gives an idea of the level of mobilization by the different types of SMOs. As we can see, in all three countries, the citizens' action groups have demobilized to a considerable extent toward the end of the 1980s. This demobilization has contributed to the deradicalization of the movements in Germany and the Netherlands, but not in Switzerland, since the Swiss citizens' action groups have always been rather conventional and since they have above all reduced the conventional part of their activities. In Germany and Switzerland, the demobilization of citizens' action groups was accompanied by a parallel increase of the protest activities of the professional SMOs. As far as the latter are concerned, their mobilization was almost exclusively conventional in Switzerland, some-

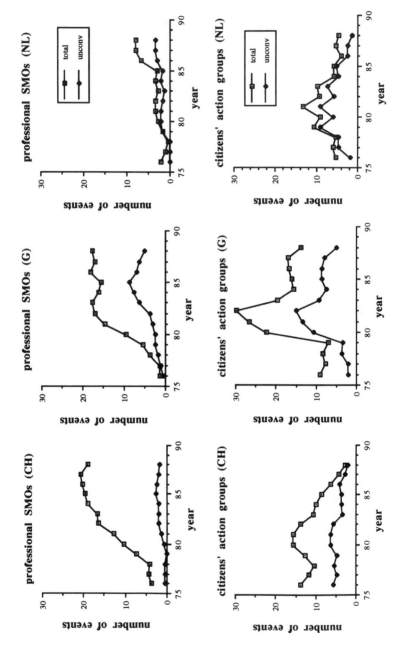

Figure 7.7. Development of the action repertoire of the SMOs of the ecology movement: professional SMOs and citizens' action groups in the four countries.

what more radical in Germany. In the Netherlands, finally, the initiative did not go over to the professional SMOs. With the demobilization of the citizens' action groups, the whole movement seemed to demobilize. This difference between Germany and Switzerland, on the one hand, and the Netherlands, on the other hand, may be interpreted in the light of an earlier result: As we have seen, the Dutch ecology movement has been integrated into established systems of interest intermediation; it is recognized and subsidized by the authorities to an extent which is as yet unknown in Switzerland. In other words, the Dutch professional SMOs no longer need to mobilize at all, in order to introduce their points of view into the political process and to get things done. In Switzerland and Germany, the movement has also gained more access to the system, which is reflected in the conventionalization of its action repertoire. But even the professional SMOs still rely on (mainly conventional) mobilization of protest in order to get things done. If the ecology movement as a whole is by far the most institutionalized movement among the five compared, the SMOs of the Dutch ecology movement seem to have traveled farthest in the direction of becoming established interest groups.[30]

CONCLUSION

In this essay I have analyzed the internal and external determinants of the organizational development of NSMs, putting most emphasis on the impact of the political context without, however, focusing exclusively on political factors. If the general political setting and the configuration of power in the political system are important for the development of the organizational infrastructure of NSMs, they are not the only factors of some relevance. First, this analysis has confirmed the idea that the internal structuration mainly follows internal organizational dynamics. Moreover, it has also indicated that there exist important differences between the organizational development of different movements, which are independent of the political context. Thus, the ecology movement is typically the most richly endowed, whereas the peace movement, the gay movement, and the urban autonomous movement have generally only few resources. We have also found movement-specific differences of external support: in general, the peace and solidarity movements are strongly supported by the Left – including unions – and by churches, whereas the gay movement, as a result of the AIDS crisis, receives public aid in all the countries. In addition, as we have expected, the different types of movements typically undergo different forms of transformation: although our indicators are far from optimal, they support the hypothesis that subcultural movements tend to commercialize or to follow the path of involution, while instrumental movements tend to institutionalize. Among the latter, the solidarity and peace movements typically have more difficulties stabilizing than the ecology movement, given their particular problem structure, which makes them susceptible to conjunctural variations in public attention cycles and party politics. The ecology movements have typically gone farthest in the direction of institutionalization as an interest group.

There are exceptions to these general patterns – exceptions which can be accounted for by country-specific variations in the political context. Thus, the particular weakness and the low level of institutionalization of the ecology movement as well as the comparative strength of the solidarity movement in France have been related to the specific strategies of the socialist government. The unexpectedly weak professionalization of Swiss SMOs made sense, if interpreted in terms of the prevalence of the militia system in Swiss politics, and the unexpected impact of an SMO's age on its resource level in the case of Germany could be interpreted in the light of the distant relationship that traditionally existed between the state and society in that country. But the political context is not only relevant for the explanation of deviant cases with respect to movement-specific patterns. Its impact on resource levels, external structuration, and the transformation of goal orientations and action repertoires has been shown to be pervasive and systematic. Thus, the French SMOs are generally weak, most radical, and most strongly politicized by their partisan environment. By contrast, the SMOs in the two smaller European democracies have a comparatively large membership, are relatively well endowed with resources, relatively well integrated into established systems of interest intermediation and comparatively moderate. The Dutch SMOs not only have the highest resource levels (in absolute terms), but they also have the most elaborate relations with authorities. The Swiss SMOs are different from the Dutch to the extent that they have the most diversified alliances and political recruitment patterns, but receive hardly any support from authorities. German SMOs finally take an intermediary position with respect to most aspects of the organizational development we have been discussing here. These results generally confirm the relevance of the political context for the mobilization of NSMs as well as the specific hypotheses that have been formulated with regard to context-specific differences in the organizational development of these movements.

The impact of national contexts on social movement structures: A cross-movement and cross-national comparison

DIETER RUCHT

Political opportunity theorists have mainly dealt with mobilization for protest as the primary dependent variable. Opportunities were clearly assets of their environment and not properties of the protest groups themselves. Thus, the crucial question was: "Which opportunities facilitate or restrict the kind and/or extent of mobilization?" Some authors have treated the level of mobilization (Kriesi, 1989b, 1991; Tarrow, 1989b, 1991b) or the strengths of movements (Rucht, 1995) as the dependent variable. Others focused more specifically on movement strategies (Eisinger, 1973; Kitschelt, 1986), behavior (della Porta and Rucht, 1991), or outcomes (Kitschelt, 1986). Underlying all this work is the explicit or implicit assumption that external opportunities have a direct effect on these dependent variables. However, the literature neglects the role of the structural basis for mobilization. This is surprising, because few social movement scholars doubt that movement networks and organizations have a strong impact on strategies, mobilization, and success.

Resource mobilization theorists have emphasized the role of social movement industries, movement organizations, and movement entrepreneurs in the process of mobilization (Zald and Ash, 1966; McCarthy and Zald, 1977; Zald and McCarthy, 1980). They have not only formulated a variety of hypotheses about these explanatory factors for mobilization as the dependent variable but also demonstrated their weight in many empirical studies. However, not much work in this research tradition analyzes the societal context that may influence social movement organizations (but see Garner and Zald, 1985; McCarthy, Britt, and Wolfson, 1991).

As a rule, political opportunity approaches have neglected the structural basis for resource mobilization, whereas resource mobilization approaches have largely ignored the broader political environments in which social movement organizations are embedded. In linking both research strands, we can achieve a fuller understanding of factors that directly or indirectly influence social movement mobilization. With this in mind this chapter analyzes the impact of external opportunities on movement structures which, in turn, influence the kind and level of mobilization. First, after defining some key categories, I will present a general model to explain variances in social movement structures. Second, I will compare the structures of the women's and environmental movements in the United States, France, and West Germany during recent decades – the dependent variable. Third, I will apply the explanatory model to these cases. The conclusion provides an argument summary and an outline of a more refined explanatory approach. Given the complexity of this threefold comparative scope – which includes cross-movement, cross-national, and cross-temporal perspectives – the emphasis will be more on the conceptual than the empirical level.[1]

TOWARD AN EXPLANATORY CONCEPT

For the sake of clarity, it might be helpful to specify some key categories that are used in the descriptive and explanatory sections of this chapter.

Key categories

Social movement. In a very restrictive sense, a *social movement* consists of two kinds of components: (1) networks of groups and organizations prepared to mobilize for protest actions to promote (or resist) social change (which is the ultimate goal of social movements); and (2) individuals who attend protest activities or contribute resources without necessarily being attached to movement groups or organizations. *Mobilization* is the process of creating movement structures and preparing and carrying out *protest actions* which are visible movement "products" addressed to actors and publics outside the movement. For large-scale and sustained movement activities, mobilization requires *resources* such as people, money, knowledge, frames, skills, and technical tools to process and distribute information and to influence people.

Movement structure. The organizational bases and mechanisms serving to collect and use the movement's resources can be called the *movement structure.* Although movement structure is mainly designed for mobilization, it may also serve other purposes such as disseminating information within the movement, forging a collective identity, or satisfying the personal interests of the movement leaders. I therefore distinguish between the more encompassing movement structures and, as a part of these, the mobilization structures as defined in McCarthy's introductory essay in Part II of this volume. Whereas large and complex movements tend to develop specific structures particularly designed for mobilization, in smaller and/or less mature movements general structures may in parallel or in sequence fulfill various functions including that of mobilization.

As any other structure of a large collective actor or organization, a move-

Table 8.1. *Typology of mobilizing agents*

	Social movements	Interest groups	Parties
Mode of operation	Protest actions	Representation of members in polities	Occupation of political offices
Main resources	Committed adherents	Expertise, money, access to decision-makers, refusing to cooperate	Voters
Structural features	Networks of groups and organizations	Formal organization	Formal organization

ment structure can vary along several relevant dimensions. It has an overall configuration based on relatively stable patterns of interrelations, which may encompass many interconnected components as described in network analyses. These components may vary in size, internal cohesion, degree of formalization, amount and kind of resources, and so forth.

In modern democratic societies, I identify three elementary types of mobilizing agents that are designed to promote collective interests in order to influence political decision-making and, ultimately, social change. These types are social movements, interest groups, and political parties. Analytically, these three collective agents can be clearly separated. Each relies on a different mode of operation and on different resources (Rucht, 1992a). Moreover, these three types have different structural features. Whereas interest groups and political parties are basically formal organizations, social movements typically lack formal rules to define a clear-cut membership and to regulate the internal process. The ideal-typical form of a social movement, then, is a network of more or less informal groups, at least groups that are not formally and hierarchically coordinated.

Though distinguishable on an analytical level, in empirical terms it is often hard to draw a clear boundary between these three types of collective actors for several reasons. First, interest groups and parties may conduct protest activities without necessarily belonging to a social movement. Second, interest groups and parties may develop an organization which is less hierarchical and less formalized than usual. For instance, consider the differences between political parties in Western Europe and the United States. Third, because social movements have no constitution, no formal division of labor, and almost no means to foster the development of just one uniform and coherent organization, they can encompass rather heterogeneous organizational components (Heberle, 1951). Movements tend to provide ample space to the mushrooming of different structures, ongoing organizational experiments, and flexible forms of cooperation. This makes it hard to grasp social movements on an aggregate level, where observers tend to overemphasize the most visible or most accessible parts, which are usually the largest and more formally organized components.

Given this heterogeneity of movement structures, it is no wonder that we may find *within* movements also those organizational forms which we have analytically separated from movements, that is, interest groups and political parties. Only when one of these organizations succeeds in reaching a hegemonic position – controlling virtually all collective resources – would I no longer consider it a movement.

When we acknowledge the possible coexistence of grassroots groups, formal interest groups, and parties within the framework of a movement, then, from an empirical perspective, this also has consequences for the concept of a movement structure. Based on the relative predominance of these elements three elementary types of movement structures can be differentiated:

1. The *grassroots model,* characterized by a relatively loose, informal, and decentralized structure, an emphasis on unruly, radical protest politics, and a reliance on committed adherents;
2. The *interest-group model,* characterized by an emphasis on influencing policies (via lobbying, for instance) and a reliance on formal organization;
3. The *party-oriented model,* characterized by an emphasis on the electoral process, party politics, and, as well, a reliance on formal organization

These three forms can vary in their distinctness, scope, relative weight, kind of linkages, and so forth, and therefore should be perceived in a comparative perspective.

Context structure. It should be obvious that the emergence and further development of a movement structure cannot be seen independently from its larger environment. This draws our attention to those factors in a movement's environment which facilitate or limit the building of a specific movement structure, resource collection, and the eventual carrying out of protest activities. I refer to this environment as the *context structure* rather than "political opportunity structure" in order to avoid the connotation of opportunities in fleeting chances, and to encompass more than the political context. Political contexts are probably the most important, but they are not the only relevant part of such an environment.

Certainly the political opportunity structure perspective is a major breakthrough in recent research on social movements. Nevertheless, it still suffers from some deficiencies (which are not inherent in the concept per se): (1) Proponents of the concept have not adequately clarified what they mean by structure, and the selected variables are not bound together by an overarching principle or theory. (2) The concept is best suited for movement types that focus on the political realm and, consequently, on questions of political power. However, there is good reason to believe that the strengths and forms of movements, at least in some cases, may heavily depend on social and cultural factors as well. (3) From a cross-national perspective, the concept seems to deal with stable opportunities without taking into account that national opportunities may quickly change over time (see McAdam, 1982; Rucht, 1990; Joppke, 1993).[2] (4) Scholars have tended to treat opportunities as objectively existent rather than socially constructed. They are socially constructed in two ways: Their perception depends on the process of framing and interpretation (Snow and Benford, 1988; Gamson and Meyer, Chapter 12 in this volume) which eventually may lead to a "cognitive liberation" (McAdam, 1982); and opportunities may themselves become targets of social movements, and undergo processes of strategic intervention. In summary, the concept of political opportunities needs to be broadened, specified, and refined.

Structure cannot be observed as such. It is a construct of the analyst who states principles of regularity and order based on observable pieces of information showing a common pattern. By definition, structure is a relatively stable configuration of elements. It remains despite changes in some of its individual elements. For example, we identify social classes in a society, or informal hierarchies within a small group. Hence, the notion of structure implies (1) a reference point (such as distributions of wealth, power, or roles) and (2) the assumption that some sort of social mechanism or organizing principle maintains the pattern over time.

In the case of the structural setting of a social movement, we are looking for those ecological elements that shape the movement's forms and activities. More concretely, we are interested in those conditions external to a given movement (or set of movements) which either restrict or facilitate the building and maintenance of movement structure devoted to conducting protest activities. What makes this context relevant to the movement is that it involves resources and conditions beyond the movement's immediate control. The movement can realize its potential to be strong and successful to the extent it takes this context into consideration and makes it resonant by structural attunement, strategic calculation, and clever use of leverage points. This requires an identification and "exploitation" of patterns that work in favor of the movement (e.g., dissatisfaction of people with the established elites) and the avoidance of that which could weaken it (e.g., loss of powerful allies). But which contextual dimensions are most crucial in this regard?

In my view, the overall context structure of a social movement, a social movement family (for this concept, see della Porta and Rucht, 1991), and a social movement sector (Garner and Zald, 1985) has three basic dimensions: cultural, social, political contexts. The *cultural context* refers to the attitudes and behaviors of individuals who may (or may not) provide support such as money, organizational help, or participation in protest events. These various kinds of support will mainly depend on how resonant a movement's issues and demands are with the experiences and interests of larger sections of the population. This resonance is a function of the distribution of cultural patterns among certain groups in the population and the framing of the problems at stake. Here both general values and more situationally bound issue perceptions come into play. In an empirical perspective, one would have to assess to which extent central values (e.g., leftist versus rightist; materialist versus postmaterialist; individualistic versus collectivistic) resonate with the values promoted by the movement in both public discourse and individual attitudes. This degree of resonance could be located on a scale ranging from dissonant to consonant.

A second dimension, *social context,* is the embedding of social movements in their social environment. Social milieus and networks which either facilitate or restrict the forming of collective identity and the building of movement structures are one aspect of this dimension. Such networks provide the background for socializing potential activists in a similar way and for bringing them together in a more directed and issue-focused interaction. Such networks are particularly crucial for the emergence and stabilization of an initial mobilization structure, which serves as the nucleus for inducing the creation of other groups and for attracting people at or outside the margins of these groups. In turn, the building of social networks depends on ecological factors, including the material conditions of a society. For example, population density or means which facilitate communication or mobility may impact on the forming of networks. A second aspect of the social context is the overall social stratification or class structure of a society. This becomes particularly important when a movement's central concerns are related to these structures, such as with poor people's movements or workers' movements.

Third, social movement groups interact with authorities and countermovements which, among other things, are parts of its *political context.* The political context is where conceptions of political opportunity structure have focused, singling out factors like access to the polity, political alignments, presence or absence of allies, and conflict among elites (Tarrow, 1989b; 34ff.). Drawing on the existing literature I consider four variables:

1. *Access to the party-system and policy decisions* includes both the formal and informal channels to influence political decisions via direct participation, or indirect means such as lobbying or litigation. It can be assessed along a scale ranging from open to closed.
2. *Policy implementation capacity* is the power of authorities to implement adopted policies, regardless of internal or external resistance. It can be assessed along a scale ranging from low to high.
3. *Alliance structure*[3] is the configuration of allies which may provide substantive and/ or symbolic support for the movement. It can be assessed along a scale ranging from weak to strong.

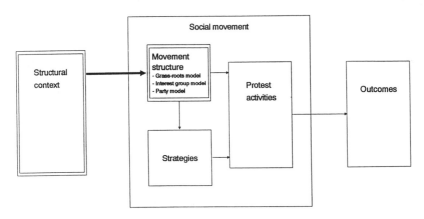

Figure 8.1. The impact of a social movement's structural context.

4. *Conflict structure* is the configuration of opponents which have the capacity to limit, undermine, or repress social movement mobilization. It can be assessed along a scale ranging from weak to strong.

Explanatory scheme

How can the relationship between these various pieces be conceptualized? In contrast to the conventional political opportunity structure approach (which directly links opportunities, on the one hand, and strategy, mobilization, or even outcomes on the other), we should pay attention to the movement structure as a crucial intervening variable. Opportunities are one of the major factors that shape a movement's structure; in turn, that structure has an impact on strategies, kinds and levels of mobilization, and eventually on movement outcomes. In other words, if we conceive of strategy as a kind of software application used by movements, we realize that the software cannot "run" without the hardware called movement structure. Although several strategic options may exist at any one time, hardware is not easily changed and thus limits the applicable software.

My assumption is that the degree to which a movement exhibits elements of any of the three organizational models outlined above depends largely on its context structure. We can visualize these relations in a scheme (see Figure 8.1). Such a perspective, of course, is only a reductionist way of modeling factors whose relations are empirically complex. They by no means form a one-way causal chain. In discussing the relationship between the structural context and the movement structure, my emphasis is on the absolute and relative weight of the movement structure's various components. I believe such a pattern is basically a function of the context structure and the type of movement.[4] My *first general hypothesis* is that the overall movement structure is stronger in terms of resources: the more open the access to the decision-making system, the lower the policy implementation capacity, the stronger the alliance structure, the weaker the conflict structure, and the more consonant the value structure. (At this point I am leaving aside the problem of curvilinear relationships which may exist at the extreme poles of some of the variable scales.)

While this hypothesis seems quite suggestive for predicting quantitative changes, it is more difficult to formulate plausible assumptions about how these variables shape the quality of the movement structure. I expect that the distribution of grassroots, interest-group, and party model elements are strongly influenced by the political context, whereas I would not expect a significant impact from the cultural and social context. Thus, my *second general hypothesis* is that a movement structure will be more formal (also in the sense of tending toward the interest-group and party models): the more open its access to the party system and to policy decision, the weaker the policy implementation capacity, the weaker the alliance structure, and the stronger the conflict structure.

Because some of the suggested relationships may seem arbitrary, I will briefly describe the underlying reasoning. First, open access continuously invites challengers such as social movements to take chances and attempt to influence the system of party politics and policy decision-making. In the long run, this encourages the formation of centralized and professional interest groups within movements (and movement parties). Second, a weak policy implementation capacity of administrative bodies is usually connected with relatively high legislative and judicial power (as compared to executive power) and high administrative decentralization. As mentioned, these features invite a continuous engagement at institutional leverage points via more formal movement organizations. By contrast, strong executive power structures in a given political system tend to induce a fundamental critique of bureaucratic and hierarchical political forms, which is then reflected in the movements' emphasis on informal and decentralized structures. Third, a weak alliance structure (particularly a lack of established parties, unions, and other interest groups as conventional allies) forces a movement to compensate by developing its own organizational bases for ongoing and quick political intervention. In contrast, a movement with strong and well-organized allies can keep its informal structure and thus profit from a division of labor based on differential resources (analogous to the "radical flank effect" as discussed by McAdam, McCarthy, and Zald in the introduction to this volume). Finally, a strong conflict structure, represented by powerful opponents, encourages the building of strong movement organizations, which allow for immediate and strategically oriented responses.

COMPARING MOVEMENT STRUCTURES

Turning to the empirical cases, I will first describe the structure of the women's and environmental movements in the countries selected, assessing similarities and differences. Since the two movements belong to the same family of new social movements in three Western capitalist societies with roughly the same degree and patterns of modernization, it should not be surprising that many similarities in the movement structures can be found. Identifying and explaining their differences will be the more challenging task. Also, a fuller description should take account of variation over time, which will be emphasized in conceptual rather than empirical terms.

Cross-movement variation

The (new) women's and environmental movements which began emerging in the late 1960s are often attributed to the same family as "new" or "Left-libertarian" movements,[5] although there is little organizational overlap between them. In pointing out similarities, scholars have referred to ideologies, goals, social recruitment, organizational forms, and action repertoires. Not all these criteria need to be met to identify a distinct social movement family. However, like different parties which are subsumed under one specific party family (e.g., the conservative parties), we would expect at least a convergence regarding these movements' background ideologies. For example, Alain Touraine (1969) has characterized "the struggle against technocracy" as the common underlying theme of all new social movements, notwithstanding the differences in their more concrete goals. In a similar vein, others have referred to various progressive U.S. movements in the 1960s as "the Movement," or to various recent xenophobic movements as the "New Right." In each case, the assumption was that there is a broad ideology which unites particular movements.

But can we also assume a convergence of structure in the various movements belonging to the same movement family? As long as the overall ideology of the movement family is concerned with procedural and structural societal problems, we should expect a certain consistency between means and ends. For example, we can hardly imagine a fascist movement with a highly decentralized structure based on consciousness-raising groups. Similarly, it is unlikely that a peace movement would deliberately use violent means to achieve its goal.

Many scholars have emphasized the broad variety of the structural forms of the new social movements family, but it is not a completely incoherent pattern. Overall, the structures tend to be highly decentralized (Gundelach, 1984; Lofland, 1985) or even fragmented, but with some formal organizations included. On the whole, there are remarkable differences between the structure of these movements and, for instance, the labor movements of the twentieth century or fascist movements. With their strong emphasis on autonomy and self-determination, we should not be surprised to find among new social movements strong indications of a grassroots structure, and relatively few signs of bureaucratic apparatus and authoritarian leadership.

Many similarities are immediately obvious when specifically comparing the movement structures of the new women's and environmental movements. Both have a decentralized structure and lack organizations holding hegemonic positions, and both lack authoritarian or even charismatic leadership. But a closer look reveals some differences as well.

In terms of size, the environmental movements have a larger membership than the women's movements in France, Germany, and the United States. This is true even after considering that formal association membership may be misleading, since the share of informal local groups is probably greater in women's movements than in the environmental movements.[6] At least for West Germany, we have reliable survey data collected in 1987 showing that the active adherence in the women's movement was 1.6 percent (passive: 8.9) compared to 3.9 percent (passive: 14.9) for the antinuclear movement, which largely overlaps with the broader environmental movement (Pappi, 1989). Also, data on participation in protest events show that 6 to 20 times more people were mobilized by environmental movements compared to women's movements in the Netherlands, France, and West Germany from 1975 to 1989 (Koopmans and Duyvendak, 1991: 236).

Second, it is obvious that the new women's movements exhibit only marginal elements of the party-model structure. Whereas Green parties have emerged in many Western democracies either within or closely linked to environmental movements, there are hardly women's parties, and none of these are significant.[7] With the probable exception of abortion (in a few countries) and ERA (only in the United States), women's issues are not important items on the electoral agenda.

Third, women's movements tend to rely on a highly decentralized structure (with the partial exception of the United States). Strongholds are small and informal groups at the local levels, although there are national organizations as well. Emphasizing personal change via consciousness-raising and self-help, women's groups operate mainly in face-to-face interaction. At least in the radical branch, there is often a sense of familiarity, intimacy, and "sisterhood," an explicit focus on personal relations, and the avoidance of hierarchy and bureaucratization (Evans, 1980). In contrast, environmental movements tend to be more instrumental, trying to build effective and powerful organizations, and giving less weight to consciousness-raising and expressive behavior.

Fourth, the women's movement is primarily organized according to the autonomy principle. This implies not only the exclusion of men but also independence from other established organizations within and outside the movement. Internally, the women's movements are mainly linked through informal networks, whereas environmental movements are linked by more formal alliances or umbrella organizations.

Overall, the women's movements come closer to the grass-roots model than the environmental movements, which tend to include more elements of the interest-group model and the party model. But these differences should not be exaggerated. On the one hand, we find a liberal strand within the women's movement which is more open to instrumental action; on the other hand, we find more expressive, countercultural, and even spiritualistic groups within the environmental movements. For example, the strand of "deep ecology" in groups such as *Earth First!* differs widely from formal environmental organizations. I would argue that the mainstream of both movements have perceptible structural differences which are probably less pronounced in the United States compared to Western Europe. If this argument holds, then we should expect that a movement's mobilizing structure would be impacted both by context structures and by the movement's specific theme or "logic" (Rucht, 1988).

Cross-country variation

The picture of the organizational structure of women's and environmental movements becomes more differentiated when we look at these movements in individual countries in recent years. In *France,* the women's and environmental movements are both relatively scattered and weak (Rucht, 1995). Some observers claim the French women's movement no longer exists. It is clear that even in major cities like Paris, there are fewer and fewer women's groups. "Less than 1 percent of adult women belonged to it [the movement] and they formed a tiny fringe of French society. According to Sauter-Bailliet, the entire MLF [Mouvement de Libération des Femmes] at best consisted of around 4,000 women" (Kaplan, 1992: 764). Nationwide organizations such as Choisir, while present in the public discourse on women's issues, do not have a strong resource base. Partly because of this weakness, there was always a tendency to lean toward leftist parties, except for the movement's small radical wing. Particularly during the 1980s, some influential feminists have promoted an alliance between the movement and the Socialist Party. Several have joined the party, accepted positions in government, or work in local administrative bodies such as centers for family help and contraceptive and abortion advice. However, no significant efforts have been made to create a separate women's party.

Clearly the French environmental movement is organizationally stronger than the women's movement. Its real strongholds are regional associations that are part of groups in a national umbrella organization called France-

Nature-Environment, which claims 850,000 members and is partly state-financed. Since the Left-Right cleavage is relatively salient in France, environmentalists have struggled not to be overwhelmed by this cleavage. One strategy was to form distinct electoral bodies to compete with established parties, and as early as 1974 the environmental movement was engaged in elections. Although relatively successful in some places, the real breakthrough came only in the late 1980s (Boy, 1990; Sainteny, 1991; Bennahmias and Roche, 1992). In the early 1990s, the two existing ecological parties, Les Verts and Génération Ecologie, had an electorate of more than 10 percent, which then was probably the highest in Europe. Yet both parties are organizationally weak. Les Verts has only 5,000 members and a high fluctuation in membership. Génération Ecologie is still weaker and is more a network of individuals than a real party. The movement's second strategy was to ally with existing, preferably leftist parties. Besides the small left-wing Parti Socialist Unifié (PSU), which became a close ally of the movement's, the Socialist Party (PS) remained an important (though ambivalent) reference point for the movement. Particularly during the 1980s, the PS not only managed to swallow the PSU, but also absorbed parts of the environmental movement. Génération Ecologie, headed by former activist Brice Lalonde (who later became minister for the environment for the Socialist government, but quit in 1992), was an attempt by environmentalists close to PS to compete directly with Les Verts. However, in November 1992, both Green parties agreed to form a coalition for the national elections in March 1993.

On the whole, the French women's and environmental movements have invested much energy in elections and party politics. This has led to significant elements of a party-model structure at the cost of those elements which are closer to the movement model and the interest-group model.

In *Germany*, we find strong movements with an elaborated infrastructure, significant organizational overlaps, and individuals with multiple movement affiliations. Whereas the network of grassroots groups clearly dominated the early periods in both women's and environmental movements, formal movement organizations have gained some complementing (but not replacing) relevance. Interest groups which focus on lobbying activities have emerged, but do not as yet play a major role.

The German women's movement has maintained its loose and decentralized structure. No single organization represents the movement or even a significant internal strand. Professional women's organizations and women's sections within the parties and trade unions are not integrated into the movement, but tend increasingly to cooperate with the grassroots groups. Although their activities are not spectacular, one should not underestimate the number and variety of these groups. For example, a survey of the Wissenschaftszentrum Berlin found more than 300 such groups in West Berlin in 1989, which certainly exceeds the total number of autonomous women's groups in France. A 1992 women's calendar lists 1,702 women's groups in West Germany and West Berlin, and formal women's associations are excluded. Knowing by selective tests that the list is incomplete, I estimate there are roughly 3,000 groups in West Germany. So the fact that a women's party did not come into existence was not due to lack of resources, but a deliberate choice by feminists not to invest much energy in party politics.

The German environmental movement is also decentralized, but in contrast to the women's movement it includes increasingly powerful membership organizations (Rucht, 1989a). The environmental groups represented in the national umbrella organization Deutscher Naturschutzring claim approximately 2.5 million members. Single organizations, such as German Greenpeace or the World Wide Fund for Nature, are among the strongest in the world, and the German Green Party is relatively strong in electoral power, size (approximately 38,000 members), and financial resources (Raschke, 1993). However, the backbone of the environmental movement continues to be the numerous, relatively informal groups which form their own regional and national networks according to their specific concerns. For example, a 1991 survey of a university town with a population of 70,000 found sixty-two local environmental groups. Of these, thirty-eight were local chapters of larger organizations and twenty-four were independent groups (Christmann, 1992: 128).

On the whole, both German movements include many elements of the grass-roots model, but conventional movement organizations and the Green Party are also strong. In the Green case, it is important to realize they are not a single-issue party but are also heavily engaged in other issues, such as promoting feminist concerns.

The *United States* has a broad variety of organizational forms, including many grassroots movements. Although grassroots movements have been widely neglected in recent work (for a critique, see Mayer, 1991), there is no doubt that on the whole both the women's and environmental movements are dominated by professional movement organizations (McCarthy and Zald, 1973). Many of these are virtually indistinguishable from conventional interest groups. It is not by chance that most of these organizations locate their headquarters in Washington, D.C.

A key organization in the women's movement is the National Organization for Women (NOW), which has a considerable membership and staff (Staggenborg, 1991: 165–67). There are many other important women's organizations which could be seen as parts or allies of the women's movement (Hallgarth, 1992) – altogether, eighty or ninety national groups. Membership of selected women's groups during 1958 through 1986 peaked in 1982 at 800,000 members (Costain, 1992: 96). Women's groups on national and state levels have become more professional (Staggenborg, 1991; Schlozmann, 1990), and Marita Haibach, a German feminist, recently praised the professional strat-

Table 8.2. *Movement structures of the women's and environmental*
movements in a cross-national perspective

	France	West Germany	United States
Grassroots groups	Very weak	Very strong	Strong
Interest groups	Weak	Strong	Very strong
Movement parties			
Organizational level	Weak	Strong	Very weak
Electoral level	Strong	Strong	Insignificant

egy of resource mobilization within the U.S. movement as a model for Germany. But because of the relatively strong anti-institutional bias that still dominates the German women's movement, this suggestion found mixed reactions.

Still stronger is the U.S. environmental movement's organizational basis. It includes several major nationwide organizations (Mitchell, 1985; Mitchell, Mertig, and Dunlap, 1991; Sereditch, 1991) and many other local or regional organizations (Freudenberg and Steinsapir, 1991). The importance of these organizations has been emphasized in other studies, but in comparative perspective it becomes clear that U.S. environmental movement organizations are supposedly the strongest and most professionalized (in every sense) in the world.

In sum, the U.S. movements are backed by relatively powerful formal movement organizations which tend to have a clear division of labor and quite often collaborate, despite their competition for resources. But because of the particulars of the U.S. party system, movement parties remain completely marginal. For example, the Green Party has so far managed to establish itself only in a few states, such as California, Hawaii, and Alaska, but even there having no influence on established politics.

The main organizational characteristics of the two movements in the three countries are summarized in Table 8.2.

Cross-time variation

The implicit assumption in the previous discussion is that the characteristics attributed to the movements in the three countries are stable over time. Though the overall description applies primarily to the 1980s and early 1990s, a closer look at this period, as well as in an expanded time perspective, reveals that changes occurred in the movements' mobilizing structures. Several examples may illustrate the significance of variation over time.

In the women's movement in France, the infrastructure and organization were stronger in the 1970s than the 1980s, although they never were as strong as in the United States. A second example is the rapid rise of the Green Party in West Germany. Only three years after coming into existence, this movement party has already entered the national parliament. Also other environmental organizations such as Greenpeace Germany and Bund für Umwelt und Naturschutz Deutschland grew extraordinarily after their beginnings in the mid-1970s. Further examples can be given for the United States. Consider the environmental movement organizations which tended to stagnate by the late 1970s, but once they came under heavy pressure from Reagan administration policies, "the national environmental lobbies were transformed into almost corporate identities" (Bosso, 1991: 163). They experienced a rapid growth in membership and other resources. Finally, we could identify remarkable strategic shifts in some of these movements over time, as was the case in the late 1970s when the U.S. antinuclear movement turned to direct action (Mitchell, 1981: 81), in the early 1980s when the U.S. women's movement tried to put pressure on the electoral level (Mueller, 1987), and in the second half of the 1970s when the German antinuclear movement shifted toward disruptive and even violent actions (Nelkin and Pollak, 1981: 77f; Joppke 1993). Behind these shifts was also a change in organizational structures, such as the emergence of dozens of loosely coupled alliances in the U.S. antinuclear movement.

Obviously, these examples cannot be explained by a stable context structure. As long as changing movement properties are not assumed to be due only to internal factors and/or external incidents, an explanatory concept which takes *change* of context structure into account must be elaborated. It is in this regard that the term "opportunities" perfectly applies.

EXPLAINING DIFFERENCES IN MOVEMENT STRUCTURES

The brief empirical discussion of movement structures as the dependent variable has shown that differences can be found across movements, countries, and time. Although the first and last dimensions should not be downplayed, cross-national differences are the most pronounced. (A condensed assessment of the six variables in all three countries is found in Table 8.3.) To what extent does the context structure explain the respective mobilization structures of the movements in the three countries?

In the *French case,* consistent with earlier empirical statements, most of the factors I have listed do not support a powerful and diversified movement structure. Specifically, there is a fairly closed party system (at least on the national level) as well as an extremely closed decision-making system (on all levels). Parties that gain only a small percentage of the vote are not represented in the National Assembly, and new parties such as Les Verts (the

Table 8.3. *Characteristics of national context structures*

	France	West Germany	United States
Access to			
Decision-making	Closed	Medium	Open
Party-system	Medium	Medium	Closed for newcomers but responsive to protest issues
Policy implementation capacity	High	Medium/low	Low
Alliances	Weak	Medium	Medium
Opponents			
Parties	Strong	Medium	Medium
Countermovements	Weak	Weak	Strong
Control agencies	Strong	Medium	Medium
Value resonance			
Public discourse	Low	Medium	Medium
Attitudes	Medium	Medium	Medium

Greens) and the National Front have succeeded in establishing themselves only in spite of such a major institutional barrier. Because in France lobbying and litigation are not promising approaches, challenger groups have invested much energy in forming new parties and gaining electoral success, facilitated by the considerable frustration with the traditional parties in the electorate. A second, striking feature of the French context structure is the absence of strong countermovements, which is probably an effect of the institutional strength of the French state. Because the powerful French state actively limits challenger movements, sometimes by repressive means, rather than being a neutral third party, there is little reason to create countermovements. Their potential task is performed by the state.

In the *German case,* most context variables were rated with a "medium" value, which is in perfect accordance with the existence of strong movements. This is because we expect curvilinear relationships between context and movement structures. Both institutional impermeability with repression, and high flexibility and permeability of the established system to challenger groups, are not favorable to the development of protest movements. In Germany, however, these conditions did not exist. Moreover, we also find a modest policy implementation capacity in Germany which is due to two main reasons. First, the federal system gives considerable power to the states. As a rule, parties holding the national majority are minority parties in several states. Second, the administrative courts and other institutions provide leverage points for challenging groups, which has been particularly important in the case of German antinuclear groups (Nelkin and Pollak, 1981). Limited access to institutionalized forms of opposition is likely to induce social movement organizations to try to exploit these other opportunities. Another feature is the relative weakness of countermovements. Given that Germany is a much weaker state than France, for example, this is surprising. Perhaps the strong conservative parties in Germany are a functional substitute for either outspoken countermovements or a strong state (as in France). The strength of the German conservative parties was probably also a factor that encouraged social movements to enter party politics with their own movement party. Two additional factors may also have contributed to this engagement in party politics. First, the Social Democratic and Liberal parties tended to play an ambivalent role regarding the protest movements. From the latters' perspective, these parties could not be seen as reliable allies. Second, the rules of the political game in Germany give much weight to political parties in general. Under these conditions, it is no surprise that even strong movements would not rely exclusively on extraparliamentary politics. Ironically, the 5 percent hurdle which originally was established to keep out newcomers and to avoid a fragmented party system, in fact strengthened the new challengers. Their only chance to enter the parliament was to unify. Therefore, hopes for a hold in party politics overruled internal ideological cleavages among those groups who were willing to engage in electoral politics at all.

In the *United States,* most characteristics of the context structure are also consistent with the existence of a relatively strong and diversified movement structure. In particular, the openness of the decision-making system must be stressed (Kitschelt, 1985), which encourages strong professional movement organizations but is not particularly supportive for radical grass-roots movements. The existing party system provides virtually no opportunity for establishment of a third party. But compensating for this exclusiveness is the loose frameworks of the two major parties, which are relatively open to new issues and groups compared to the coherent parties in Europe. Therefore, there is no sharp division between U.S. political parties and more conventional movement organizations. Finally, the strength of U.S. countermovements, exemplified by antifeminist movements (Buechler, 1990: chap. 5) and the pro-life movement, could be attributed to two main factors. First, since the state is not overly strong, it does not take the wind out of countermovements' sails. Rightly or wrongly, the U.S. state was perceived more as a third party and less as the main opponent in cases involving movements and counterforces in the last decades. Second, countermovements opposing progressive movements tend to be backed and fueled by fundamentalist religious groups, which are extraordinarily strong and vital in the United States.

Overall, these evaluations are largely supportive of the hypotheses about factors determining the *strength* and *quality* of movement structure. Although scholars may find the picture oversimplified, and although some features of the context structure may be interpreted in slightly different ways, I think that this approach provides a basis for a more detailed and thorough analysis. A major step would be to move beyond the general traits of both context structure and movement structure developed here.

SUMMARY AND PERSPECTIVES

The preceding discussion should have demonstrated that the task of conceptualizing and empirically analyzing social movement contexts to explain movement structures leads beyond crude schemes. Several dimensions and factors come into play, though not all will be relevant in each empirical case. Because dependent variables such as structure, strategy, mobilization, and outcomes of a social movement do not necessarily covary, we have to be specific about the dependent variable of interest. Accordingly, we need a conceptual framework tuned for this distinct task.

This chapter has focused on movement structures, and I have sought to explain their strength and basic profile by referring to three basic structural types. In general, a social movement may include elements of the grassroots, interest-group, and party models, all to different degrees. We found that the French movements are weak compared to their U.S. and West German counterparts, and that the French movement was strongest in the party-model, the United States in the interest-group model, and the German movement a balance of all three. Only to a minor extent did these patterns seem to result from deliberate choices; each can be interpreted as an adaptation to a movement's relatively stable environment, which is here called the *context structure*. Supposedly a movement structure is an outcome of many trial-and-error processes in which more than national contexts come into play.

In a broader conceptual scheme, the movement structure can be considered an intermediate factor between the context structure and the strategies, actual mobilization, and eventual mobilization outcomes. The idea of political opportunity structures provides an important and useful starting point for conceptualizing movement contexts, but it needs to be broadened and elaborated. Comparisons across movements, across countries, and across time may be the best way to develop and improve such conceptual frameworks.

Building on the provisional explanatory model in the first section, new elements derived from both conceptual reflections and some empirical insights can now be added. First, movement structures do not depend exclusively on the political setting in which social movements are embedded. Social and cultural structures come into play as well. Second, I would argue

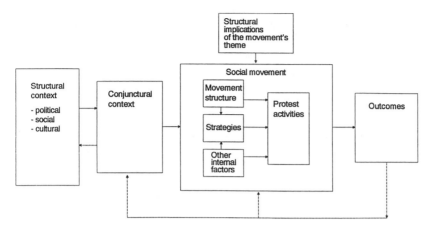

Figure 8.2. Elaborated model for context structures and social movements.

that such a structural context must be conceptualized by taking into account less inert factors which I refer to as the conjunctural structure. In addition, movement-specific opportunities, and links to and diffusion between movements within and across countries, come into play (McAdam and Rucht, 1993). Finally, one has to acknowledge that mobilization and outcomes may feed back into both movement structures/strategies and context structures. In some cases, particular elements of the context structure may even become a target of movements in order to better reach their ultimate goals. For example, a social movement may join the fight for freedom of information to improve chances of influencing a particular policy. Movement successes may create new opportunities.

Whatever such expanded and refined explanatory models look like, there is an underlying assumption: All the variables discussed are features outside of the movement under consideration. Obviously, this assumption can be challenged. The very logic of dealing with movements as distinct entities is less evident when we take into account ties and overlaps with other movements and with organizations not considered part of a movement. Presuming the distinction between "inside" and "outside" of movements is at all meaningful, the question of relevance of internal factors for shaping movement structure, mobilization, and outcome arises. As for movement structure, identifying internal features of the movement and relating them to the structure is implied. Elements that could come into play, for example, are movement ideology, central themes, and aspects of leadership. In some cases, there is certainly an independent effect of a movement's theme on its structure. It is hard to imagine movements fighting for political decentralization but having a completely centralized internal structure. Life-cycle effects may also be inherent in the movement, but this aspect is not discussed here. This does not necessarily lead back to an outdated vision of "natural" life-cycles derived from biology, but could be developed through systematic empirical research. Why should we not expect to see the effects of exhaustion after a movement tries to maintain an extraordinary level of activity?

Taking these various arguments into consideration, we can propose a more elaborate schematic model as shown in Figure 8.2.

This model is no more than a conceptual tool, helping to direct the researcher's attention and to systematize dimensions and variables in a complex field. Obviously, the danger is that the model itself suffers from overcomplexity and lacks parsimonious qualities. However, the degree of complexity is not simply a matter of scientific "style" and individual ambition, but depends largely on the scope and level of analysis. To understand the changes in movement structures, and the interplay of various sets of factors ranging from the context structure, to social movement properties, to movement outcomes, we must go beyond simple models.

9

Organizational form as frame: Collective identity and political strategy in the American labor movement, 1880–1920

ELISABETH S. CLEMENS

Modern society, according to Max Weber, is characterized by the displacement of a rationality of ends by a rationality of means. To date, much of social science has failed to pursue the implications of this claim. The study of ideology remains dominated by a vocabulary of ends, with its emphasis on substantive content, although attention to genre in discourse has begun to intrude on the margins of social history. The analysis of action continues to reference material interest in an endlessly elaborated system of class fractions and contradictory locations, although it is acknowledged that a few idiosyncratic groups such as professionals may have an interest in specific forms of social organization. For the most part, however, means are discussed in terms of presence or absence, resources in terms of more or less. The "how" of organization remains secondary to the "for what?" and "for whom?"

This claim may seem overstated, particularly in the field of social movement theory, where resource-mobilization approaches have been criticized for overemphasizing the mechanics of mobilization at the expense of the questions of collective identity that are central to the new social movement perspective (Klandermans and Tarrow 1988). But if one looks more closely, the role attributed to organization in movements has been conceived quite narrowly. Frequently, organization is conceptualized in rudimentary terms: present or absent as a facilitating or blocking condition (e.g., indigenous organizations and preexisting ties, McAdam 1982; Connell and Voss 1990); more or less as a resource (McCarthy and Zald 1977); bureaucratic or not as a possible limit on the radical potential of a movement (see Jenkins 1977). These treatments of organizations fail to capture the rich and varied dialogue about organizing that suffuses social movements and to consider the theoretical implications of all this talk about "how."

In this talk about "how," organizational form appears as a movement frame which both informs collective identity and orients groups toward other actors and institutions. Understood as a movement frame, organizational form defines groups as "people who act together in a particular way" and portrays problems as amenable to a particular type of action. This view of organizational form also profits from a more elaborated understanding of opportunity structures, which moves beyond the imagery of open or closed spaces to consider distinctive configurations of opportunity (see Gamson and Meyer, Chapter 12 in this volume) and, consequently, the possibilities of "fit" with different movement frames or mobilizing structures. Tinkering, in the face of ambiguity, competition or opposition, movement activists are viewed as *bricoleurs* who reassemble familiar forms of organization in order to mobilize challenges to existing institutions.

Challenges are, of course, not necessarily successful. Indeed, the work of invoking or implementing organizational forms is seen with particular clarity when such efforts are frustrated and redirected. A series of such redirections characterized the political development of organized labor in the United States in the decades surrounding the turn of the century. As commentators bemoaned the failure of organizational models successful in Europe – why no socialism in the United States? – American organizers were forced repeatedly to find new forms of mobilization as familiar models were discredited. (See the essay by Kim Voss, Chapter 10 in this volume; also Hattam 1983: chap. 4.) At a time when the institutions of political participation and governance were objects of widespread contestation (Clemens 1990a; Skowronek 1982), diverse components of the labor movement struggled both over and with multiple forms of organization. Labels that might seem to designate different ends actually signified different identities and strategies of action. Virtually all members of the working class would agree on the value of food and sanitation, but "bread and butter unionism" and "sewer socialism" invoked different identity frames, one rooted in craft solidarities and the market, the other in political loyalties and the neighborhood.

These identities implied different strategies of collective action (bargaining with employers versus competing in elections) and orientations to the opportunities afforded by markets and politics. Struggles over organizational form focused disputes on the proper relation of labor to the market, to the polity, and to other social institutions, as well as on the distribution of power within organized labor itself. One camp, associated with Samuel Gompers and the leadership of the American Federation of Labor through the first decades of the century, was strongly committed to craft-based organizing in the labor market. As the 1888 contribution of the miners' National Progressive Union made clear, this form of organization entailed both a statement of collective identity and a set of goals and values:

Upon matters of wages and obnoxious rules that oppress and rob us, we should not look to legislative bodies for protection. It would be unmanly for us as miners to ask either national or State legislators to exercise a paternal surveillance over us and the difficulties which we ourselves can supervise and control. (quoted in Marks 1989: 189)

A second pairing of organizational form and collective identity was promoted by the socialist-influenced Wisconsin State Federation of Labor. The preamble to its constitution declared:

We, the organized laboring people of the State of Wisconsin, in convention assembled, for the purpose of common defense against the evils from which our class now suffers, declare that the ballot is labor's most effective weapon, and in its use we must be educated and united. Our only hope of industrial emancipation lies in alliance with the progressive political forces of the times. Our great error in the past has been in the support of parties pledged to the perpetuation of an industrial system which has produced an arrogant plutocracy and impoverished the people at large. (*Official Directory* 1896–97: 15)

Both groups opposed themselves to politics as usual, but proposed different identities and forms for action: the self-governance of manly producers versus the political (but not partisan) mobilization of workers as citizens. This debate over the legitimate forms of organization, identities, and strategies of collective action by workers crystallized in a series of struggles over the relation of organized labor to political parties.[1]

The outcome of this debate was not a mere formality; the struggle over models of organization determined the political capacities of labor, the passage of policies to regulate markets, the establishment of agencies to implement those policies, and, not least, the relationships between organized labor and these new state agencies. In the next two sections, I sketch models of social organization and practical action to support this claim. Insofar as "organizational form" implies both a *cognitive* model that informs identity and those *structures* of relations that characterize social institutions, form both frames actions and articulates those actions with the existing system of political organization, at times producing institutional change.[2] This process is then illustrated by the struggle over the forms of economic unionism, partisanship, and nonpartisanship within the American labor movement of the late nineteenth and early twentieth centuries.

THE MATRIX OF ORGANIZATIONAL FORM

Form frames action and identity at the same time that it determines the possibilities for articulation with other movements and institutions. One role of movement activists and entrepreneurs is to creatively recombine existing components of a society's organizational repertoire in the hope of optimizing the social potential for mobilization while attaining a working, but not too close, relation to political institutions and elites. Depending on the circumstances, this tinkering may be shaped by competition among movement organizations or between movements and political institutions. To borrow a term from the anthropologist Claude Lévi-Strauss, this cobbling together of organizational models may be described as *bricolage:*

Neither the images of myth nor the materials of the bricoleur are products of "becoming" pure and simple. Previously, then they were part of other coherent sets, they possessed the rigour which they seem to lack as soon as we observe them in their new use. What is more, they still possess this precision in so far as they are not raw materials but wrought products: terms in language or, in the case of the bricoleur, in a technological system. They are therefore condensed expressions of necessary relations which impose constraints with various repercussions at each stage of their employment. Their necessity is not simple and univocal. But it is there nevertheless as the invariance of a semantic or aesthetic order, which characterizes the group of transformations to which they lend themselves, which, as we have seen, are not unlimited. (1966: 35–36)

If *bricolage* is to do more than provide academic legitimation for telling stories about history, the critical issue is to understand in what sense organizational models are "condensed expressions of necessary relations which impose constraints with various repercussions at each stage of their employment."[3] Only to the extent that a society's repertoires of organization can be mapped as structures of constraint and opportunity can we analyze the interplay of action and institution in the development of social movements.

Such a social matrix of organizational form would capture the social distribution of organizational repertoires at three levels: normative, practical, and institutional. In the first sense, the distribution of repertoires is determined by a culture's rules or prescriptions about what actors may use what organizational models for what purposes. Organizational models may be categorized as "appropriate for men," "appropriate for politics," "appropriate for rural communities," and so forth. Combinations of models within categories are likely to provoke little resistance, but at the same time offer little potential for institutional change. Combinations across opposed categories – such as male and female – will meet with resistance, perhaps repression. Novel and potentially change-producing combinations will draw on different but more or less adjacent categories. For example, elsewhere I have argued that women's groups were able to enter the political arena *not* by appropriating the masculine and fraternal models of partisanship, but by using the clearly public but comparatively gender-neutral forms of business organization (Clemens 1993).

If everyone knew and did only, but all, that their culture dictated for them, the first and second levels of the matrix would be identical. But real life rarely follows the rules. At the level of practices, the distribution of organizational repertoires maps knowledge (either experiential or cultural) of different models of action. During the late nineteenth century, not all men shared the experience of military service, although most would have some cultural knowledge of this form of organization. Other men surely did not know the practices of a fraternal order, but had a reasonably good understanding of what went on in their wives' reading clubs. The reverse was also true, perhaps more so since the cultural privileging of men's activities meant that male models of organization were publicized and, therefore, asymmetrically available to women. The possibilities of combination at the practical level echo those at the normative level. Similarity in the organizational models employed by individuals or groups increases the possibility of coordination, while decreasing the potential for novelty or institutional change.

Finally, organizational repertoires are distributed in an institutional sense. Some models are embedded in clusters of institutions, relatively impervious to change, and often actively protected by those with an interest in those institutions. By virtue of being embedded within a relatively powerful and resource-rich movement, the model of craft unionism was fiercely defended by actors with an interest in preserving their own power and privileges. Other organizational models may be widely distributed at the normative and practical level, but not embedded within social institutions. Such models are particularly vulnerable to change.

If these three levels are combined in a single matrix, a map of organizational constraint and opportunity emerges. In some regions, organizational models are densely connected across levels. In such cases, there are clear rules about who should use a particular organizational form, members of that category actually do use it, and mobilization in this form is actively supported, legitimated, and reproduced. The association of adult white males and party politics, a product of intense socialization and cultural elaboration in the nineteenth century (Baker 1983; McGerr 1986), is one example of a configuration of rules, experience, and institutions that restricted some forms of political action and facilitated others. Elsewhere repertoires overlap and slip as one moves from norms to practices to institutions. These discontinuities represent opportunities for institutional change. By mobilizing individuals around a new (but culturally acceptable) model or inspiring them to use familiar models for new purposes, social movements serve as catalysts for the rearrangement and possible transformation of the array of organizational models that characterizes a society.

ORGANIZATIONAL FORM AS FRAME

The language of framing (Snow et al. 1986) provides a valuable tool for addressing the dynamic of organized challenge and institutional change. Although discussions of master frames and ideologies have tended to emphasize their cognitive and normative aspects – What is the world like and what in it is to be valued? – these aspects should not be divorced from considerations of practical action. Answers to the pragmatic question of "How do we organize?" reverberate inward to the shaping of collective identity and outward to link movements to institutions or opportunity structures.

Framing and practical action

By pointing to the links between the forms of social organization and the frames with which we orient ourselves to social experience, I begin by ignoring one of Goffman's first qualifications to his discussion in *Frame Analysis*. "This book," he argued, "is about the organization of experience – something that an individual actor can take into his mind – and not the organization of society" (1974: 13). Thus, his discussions of framing concentrate on the varieties of primary frameworks – natural or social – and their reinterpretation of "keying" as different orders of reality: play, rehearsal, or fantasy. Play and rehearsal, however, are forms of social organization as well as orders of reality.

So what are the possible connections between interpretations of social reality and the reality of social structure? One possible answer is found in the work of Pierre Bourdieu who developed the concept of *habitus,* an internalized disposition or conditioning that generates actions which tend, in turn, to reproduce social structures or fields of practice. The analysis of *habitus* is an alternative to accounts that portray action as generated by "a *repertoire of rules*" (1984: 101–2; 1977: 2). In complex societies, however, where many relations and practices are institutionalized and enacted as conventions (of which an understanding may be acquired or transmitted), much action does take on the qualities of rule-following. Some of these rules may be abstract, but many are exemplary, more like recipes than laws. To analyze action under these macrosocial conditions, theorists have developed models of practical action intermediate to the application of abstract rules or the enactment of an internalized disposition. Invoking terms such as script, toolkit, or exemplar, these arguments suggest that action entails the use of generalizable yet concrete models, based on a culturally acquired understanding of which models are appropriate to which actors and situations (Bourdieu 1977: 200 n. 20; DiMaggio and Powell 1991; Goffman 1974; Kellerman 1991; Swidler 1986).[4]

This line of argument has been developed in order to explain action, but models of action also imply models of organization. If figure and ground are reversed, a script for action is simultaneously a set of expectations about relations to other actors. In modern societies, scripts for action and models of organization are not only learned through lived experience but transmitted through formal institutions and the mass media. Commenting on the behavior of the boys in her class, a Chicago kindergarten teacher observed: "Half of the boys have seen *Star Wars* and *The Empire Strikes Back* and they teach what they know to the other boys. There is enough chapter and verse to add a new twist to the serialized version acted out daily." In the process, the boys internalize particular understandings of values (good and evil) and roles or scripts (heroes and villains), but they also learn about the models of organization that are relevant to the pursuit of such values or the enactment of such roles:

Now Franklin ties up the loose ends, giving Power Droid greater authority and placing him on the good side. "Sandman is the boss of the Jawas. Power Droid is the boss of the Sand People. Obi-Wan Kenobi is the boss of Power Droid. And Obi-Wan Kenobi don't have a boss."
The children think a great deal about leaders and followers. They are increasingly aware of the social order that exists beyond their control. This is particularly true of the boys, whose tendency to play in large groups makes the establishment of leaders essential. The huge Star Wars cast enables everyone to be someone's boss. In the playground after lunch, Jonathan announces that he is Sandman. "I'm the boss of the Jawas!" he says, although no one present is identified as the Jawas. (Paley 1984: 21–23)

Repertoires of organization are thus one form of cultural competence. Like Bourdieu's cultural capital or Swidler's cultural toolkit, organizational repertoires may be characterized by their distribution across different social groups and their relation to existing social or political institutions. This distribution will be the product of socialization, exposure to various organizational models, and the fit or resonance between the two. Thus repertoires of organization vary across groups within a society, among societies, and over time.

This account of practical action is compatible on a number of levels with recent analyses of social movements. As Tilly suggested with the concept of "repertoires of collective action," action is shaped by and coordinated through the development of those models or scripts shared within a particular society at a particular historical juncture (1978).[5] As a resource, the presence of shared models facilitates mobilization. These models may also inform the development of collective identity. The answer to "Who are we?" need not be a quality or a noun; "We are people who do these sorts of things in this particular way" can be equally compelling. Finally, attention to the relation between the organizational models deployed by social movements and the social distribution of organizational repertoires echoes the analysis of "frame resonance" by Snow and Benford: "Hypothetically, if a frame is empirically credible, experientially commensurable, and narratively resonant, the stronger the consensus mobilizations and the more fertile the soil for action mobilization" (1988: 211). Translated into the language of organization, to the extent that the proposed model of organization is believed to work, involves practices and organizational relations that are already familiar, and is consonant with the organization of the rest of those individuals' social worlds, mobilization around that model is more likely.[6]

Organizational form and institutional change

In the context of social movement theory, the spread of organizational forms across arenas of social life may be reconceived as a process of frame alignment (Snow et al. 1986). Just as activists construct links among diverse accounts of grievances, knitting them together in the context of some "master frame," so a common organizational form may serve as a foundation for alliances among groups with seemingly distinct interests. Thus, many nineteenth-century farmers and workers sustained a common identity as the "producing classes" well into the period of industrialization, aided by their reliance on a common organizational form, the fraternal order, as the template for both the Patrons of Husbandry (aka the Grange) and the Knights of Labor. Through a process analogous to frame-bridging, an organizational model may become embedded within a reinforcing cluster of institutions (Jepperson 1991) when actors discover that they share a particular set of practices or social arrangements. The overall robustness of that model is enhanced both through interaction and insofar as one actor can point to the organizational practices of the other as a source of legitimation.

A dynamic akin to frame amplification characterizes periods of debate or contestation over organizational models. As will be evident throughout the attempts of labor activists to construct a viable model of political organization, mobilization involves explicit debate and dramatization of taken-for-granted, socially embedded, models of organization. As such debates intensify, strategic choices between organizational models reveal themselves to be also choices between goals and collective identities. Finally, the processes of frame extension and frame transformation point to the displacement of organizational models from one arena of social activity to another. To the extent that one accepts a modified version of *bricolage,* where one's materials include very little that is new, the difference between extension and transformation is essentially one of focus of attention. When the group or groups studied attempt to export a model of organization to new arenas, we speak of extension. When a new model appears within the scope of a study, we speak of transformation or, perhaps, replacement. The probability that any given reframing will take hold and shape the relations of practices of a group will be determined largely by the local distribution of organizational repertoires and their compatibility with the newly introduced frame (Jepperson 1991).

Resonance with respect to organizational form recalls a powerful and pessimistic line of argument within political sociology. Represented by Michels's "iron law of oligarchy" and Weber's "routinization of charisma," resonance or isomorphism at the level of organizational form is associated with cooptation, not with the mobilization of movements outside routine political channels. But this apparent contradiction reflects the different foci of the two literatures. The discussion of framing in social movement research has concentrated on the resonance of movement frames with widely held beliefs and ideologies, while political sociologists emphasize the relation of challenging movements to formal political institutions.

This division of labor has been further reified both terminologically – since movements with regularized relations to the political system are defined as "*non*social movement organizations" (Klandermans and Tarrow 1988: 13, 23; but see Gamson 1975) – and theoretically to the extent that the new social movements approach has built on Habermas's analysis of modern society as characterized by an increasing divergence of "system" and "life-world" (Habermas 1981; Rucht 1988). But this conceptual distinction may be fruitfully redefined as a matter of the degree of difference between the organizational repertoires of everyday life and those embedded in political institutions.

To the extent that the organizational models deployed by a movement resonate with the repertoires of organization familiar to members of a society, the mobilization potential of that movement is increased. But insofar as a movement invokes models isomorphic to those of formal political institutions, it is vulnerable to cooptation (of course, insofar as a movement uses models incompatible with formal politics – such as terrorism – it attracts increasingly repressive responses, see the essay by Donatella della Porta in Chapter 3 this volume). Yet some degree of isomorphism is necessary if movements are to gain access to, and leverage over, established political elites and processes. The conceptual abyss between movements and politics may be bridged if one begins with an image of the social world as comprising multiple more or less bounded, more or less compatible organizational fields (Clemens 1993).

To the extent that a movement's identity and actions are bound up with particular models of organization, one of the most important consequences of movement activity is the displacement of organizational models from one sphere of life to another. Movements, like individuals, may try to remake the world in their own image. Insofar as movements are grounded in the forms of everyday life, the practices of family, community, and fraternal lodge may shape the vision of a transformed polity that guides action. Of course, it is equally true that insofar as movements appropriate the practices of formal political institutions, the organizational models informing social life may be similarly displaced. At an organizational level, the practices of social movements correspond to what philosopher Nancy Fraser has termed the "'discursive political' or 'politic*ized*' – [which] contrasts both with what is not contested in public at all and also with what is contested only by and within respectively specialized, enclaved, and/or segmented publics" (1990: 204). In trying to reorder the world, movements select, recombine, and transform the organizational models and practices that undergird institutions.[7]

The availability of alternative forms or models of organization will have comparatively few consequences for action in the highly institutionalized arenas of formal politics. Defining institutions as "those social patterns that, when chronically reproduced, owe their survival to relatively self-activating social processes," Ronald Jepperson argues that the structured relations among these orders or patterns (of which "organizational models" are a subset) determine the probabilities of institutional change:

> A given institution is less likely to be vulnerable to intervention if it is more embedded in a framework of institutions. It is more embedded if it has been long in place (so that other practices have adapted to it) or more centrally located within a framework (so that it is deeply situated). It is more embedded if it is integrated within a framework by unifying accounts based in common principles and rules. Further, the greater the linkage of this institution to constraints conceived to be socially exogenous – namely to either socially exogenous (transcendental) moral authority or presumed laws of nature – the less the vulnerability to intervention. (1991: 145, 151–52)

The impetus for institutional change – the substitution of one set of self-reproducing patterns for another – is, therefore, most likely at the margins of elaborated and integrated institutional fields. And to the extent that such fields are buttressed by "unifying accounts" and "moral authority," challengers will be most favored when they appeal to an alternative but widely accepted set of accounts and principles. If, at the level of discourse, an "arena of contesting [interpretive] packages . . . is the battleground for forming mobilization potentials" (Gamson 1988: 223), conflicts over organizational models are likely to be most heated and productive of change in the interstices between highly institutionalized fields of social action.[8]

The next section addresses one particular institutional change – the establishment of extrapartisan, interest-group politics in the United States – from the perspective of one social movement or movement industry: organized labor. For the purposes of this analysis, I use "organized" in its broadest sense; the puzzle is to understand how a highly variegated history of collective action condensed into a particular institutional form: the labor-market union, organized around distinctive craft skills, with indirect ties both to political parties and state agencies. The answer, I argue, is to be found in the efforts of activists to adopt and adapt models of organization that both resonated with existing repertoires of social organization and articulated with established political institutions.

COLLECTIVE IDENTITY AND POLITICAL STRATEGY IN THE LABOR MOVEMENT

The profound politicization of American labor since the late nineteenth century has often been overlooked, in part because it is viewed against the development of strong labor or socialist parties in European industrial democracies, in part because modern union politics appear much less explicitly political than the campaigns of the Knights of Labor, the Union Laborites, and the innumerable Workingmen's parties of the previous century. But this narrow focus on the campaign trail and the ballot box misses the fact that "unions today are oriented to politics in a way undreamt of in the years of their early growth." As members of a "legislative polity" (Orren 1991: 218), they participate in the decisions of state agencies, lobby for and against legislation, mobilize money and votes for candidates. In both Europe and the United States, the origins of this intense politicization of labor lie in the period prior to World War I, in the growing "interpenetration of labor market institutions and the state, of economics and politics" (Marks 1989: 15–17).

The story is further complicated since it begins with efforts at *depoliticization*. Although comparative macrosocial accounts typically sketch a steady expansion of political participation and state intervention into ever more realms of social life, by the first decades of the nineteenth century national politics already pervaded the social world of adult white men in the United States. By this, much more is indicated than simple universal (white) manhood suffrage. The development of the party organization during the 1820s and 1830s entailed the invention of social practices, rituals, and a system of organized relations that structured community life. Through caucuses and conventions, local mobilization was linked to the biennial and quadrennial elections of Congress and the president. The affective hold of these institutional arrangements is suggested by the frequency of organizational borrowings from and metaphorical appeals to religion: "Even the procedures of voting replicated ecclesiastical habits, with communicants approaching a designated window (sometimes even called an altar), demarcated by rail, rope, or board" (Baker 1983: 271). Political independence or nonpartisanship was labeled heresy (Silbey 1991: 129) and, by the end of the century, commentators felt that party had gone so far as to outstrip religion in the loyalties of many citizens:

With the great mass of the voting population of this country the political sentiment which binds them to the party organizations is as strong and enduring as the religious sentiment cherished among Christians of the various sects, and it is not improbable that there are more backsliders among the Christian converts than are found among the adherents of the great parties. (Brown 1897: 8)

However powerful the affective ties between citizens and party, the system nevertheless excluded many of the grievances and concerns of otherwise avid partisans. Constructed as organizations to maximize votes in national elections (and thereby to control patronage within the federal government), the parties conducted local elections in national terms and nominated local candidates on the basis of partisan contributions rather than for their positions on issues of local relevance. In the decades following the Civil War, these excluded concerns and constituencies fed into multiplying social movements and third-party efforts: agrarian discontent, labor mobilization as well as occasional violence, utopian efforts, the temperance movement, and an unprecedented mobilization of women. Yet the institutionalized arrangements of the party system ensured that these grievances would not be easily translated into political power. Even those with the organizational skills to mount a third-party challenge within established channels had little incentive to do so:

Why, however, does it so seldom happen that the professional politicians, who "know the ropes," and know where to get the necessary funds, seek to wreck a party in order to found a new one more to their mind? Because they are pretty well satisfied with the sphere which existing parties give them, and comprehend from their practical experience how hazardous such an experiment would be. (Bryce 1895: 50–51)

From senators to precinct captains and ward-heelers, the party system presented a powerful set of disincentives to mobilization around collective grievances rather than partisan loyalties. The litter of failed third-party movements provided an additional cautionary lesson. Therefore, the first requirement for the mobilization of labor (or any other social group) around a set of grievances or interests was the elaboration of forms of social solidarity independent of party.

The fraternal model

One template for organization outside the party system was provided by the Masons. In the United States, the second half of the nineteenth century saw a flowering of fraternal organizations. According to estimates from the 1890s, the fraternal orders enrolled one in five to eight American males (Carnes 1989: 1) and the model of fraternalism was adopted by the Patrons of Husbandry and by the Knights of Labor, as well as by professional and craft associations. The by-laws of fraternal organizations routinely forbade the discussion of politics and celebrated the distinctive solidarity that resulted. In 1880, the *Freemason's Repository* queried:

Is it not a matter of rejoicing that Masonry knows neither sect nor party, and that the Lodge-room is the one place where men of all opinions can meet in a blessed communion? In these days when there is so much excitement in the political world, it surely counts for something of good that so restful an atmosphere pervades the place of Masonic meeting, and the brethren who oppose each other on party grounds can here enter into sweet fellowship, and strike hands together for the advancement of those interests and principles which attach to the Institution. (Quoted in Dumenil 1984: 102)

This insistent separation of interests and politics strikes a contemporary reader as odd and implausible. The model of interest-group politics, after all, presumes an almost natural connection between the two. But the widespread appropriation of fraternal organizational models reproduced this disarticulation of solidarity and political action throughout the associational web of late nineteenth-century American life: "The conscientious Knight [of Labor] at one moment was advised to 'let political parties and political clubs, of whatever name, severely alone'; the next moment he was told to 'organize, co-operate, educate till the stars and stripes wave over a contented and happy people" (Fink 1983: 24–25).

Other elements of the fraternal model created further obstacles to its deployment as a vehicle for collective action. If the lodges offered an alternative to partisan solidarity, they did not offer a *political* alternative to partisanship. Rather than aggregating preferences and grievances within electoral units, the lodge form tended to fragment communities and blur potential lines of political conflict. In addition to the predictable divisions of occupation, ethnicity, and even military service, most towns and cities featured the distinctive totemic divisions of Victorian America: the Knights of Pythias, the Improved Order of Red Men, the Independent Order of Odd Fellows, the Modern Woodmen of America, and innumerable others, above all the Masonic orders. These fraternal orders blurred lines of class conflict on both cultural and organizational levels. The rhetoric and ritual of the orders, with their progression through elaborated ranks and degree sequences, enacted a model of social mobility as available to all and further suppressed occupational identities by dramatizing differences of gender and race (Carnes 1989; Clawson 1985, 1989). Organizationally, fraternal orders linked localities and bridged class differences. Both elite and would-be politicians frequently boasted multiple affiliations,[9] ties that connected them, however tenuously, to their less-privileged constituencies: "The turn-of-the century fraternal order enabled men at considerable social distance from one another to think of each other as brothers, thus articulating their unity of interest and common identity" (Clawson 1985: 690).

The fraternal model of organization thus played a highly ambivalent role in the political development of labor in the United States. In its own right, as Mary Ann Clawson argues, fraternalism tended to depoliticize the working class by generating cross-class ties of brotherhood, taking energy away from more narrowly framed labor mobilization, and enacting a vision of unconstrained social mobility (1985: 674). At the same time, however, the widespread availability of the fraternal model made possible the development of forms of social solidarity outside the party system. Two of these quasi-fraternal organizations, the Knights of Labor and the Patrons of Husbandry (a.k.a. the Grange), were central to the mobilization of industrial and agrarian discontent from the 1870s through the 1890s. But the legacy of the fraternal model, its insistent exclusion of partisan divisions, prevented the articulation of these organizations with the political system and the translation of mass mobilization into electoral or legislative success. Even as they enjoyed a series of victories in local elections during the 1880s, the Knights of Labor avoided "the continuing official ban on 'direct' political activity by forming shadow 'progressive' committees or political clubs'" (Fink 1983: 26). If the labor movement was to gain leverage over elected office at all levels of government, an organizational form that both consolidated strength in localities and transcended localism in the name of a common endeavor was required. American men had all too vivid a familiarity with an organizational model meeting these requirements: the army.

The military model

The Civil War of 1860–65 is often described as the first modern war, complete with mass mobilization of the citizenry. Of northern men between fifteen and forty-four, more than one-third served in this army; the proportion was considerably higher in the Confederate states. Even as late as 1910, as many as 40 percent of elderly men in some northern states received Civil War pensions, a figure that reflects both the extent of service and the intense political dynamic expanding the pensions system in the late nineteenth century (Skocpol 1992: chap. 3). Military practices pervaded social life following the war. As Ralph Waldo Emerson explained in 1863: "War organizes. . . . [M]y interest in my Country is not primary but professional" (quoted in Bledstein 1976: 30).[10] Parties intensified their use of military metaphors and practices as campaigns focused on "waving the bloody shirt" (Silbey 1991: chaps. 5 and 12). And veteran status was the requirement for membership in one of the largest and most influential of the period's quasi-fraternal associations, the Grand Army of the Republic. With the military model providing a primary, and fundamentally political, identity, fraternal practices could then be imported since it was assumed that members had no partisan differences to be left at the lodge-room door.[11]

Unlike fraternalism, military status transcended identities grounded in occupation, locality, ethnicity, religion, and, potentially, even race by invoking a political rationale (common national interests) rather than a mythical brotherhood detached from other social relations and identities. But in a literal translation to civilian life, the military model presented the same obstacle to labor mobilization as had the fraternal orders: In its familiar deployments, the military model crossed classes and required hierarchical relations.

Yet in the American context, a more egalitarian version of the military model was available in the mobilization of the citizenry into militias, a form of organization that meshed neatly with two political tactics that aggregated individual actions or opinions into collective action, the march and the petition. In response to the devastating economic depression of 1893, Jacob Coxey combined his promotion of federal funding for good roads and other public works with Carl Browne's experience in organizing protests and marches of the unemployed. Out of this synthesis came Coxey's Army, the "petition in boots." Culminating in a march on the U.S. capital on May 1, 1894, by a fraction of the thousands who had joined eight different "armies" mobilized in the western and midwestern states, the movement transcended local identities[12] while drawing freely on tactics and organizational models familiar to Americans. Indeed, the repertoire of action employed by the marchers reads like a listing of summer movies: A contingent from the Pacific Northwest hijacked a train, chased by representatives of law and order; other groups built rafts – Kelly's "navy" floated through Iowa while a Denver contingent struggled down the Platte to Omaha and eventually reached St. Louis; another contingent of Kelly's army (including the author Jack London) worked its way across Iowa with a series of exhibition baseball games.

By embedding a radical demand for federal intervention to support the unemployed in familiar organizational models and narratives, the Coxeyites secured a rather surprising immunity from direct repressive responses in an era when violent suppression of labor was not uncommon (although contingents making their way through the Southwest were less fortunate as authorities marooned their boxcars in the middle of the desert, a tactic later used to suppress the region's Industrial Workers of the World). Local support for the marchers also drew on familiar forms, notably as women "served as members of home guard units and . . . auxiliaries, patterned after Civil War organizations that women had formed to send the amenities of life to soldiers on the battlefield" (Schwantes 1985: 127). This strategy of organization mapped onto popular expectations while also matching the requirements of an expanding national media system:

What Coxey and Browne essentially did was to create an unemployment adventure story that the press found irresistible. With characters sufficiently colorful and the perils of the journey sufficiently great, curiosity alone drew to the drama readers who cared little or nothing about complex economic issues or what it all portended. (Schwantes 1985: 46)

Indeed, Coxey's Army marked a turning point in the role of the media in movement mobilization and influence. As Coxey's own contingent out of Massillon, Ohio, floated down the Chesapeake and Ohio Canal toward the capital, they were followed by a "press boat," a barge rechristened the "Demon Flyer" after Browne's charge that reporters were "argus-eyed demons of hell." In the now familiar pattern, reporters responded to the novel challenge of managing the collective coverage of a movement by drawing on fraternal organizational models: "The reporters covering the march organized a fraternity – the AEDH – led by archdemon Austin Beach of the *Pittsburgh Times,* and made honorary members of the Western Union telegraphers who accompanied them" (Schwantes 1985: 77). The unprecedented coverage – reporters simply tapped into telegraph lines along the way to send out a constant stream of stories – in turn contributed to the nation's developing repertoire of organization. In the following decade, labor activist "Mother" Jones would organize "children's marches" and advocates of women's rights would lead "suffrage hikes" to publicize their causes.

The impressive potential of Coxey's Army for mobilizing both participation and public support reflects the synthesis of the familiar and the novel at the level of both norms and practices of organization. As Carlos Schwantes argues:

Ostensibly a crusade for jobs and an advocate of what we now call the modern welfare state, its methods and traditions were largely those of the classic frontier; and the transcontinental odyssey undertaken by the Kelleyites and other argonauts from the Pacific Slope was basically a variation on a familiar theme. It was a late nineteenth-century version of the journey overland by pioneer seekers of El Dorado or the new Garden of Eden. (1985: 261)

By appealing to the same "unifying accounts based in common principles and rules" that had framed the nation's westward push across the continent (Jepperson 1991; Johansen 1967; Starr 1981), the militialike mobilization of Coxey's Army resonated with popular political culture, thereby acquiring a legitimacy that protected the movement from being reframed in terms of tramps and vagabondage.[13]

But while the military model was powerful in the service of mobilization, it raised problems with respect to political tactics. After all, what armies do is conquer, and those attacked may legitimately resist. Therefore, to march on the Capitol in the form of an army seemed to invite repression and, even if the peace was preserved, it was unclear what an army would do to influence a legislature. So, on May 1, 1894, the first contingents to arrive organized a parade to Capitol Hill, met with violent repression by the police, distributed a statement to the press, and retreated to set up an encampment nearby. By late summer, Maryland policemen and the Virginia militia would drive out the remaining Coxeyites. As the Bonus Army would learn four decades later, to voice grievances by mounting a military march on Washington was to invite repression.

In its efforts to construct a political vehicle outside the party system, the labor movement enjoyed mixed success in the case of Coxey's Army. The Army's appropriation of familiar organizational models and "legitimate" tactics gave it a quite remarkable potential to mobilize participation and consensus around the politically radical goal of unemployment relief through federally supported public works and irrigation projects. As a statement of collective identity, military metaphors would also continue to define categories of persons deserving extraordinary public support. In presenting a bill for a national old-age pension in 1910, Socialist Congressman Victor Berger of Milwaukee "told the House of Representatives that his object was to provide a pension for veterans of the industrial wars who, unlike Civil War veterans, had been forgotten" (Miller 1973: 53). In a few western states, this logic did triumph, but only for veterans of territorial settlement; old age homes and pensions were granted not to workers but to "pioneers," a status that typically required twenty-five years' residency in a single county. But the military model had self-defeating implications for political action. Armies come to conquer; therefore, the use of this organizational model tended to legitimate a violent response by established political authorities. Another model of articulating the grievances of workers with the nation's political institutions would have to be constructed.

Unions in politics

At first glance, the most obvious path would be to connect the fundamental units of the nineteenth-century labor movement, craft-based locals, with political mobilization. But in the United States, craft unionism and political institutions are organized around very different principles. Like the fraternal orders, craft unions fragmented communities while linking locals into national or international associations. The organization of politics, by contrast, is profoundly territorial. To secure power, a movement must be able to produce electoral majorities within geographically defined constituencies. If unions were to become political players, the structure of organized labor itself would have to be challenged, and with it the power and perquisites of the established leadership. Not surprisingly, efforts to construct a model of political action for unions were a source of sustained controversy within organized labor.

These tensions were reflected in the weak form of political engagement advocated by the leadership of the American Federation of Labor, the "friends and enemies" strategy that was finally adopted only in 1906. Disavowing both affiliation with one of the major parties and those third-party strategies discredited by repeated failure in the nineteenth century, the AFL concentrated on endorsing candidates and developing a lobbying capacity at the national level – although, at that time, most labor legislation fell within the realm of state governments.[14] If the political influence of labor was to be expanded outside the jurisdiction of the federal government, union action also had to be coordinated at the state and local levels. As the California State Federation of Labor proclaimed at its first convention:

We declare our purposes to be to devise means for the complete organization of labor in California; to establish better communication between the labor unions of the State; to secure united and harmonious action in all matters affecting our welfare; to circulate labor literature and promote economic intelligence; to create a public sentiment more favorable to trade unions; to prevent unfavorable legislation and make known the enemies of organized labor; to collect statistics concerning California labor for the better information of our law-makers; to see to the enforcement of all laws calculated to benefit the laboring people . . . (*Proceedings* 1901: 3)

The claim that a political rather than purely economic identity should be central to organization of labor was not limited to avowed socialists but informed the actions of many state and local groups. Efforts to map models of organization onto the structure of the federal system were crucial to the success of other movements, including the political efforts of formally disenfranchised women (Clemens 1990, 1993; Skocpol 1992). But such a reorganization seriously threatened the power of the national leadership of the AFL as well as the leadership of each national or international craft union.

Analyses of the American labor movement have tended to stress the clash between craft and industry as the basis for organization, but this approach ignores the struggles among labor activists over citizenship versus craft as primary principles of identity. In part, this bias reflects the considerable success of the AFL leadership at suppressing forms of labor organization based on the constituencies recognized by the system of electoral politics; representation and voting privileges at national conventions minimized the role of city centrals and state federations while privileging the craft-based internationals. But the representation of such geographically defined labor organizations within the AFL was not nearly so threatening as the repeated efforts to create ties among these organizations that were not mediated by the craft unions.

A number of these attempts were led by Social Democrats in the Wisconsin labor movement, a constant source of opposition to the established AFL leadership.[15] In 1902, the Milwaukee Federated Trades Council invited city central bodies of the AFL to join in a National Municipal Labor League, a proposal that the AFL squashed (Gavett 1965: 100–1). Three years later, the Wisconsin State Federation of Labor sent out invitations to all state federations to attend a national conference to promote uniform labor legislation: "Past experience has taught us, and we have become convinced that legislation of great importance is difficult to obtain in a single State, but perhaps possible by a general demand by all State Federations all along the same line, at the same time." The equivocal response from California suggests the difficulty of constructing acceptable means for joint action: "While we are in perfect sympathy with the objects herein sought to be attained, we do not believe it advisable at this time to send a delegate to such convention." The WiSFL did not give up and continued to urge delegates of state federations to meet separately at the annual AFL convention or to use the AFL newsletter as a way of coordinating their actions (CaSFL *Proceedings* 1906: 24–25; WaSFL *Proceedings* 1913: 87; WiSFL *Proceedings* 1905: 36; 1906: 18; 1911: 67–68; 1915: 55). In each case, the AFL blocked the development of a system of federal relations within the labor movement. Having built an integrated set of institutions on the model of the craft union, the AFL successfully resisted restructuring in accordance with different principles or identities.

Prevented from building a truly federated political movement, individual city centrals and state federations constructed new models of organization to secure influence in their own locales. In Washington State, both the Spokane Trades Council and the Seattle Central Labor Council opposed AFL craft policy. In Seattle, the council developed a politically powerful form of organization midway between "simple" craft unions and politicized industrial unions. Named after a prominent local labor leader, "Duncanism"

consisted of three elements: (1) strong central control of all unions in the area by the central labor council; (2) close cooperation of allied trades in an industry through the trades councils, cooperation of trade councils, and their informal allegiance to the Central Labor Council; and (3) the attempt to get all agreements between management and the various craft locals within a single industry to expire simultaneously so that labor could bargain as a unit. Duncanism, therefore, led to the accumulation of vast power in the hands of the Central Labor Council – power which reduced the hold of the international unions over their Seattle locals. Until 1920, Duncanism operated informally in order to avoid giving the AFL Executive Central grounds for punitive action against the Seattle Central. (Friedheim 1964: 48–49)

Similar efforts to strengthen the city central were made in Los Angeles (Stimson 1955: 199, 276) and the California State Federation of Labor adopted a resolution recommending to its affiliated unions that where such unions are closely allied, when they enter into contracts with employers, such contracts be uniform in regard to time of expiration (*Proceedings* 1907: 36). Given the character of local organization, it is perhaps not surprising that Seattle was the site of one of the largest general strikes in the nation after World War I and that Los Angeles labor was part of a movement that nearly elected a Socialist to the mayor's office in 1910, a show of strength that prompted an intensification of the repressive open shop movement.

This struggle over organizational form was also a struggle over identity. Should an organization combine workers who possessed a distinctive craft or citizens who were also workers? In their efforts to construct a model of collective identity and organization around the citizen-worker, state and local activists were repeatedly blocked by the entrenched AFL leadership and craft unions. Gradually, however, an alternative strategy emerged built around the citizen-worker identity as applied to individuals rather than a collectivity. In one sense, this strategy marked a return to the premises of the party system, building on the central institutionalized practice of American democracy: voting. But this practice was to be linked to a new understanding of political identity consciously cultivated by labor organizations. If voting was to serve labor, workers had to learn to vote in new ways:

Under our present political system it seems almost impossible to arouse a sense of duty in the public mind that will compel *adequate* restrictive legislation. As long as we *will* vote for party candidates as such regardless of the individual and the influences behind him, it is, perhaps, unbecoming to complain of their shortcomings as officials of state. The voters of California for years have been cognizant of the fact that the machinery of the great political parties is manipulated and controlled almost entirely by corporation influences, and yet with each succeeding election they harken to the pleadings of the political shyster and place in high office individuals who, to all appearances, are mere tools in the hands of their corporation masters. (CaSFL *Proceedings* 1908: 50)

In order to limit the power of the "corporation masters," the growing labor lobby in California needed to link individual electoral decisions to legislative outcomes: "We must weigh carefully the records and character of all candidates for our suffrage before, and not after, election day." Consequently, a system was needed whereby "in the future past records of those seeking support should be accepted for our guidance, rather than mere catch-penny promises." To this end, labor and other associations broke with a basic model of democratic representation in which – in theory – one was to elect honorable men in the expectation that they would follow their conscience and pursue the common good rather than specific interests. Instead, the legislative agent began to include votes on labor legislation by roll call in his annual report and named those "Senators and Assemblymen who stood ready to work and vote in the interest of the wage earners" (CaSFL *Proceedings* 1908: 33, 94–97; 1915: 38–39). These reports were soon published separately as the "Report on Labor Legislation and Labor Record of Senators and Assemblymen." A parallel effort to coordinate labor's use of direct democracy was made by printing the entire text of many of 48 amendments, initiatives and referenda put to the voters in 1914 with an "X" in the recommended box (CaSFL *Proceedings* 1914: 75–78).

In the place of a system in which party loyalty determined one's opinion on everything from monetary policy to foreign affairs, state labor leaders developed techniques for cultivating a sharply delimited, interest-based political identity. In order to avoid ideological splits within labor, the president of the CaSFL advised that "there should be no entangling alliances with other labor bodies seeking the advancement of their own pet measures" (CaSFL *Proceedings* 1910: 46). This move toward a narrowly constructed identity was evident in the procedures for publishing legislative votes: "If Labor desires to obtain a correct and unvarnished record concerning the attitude of individual legislators, the record must be taken on those legislative propositions which emanate directly from Labor and which have not other backing than the principles and influence of organized Labor" (CaSFL *Proceedings* 1915: 100). Commitments to moral reform, social justice, women's rights, foreign policy, and a host of other concerns were normatively and practically excluded from the political identity of labor.

Once developed, these practices could be linked with various collective identities. In Washington State, an unusual alliance of organized labor, farmers, women's associations, and social reformers was embodied in the Joint Legislative Council. This broad alliance deployed practices similar to those used in California for the narrow interests of organized labor. The importance of these new practices of political control is evident from the detail in which the new methods were described. In 1913, the WaSFL president explained:

At both the Farmers' Union and State Grange conventions I presented a pencil copy of a proposed tabulated legislative review, so arranged in two colors that any one could tell at a glance whether a legislator voted for or against the people's interests, recording votes on important amendments and final roll calls on Initiative, Referendum and Recall Amendments, Compensation Act and Women's Eight-hour Law. All who saw it expressed the conviction that it was just what was needed to educate the public as to how their senators and representatives voted. With the approval of these organizations and our Executive Committee, this Tabulated Legislative Review was printed and placed in circulation. It proved to be the most influential piece of campaign literature we ever issued, over 100,000 being printed and circulated in response to demands for the same. (WaSFL *Proceedings* 1913: 37)

Such broad reform alliances were rare and unstable, easily fragmenting into their component associations. And so, out of decades of experimentation with organizational models and political identities was born that curiously ahistorical creature who now populates political science: the individual self-interested rational voter.

The language of individualism and self-interest so permeates contemporary American political culture that it often appears, if not natural, at least original with the ideological and institutional founding of the nation. But revolutionary beliefs and practices were republican, stressing virtue and public service while avoiding the vices of faction. By the early twentieth century, both the normative and organizational underpinnings of this system had been transformed. Men learned not only to vote in their own interests, but to feel good about it and to believe that their individual actions would be aggregated into a maximization of goods, if not into a common good. But this learning was not the individual accomplishment of isolated workers; it was the product of membership in a new form of organization, one which constructed identities on the basis of role-based interests.

THE RATIONALITY OF MEANS AND THE RULE OF THUMB

If grievances generate movements only when resources are available, the lesson to be learned from American labor history is that the form as well as the quantity of those resources has consequences. The organizational repertoire of American workers in the late nineteenth century presented a number of possible models for organization, familiar scripts for collective action that would reduce coordination costs while providing a measure of cultural legitimacy and immunity from repression. But these models implied quite different constructions of identity and orientations to political institutions and opportunities. These were discovered in practice, as labor activists tried one organizational recipe after another.

This experimentation with familiar forms in novel settings, this *bricolage,* was not limited to organized labor. Elected to the presidency of the University of Minnesota in 1869, William Watts Folwell complained that "We are building our great national fabric according to the rule of thumb" (quoted in Bledstein 1976: 284). But this indignant outburst against the "rule of thumb" presumes a model in which action is guided by the rational or reasoned pursuit of ends. In contrast, a rationality of means suggests that what we do is determined by what we already know how to do as much as by what we, in some ultimate sense, desire to achieve. By extension, the probabilities of different types collective action are shaped by the distributions of models of organization within a particular society at a particular point in time. These distributions, in turn, can be characterized at three levels: normative, practical, and institutional. Both individual and collective action are shaped by what people believe about how they should act, by those forms of action which they have mastered at a practical level, and those forms of action which are embedded in institutionalized arrangements of power and resources.

This focus on the social distribution of organizational means suggests a continuum of possible relations between social movements and institutional politics. Movement activists construct organizational forms and strategies that, if effective, will partially overlap with both the mobilizing structures embedded in society and the institutionalized channels of political access. Too much overlap in either direction can result in the social or political co-optation of a movement, too little in failed mobilization or state repression. Just as the ideological frames used by movement activists must make mobilization meaningful for participants at the same time that they frame the movement's claims in terms comprehensible within a broader political arena, the selection of organizational forms must be familiar but not too much so.

The collapse of a social movement: The interplay of mobilizing structures, framing, and political opportunities in the Knights of Labor

KIM VOSS

Failure is an unpopular subject among social movement scholars. Like death and taxes at social gatherings, it is a topic that many of us avoid. In contrast, the birth of insurgency is eagerly debated. As a result, our theories of movement emergence are much more sophisticated and convincing than our models of movement development and decline.

However, while social movement failure is a neglected topic theoretically, in the empirical world it occurs frequently. For example, in his study of American social movements William Gamson (1990) found that over half the organizations in his representative sample failed partially or completely. In light of its frequency, it is important that scholars of social movements begin to construct better theoretical frameworks for understanding the causes and consequences of movement decline.

This chapter contributes to this effort by examining an important failed social movement: the Knights of Labor. The Knights of Labor is an especially significant case, both historically and theoretically. Historically, the collapse of the Knights of Labor was critical in shaping the "exceptionalist" course of the American labor movement (Voss, 1993). Before the collapse of the Knights, the American labor movement developed along lines that were broadly similar to labor movements in England and France. All three originated in the 1830s as movements of skilled craft workers, and all three began, in the last quarter of the nineteenth century, to adopt new inclusive labor ideologies and organizational forms through which less-skilled wage earners were incorporated into the labor movement. After the failure of the Knights, however, the American labor movement began to stand apart. But while the

Using social movement concepts, this chapter reframes and expands on material that appeared in Voss 1992 and 1993. I am indebted to the editors and the participants at the European/ American Perspectives on Social Movements Conference, Washington, D.C., August 1992, for comments on earlier versions of this essay. The Institute of Industrial Relations at the University of California provided financial support for this project.

new union structures and ideologies launched in England and France laid the basis for a permanent broadening of the social base and political horizons of the labor movement, efforts by the Knights of Labor to similarly reshape the American labor movement ultimately collapsed. After the Knights of Labor disintegrated, the American labor movement once again became the domain of a small group of skilled workers, organized primarily along craft lines. As such, it was increasingly out of step with labor movements on the other side of the Atlantic.

Theoretically, the Knights of Labor illustrates some of the pitfalls social movement scholars confront by focusing so exclusively on movement emergence. Initially, the Knights of Labor was extremely successful at mobilizing workers. However, some of the very framing and organizational innovations that underlay its success later contributed to the Knights' decline. A careful examination of the interplay between mobilizing structures, framing, and political opportunities in the Knights of Labor will serve, therefore, to illustrate how the organizational and framing choices activists make have consequences not only for gaining adherents but also for shaping movement outcomes.

In addition, an examination of the collapse of the Knights of Labor draws our attention to the theoretical problem of how failures of social movements can alter the shape and likelihood of future collective action. In the wake of the collapse of the Knights of Labor, the labor activists who had once championed radical reform and classwide organizations were demoralized, the organizational forms which had been used for the purpose of incorporating less skilled workers into the labor movement were discredited, and the strategic frame that had been constructed by the Knights lost its power to mobilize workers.

In this chapter, I explore the causes and consequences of the Knights' failure. In the first section, I describe the initial mobilization of the Knights, emphasizing the new organizational forms and collective action frame developed by Knights activists. This section also places the Knights of Labor in a comparative context. A statistical analysis of the Knights' collapse in one American state, New Jersey, follows. This analysis highlights the destructive impact of employers' associations, an impact that is investigated through a comparative examination of employers' organizations and government tolerance of their actions in the United States, France, and England. Concluding that American employers' associations were stronger, but that this alone is an unsatisfying explanation for the Knights' demise, the remainder of the chapter examines the relationship between workers' organization, Knights' ideology, and employers' actions in one New Jersey city, Newark. A conclusion draws out the implications of the empirical studies for our understanding of the Knights and for our efforts to construct improved models of social movement development and decline.

THE GROWTH OF THE KNIGHTS OF LABOR: NEW MOBILIZING STRUCTURES AND COLLECTIVE ACTION FRAMES

The Noble and Holy Order of the Knights of Labor was the largest labor organization of the nineteenth century and the most successful working-class movement in the United States before the 1930s. At its peak in 1886, it enrolled almost 750,000 workers, including 60,000 blacks and 65,000 women (Ware, 1929: 66; Grob, 1969: 53; Levine, 1983: 325). Measured either in terms of numbers or diversity of membership, the Order was initially more successful than similar new unions in late-nineteenth-century England and France.

The growth of broad-based labor movements in all three countries reflected changes in the economy that undermined long-standing divisions between skilled and less-skilled workers.[1] But these changes did not automatically lead workers to adopt broader identities or provide a set of organizational strategies guaranteed to generate successful unions. Labor activists in each country had to construct new, inclusive union structures and ideologies. The relative success of the Knights of Labor in meeting these challenges is especially impressive when one considers the greater swiftness of industrial development and diversity of the labor force in the United States (Voss, 1993: chap. 2). Industrialization's rapid rearrangement of work disrupted many informal network structures, while the multicultural makeup of the labor force created a dizzying array of micromobilization contexts.

The Knights expanded rapidly in spite of these especially difficult circumstances because of the new organizational structures Knights leaders cobbled together as they attempted to build an inclusive labor movement, and because of the new interpretive frame Knights activists developed as they attempted to recruit supporters.

Before the Knights of Labor, the predominant organizational unit of the American labor movement was the craft local. For decades, it had allowed skilled craft workers in many trades to achieve stable organization, relatively high wages, and a large degree of control over working conditions. But it also sharply divided craft workers from less skilled workers.

The seven skilled garment cutters who founded the Knights in Philadelphia in late 1869 explicitly rejected the craft model of labor organization. As their leader, Uriah Stephens, argued, craft unions were powerless to address the true cause of labor's degradation, which lay in the "present arrangement of labor and capital" whereby "capital dictated" while "labor submitted." Only by organizing more broadly, he suggested, would workers be able to "emancipate" themselves from "the thraldom and loss of wage slavery" (quoted in McNeill, 1887: 402).

The new organizational forms that would eventually be used to achieve Stephens's broad-based vision were not, however, instituted overnight. At first, the only real differences between the Knights and the established craft unions were the Order's inclusive ambition and its endorsement of secrecy and ritual. The secrecy and ritual, borrowed from the fraternal organizations to which many craft workers belonged in the nineteenth century, were adopted as a means of bolstering organizational stability and member loyalty. Secrecy, of course, also provided a shield from employers' blacklists, which often undermined unions in this period.

The Order's secrecy made centralized control difficult, and groups of workers who joined the Knights came to enjoy wide latitude in who and how they organized. The founding local adopted the Masonic practice of using "sojourners" – nonvoting members of other crafts who, it was hoped, would learn the Knights' principles and rituals and then create locals in their own trades. This custom eventually evolved into the practice of allowing members to create locals which were open to all workers in an industry or locality.

By 1879, locals were adopting a variety of organizational forms. They were organized along occupational, industrial, and territorial lines, depending on the needs and identities of the group of workers involved. Some locals (termed "mixed assemblies") were open to all comers (with the famous exceptions of lawyers, bankers, professional gamblers, stockbrokers, and liquor dealers),[2] while the majority (termed "trade assemblies") were organized on the basis of occupation or industry, with the members themselves defining the scope of the industry or occupation. Tactical flexibility was also tolerated and local assemblies employed an extensive array of tactics to further their interests: cooperation, political action, boycotts, strikes, arbitration, collective bargaining, and other activities. Coordination was provided by district assemblies, which were organized territorially and sent representatives to the national convention.[3]

At the end of the Long Depression, the Knights shed its policy of secrecy. This, along with the improved economic climate and the Knights' organizational flexibility, laid the groundwork for steady membership gains in the early 1880s. Then, in 1884 and 1885, membership expanded rapidly as highly publicized strikes by Knights of Labor railroad workers culminated in a victory over the financier Jay Gould, perhaps the most hated of the robber barons. Something akin to what Doug McAdam (1982: 48–51) terms "cognitive liberation" occurred as a result: workers who were ordinarily fatalistic began to demand change and to develop a new sense of power and efficacy. Thousands of previously unorganized workers initiated local assemblies, and the agitation touched off by these gains carried over to the 1886 eight-hour campaign, setting off a new wave of membership gains. By 1886, workers of virtually every nationality and race and nearly every industry had become Knights members. Geographically, locals had been established in almost every city and midsized town in the country. For the first time in American history, a national labor movement had been built from the grass roots –

or to use the language of social history – from the bottom up (Oestreicher, 1987: 47).

While the publicity generated by this unrest spread the Knights' solidaristic message, the underlying pattern of mobilization was one that built initially upon craft loyalties and then spread through community ties between skilled and less skilled workers (Voss, 1988). The workers with the strongest pre-existing networks, both formal and informal, were skilled craft workers. Typically, they were the first to organize in a community. Later, through the use of paid organizers and the activation of informal community ties, less-skilled workers were encouraged to initiate local assemblies.

In England and France organizational innovation was also closely associated with efforts to build an inclusive labor movement. In England, the so-called new unionists built general unions, which were open to less-skilled and other previously unorganized workers, often in a number of industries (Hobsbawm, 1964, 1984). They adopted this form in large part because strong and exclusive craft unions already existed in England's basic industries, and, as a rule, these established unions were hostile to the new unions. Thus, new unions had to organize under and around existing unions. In France, craft unionists began to support the strikes of less-skilled industrial workers in their local communities, and often these actions led to the founding of industrial unions, both locally and nationally (Hanagan, 1980). Eventually, the *Confédération Générale du Travail* began to impose the industrial union model on member organizations (Friedman, 1985: chap. 2). Thus, while both English and French labor activists created new organizational structures, in neither country was there as much flexibility in organizational forms as there was in the Knights of Labor.

Organizational flexibility was one important reason why the Knights grew so rapidly in the mid-1880s. Another reason was the collective action frame forged in the crucible of spiraling conflict as Knights activists strove to explain their movement to prospective supporters and the public.

The set of beliefs that fueled the Knights' rapid growth was one that stressed labor solidarity and cooperative social relations. Its vision was of a "workingmen's democracy" in which a broadly organized labor movement would champion the public good within a regulated cooperative economy (Fink, 1983: 228). This vision invoked the nation's republican heritage and built upon traditional labor rhetoric while pushing both republicanism and labor rhetoric in more inclusive, democratic, mutualist, and oppositional directions than had ever been attempted before.

Republicanism was a common interpretative frame in the nineteenth century; groups and individuals of quite different circumstances and persuasions claimed its mantle to pursue their interests and goals. However, the Knights amplified the frame in their efforts to mobilize the commitment of wage earners and the support of the larger public (Snow et al., 1986). They did so primarily by tieing workers' economic and shopfloor difficulties to a larger political threat to American democracy. As one Knights member testified before Congress in 1883, "owing to the degradation of labor, the political structure of this country is resting on a sand heap" (U.S. Senate, 1885: 218). George McNeill, an influential Knights official, put it most sharply in a widely quoted statement that declared "an inevitable and irresistible conflict between the wage system of labor and the republican system of government" (McNeill, 1887: 459).

American labor activists had long argued that wage labor threatened the independence necessary for good citizenship, but the Knights went beyond this traditional argument. Rather than simply calling for a return to the old days of independent proprietorship as had earlier union activists, the Knights argued that because of economic changes, citizenship rights must now include a basic set of economic guarantees for all wage earners. Unless democracy was extended to the workplace, ensuring all citizens equality at work as well as equality before the law, it would be impossible to maintain a republican form of government. As the Knights' preamble insisted, the "alarming" concentration of "great capitalists and corporations" must be "checked" because the dependence it engendered was corrupting workers' economic independence and their ability to function as competent citizens (Wright, 1887: 157–59).

Aside from amplifying the republican theme, the Knights also amplified and extended traditional labor ideology. First, they pushed labor rhetoric in a much more inclusive direction. Earlier in the century, organized labor had spoken for the independent artisan and disdained the craftless workers; the Knights, by way of contrast, repeatedly described themselves as the "masses" – the "toiling," "industrial," "working," and "laboring" masses. Moreover, their slogan, "An injury to one is the concern of all" was a clarion call for solidarity across skill, ethnic, and gender lines.[4]

Second, the Knights extended the limits of earlier labor ideology by arguing that state action would be required to "secure for workers the full enjoyment of the wealth they create." At the national level, the Order demanded public ownership of the communication, transportation, and banking systems. At the state level, the Order sought health and safety laws, bureaus of labor statistics, and the "abrogation of all laws that do not bear equally upon capital and labor" (Cook, 1886). In a country and an era in which state action was looked upon with great suspicion, granting the state even this limited role was a radical step.

However, although the Knights were more willing than most of their fellow citizens to use the state as an instrument of social progress, they looked above all to direct action, example, and agitation to bring about their aims. Their call for self-organization and self-help extended beyond anything that the working class had previously attempted. Members built a dense network of alternative institutions and practices, including local assemblies, boycotts, reading rooms, bands, parades, lecture circuits, sporting clubs, cooperatives, and labor parties. The Order even established its own court system (Garlock, 1978). These courts, organized at the local and district levels, heard cases involving violations against both the Order (such as scabbing and accepting substandard wages), and the civil law (such as wife-beating and failure to pay boarding bills). Such institutions heightened workers' class awareness, gave them practical experience of mutualism, and helped make the Knights' vision of a producers' self-governing republic tangible to members.[5]

Third, the Knights extended earlier labor ideology by offering an elaborated vision of the alternative society they endorsed. Labor activists in the United States had long endorsed cooperatives as the best means to abolish the dependence of "wage slavery," but earlier, activists had advocated them primarily as a means to uphold customary production practices. The Knights, in contrast, argued that cooperatives were the way to "republicanize" industry; that is, the way to reorganize work so that all workers – skilled and unskilled alike – would have an equal voice in deciding what to produce and how to produce it. In addition, the Knights' experience with cooperation was much more extensive than any other labor union: They successfully established many more cooperatives and sustained them much longer than had earlier unions (Leikin, 1992). These cooperatives were seen both as a practical means of self-help and as a way to demonstrate the moral superiority of a cooperative over a competitive economy.

Scholars have differed sharply in their assessment of the radicalism of the Knights' beliefs. Some have argued that the Order advocated a "backward-looking," "producerist" ideology that doomed the organization, while others view its program as evidencing working-class consciousness, or even proto-socialism (Aveling and Aveling, 1891; Grob, 1969; Fink, 1983; Oestreicher, 1986; Hattam, 1992). Some of the variation in assessments stems from the fact that the Knights' beliefs were often vague or open to multiple interpretations. It is clear, for example, that members were profoundly ambivalent about capitalism: While some who joined were socialists, most were sure only that they had to redefine the social balance of power between labor and capital. Moreover, the beliefs evolved over time, especially as membership grew and strike activity increased, and this too contributes to the controversy, because scholars rarely examine this evolution. Along with heightened conflict, for example, came a steady sharpening of the boundaries drawn between workers and employers. At first, most Knights members spoke the language of producerism, tending to define their opponent as "monopolists" and themselves as "producers" – a category that included small employers as well as workers. In the Knights' initiation ceremony, which was written in 1869, the Order declared that it had "no conflict with legitimate enterprise, no antagonism with necessary capital" (Cook, 1886: 30). By 1883, when Robert

Layton, the national secretary of the Order, testified before Congress, he stated that *capitalists* were ineligible for membership although employers could join who had once themselves been wage earners, who continued to respect labor, and who paid union wages and abided by union rules (U.S. Senate, 1885: 5).[6] And by 1886, Knights members in Newark, New Jersey, were preventing *all* employers from marching in Labor Day parades (*Newark Evening News* 9/6/1886; 9/7/1886).

Disagreement over the radicalism of the Knights' collective action frame can also be traced to the fact that the Knights amplified and extended existing interpretive frames (republicanism, producerism) rather than creating new ones. In particular, this provides the basis for dismissing the Knights' beliefs as backward-looking. However, social movement scholars have learned, thanks to the work of David Snow and his collaborators, that social movement organizers seldom invent new belief systems out of whole cloth (Snow et al., 1986; Snow and Benford, 1988, 1992). Instead, they most often build on, amplify, and extend existing mentalities and political beliefs. The Knights built upon a republican frame to create a radical organization that clearly challenged the status quo.

The indictment of the Order as backward-looking also exaggerates the extent to which the discourses of comparable movements broke radically with the conceptual categories of the past, thus exaggerating the extent to which the Knights' ideology differed from the ideology of successful contemporary labor movements in other countries. In both its producerism and its vision of an alternative cooperative society, the Knights of Labor shared much with both the French and English labor movements in this period. French labor activists used a similar republican language, their speeches and declarations were peppered with references to "producers," and the alternative society they wanted to create bore a striking resemblance to the Knights' notion of a cooperative commonwealth (Perrot, 1987: esp. 223; Moss, 1976; Reid, 1985).[7] Producerist values also lingered among English workers, and union writers frequently spoke of the need to differentiate between good and bad employers, useful industry and speculative capital (Joyce, 1991, esp. 117–20; Hobsbawm, 1984: 260). Of course, there were important differences in tone and outlook as well. In Britain, the "new" unions endorsed a reformist, pragmatic socialism, and in France, many of the activists who pushed for a broad, inclusive labor movement espoused revolutionary syndicalism. But in all three countries, producerist categories and cooperative alternatives continued to shape both workers' and activists' understandings of their situation. French, English, and American workers all combined old and new terms and categories as they attempted to make collective sense of new social realities. It was, after all, a period of experimentation, even ideological vagueness; workers and sympathetic intellectuals in each country struggled to find a common language and workable program which would be capable of rallying diverse groups of workers against the onslaught of industrial capitalism.

As we have seen, the Knights of Labor were initially successful at mobilizing workers to their cause. Ultimately, however, they failed. The decline began in mid-1886 during a campaign for the eight-hour day. At a public demonstration in Haymarket Square, Chicago, a bomb exploded. Over seventy policemen were injured, one fatally, and the police opened fire and killed or injured an indeterminate number of demonstrators. Anarchist leaders who were addressing the crowd when the bomb exploded were immediately blamed for the bombing. Despite a lack of evidence that the anarchists or the Knights had anything to do with the bombing, intense antilabor sentiment swept the nation, demonstrating that the "radical flank effect" is not always positive. On the night of the bombing, the national officers of the Knights, negotiating in the course of a third railroad strike, called off the strike without achieving a single demand. Combined with the failure of the eight-hour campaign, these developments suddenly reversed the Knights' explosive growth (Salvatore, 1982: 68–69).

Membership began to drop off in the aftermath of these defeats, and the Knights became embroiled in both an internal factional battle, as well as a bitter conflict with a growing number of unaffiliated trade unions. By 1890, membership had plummeted to 120,000 and by 1893, when the national organization served briefly as a vehicle for an agrarian-socialist alliance, its membership was under 80,000 (Oestreicher, 1984). The Order remained a powerful force in many areas through the 1890s, but never again attained anywhere near the membership or influence it had in the mid-1880s.

WHY DID THE KNIGHTS COLLAPSE?
EXISTING EXPLANATORY APPROACHES

The Order's dramatic history has long fascinated scholars and several have offered explanations for its decline. The standard historical account focuses on internal movement dynamics to explain the Order's collapse. It treats the Knights as a single, unified, national entity, and analyzes the order in relation to the organization that would eventually supplant it, the American Federation of Labor. The most influential variation is one offered by Selig Perlman (1918), a student of John R. Commons. In his view, skilled workers in the United States were unwilling to jeopardize their stronger bargaining position in order to improve the situation for less-skilled workers; thus, when less-skilled workers flooded into the Knights, skilled workers fled the Order and joined the trade unions of the American Federation of Labor. Subsequent work by Ulman (1955: esp. 374–77) strengthens the plausibility of Perlman's account by providing a reason why American workers might have been particularly craft conscious. He points out that economic development involves twin problems for any labor movement: It simultaneously deskills workers while extending labor and product markets. By stressing the first of these problems at the expense of the second, Ulman argues, the Knights essentially gambled that the leveling influence of technological change would be great enough to make allegiance to the Order a matter of self-interest for skilled workers. But, in Ulman's view, the impact of the market turned out to be greater than the impact of technological change in the United States, thus dooming the Knights.

Philip Foner (1955: 157–60), on the other hand, rejects the argument that the Order failed because its structure could not be adapted to the needs of skilled workers, showing that the Order was actually highly flexible in meeting the organizational needs of its varied membership. He argues that the Knights were destroyed by the national leaders and the ease with which non-working-class members could obtain membership. These middle-class members, he claims, betrayed the rank and file.

Recently, labor historians associated with the "new labor history" have rejected both these explanations. They argue, quite persuasively, that any explanation which treats the Knights as a single, national organization – as Perlman's, Ulman's, and Foner's do – is both misleading and incomplete because it necessarily distorts our interpretation of what was actually a varied, decentralized association. Therefore, they insist, to understand the Knights, one must see it as composed of thousands of local assemblies, each pursuing, with relative autonomy, local goals and strategies. In their effort to rewrite a history of the Order that avoids the pitfalls of the older accounts, they have undertaken detailed studies of the Knights in industrial cities, like Detroit and Cincinnati, as well as in smaller communities, like Rutland, Vermont (Fink, 1983; Oestreicher, 1986; Ross, 1985). To one degree or another, each of these studies take the Perlman view as a point of departure, and together they present much evidence to refute the view that the Knights were unable to serve the interests of skilled workers, or were somehow unfitted to the American environment. And they have added greatly to our understanding of the importance and meaning of the Knights. But they have been less helpful in providing a general explanation of the Knights' collapse because their local focus tends to generate highly specific interpretations.[8] To the extent that a general theme has emerged, it is one of internal dissension, although not along the simple dichotomous lines suggested by Perlman, Ulman, or Foner. Instead of the significant division being between the Knights and the American Federation of Labor, or between skilled and less-skilled workers, they see the roots of factionalism lying in industrial diversity and ethnic difference. The clearest implication of their work is that the interaction between differing industrial circumstances and varying ethnic combinations will lead to distinct factions in different communities.

"New" labor historians, then, present a fundamentally different account of the Knights' demise but one which, like that of their predecessors (the "old" labor historians), focuses exclusively on internal movement dynamics.

Factors external to the labor movement, such as the actions of employers or the changed political climate in the wake of Haymarket, are frequently mentioned but rarely singled out as primary causes of movement decline.[9] Their work, however, raises the question of whether factionalism is a cause or a symptom of collapse. As social movements fall apart, they often disintegrate into factionalism, but this does not mean that factionalism alone leads to the failure. We need to know whether ethnic and industrial diversity always led to factionalism and collapse in the Knights, or whether other factors, like political opportunities and countermovements, encouraged both the factionalism and the collapse. The best way of finding out is to undertake a systematic study of the general conditions that led to the collapse of Knights locals.

A QUANTITATIVE EXPLORATION OF THE KNIGHTS' COLLAPSE

In an effort to uncover the general conditions that led to the collapse of Knights locals, I have undertaken a systematic empirical study of local variation in the failure rates of Knights local assemblies in New Jersey. This analysis is designed to assess how well the various explanations given for the Knights' demise account for the pattern of local assembly failures in New Jersey. The circumstances that led to the collapse of local assemblies are examined using event history analysis (Tuma and Hannan, 1984). Specifically, a loglinear specification is used to estimate how vectors of independent variables altered the rate of collapse of Knights of Labor local assemblies.[10]

Since the defection of skilled craft workers looms so large in the Commons-Perlman-Ulman accounts of the Knights' demise, I concentrate on local assemblies which pursued a craft strategy of organizing only skilled workers along narrow, occupational lines. All such assemblies that were active in New Jersey towns between 1879 and 1895 are included in the analysis.[11] Two features of this investigation should be borne in mind. First, it is formal dissolution that is being examined, not incremental membership loss (for which data is simply unavailable). Some locals lost large numbers of members and fell on hard times yet persisted as organizational entities; in this analysis such locals are indistinguishable from more successful assemblies.[12] Second, the term "longevity" is used in a relative sense – while a few locals remained in existence a decade and a half, the majority were in existence only a few years. (The average life of skilled locals was approximately four years.)

New Jersey was selected because it was an important center of manufacturing with a diverse industrial base. Moreover, the New Jersey Bureau of Statistics collected crucial information about the occupational composition of the Knights that is not available for other states. In addition, it was a state in which the Knights enjoyed a fairly typical level of success: At the Order's height in 1886, the Knights represented between 13 and 15 percent of the state's total manufacturing work force (Voss, 1993: chap. 3). This percentage of the work force would not be unionized again until the massive organizing drives of the CIO in the 1930s.

Independent variables were chosen which, given available evidence, would allow an assessment of the arguments put forward to explain the Knights' collapse. Included are measures of the community and industrial context in which the local assembly operated; indicators of whether relevant types of Knights of Labor local assemblies and trade union locals were present in the community and industry at the beginning of each year; an indicator of the presence of employers' associations; a measure of labor's electoral successes; a marker of the years prior to 1887, when the political opportunity structure was most favorable to the Knights; and a measure of the varying fortunes of the Knights' national organization. Detailed variable descriptions are given in an appendix to this chapter.

One important independent variable is absent in this analysis – the Knights' collective action frame. As noted, some scholars have implicated the Knights' beliefs in its decline (Grob, 1969; Hattam, 1993). However, the kinds of quantitative data available will not allow exploration of this issue. Instead, an evaluation of the role of framing in the Order's downfall will be presented when the case study is discussed farther on.

FINDINGS

Table 10.1 presents the results of the event history analysis. Rather than reporting the fully specified model, the table includes only the coefficients and standard errors for the reduced model.[13] These are shown in the first two columns. Interpreting the coefficients in the table is much like interpreting unstandardized regression coefficients. Positive coefficients indicate that the independent variable increased the probability of organizational failure, and negative coefficients indicate that the variable decreased the likelihood that the local assembly would collapse. The table also presents an "impact" column. This indicates the factor by which a "standard change" in the value of each independent variable multiplies the rate of organizational collapse when other variables are held constant at their mean values. The "standard change" used is the shift from "0" to "1" for dummy variables, and the shift from one-half a standard deviation below the mean to one-half a standard deviation above the mean of continuous variables.

Overall, the results suggest little support for the standard explanations of the Knights' collapse. This can be seen most readily by looking at the first column of the table. None of the labor-organization variables had a significant effect on assembly failures: Neither the presence of less skilled Knights' assemblies nor the presence of trade union locals had any impact on the

Table 10.1. *Rate of failure of skilled Knights of Labor locals, 1879–1895[a]*

Independent Variables	Reduced Model		
	Coef.	S.E.	Impact
Intercept	−6.74	2.66	
Industrial factors			
Wage differential	—	—	—
Number of establishments	−.11	.22	.86
Establishment size	−.0022	.0020	.73
Technological change	−.88*	.39	.78
Capital-to-labor ratio	.17*	.08	1.56
Percent females	—	—	—
Community factors			
Population	.40	.28	1.72
One-industry town	1.45*	.62	4.28
Ethnic diversity	—	—	—
Election victory	−.78	.65	.46
Organizational factors[b]			
KOL craft assem. in local industry[c]	—	—	—
KOL craft assem. in community	.66	.45	1.93
KOL less-skilled in local industry	—	—	—
KOL less-skilled in community	—	—	—
Trade-union craft in local industry	—	—	—
Trade-union craft in community	—	—	—
Employers' association	.90*	.41	2.47
Time factors			
Prior to 1887?	−.60	.40	.55
National factors			
National KOL death rate	.0012*	.0005	1.42

*$p < .05$ (two-tailed test).

[a]Only coefficients for the reduced model are reported. Variables that were clearly nonsignificant were eliminated in order to obtain stable coefficient estimates for the significant factors. Overall x^2 of reduced model is 37.77 with 11 degrees of freedom (significant at the .001 level). Number of local assemblies (N) = 45. (Three local assemblies were dropped because of missing data.) Number of spells = 206.

[b]Organizational factors measure whether locals of each type were present in the community or industry at the beginning of the calendar year.

[c]Indicates the presence of at least one less-skilled assembly in the local industry in addition to the assembly being analyzed.

failure of skilled Knights assemblies. Thus, the Commons-Perlman argument is not confirmed; there is no evidence that skilled workers left the Knights to join the trade unions when less-skilled workers joined the Order in large numbers. Some indirect support is found for Ulman's reasoning that the Knights appealed to skilled workers undergoing technological change. On the significance of the technological change variable, keep in mind that failure is being modeled, and hence a negative sign indicates that the variable increases the likelihood of survival. But additional analysis of industry differences (not reported here) shows no support for the other half of his argument: To the extent that one can measure variations in product and labor markets by industry, there is no evidence that the skilled left the Knights in response to the development of the market.

In a very indirect sense, the significance of the national failure rate measure provides some support for Foner's argument that national level leadership policies and problems undercut the Knights. Local assemblies in New Jersey tended to fail when the national failure rate was high. However, this variable does not overshadow the effects of the other variables in Table 10.1, which suggests that national level events occurred within the context of, and interacted with, local conditions. Foner's other argument, that the Knights were betrayed by increasing numbers of middle-class members, fares less well when confronted with available evidence. The New Jersey Bureau of Statistics of Labor and Industries provides a list of all the occupations represented in New Jersey's local assemblies in 1887. Out of a total of 40,000 workers, only 113 have middle-class occupations, which hardly seems large enough to have betrayed the Knights.

The table suggests that ethnic diversity (at least at the community level) had no effect on the survival of Knights locals. Similarly, electoral failure does not seem to have contributed in any direct sense to the collapse of the Knights.

Instead, these results indicate that the failure of the Knights among skilled workers had more to do with employers' strategies and the industrial situation than it did with trade union exclusiveness or the entrance of less-skilled workers into the Knights of Labor. Skilled locals lived longest when they were organized in labor-intensive settings and when technological change was rapid. Locals organized in one-industry towns, on the other hand, tended to be short-lived, just as they did when employers initiated employers' associations. The negative effect of one-industry towns calls into question recent arguments about the fragmenting effects of industrial diversity, as does the fact that population had no effect on longevity. Indeed, skilled locals were over four times more likely to fail when they were organized in one-industry towns.[14] Employers' associations also had a devastating effect on skilled locals – they collapsed two and one-half times faster when the employers organized.

Results reported elsewhere on the collapse of less-skilled locals provide further evidence that the Knights' decline was not the result of failed solidarity between skilled and less-skilled workers (Voss, 1992). Nor was it the consequence of competition between the Knights and the trade unions. Instead, the investigation of less-skilled locals suggests that there were two variables which had an equally devastating effect on both skilled and less skilled locals: the national failure rate and the presence of an employers' association.

While it is no surprise that the national decline of the Knights tended to rebound on New Jersey locals, the negative impact of employers' associations on both skilled and less-skilled locals should be emphasized and analyzed further. It suggests that those of us who seek to understand the American labor movement too often focus on its internal dynamics. Instead, we need to look more carefully at the activities of employers.

THE KNIGHTS, EMPLOYERS' ASSOCIATIONS, AND THE STATE

As we have seen, employers' associations played a key role in the collapse of the Knights in New Jersey. New Jersey is certainly not the nation, and we would want to know a great deal more about the importance of employers' associations elsewhere in the United States before placing undue emphasis on their role, but if we assume for the moment that this New Jersey finding can be generalized, it raises an intriguing possibility: Perhaps the reason the Knights collapsed completely, while the new broad-based unionism in Britain and France survived, has more to do with the consciousness and actions of employers than with the consciousness and actions of workers. Perhaps employers in the United States organized more rapidly, brought more resources to the battle, and fought more bitterly than their European counterparts. Perhaps, in other words, it is time to turn the old arguments about the "exceptionalism" of American labor on their head.

This is the conclusion of a small but growing body of literature. For example, James Holt (1977), in a comparison of iron- and steelworkers in the United States and Britain, concludes that American employers simply had greater financial resources and political power with which to fight unionism, and that this is the primary reason why British steelworkers forged a successful union (and one that was eventually open to less-skilled workers) in the late nineteenth century while American workers did not. Sanford Jacoby (1991) reaches a similar judgment after reviewing the evidence on management practices in England and the United States (see also Zeitlin, 1987).

Aside from the explicitly comparative literature, additional support for this line of argument can be gleaned from the literature on the new unionism. Several historians have noted that in Britain the employers' counteroffensive against the new unions was feeble. Eric Hobsbawm (1984: 161), for example, explicitly argues that the new unions were still in existence in 1911–13, when a second period of explosive growth occurred, because employers made few attempts "to eliminate unions altogether or to deny their right to exist." Similarly, Alan Fox (1985: 189–90) notes that while a few "unrepresentative" British employers founded associations specifically to destroy the new unions, most "had little stomach" for "American-style" union busting, with its "attendant unrestrained brutality and lawlessness." British employers were "ever ready to grumble about the unions and resent them for most of their industry's ills," he notes, but few were willing to pursue a "knock-down, drag-out fight" to defeat them.

Further, Peter Stearns's (1968) and Gerald Friedman's (1991) studies of French employers provide grounds for believing that American employers were unusually successful at uniting to defeat labor unions. French employers, although notably hostile to the organizational efforts of their employees, were themselves very slow to organize and tended to initiate weak, low-dues associations once they did combine. Available evidence suggests that American employers were able to organize with less difficulty, and that the associations they established tended to require high dues (Friedman, 1991; Bonnett, 1956). This made them formidable opponents in battles with unions.

One need not try to explain international differences in the success of labor movements by appealing exclusively to variations in employer strength. Indeed, it would be a mistake to open up our discussion of the development of the American labor movement by including employers while forgetting the larger political opportunity structure. Again, Friedman's (1988) work is instructive in this regard. While he agrees that employers were better organized in the United States, he points out that French workers owed their success as much to the French state as to employer weakness or labor's strength. In France, the state feared any unrest that might precipitate yet another constitutional crisis, and thus when strike action involved large numbers of workers, the state tended to intervene. Intervention generally resulted in shorter strikes and at least some employer concessions (Shorter and Tilly, 1974: 28–45). In the United States, on the other hand, neither the federal nor the state government intervened directly with any frequency, even when strikes were massive.[15] And on the occasions when the government did intervene, it acted – often violently – against the strikers. Thus, in the United States, workers could not count on state action to neutralize intransigent employers. So, even if employers' associations had been equally strong in France and the United States, their impact on the labor movement would have been greater in the United States.

When we consider the possibility that employers' associations were unusually strong and well organized in the United States together with the existence of a state that set the rules for industrial conflict and then generally refused to intervene in labor disputes, I think that we are much closer to understanding the reasons why employers' associations had such a devastating effect on the New Jersey Knights. This account, of course, accords well with other studies which demonstrate the effects of both political opportunity structures and countermobilization on the fate of social movements (Kitschelt, 1986; McAdam, 1983a; Zald and Useem, 1987; Rucht, this volume).

However, the account given so far says nothing about the dynamics of the contest between the Knights and the employers. Yet dynamics are crucial because, as the editors to this volume note, they hold the key to understanding the fate of social movements. To fully grasp the Knights' collapse, we need to know more about how the employers were able to mobilize so effectively. We also need to find out what actions the Knights engaged in when confronted with organized employers. Finally, if we also want to understand the consequences of the Knights' demise, we must examine how the Knights' leaders and members dealt with their defeat at the hands of organized employers.

Looking more closely at a local conflict between the Knights and an employers' association should help illuminate these matters. In addition, it should help to clarify the role framing processes played in the Order's collapse. The case discussed is that of a lockout of leather workers in Newark, New Jersey. It was chosen because it is one of the cases that makes up the findings reported in Table 10.1 and because it is a case in which the conflict between Knights members and an employers' association can be traced through reports in the local press.[16]

EXTENDING THE INVESTIGATION: AN EXPLORATION OF THE 1887 LOCKOUT OF THE NEWARK LEATHER WORKERS

Between 1883 and 1886, Newark's leather workers joined the Knights of Labor, along with most other members of the city's large and diverse industrial labor force. The leather workers established five local assemblies, three organized along skilled, craft lines, one open to all leather workers, and one composed of less-skilled German tanners.

With organization came an increased readiness to use collective action to redefine the employment relationship. In a series of unprecedented strikes, Newark's leather workers won an impressive amount of collective control over their work lives. By January 1887, leather workers had abolished subcontracting, had equalized pay across the industry, had increased wages, and had created a system of shop stewards. Two things are especially notable about these strike victories. First, they were successful because workers carefully built support across skill and ethnic lines. Second, workers prevailed in the first and most hard-fought strike because three small firms broke ranks with the other employers and settled with the Knights.[17]

These strikes and their victorious outcomes were part of a larger trend.

Throughout Newark, Knights' organizing ushered in increased conflict, new collective demands, and new levels of solidarity. While important divisions remained (notably, over political strategy), it was apparent that Newark workers, both within and outside the leather industry, were developing the sense that, as a group, they shared a common fate.

This flourishing sense of working-class identity was accompanied by a sharpening attitude of opposition to employers. In September 1886, as noted earlier, Newark workers refused to allow employers to march in the Labor Day parade. Then, in December 1886, the Knights-dominated Essex County Trades Assembly passed a resolution barring even small employers from serving as delegates.

The strikes and organizational gains soon aroused a reaction on the part of employers. In 1886, harness, clothing, brewing, and hat manufacturers all organized. In addition, Newark's Board of Trade (a citywide organization of Newark's leading manufacturers) began a lobbying effort to reassert employers' political clout. It began a campaign to induce the legislature to reenact the conspiracy laws that had traditionally been used by employers in New Jersey to severely limit the legal actions of labor unions. Only in 1883, after a hard-fought legislative battle, had the Knights and their allies attained the repeal of these laws.

Leather employers did not join the ranks of those who established employers' associations until the spring of 1887. Earlier, leather manufacturers had attempted to coordinate efforts to defeat Knights strikes, but they had a difficult time maintaining solidarity, especially between small and large employers. By formally organizing, they hoped to be more successful. The owners of the largest leather firms were activists in launching the Leather Manufacturers' Association of New Jersey (LMANJ). A few months after the first meeting, the association selected one of its members, R. G. Salomon, to violate his contract with the Knights by ordering his men to complete extra work each day over the agreed-upon limit. The LMANJ assisted Salomon in hiring strikebreakers (when, as expected, all 125 employees struck over the demand), and turned over to him a large portion of the work of other members to ensure his continued business during the conflict (*Newark Evening News* [hereafter *NEN*] 6/8/1887; New Jersey Bureau of Statistics of Labor and Industries [hereafter NJBSLI], 1888: 228–29; *Journal of United Labor* 9/24/1887; Perlman, 1918: 415). The Knights were able to induce some of the strikebreakers, recruited from Salem, Massachusetts, to leave, but Salomon successfully obtained others, and the strike was eventually lost. None of the strikers were rehired (*NEN* 6/11/1887, 7/25/1887; NJBSLI, 1887: 258–61).

This was the first important strike the Newark employers had won since the leather workers had organized Knights' assemblies. It signaled the strength and resolve of the LMANJ to the Knights, but equally important, to the manufacturers who did not yet fully support the association. By putting aside their individual, short-term interest in gaining a competitive advantage over Salomon, the members of the LMANJ demonstrated that they had both the solidarity and the financial resources to potentially drive the Knights out of the leather industry. This undoubtedly led employers outside of the LMANJ to reconsider any conclusions they had drawn about the Knights being a permanent force in Newark's leather industry. Moreover, Salomon's victory demonstrated to leather employers in general that the price of breaking ranks could be high. If the members of the LMANJ were willing to forgo short-term advantages to defeat their employees, they might also be willing to set them aside to defeat manufacturers who did not join or who defected from the employers' association.[18] Thus, with a single victory, the LMANJ successfully made both the risks of nonmembership and the benefits of solidarity much higher. This probably goes a long way toward accounting for how, after the strike, the LMANJ was able to convince a group of employers who had previously been unwilling to join the association, to put up bonds of between $2,000 and $5,000, ensuring their compliance with the association in future actions (*NEN* 7/14/1887).

Buoyed by their victory, the LMANJ announced in mid-July that they were going "to fight the Knights of Labor for control over the shops." Beginning August 1, manufacturers would no longer allow their men to return to work unless they agreed to quit the Order (*NEN* 7/14/1887; *John Swinton's Paper,* 7/31/1887; NJBSLI, 1888: 228–29). Charles Dodd, the leader of the Newark District Assembly (DA 51), moved immediately to avert trouble by writing to the president of the LMANJ, suggesting a meeting between the two men to settle any difficulties between their respective organizations. When the president of LMANJ refused to see him, Dodd sent a letter to every manufacturer requesting either a meeting or notification that the manufacturer did not intend to "anul" his contract with the Knights (*NEN,* 7/26/1887). Most manufacturers responded to Dodd's request, the majority saying that they intended to abide by the decision of the LMANJ, but a few stating that they might not. Even some of those expecting to go along declared, however, that "they had no grievance against the Knights of Labor and that the proposed shutdown ... was solely for the purpose of adjusting trade matters." The Knights seized upon this seeming support, and attempted to reframe the conflict as one which would hurt the small employers as well as the Knights. As one official said,

We have been expecting this thing for months, and we are fully prepared to meet it. Our different [KOL] associations knew that the formation of the Manufacturers' Association meant an effort to crush out unionism for one thing, *and also to crowd out of the business a few of the smaller firms, in order to give a monopoly of the leather business to the big firms.* (*NEN* 7/26/1887; emphasis added)

The LMANJ, however, dismissed the sincerity of its members' expressions of friendliness toward the Knights.

Between the manufacturers' announcement of the lockout in mid-July and August 1, when the lockout was to be enforced, the Knights debated over whether they should strike before they were shut out. If they struck immediately, some argued, the workers would have a strategic advantage because employers would be left with hides midway through the tanning process. But Dodd and the other leaders of DA 51 were anxious to avoid any appearance of responsibility for the trouble; if that happened, it would almost certainly turn public sympathy against them (especially since they had contracts with many of the firms), and would have the added disadvantage of further uniting the manufacturers. In addition, the officers of DA 51 were worried about the high cost of supporting the leather men and wanted to avoid a confrontation for as long as possible. The Knights had grown very quickly in Newark and with growth had come dramatic increases in strike activity. At first, many of these strikes had been successful, but following Haymarket, the success rate had fallen precipitously. This had dangerously stretched the Knights' resources for carrying out what would surely be one of the largest confrontations yet seen in Newark (Voss, 1993: chap. 7).

The actual conflict began more like a poker game than like the pitched battle between capital and labor that the Knights expected. On August 1, the manufacturers took no immediate action, and the leather workers were momentarily jubilant, believing that the inaction signaled internal dissension among the manufacturers. If so, the events of the next few days played into the employers' hands. When it became obvious that the anticipated shutout was not going to occur, a few leather workers attempted to call the bluff of one employer who had heatedly denounced the Knights just a few days earlier. But the shop was not one of the Knights' strongholds, and the other workers, who might have stuck with the Knights in the event of a lockout, resented the minority for trying to precipitate a strike. They refused to follow the militants out of the shop (*NEN* 8/1/1887, 8/2/1887, 8/3/1887). Over the next few days, rumors of dissatisfaction with DA 51 appeared in the newspapers, and manufacturers told reporters that they had canvassed their workers and found that most were "willing to give up the order rather than lose their work" (*NEN* 8/4/1887). The manufacturers added that they had prepared for the confrontation, having stopped the preparation of new hides for processing the week before.

Increasingly, it was becoming clear that the Knights were being maneuvered into position where inaction appeared to be weakness. Only by calling out the leather workers could they prove what, just a few days earlier, had been a foregone conclusion: that they had the support of their members. Yet in doing so, they would be the first to break the contracts still in effect between the Knights and the employers. On August 6, the District Assembly called out workers in two firms, hoping that a demonstration of their members' loyalty would induce the LMANJ to negotiate. But although most of the workers heeded the strike call, the LMANJ countered two days later by announcing that it had set a new lockout date, August 13.

The next several days brought increased framing activities and strategic maneuvering on both sides. Employers whose shops had already been struck began to hire strikebreakers (*NEN* 8/11/1887; *New Brunswick Daily Home News* 8/8/1887, 8/11/1887). In one case, policemen were retained to guard the strikebreakers, a move that outraged workers who angrily denounced it, both because it gave the false impression that workers were threatening violence and because it made it appear that the police and the local government were on the side of the employers. In addition, the LMANJ announced that it had agents in England, France, and Germany, and that they had found skilled leather workers "only too willing to come here for bigger wages than they could ever earn at home" (*New Brunswick Daily Home News* 8/11/1887; *NEN* 8/15/1887).

The manufacturers also worked hard to maintain unity. The LMANJ reminded its members that they had to conduct their business without recognition of the Knights of Labor or forfeit their bonds (*NEN* 8/8/1887). Employers who worried about the loss of their skilled leather workers were assured that they would be helped in every possible way. Even though leather making was a highly competitive industry, association leaders went so far as to promise that they would rotate among firms the skilled workers who remained on the job.

For its part, the District Assembly struggled to find an effective strategy for dealing with the much greater resources of the LMANJ. An effective communitywide boycott was organized to prevent the sale of food and supplies to strikebreakers, forcing at least one employer to set up both a cafeteria and sleeping quarters inside his factory (*NEN* 8/11/1887, 8/23/1887). Workers were also successful in inducing some strikebreakers to leave – eventually, the Knights would even pay return passage to England for a few of the strikebreakers (*NEN* 8/29/1887). But while such tactics helped to maintain day-to-day solidarity, the Knights knew that they had to find a way to break the employers' resolve. Paying for strikebreakers to return home would soon deplete DA 51's treasury. Moreover, it was becoming painfully obvious that some of the employers were willing to do almost anything to break the Knights; not only were they voluntarily giving up months of profit, they were also spending large sums of money to recruit skilled replacements from as far away as Germany. The Knights talked of a nationwide boycott of all leather made in Newark, but, as one manufacturer soon pointed out, it had little chance of success because the markets for Newark's leather industry were worldwide (Popper, 1951: 73). Thus the leaders of DA 51 began to believe that their only hope was to undermine employer solidarity.

Both pragmatic and ideological considerations led DA 51 to devote most of their energies to dividing the employers. Pragmatically, they had few choices. Although they assured both the leather workers and the press that they had the financial reserves to maintain the strike, they actually had little money in the treasury. As an organization geared to the unionization of poorly paid workers, the Order's dues were very low – not enough to support a strike fund. The only way to support strikes once the dues revenue was gone was to appeal to the local assemblies and trade unions (NJBSLI, 1888: 42–46). It was summer, however, which was the slow season for many of Newark's workers, and DA 51 could count on the working-class community for only limited funds (*NEN* 8/16/1887). The Knights' national executive board promised to help, but its reserves, too, had also been depleted in the many conflicts it had been involved in during 1886 and 1887.

However, pragmatic reasoning alone did not dictate the Knights' strategy. As the officers of DA 51 viewed the forces arrayed against them, the clearest cause of their predicament was indeed concentrated capital. This was shown most clearly by the manufacturers who had initiated the LMANJ and who were now directing the lockout: They were the owners of the three largest leather firms in Newark (Voss, 1992). It also seemed quite possible that the small employers might yet be persuaded to take a conciliatory stance toward the Knights. Not only, as we have seen, had the smaller manufacturers settled first in the 1886 strike, but it was disproportionately the smaller firms who refused to join the employers' association, or, if in the association, who delayed posting the lockout notice (*NEN* 8/9/1887, 8/10/1887). Much of the small employers' reluctance to go along with the LMANJ lay in their greater economic insecurity; because leather manufacturing was a highly competitive industry, they faced bankruptcy when production was disrupted for even a short time.[19] Thus, the small employers were susceptible to the argument that concentrated capital was as much their enemy as the Knights of Labor. Reports on August 12 that a few members of the employers' association had approached a lawyer to find out whether or not the manufacturers' association really had the legal ability to enforce discipline by keeping their bonds added plausibility to the Knights' belief that the employers' solidarity might be crumbling. Further evidence that the LMANJ was itself worried about winning and keeping the smaller firms was demonstrated when it was reported that the LMANJ had assured the small manufacturers that they would be lent skilled workers if necessary to meet production. Thus, it was not unreasonable for the Knights to believe that, if they could successfully frame the conflict as one of labor and enterprise against monopoly, they might be able to break up the LMANJ and avoid losing the conflict.

But reframing the conflict in this way had two significant drawbacks for DA 51: It tended to discourage the Knights from exploiting their ability to disrupt production, and it ran the risk of intensifying internal tension within the labor movement. It discouraged the Knights from walking out during critical periods in the leather production cycle because workers hoped that, if they avoided hurting employers, the latter might be more easily convinced that labor was good, while monopoly was corrupt and unfair. It ran the risk of heightening internal divisions because the Knights' leaders were taking a view of labor's opposition that had by 1887 become the minority position. Indeed, very early in the conflict, it became clear that there were two factions among the leather workers: a conservative faction which supported DA 51 for the way it was managing the conflict, and a radical faction which was unhappy about DA 51's moderation. Since these two factions also had ethnic overtones (the radical faction tending to have more German adherents, and the conservative faction having more Yankee, English, and Irish adherents), when DA 51 escalated its attempts to rhetorically include the small employers in labor's camp, the result was increased ethnic conflict along with increased division over labor's vision of itself.

Given the Knights' strategy and their financial constraints, they needed to break the manufacturers' unity fairly early if they were to prevail. The longer the lockout lasted, the more difficult their financial situation would become, and the greater the probability would be of internal division. But this early settlement was not forthcoming. By the eve of the lockout, nearly 800 men were already out, and some of them had been without a job for almost a week, which meant that they would soon need financial support (*NEN* 8/11/ 1887). On August 13, the official beginning of the lockout, an additional 455 men were thrown out, bringing the total number of locked-out workers to 1,255 (out of a labor force of 1,800) (NJBSLI, 1888: 258–61).

On August 15, DA 51 received more disappointing news: All of the employers who earlier had promised Dodd that they would not participate in the lockout did so despite their previous statements to the contrary. Nonetheless, the Knights kept up their efforts to win over manufacturer support even in the face of this setback – sending some employees back temporarily so that they could take care of leather hides that might be ruined by the cessation of production (*NEN* 8/15/1887). They also sent workers to the immigration headquarters at Castle Rock, New York, where they alerted the commissioner of immigration that leather workers might be entering the country illegally as strikebreakers (*NEN* 8/11/1887, 8/15/1887, 8/19/1887).

By the second week of the lockout, it was becoming increasingly clear that the Knights' appeal to the small manufacturers was not having the desired effect. While the eight small manufacturers who from the beginning had refused to join the employers' association did not lock out the Knights, the leather workers were unable to convince any of the thirty-three member manufacturers to break with the association. And, on August 19, the LMANJ moved to intensify pressure on the eight holdouts. It threatened that, if the eight did not join in the lockout, the association would cut off supplies of raw hides and call in all outstanding notes and claims held by members of the LMANJ against these small firms.

DA 51, in what was surely an act of desperation, responded with a circular addressed to the businessmen of Newark which argued, in part,

Gentlemen: The enforced idleness of 1,200 men, citizens of this city who, with those depending upon them for support number 4,000 persons, is a matter which directly affects your interests. Opposition by the manufacturers to a perfectly legal organization of labor, is the cause of this unfortunate state of things, hurtful not only to all those immediately concerned, but to the business community at large; *for what injures one portion in a degree injures all.* (*NEN* 8/20/1887; emphasis added)

Imagine what effect the italicized passage would have had on those workers who had voted a year earlier to exclude employers from marching in the 1886 Labor Day parade! Here were the leaders of the leather workers attempting to stretch the Knights' motto, long a clarion call for labor solidarity, into a plea for help from the very men who were daily hiring strikebreakers and waging the strongest assault ever mounted against labor in the city of Newark. Angry dissatisfaction with the leadership of DA 51 was reported in the press, and internal dissension broke into the open when six days later one of the nonleather assemblies disbanded, disgusted with DA 51's handling of the strike.

By mid-September, it was clear that the leather workers had suffered an absolute defeat. Some reapplied for their old jobs, but at least half were turned away, and all the shop stewards were blacklisted. Other leather makers left Newark to find work elsewhere. About 350 still remained out of work at the beginning of November (NJBSLI, 1888: 258–61).

The defeat of the leather workers in the 1887 lockout ended union organization in Newark's leather industry and had serious repercussions for the city's labor movement. Both organizationally and ideologically, the loss was devastating. Of the three local assemblies directly involved in the lockout, two collapsed when the workers went back to work, while the third disbanded a few months later. Other local assemblies experienced similar failure rates. At the beginning of 1887, there were forty-eight local assemblies of manufacturing workers in Newark, while at the end of 1888, only twelve of these were still active. Moreover, the Knights' inability to prevail over the leather manufacturers severely undermined the influence of those local assemblies that survived, as evidenced in the disarray that accompanied the Knights' strike efforts in 1888 and in the precipitous decline of the Essex County Trades Assembly beginning in late 1887.

Ideologically, local leaders were unable to offer a convincing argument for how the exercise of working-class solidarity might lead to anything other than another defeat in the future. Indeed, aside from statements in which locals' leaders blamed each other for the failure of the strike, no analysis at all was offered. As a result, the Knights' vision was discredited in Newark. When the labor movement rebounded again at the end of the 1890s, it did so by eschewing both the inclusion of less-skilled workers and the Knights' alternative vision of a "workingmen's democracy."

THE COLLAPSE OF THE KNIGHTS OF LABOR: EMPLOYERS' ASSOCIATIONS, KNIGHTS' MOBILIZING STRUCTURES, AND FRAMING

The Knights' experience with the leather manufacturers in Newark provides further evidence that employers' associations played a key role in the decline of the Knights. Once organized, employers had many more resources and a great deal more maneuvering room than workers. Indeed, it is difficult to see how the Knights, no matter what tactics they tried or frames they used, could have prevailed against the employers so long as the manufacturers were unified and willing to commit so much of their energy and capital to defeating the Knights.

The case study also illuminates some of the strategies which allowed American employers to organize so effectively. Employers confronted many of the same types of obstacles to mobilization that workers faced: They were in a highly competitive environment, were often suspicious of each other's motives, and were internally divided. Their success depended on overcoming their short-term interest in stealing their competitors' markets and on their ability to maintain solidarity. Certainly, as Offe and Wiesenthal's (1985) work on the logic of collective action suggests, their smaller numbers eased mobilization. But small numbers alone were not sufficient to overcome all obstacles, especially not the divisions between small and large employers. Those most committed to the employers' association, the large employers, had to find a way to encourage or coerce the small employers to stay solidary even when it did not appear to be in their interests to do so. Here, the bond, a tactical innovation, provided a sufficient deterrent to breaking ranks, resolving the solidarity problem that had earlier plagued the employers. Once solidarity was ensured, the very monopolization and concentration that the Knights so abhorred was the source of the capital reserves which financed the lockout.

Moreover, the case suggests that the Knights' rapid mobilization also contributed to its decline in Newark. The dramatic increase in recruits and strike activity clearly depleted the organization's resources and energies. In addition, rapid growth in the number of local assemblies made it difficult to communicate and reconcile the steadily growing sense many members had that their battle was with *all* employers, rather than with only the unproductive, monopolistic employers. And, of course, it was the Knights' rapid growth, along with their ability to build alliances across the skill divide, that sparked the employers' reaction in the first place.

The case study also helps to clarify the role that framing played – or more precisely, did not play – in the Order's decline. Often, the Knights' producerism is denigrated as backward-looking. The implication of this critique is twofold. First, it suggests that the world had so completely changed by the 1880s that any talk of strategic alliances with small employers was a hopeless dream, a throwback to a long-gone era. Second, it implies that the Knights' use of producerist categories prevented the organization from acting on the basis of working-class interests. Neither of these arguments is supported by the Newark case. In 1886 and early 1887, Newark workers were able to divide the small employers from the large ones, and achieved strike victories as a result. Moreover, in Newark, the Knights' ideology did not impede workers from constructing a working-class identity. This was demonstrated especially when Knights members offered strike and organizational support across the skill line that had for so long divided the working class. The fact that Knights spokesmen sometimes expressed sympathy for the plight of the small employer, arguing that he, too, was victimized by large-scale capitalism should not blind us to the distinction workers made between themselves and the small employers.[20] Knights members struck small employers as well as large, and they insisted on the same pay scales and working conditions in both small and large shops.

Producerism, and the Knights' injustice frame more generally, I am arguing, did not prevent Newark leather workers from acting collectively as a class. What it did, instead, was shape the Knights' strategic choices and its conceptual resources for framing defeat. Strategically, it led Knights' leaders in Newark to believe that, once again, they might be able to shatter employer unity by stressing the victimization workers and small employers shared at the hand of large employers. This time, however, the employers' association had destroyed the basis for a strategic alliance between the Knights' members and small employers. Some workers understood this more quickly than others, and this became a fault line that ruptured in internal dissension.

FRAMING AND "FORTIFYING MYTHS"

The Newark case demonstrates that the Knights' collective action frame was not the determining factor in the Order's collapse, as some have argued. This is not to say, however, that framing played no role. It probably accelerated the Order's collapse. But more critically (and more speculatively), it shaped subsequent activism.

The Knights' collective action frame left Newark workers with very pessimistic conclusions about labor's ability to reshape society. Working-class republicanism was a set of beliefs that gave to workers the mission of rescuing the nation, while suggesting that they would be able to accomplish this enormous task by organizing thoroughly, and demonstrating their moral and numerical power. If they did this, the Knights believed, they would be able to convince the middle class of the essential truth of their cause. It was not that the Knights did not expect opposition or class conflict: they did. But they also anticipated that once they won workers over to their cause, they would be able to attract the support of others, especially the middle class. When the moment of truth came, and they were unable to convince the small employers of the justice of their cause, they were left, ideologically, with only themselves to blame. As Gregory Kaster (1990) has suggested, this had always been the dark side of American labor's language of dissent in the nineteenth century. Implicit in its terms was the idea that ultimately workers were to blame if they were unable to take charge of their destiny. While, as I argued earlier, the Knights' collective action frame was one that extended earlier labor rhetoric in several important respects, it was not a frame that transformed labor's attributional orientation. The Knights' master frame was not conducive to what Snow et al. (1986: 474) term the "externalization of responsibility," even in the face of organized capital.

Also important in this regard is the Knights' suspicion of state activism. While the Knights' ideology accorded a larger role for the government than had most earlier versions of labor republicanism, the Order's suspicion of strong centralized authority tended to blind its leaders to the possibility of calling for state intervention to counter employer power. Again, workers were left with only themselves to blame for the defeat of the Knights.

Thus far, I have been analyzing only what happened in Newark. How plausible would it be to generalize more broadly to the nation at large? It is, of course, difficult to know, but it is beyond dispute that the organization of the leather manufacturers was part of a much larger trend (Bonnett, 1956; Perlman, 1918: 414–16). In addition, the curious silence of local Knights leaders that followed the defeat of the leather workers in Newark can also be found in the labor press in other cities, as well as in the biographies of relevant labor leaders.[21] Aside from the inevitable blaming war that went on between a few national leaders of the Knights as the Order declined across the nation, there are virtually no articles or published speeches assessing the reasons for the Knights' collapse that appeared anywhere in the country. Neither are there martyrs, nor brave projections of how, next time, the working class would triumph over its enemies. Indeed, there is no sense at all of a next time. It is as if the very opposite of what McAdam terms "cognitive liberation" occurred: instead, what we might call "cognitive encumbrance" took place.

It is instructive in this regard to compare working-class republicanism's implicit doctrine that workers are responsible for any failure to change society with socialism's doctrine that the triumph of the working class is historically inevitable. Socialism included what might be called a "fortifying myth," that is, an ideological element that allows activists to frame defeats so that they are understandable and so that belief in the efficacy of the movement can be sustained until new political opportunities emerge.[22] Working-class republicanism did not have such a "fortifying myth." Ultimately, working-class republicanism simply provided the Knights of Labor with too few ideological resources for explaining what had happened, in Newark or elsewhere. And because the Knights had achieved greater solidarity than had any previous organization, their failure and, hence, responsibility was all the greater.

LONG-TERM REVERBERATIONS
OF THE KNIGHTS' COLLAPSE

The history of the American labor movement in the forty years after the Knights' collapse suggests that the Order's defeat had implications for workers' collective action extending far beyond the immediate decline of the Knights. After the collapse of the Order, Knights activists were disheartened, the organizational structures they had built were scorned, and the collective action frame they had devised was rejected. This made it difficult for radical labor activists to recognize and act on new political opportunities when they occurred. In the 1890s, for example, a large populist movement provided the opportunity for farmer-labor cooperation at the same time the American electoral system underwent a critical realignment, offering an even more opportune moment for mass insurgency than had existed in the 1880s. But chronic despair clouded the vision of those who might earlier have attempted to mobilize a movement, and those who had earlier spoken out in favor of a broad-based labor movement were silent.

At the same time, those in the labor movement who promoted moderate politics and sectional labor unions were empowered. A new group of labor activists achieved prominence in wake of the Knights' defeat, the majority of whom eschewed the organization of less-skilled workers, and rejected the vision and program of radical working-class republicanism. These newly empowered activists drew lessons from the Knights' failure. As Samuel Gompers, the best known of these activists and leader of the American Federation of Labor, stated when justifying his conservative policies, he had seen "how professions of radicalism and sensationalism concentrated all the forces of organized society against a labor movement and nullified in advance normal, necessary activity" (Gompers, 1925: 97). The lesson he and others like him drew from the failure of the Knights was that only closed craft unionism and pragmatic, nonradical politics could succeed in the United States.[23]

The contrast with the British new unionism is telling. The new unions, like the Knights of Labor, experienced a big fall-off in membership after the first dramatic membership gains. However, as we have seen, employers did not go all out to eradicate the new unions. Thus, the new unions survived, if in weakened form. But the collective action frame used by new union activists included the socialist fortifying myth that the working class would eventually win. When a new wave of industrial unrest took place in 1911–13 and fresh political opportunities arose, new union activists were able to provide leadership, a collective action frame, and an organizational base to mobilize a revitalized labor movement. Many in the old unions eventually came to look favorably on Left politics and general unionism as a result of the tenacity and incremental successes of the new unionists (Hunt, 1981: 311–15; Marks, 1989: 210–11).

In the United States, in contrast, the Knights as a national organization did not survive the depression of the 1890s, and were not around when there was again an upsurge of industrial unrest beginning in 1909.[24]

CONCLUSION

This essay has offered a new explanation for the failure of the Knights of Labor and suggested some of the ways the Knights' collapse shaped workers' subsequent collective actions. Based on the history of the Knights in one important industrial state and comparative evidence about the development of similar labor movements in England and France, this essay demonstrates that the Knights of Labor failed because its rapid growth and early successes resulted in the countermobilization of powerful employers' associations. Unlike their counterparts in England and France, these associations had the benefits of rapid economic concentration at their disposal and no interventionist state to constrain them. Employers' disproportionate resources and strategic leverage put the Knights in a nearly hopeless situation, against which they struggled by reframing their conflict so that small employers would ally with the Knights. This strategy, which drew upon the ideology of working-class republicanism, did not work, and it led to internal schisms that rent apart the organization.

In the wake of the employers' effective countermobilization, Knights leaders were unable to innovate new strategies or to come up with an account of what had happened that would allow Knights members to believe that their collective action would lead to a different outcome in the future. Instead, a process of what I have called cognitive encumbrance seemed to occur, in which Knights participants blamed themselves for their failure to achieve a "workingmen's democracy."

The Knights' collapse mattered for the subsequent development of the American labor movement for two reasons. First, it strengthened employers' sense of collective identity and bolstered their organizational abilities. In future labor conflicts, they would be an even more formidable opponent. This is not the effect the Knights intended, but it is one way in which they affected subsequent class relations in the United States.

Second, workers drew lessons from the failure of the Knights about what kinds of strategies and organizations were likely to succeed in the future. Those who argued that craft unionism was the best organizing strategy for the American labor movement were empowered, and those who argued for broader-based organizing structures and political visions were marginalized. As a result, it would subsequently prove to be much more difficult to build upon craft ties to forge industrial unions.

Beyond the evolution of the American labor movement, this study has implications for our collective efforts to build better theories of social movement development. It demonstrates the usefulness of the theoretical framework presented in the introduction to this volume. By attending to the interplay of political opportunities, mobilizing structures, and framing processes, it has been possible to provide a more convincing explanation for the Knights' collapse than has been offered by others.

At the same time, however, this study also suggests that these three factors may not provide a sufficient theoretical framework when scholars move beyond the emergence phase of social movements and attempt to explain development and decline. In later phases of social movements, the appearance and actions of countermovements can be decisive. Certainly, McAdam, McCarthy, and Zald include countermovements in their discussion, but theoretically, they locate countermovements under the rubric of political opportunities. My analysis of the Knights suggests that subsuming countermovements under the more general category of "political opportunities" is inadequate. More theorizing about the dynamics of countermobilizaton is needed.

More speculatively, this study proposes some of the specific ways in which framing processes might shape the outcome of social movements. First, it is possible that the kind of "cognitive encumbrance" that helped to account for the speed of the Knights' demise might also befall other movements. Second, this study raises the possibility that "fortifying myths" are one framing element that might mitigate against the occurrence of cognitive encumbrance. Fortifying myths provide a ready set of arguments for activists to interpret defeats so that they are seen as setbacks, not final episodes.

Finally, this study draws attention to the ways in which social movements prepare the ground for future collective action. Many have pointed to the ways in which social movements can sometimes facilitate other movements, as for example happened when the women's movement built upon the civil rights movement (Evans, 1980; McAdam, 1988a). But, as this study of the Knights of Labor indicates, the relationship is not always beneficial. Sometimes social movements limit the course of future collective action by constraining activists' choices of plausible mobilizing structures and collective action frames.

Appendix. *Description of independent variables*

Variable	Description
Industrial factors[a]	
Wage differential	The percentage difference between the wages paid to skilled workers and the wages paid to "ordinary laborers" in the local industry (*local industry* is defined as the workers in a single industry in a single town. For example, the workers employed in Paterson's silk industry constitute one local industry and the workers employed in Jersey City's silk industry compose another.)
Number of establishments	The (logged) number of factories in the local industry
Average establishment size	The average number of workers per establishment in the local industry
Technological change	The increase in horsepower per worker between 1880 and 1890, a measure intended to reflect the intensity of mechanization
Capital-to-labor ratio	The number of dollars invested in the local industry divided by the annual wage bill for the local industry
Percent females	The percentage of female employment in the local industry
Community factors[a]	
Population	The log of the township population, measured in 1875 and 1885
One-industry town	A variable coded "1" when a single manufacturing industry dominated the locality (following Shorter and Tilly (1974) a locality was considered a one-industry town if one manufacturing industry employed more than 50% of the total manufacturing work force and there was no other manufacturing industry with more than 15% of the work force; the community was also classified a one-industry town if a single manufacturing industry had more than 60% of the work force, and the next largest industry had less than 20%)
Ethnic diversity	Calculated for each community, based on the proportion of residents born in the United States, Germany, Ireland, and "elsewhere" (the following formula was used: $H_i = 100(1 - \Sigma p_i^2)$, where p_1 is the population in that community born in location i)
Organizational factors[b]	
KOL less-skilled assembly in the local industry	A variable coded "1" when a local assembly of less-skilled workers was present in the local industry

Appendix *(continued)*

Variable	Description
KOL less-skilled assembly in the community	A variable coded "1" when a local assembly of less-skilled workers was present in the community but outside the local industry (the distinction between community and local industry was made because earlier work on the Knights' emergence indicated that different dynamics operate at the community and industry level)
KOL craft assembly in the local industry	A variable coded "1" when an additional craft-type Knights local is present in the local industry
KOL craft assembly in community	A variable coded "1" when a craft-type Knights local is present in the community
Trade-union craft in local industry	A variable coded "1" when a non-Knights craft local was present in the local industry
Trade-union craft in community	A variable coded "1" when a non-Knights craft local was present in the community
Employers' association	A variable coded "1" when a manufacturers' association was present in the local industry
Election victory	A variable coded "1" when labor party candidates won
Time factors	
Before 1887?	A variable coded "1" for years prior to 1887 (after the Haymarket bombing and the loss of the third railroad strike against Jay Gould, the Knights had a much more difficult time maintaining membership and sustaining organization)
National factors	
National KOL death rate	The crude death rate for local assemblies in the national Knights of Labor (this variable, which is measured for all years of the Order's existence, is included as a control for the possibility that local variation in the failure rate of Knights assemblies merely reflects the Knights' national pattern of collapse)

[a]Coded from the U.S. Tenth Census, 1880, manufacturing manuscripts; and the New Jersey State Census, 1875 and 1885.

[b]All organizational variables are constructed as time-varying covariates. Together, the labor movement variables describe the types of union organization located in each industry and community at the beginning of each year. They are coded from a variety of sources including Garlock (1973), New Jersey Bureau of Statistics of Labor and Industries (1888, 1901), and various issues of the *New Jersey Unionist, Paterson Labor Standard,* and local New Jersey newspapers. See Voss (1993) for details. Information on employers' associations was compiled from Bonnett (1956) and local New Jersey newspapers. Election data was gathered from Fink (1983: 28–29), *John Swinton's Paper,* and local newspapers. I am indebted to Leon Fink for providing additional information about the dates of elections reported in his book.

PART III

FRAMING PROCESSES

11

Culture, ideology, and strategic framing

MAYER N. ZALD

The recent focus on the strategic framing of injustice and grievances, their causes, motivations, and associated templates for collective action, has served to reemphasize the central importance of ideas and cultural elements in understanding the mobilization of participation in social movements and the framing of political opportunity. While conceiving of culture and framing as strategically produced represents a substantial break with past conceptions of ideas in movements, which tended to emphasize their embeddedness in community and as crescively emergent, still the notion of strategic framing is quite vague in terms of its constituent elements and general processes. This introduction to Part III focuses first on the larger evolution of the analysis of ideas and culture in academic scholarship and as it was entailed (or not) in the study of social movements. Recent decades have seen the emergence of modes of analysis of culture, of frames and scripts, of rhetoric and dramaturgy, and of cultural repertoires and tool kits that substantially enhance our ability to analyze the role of culture, ideology, and frames in social movements. The literature on culture and framing in social movements has been somewhat amorphous. I sketch six basic topics in the interplay of movements, framing, and the larger society. First, I discuss the *cultural construction of repertoires of contention and frames.* Second, since framing takes place in the context of larger societal processes, I discuss the contribution of *cultural contradictions and historical events* in providing opportunities for framing. Frames are generated by a diverse set of actors in relation to a variety of audiences inside and outside of a movement. Thus, the third topic for attention is *framing as a strategic activity.* Moreover, frames are contested – within the movement by leaders and cadre debating alternative goals and visions for the movement, and externally by countermovement actors, bystanders, and state officials who oppose the movement. Thus, fourth, I discuss *competitive processes* that represent the context in which frames are selected and come to dominate. Fifth, frames are transmitted and reframed in the *mass media.* Ever since the development of the broadside and early newspapers, movements have depended on the media for the promulgation of images of movements. Understanding frame transmission and success depends in part upon understanding the production routines of the media and the potential impact of different kinds of media. Finally, we must understand how political opportunity and mobilization intersect to shape the *outcomes* of framing competitions. Outcomes are both short term and long term, on policy and on the cultural stock.

CULTURE, IDEOLOGY, AND FRAMES IN CONTEMPORARY SOCIAL MOVEMENT THEORY

Culture, ideology, and strategic framing is our broadest and loosest conceptual cluster. They are linked because they are the topics that deal with the content and processes by which meaning is attached to objects and actions. Roughly speaking, as we use the terms, culture is the shared beliefs and understandings, mediated by and constituted by symbols and language, of a group or society; ideology is the set of beliefs that are used to justify or challenge a given social-political order and are used to interpret the political world; frames are the specific metaphors, symbolic representations, and cognitive cues used to render or cast behavior and events in an evaluative mode and to suggest alternative modes of action. Although it has been common to see culture as a long-enduring set of symbols and beliefs, it is also possible to treat the emergence and creation of culture. Ideologies tend to be more complex and logical systems of beliefs than frames, though frames may be embedded in ideologies. Moreover symbols, frames, and ideologies are created and changed in the process of contestation.

In the recent development of social movement research, following the decade of the sixties, the systematic study of culture, ideology, and frames developed last, after the resource mobilization and political process approaches had already developed some momentum. However, a longer and more sociological view reveals a different and more complex process of differentiation and attention to the study of ideology and beliefs.

Before the advent of the discipline of sociology and especially the development of the Chicago School, the study of social movements was treated as part of political philosophy and the history of ideas. Historical studies of movements and revolutions often focused upon ideology and beliefs, especially the ideologies and beliefs of key historical actors – whether Martin Luther or Karl Marx, whether the philosophes or the political economists. However, the recounting of the ideas promulgated by key figures was typically treated developmentally, as a sequence of ideas in the heads of movement leaders, or in terms of historical diffusion, the spread of those ideas. The core elements of movement beliefs might be played out against the social situation and conditions in which the movement leader developed, but a kind of determinism or epistemic realism guided the analysis. That is, ideas were treated as real in themselves; analysis of the play of ideas, the strategic understanding of the range of alternatives, the intricate analysis of metaphor and symbol, a differentiated view of the layers of audience reception, attention to the silences of ideas were beyond the reach of the traditional history of ideas.

That kind of intellectual history has continued and movements can still be described in terms of the careers, beliefs, and ideologies and critical events surrounding movement leaders. (It is not as if the transformation of academic studies leads to the total displacement of earlier modes of analysis.) The development of sociology, however, especially in America, led to a different approach to the study of collective behavior and social movements. Concerned with general patterns of social relations and behavior and shaped by a profound concern for the social changes generated by industrialization and urbanization, Chicago sociologists, especially Robert Park and, then, Herbert Blumer, developed the field of collective behavior (including social movements) to examine the responses to social change that occurred outside of formal institutions and well-institutionalized processes. The key phenomena linked under this rubric were public opinion, fads and fashions, riots and panics, and social movements and revolutions.

Each of these phenomena has a cognitive or ideological component. For instance, public opinion involves attitudes and beliefs about shared objects. Even riots and panics, the phenomena with least apparent cultural and symbolic content, have cognitive and perceptual components in that they require social situations to be defined as threatening or as requiring very active physical behavior. Too, situations calling forth riots (e.g., bread riots, soccer riots) develop cultural traditions of patterned behavior. Moreover, Chicago sociology also gave birth to the important school of symbolic interactionism. Yet the dominant thrust of the study of collective behavior, as in most of sociology, was to focus upon structure and process, treating the *content* of ideology or beliefs as either outside the realm of analysis or as a constant.

The point may be overstated. After all, symbolic interactionists Ralph Turner and Lewis Killian (1957) treated emergent norms as one of the defining features in the transformation of random or disorganized responses to problems into collective and organized behavior. Similarly, Neil Smelser (1962) argued that different kinds of generalized beliefs were essential for each kind of collective behavior. Nevertheless, the analysis of collective behavior and social movements until very recently focused largely on structure and process.

In part, culture and ideology were downplayed because sociologists of those decades had few tools for analysis. Although symbolic interactionism asserted the centrality to social life of symbolic communication and shared meanings, it focused more on interaction and less on the content and force of symbols. Sociologists of social movements, preoccupied with distancing themselves from what were perceived to be the limits of the earlier tradition of collective behavior analysis, began to focus upon the organizational and political aspects of collective action, even though in other parts of sociology and social sciences a turn toward culture, frames, and symbols was beginning to occur. (See Zald in Morris and Mueller, 1992.) These developments have led to a revolution in our ability to analyze culture. We have had a major invigoration of our ability to analyze culture, to understand meaning, to dig beyond the surface rendering of language, representation, and metaphor.

The turn to culture and language in contemporary social science has several sources – the development of French structuralism, the growth of semiotics, the development of hermeneutics and discourse analysis, Gramscian Marxism, psychoanalytic theory, feminist theory, postmodernism, the analysis of accounts, and so on. However, four not entirely separate streams have had a direct impact on the study of social movements and on essays in this volume: (1) the depth analysis of culture and symbols that developed first in anthropology; (2) the analysis of frames and scripts stemming from the cognitive revolution in psychological social psychology and from Goffman's work in sociology; (3) the turn to dramatistic and rhetorical analysis; and (4) the analysis of culture as repertoires of action and as tool kits.

Depth analysis of culture

Never has so much been made out of one set of cockfights! Clifford Geertz's (1973) analysis of the cultural meaning of cockfights in Bali, of how the social patterning of betting and of bettors recapitulated social patterns and relations of the larger Balinese society, was part of the reinvigoration of our understandings of how cultural patterns deeply penetrate everyday life. Of course, the deep understanding of culture, of latent meanings, of the relationship of symbolic form to social structure would have occurred without Geertz's trips to Bali, since his work fed into and off of larger intellectual currents. However, anthropological perspectives on culture and symbols, especially the work of Geertz and Victor Turner, have infused analysis of both the continuities of movement ideology and language with preexisting understandings in different groups in society *and* an understanding of how movements change the culture, providing new terms, iconic symbols, and glosses on social relations. The French Revolution has provided especially fertile grounds for this analysis. (See William H. Sewell, 1980, and Lynn Hunt, 1984.) William Sewell's (1985) debate with Theda Skocpol (1985) has especially illuminated two alternative views of the role of ideology in large national revolutions. Sewell shows how Skocpol's original comparative work on revolution ignored the importance of culturally consonant ideologies in shaping the directions and alternatives, while Skocpol argues that the anthropological approach to ideology is too passive and deterministic. She favors, instead, an approach which sees ideology as more active and strategic.

Cognitive processes and framing

Where anthropological perspectives have led to a focus upon cultural continuities and transformation in meaning systems and in the cultural stock, social psychological perspectives have led to a focus upon the cognitive processes involved in interpreting, classifying, and characterizing behavior and situations, and the functions of these frames in evoking responses and charting alternatives. Prior to the 1970s, the social psychology of social movements focused largely on motivational matters. Thus, the whole debate about deprivation, relative deprivation, and rising expectations zeroed in on the question of the social conditions that generate the energy for participation in movements. Although relative deprivation and rising expectations both have an explicit perceptual component – that is, they depend upon cognitive awareness of contrasts – cognitive analysis stopped there.

Social psychology then took a cognitive turn. Beginning with cognitive dissonance theory, then turning to attribution theory, and the analysis of scripts and schemas that operate to pattern and cluster chains of behavior, psychological social psychology moved cognitive processes to center stage. Sociological social psychology was affected by Erving Goffman's (1974) subtle analyses of how changes in social-physical context, often minute, reshaped the possibilities for behavior. Frame analysis, which resonates with gestalt psychology, becomes an entry point for how socially defined markers (from subtle physical changes such as desks and curtains, to symbols and ideologies) make sense of the world and provide alternative pathways for behavior. Frame and script are connected, since elaborated scripts are organized around core schemas, which serve as central frames.

Rejuvenating symbolic interactionism, frame analysis is directly applied to social movements by Snow and his colleagues (Snow et al., 1986; Snow and Benford, 1992), who developed a number of related concepts (e.g., frame resonance, master frames, diagnostic frames, prognostic frames) to show how ideologies and symbols work in the service of social movements. Frames help interpret problems to define problems for action and suggest action pathways to remedy the problem. Scripts and schemas are used by Gamson and associates (Gamson and Modigliani, 1989; Gamson, 1992a, 1993) to analyze the transformation of political debates in areas as disparate as nuclear power and weaponry, welfare politics, and abortion politics. Frames can be contested. Activists in movements and countermovements have a stake in developing metaphors, images, and definitions of the situation that support alternative programs.

Analysis of rhetoric and dramaturgy

The cognitive turn has been accompanied by increasing attention to the ways in which behavior is plotted and shaped by rhetoric and dramatistic modes.

Related to symbolic interactionism, but reaching out to literary theory and theories of persuasion, dramaturgical and rhetorical analysis is introduced to the study of social movements by the political scientist Murray Edelman (1967, 1971) and, more immediately, by Joseph Gusfield (1969, 1981). Dramaturgy and rhetoric are employed by social movement actors to enplot their worlds and to persuade their audiences, and by scholars to analyze their actions. Further, the scholars themselves use rhetorical and dramaturgical tools to render their analyses and persuade *their* audiences.

Repertoires and tool kits

Finally, issues of how social movements innovate and change have been linked to cultural analysis through the notions of repertoires of contention (and of organization) and of cultural tool kits. Although Charles Tilly is largely considered a structuralist, his notion of "repertoires of action" (1978; see also Tarrow, 1994) recognized and gave legitimacy to the notion of innovation and learning of repertoires of contention. More recently, Ann Swidler's (1986) idea of "culture as tool kit" gives us a framework for thinking about institutional learning and the *bricolage* process by which components of the cultural stock are assembled into specific models, or exemplars, of socially defined behavior.

THE DYNAMICS OF FRAMING

Armed with new modes of analysis, scholars have increasingly incorporated cultural and symbolic themes in their analysis of social movements. A 1994 volume edited by Laraña, Johnston, and Gusfield includes many essays focusing on ideology and symbols in social movements. McAdam in that volume provides an overview of the impact of culture on social movements and social movements on culture. Potentially, this is very large and amorphous terrain. Here we focus on the societal and media context of framing and framing as a strategic activity. I briefly sketch several topics that need to be highlighted in understanding repertoire and frame dynamics.

Cultural construction of repertoires of contention, mobilizing structures, and frames

Social movements exist in a larger societal context. They draw on the cultural stock for images of what is an injustice, for what is a violation of what ought to be. For instance, a phrase popular in the women's movement, "A woman's body is her own," frames a problem and suggests a policy direction for women in relation to abortion policy and the medical establishment. But it makes sense only in a cultural discourse that highlights notions of individual autonomy and equality of citizenship rights: autonomy because it focuses upon individual choice, equality because it presumes that women are equal citizens. It would make little sense in a society in which most people, male and female, were slaves, or believed to belong to the family or the collective. It would make little sense in a society in which women were largely and legitimately conceived of as dependent on, first, fathers, and second, husbands. Contemporary framing of injustice and of political goals almost always draw upon the larger societal definitions of relationships, of rights, and of responsibilities to highlight what is wrong with the current social order, and to suggest directions for change.

Similarly, movements draw on the cultural stock of how to protest and how to organize. Templates of organization include skills and technology of communication (e.g., writing newsletters, running meetings), of fund raising, of running an office, of recruiting members. Repertoires of contention include bombing buildings, building barricades, organizing marches, nonviolent disruption, and the like. Templates of organization may be drawn from the whole society, while repertoires of contention are available from the whole social movement sector (including political parties and prior social movements), or similarly situated actors. For instance, SMOs may learn lobbying techniques from industry trade associations, and vice versa. (See Useem and Zald, 1982.)

Cultural stocks are not static, and over time repertoires of contention grow and change. Some items fall out of the repertoire. For instance, for a variety of reasons the neighborhood barricades, so important to the European urban revolts of the nineteenth century, have largely vanished. So, too, the sit-down strike is no longer as prominent as it once was. On the other hand, in the United States the number of marches on Washington increase as transportation costs decline, as Washington becomes more a focus of citizen and media attention, and as the skills to organize such marches are more widely disseminated.

To say that social movements draw on the larger cultural stock is not to say that all social movements have equal access to that stock. Social movements, their leaders, and participants are differentially situated in the social structure. As such, they draw upon the repertoires and frames available to and compatible with the skills, orientations, and styles of the groups that make them up. Middle-class whites do not have access to the emotional styles of the black church to facilitate solidarity in the face of fear; homeless women do not have the lobbying skills of Harvard-trained lawyers. Moreover, repertoires of contention and of organization have to "fit," to be "appropriate to" the injustice. A violent tactic such as bombing a clinic feels right to antiabortion advocates who equate a fetus with a person; it is extremist behavior to those who deny that equivalence. Again, in 1993 and 1994 Hispanic-

American students used hunger strikes as a tool to gain changes in ethnic studies programs: In the context of the example set by Caesar Chavez, this was culturally consonant; to outsiders, it seemed disproportionate.

Cultural contradictions and the flow of history

Political and mobilization opportunities are often created by cultural breaks and the surfacing of long dormant contradictions that reframe grievances and injustices and the possibilities of action. Sometimes these breaks are behavioral events that recast or challenge prevailing definitions of the situation, thus changing perceptions of costs and benefits of policies and programs and the perception of injustice of the status quo. The event, which may suddenly impose a grievance as at Three Mile Island, or the dramatic framing of an issue, as in the Anita Hill–Clarence Thomas hearings or the Rodney King decision, changes perceptions and calls attention to, and crystallizes opinion on, moral and political matters that had been dormant or ambiguous. The cultural part is that the behavioral event plays into reigning definitions and symbolic frames. For instance, nuclear power plant accidents at Three Mile Island and Chernobyl, though differing in scope and in actual damage to health and the environment, both affected perceptions of safety and the relative legitimacy of the nuclear power industry and of activists. Both parties had made claims about the value and safety of nuclear power. The events challenged the claims of the pro–nuclear power sympathizers and authorities, gave credence to the claims of the anti–nuclear power groups, and created a sense of urgency for action.

Cultural contradictions occur and lead into mobilization when two or more cultural themes that are potentially contradictory are brought into active contradiction by the force of events, or when the realities of behavior are seen to be substantially different than the ideological justifications for the movement. The modern civil rights movement grew out of the attempt to dismantle segregation in public institutions and in the law. Although no single event or person forced the contradiction of racism and democracy unto the public agenda, events following World War II facilitated that process. In particular, as the United States played an increasingly dominant role in justifying the dismantling of the colonial system and the spread of democratic systems, the contradiction between democracy and racism at home restricted the claims of the American model. Harry Truman was not known as a liberal on racial matters, yet his executive order desegregating the military signaled to the world and to domestic partisans and audiences some readiness of the United States to resolve the contradiction. Both the issues and the changing balance of power were addressed in that executive order.

Cultural contradictions in the status of women have been revealed by their participation in the abolitionist movement of the 1840s and 1850s and in the civil rights movement and the antiwar movement of the 1960s. In both cases, there were discrepancies between the ideological justifications of the movements and the treatment of women activists. The recognition and construction of those contradictions were part of the grounds justifying the suffrage movement and the modern feminist movement.

Strategic framing

Cultural breaks and cultural contradictions provide context and opportunity for movement cadre (leaders and core participants) and for activists and sympathizers. But there is an active process of framing and definition of ideology, of symbols, of iconic events by moral entrepreneurs – who may or may not be activists themselves. Journalists, ministers, community and associational leaders, politicians, and writers attempt to define the issues, invent metaphors, attribute blame, define tactics. Both cultural breaks and cultural contradictions lead to action and policy imperatives only as they are defined in an active process of cultural and movement construction.

Snow and his collaborators (Snow and Benford, 1988, 1992; Snow, Rochford, Worden, and Benford, 1986) have articulated a set of concepts for thinking about how frames work to provide shorthand interpretations of the world, to locate blame, to suggest lines of actions. Moreover, large movements, or progenitor movements, may provide master frames, which later movements may draw on. For instance, the civil rights movement provides a language that the later women's movement and the disability movement can draw upon. Whether it is the diagnostic and prognostic frames provided by large historic ideologies such as socialism, the development of a tactical solution such as "nuclear weapons freeze," or the action implications of a concrete historical event, such as the Haymarket riot or Rosa Parks's refusal to move to the back of the bus, movements actively engage in the construction of meaning, the portrayal of injustice, and the definition of pathways to change. Note that Rosa Parks was no simple cleaning woman; she had been active in the National Association for the Advancement of Colored People (NAACP) and had been secretary of the local chapter. Moreover, boycotts and resistance to segregation were not new (Morris, 1984).

Competitive processes

This active process of construction occurs in a variety of arenas. There is an external and internal competition for defining the situation and what is to be done. Externally, movement activists and leaders contest authorities and they enter into debates with countermovement activists and leaders. Movements and countermovements not only are involved in mobilization contests to demonstrate who has the most support and resources at their command, they are involved in framing contests attempting to persuade authorities and bystanders of the rightness of their cause.

At the same time, different movement organizations (MOs) and segments of a movement engage in an intramovement contest over tactics and goals. This intramovement process leads to changes in the dominant frames of a movement and a succession in MO power and influence. For instance, the influence of the NAACP receded as SCLC rose. There is, then, a twofold process of change: Specific organizations and leaders rise and fall while, loosely connected, frames and definitions succeed or recede in importance. Since no MO or leader "owns" a frame (i.e., they can be appropriated by others), the connection of MOs to cultural frames is problematic.

Framing and the media

Framing contests occur in face-to-face interaction and through a variety of media – newspapers, books, pamphlets, radio, television. Movement activists may debate in coffeehouses, in bars, or in meeting halls, but they have to change and mobilize bystander publics, many of whom may only know of the movement and its issues as portrayed in various media.

Media are not neutral to this process, since they lend themselves to different rhetorics and images, to rendering the salience and intensity of issues. For instance, an image of an aborted fetus on television has different impact than reading about abortion in a newspaper. Media differ in their ability to convey information, evoke emotional response, dramatize events, and focus attention. Since they, too, are part of a larger cultural context, this selection process will be shaped by the larger society of which they are a part. Thus, for instance, Hallin and Mancini (1984) show how Italian and American TV provide a very different set of coverages because of the differences in presidential and representational forms in the two countries.

Moreover, mass media have production routines and organizational dynamics that lead them to more than transmit information; they transform it. Thus, in capitalist democracies, the media not only "report the news" but must also respond to their owners' or controllers' wishes and to market demands. Since public interest in stories waxes and wanes, activists develop strategies for encouraging media to cover them (Ryan, 1991).

At any point in time, a specific movement has available the current social stock of media possibilities, but over time that stock changes, effecting framing potential. Changes in technology – the development of newspapers, the coming of radio, the growth of television, the development of satelites, the spread of hand-held video cameras, each changes the potential for framing movement demands and injustices.

The impact of social movements on the cultural stock

Social movements not only draw upon and recombine elements of the cultural stock, they add to it. The frames of winning movements get translated into public policy and into the slogans and symbols of the general culture. Losing movements are confined to the dust bowl of history and are marginalized (though often to return when the wheel of history resurfaces issues or cleavages submerged in defeat). For instance, racist rhetoric of groups such as the Ku Klux Klan is marginalized by the civil rights movement, only to resurface as immigration issues and changing political coalitions and power surface the issues once more. Successful movements have their tactics and frames appropriated by other movements; they become exemplars providing training grounds and models. Failing movements are less likely to provide ideological and symbolic models, we suspect, but they do provide networks of affiliation and reservoirs of experience drawn on by later movements with loose similarities. Movements such as the anti–Vietnam War movement and the student movement of the sixties that have an especially strong cultural component also feed into the general culture, leaving a set of terms and images that become part of the general cultural stock.

The important contribution of this volume is to link cultural and framing processes to mobilization and political opportunity in social movements. Essays elsewhere in the volume also deal with framing issues. In particular the essays by Elena Zdravomyslova and by Anthony Oberschall in Part I examined the interaction of political opportunity and frame and symbolic development in the transformation of the former Soviet Union and Eastern Europe. Essays in Part II by Elisabeth Clemens and Kim Voss dealt with the role of cultural models and framing in mobilization processes in labor unions and political action. The four essays in this part move components of framing and culture to center stage. They link frames to political opportunities and structures and to the mobilization of bystanders through the media.

In "Framing Political Opportunity" (Chapter 12), William Gamson and David Meyer provide a general framework for integrating long-term and short-term aspects of culture and framing with the institutional versus cultural source of political opportunities. Their chapter links macro and micro issues. They argue that political opportunities have an inevitable cultural component. That is, political opportunities require recognition and framing, thus symbolic and institutionalized cultural assumptions play into defining political opportunities. They develop a typology of opportunities, related to volatile and stable elements, on the one hand, and whether the opportunity occurs in the cultural or institutional domain, on the other. At the micro level, they show how the cognitive biases of movement cadre lead them to define opportunities for successful action when an outside observer might well think action had little hope.

Chapters 13 and 14 implicate the media in the framing of issues and in the public response to movement frames. John McCarthy, Jackie Smith, and I (Chapter 13) locate attention to movements in the context of the broad competition for space and time in the media and other arenas. We argue that

scholars often conflate several different cycles or processes that together influence how important social movements are to the public, to elections, to
government and to the media – the mobilization cycle, the tactical-protest
cycle that makes news, the relation of public opinion to newspaper reporting
of different issues, the electoral cycle and the government agenda. Each of
these arenas is organized in different terms and has a logic of its own; each
is only loosely coupled to the others. In capitalist democracies, the amount
of space given to different issues is a function of the perceptions by media
workers of both public interest and story importance. On the other side,
publics pay attention to some issues based largely on media attention to those
issues, while for some issues, such as concern about the economy, media coverage is only loosely linked to the amount of public concern. Each of these
sites has its own dynamics and incentives. Movements compete for space on
each of the agendas. Partly, McCarthy, Smith, and I deal with how the flow
of competing events shapes political opportunity and the present framing
efforts of activists. We demonstrate the usefulness of this approach by drawing on data collected from several types of movements – empowerment of
the poor, environment, peace, public interest groups, and anti–drunk driving.
These data show how differential access to arenas shapes the tactics of movements.

Bert Klandermans and Sjoerd Goslinga (Chapter 14) investigate how the
structure of newspaper stories affects audience perception and reaction to a
social welfare issue in the Netherlands. In recent times the growth of the
welfare state in Western democracies has been slowed by the fiscal crisis of
the state. These authors show how one runaway program in the Netherlands,
the disability program, has been reported in the press and how different audiences respond to that reporting. It is a microanalysis of the relationship of
the structure of stories to audience reaction. It is also a study of the social
construction of an issue.

In the final chapter of Part III, Doug McAdam critiques the "ideational
bias" of much of the discussion of frames that ignores the extent to which
movements operate in hostile environments and manipulate perceptions of
threat. He draws attention to the multiple functions of strategic frames. Mc-
Adam also shows how Martin Luther King, Jr., developed a dramaturgical
rhetoric that strategically responded to the challenges faced by the civil rights
movement. That rhetoric was tightly tied to African-American religious culture at the same time that it resonated with well-established American political themes.

In the introduction to this volume we commented that we had two major
aspirations for the volume – the stimulation of research that showed the interplay or interaction of processes suggested by juxtaposing the three major
conceptual domains of modern social movement theory and the stimulation
of cross-national research. Many chapters in the volume (e.g., those by
Kriesi, Oberschall, della Porta, and Rucht) show the interaction of processes

drawn from two domains and are comparative. It is clear, however, that comparative studies of framing processes across movements, across time, and across national/cultural contexts are relatively rare. (But see Oberschall, Chapter 4.) The literature on tactical repertoires and on framing tends to examine them within single movements, occasionally also noting the diffusion of repertoires of contention or of frames from one movement to another. I believe that a major research agenda for the future is the study of frames and culture in comparative context. Without attempting to be exhaustive, let me suggest how the general topics discussed in this section can be used to point to lines of possible research.

Cultural construction

Movement frames and ideologies grow out of existing cultural definitions, but play out in other nations and cultures as well. The rhetoric and framing of the French Revolution spreads immediately to other nations and over the ages. Similarly, the modern women's movement is received variously in different nations. Just as the structural study of revolutions can be done comparatively, so too can cultural receptivity and resonance, sharpening our understanding of the relationship of culture incorporation and transformation of master frames and symbolic imagery in social movements.

Cultural contradictions and historical events

Events such as the nuclear accidents at Chernobyl and Three Mile Island present research opportunities on at least two fronts. On the one hand, because the media, governmental reactions, and social movement mobilization processes differ between societies, they allow scholars to have an almost experimental opportunity for watching the playing out of social movements when there are similar threats or causes for movement action. On the other hand, such events can be framed differently in different societies, depending upon perceptions of the legitimacy of the state, locating responsibility and so on. Cultural contradictions related to similar processes, say the status of women, will play out differently in societies, even though they may have similar formal rhetorics.

Strategic action

The field of movement entrepreneurs and activists for movements are differently located and constrained in different movements. Gamson, Ferree, Lindgens, Neidhardt, and Rucht, in ongoing research, are studying how the abortion issue is framed and nested in the political systems of the United States and Germany. Activists in Germany are more likely to be located within political parties than in the United States, where independent social movement organizations (SMOs) are more often the rule. Similarly, the history of women's issues is substantially different in the two societies.

Competitive processes

Since societies differ in the amount and structuring of social movement activity and the control and manifestation of countermovements, the processes of competitive framing are likely to look quite different, both within movements and in relationship to countermovements. In one society countermovements may be largely state sponsored, whereas in another the state may be almost a neutral arbiter. Thus, the amount and structure of competitive framing ought to look quite different in, say, Great Britain and the United States, even if on other grounds they might look quite similar.

Media processes

We know (Hallin and Mancini, 1984) that nations with different political structures and with different media control report the news in different ways. Hallin and Mancini find, for instance, that the representation of parties and leaders is quite different in Italy than in the United States. Those differences in the media impact upon how movements are reported and how they serve as conduits for mobilization or suppression. But there has been little mapping of the range of variation beyond the gross distinction between repressive, state-controlled systems and open systems. We know little about the impact of differences in news formats and styles. How, for instance, adversarial journalism, as contrasted with "neutral professionalism," impacts on the reporting of movement activity is largely unknown. Nor do we know how mass culture affects "newsworthiness" in different cultures, thus shaping the market for movement news.

Outcomes

Comparative examination of the impact and outcomes of movements on culture and frames, as well as on policy, would be extraordinarily valuable. For one thing, the policy outcomes literature in political science has been most developed in the United States, with fewer studies of impact and outcome in other countries. Moreover, when and how movements add to or change the cultural stock are an important dimension for understanding social change in general. The cultural stock becomes the backdrop for social movement development and political choice in the next round of collective mobilization and choice. Thus, a comparative focus on outcomes contributes to locating social movements in historical process.

12

Framing political opportunity

WILLIAM A. GAMSON and DAVID S. MEYER

The concept of political opportunity structure is in trouble, in danger of becoming a sponge that soaks up virtually every aspect of the social movement environment – political institutions and culture, crises of various sorts, political alliances, and policy shifts. As Tarrow notes (1988: 430), "Political opportunity may be discerned along so many directions and in so many ways that it is less a variable than a cluster of variables – some more readily observable than others." It threatens to become an all-encompassing fudge factor for all the conditions and circumstances that form the context for collective action. Used to explain so much, it may ultimately explain nothing at all.

Part of the problem is that analysts use political opportunity structure to serve a wide variety of functions, and define it accordingly. Scholars who want to explain the emergence and influence of a movement over time use it as a set of *independent variables,* to describe dynamic aspects of the political environment that change to allow or encourage the emergence of challengers (e.g., Jenkins and Perrow 1977; McAdam 1982; Meyer 1990, 1993a). Others who want to compare the development of similar movements in different nations, states, or cities use political opportunity structure as a holder for *intervening variables* such as institutional structures or rules of representation (e.g., Amenta and Zylan 1991; Eisinger 1973; Kitschelt 1986; Tilly 1978). In cross-sectional comparisons, they use political opportunity structure to ex-

This chapter originated as a paper prepared for a conference entitled European/American Perspectives on Social Movements, Washington, D.C., August 13–15, 1992, and for the American Sociological Association Annual Meeting, Pittsburgh, August 20, 1992. The essay benefited from much good attention by members of the Boston College Media Research and Action Project (MRAP), the National Endowment for the Humanities Summer Seminar on "The Political Histories of Collective Action," led by Sidney Tarrow at Cornell University, and the Conference on European/American Perspectives on Social Movements. We also thank Sidney Tarrow and Robert Kleidman for offering detailed written comments on a draft.

plain why like movements choose different tactics or effect different policy outcomes. Finally, others who want to understand the long-term influence of movements on policy and culture point to structural opportunities that movements can create, or political opportunity structure as *dependent variables* (e.g., Burstein 1991; Freeman 1975) – although few have used the term explicitly in this context.

In fact, political opportunity structure can serve all of these uses, but we need to be more clear about our purposes, what we mean by opportunity, and about the interaction between movements and opportunities. Opportunities open the way for political action, but movements also make opportunities. If the zeitgeist of the 1960s provided new space for social movements to operate, it was in part because the movements created that space through their own actions. The voting rights won by the civil rights movement changed the opportunity for institutional political action in the United States. Opportunities may shape or constrain movements, but movements can create opportunities as well.

Like the concept of frame, opportunity balances elements of structure and agency. Frames are, on the one hand, part of the world, passive and structured; on the other, people are active in constructing them. Events are framed, but we frame events. The vulnerability of the framing process makes it a locus of potential struggle, not a leaden reality to which we all must inevitably yield.

Similarly, opportunities sometimes present themselves with no movement provenance, but movements are active in structuring and creating political opportunity. Movements often benefit from opportunities created by predecessors or other contemporary movements. Beyond this, opportunities are subject to interpretation and are often matters of controversy. Political opportunities are subject to framing processes and are often the source of internal movement disagreements about appropriate action strategies.

The second half of this chapter examines this process of framing political opportunity within social movements. But before we can take on this task, we need to unpack the terms and issues that comprise political opportunity. The essential problem is that everyone who writes about political opportunity structure refers to different variables. It is certainly appropriate for analysts of the prospects of successful civil rights mobilization, for example, to consider different factors than someone studying the environmental movement. Without more specificity, however, political opportunity structure could be defined exclusively ad hoc and after the fact. We want to integrate the disparate approaches outlined above so that we can make progress in developing a more robust concept that makes useful comparisons possible across time, space, and different issue areas. We want a concept that allows careful analysis to examine and identify opportunities even in the absence of a challenging movement.

UNPACKING POLITICAL OPPORTUNITY

We readily acknowledge the need for including the context in which movements operate in a systematic way in order to explain the development and outcomes of collective action. The resource-mobilization perspective drew analytic attention away from state or social breakdown as the cause of social protest movements, as resource-mobilization theorists emphasized activist success rather than social failure in explaining movement activity. This gives organizers credit for their work but also implicitly blames them for failures or the absence of movement activity.

Often the best efforts of the most skillful and committed organizers are not enough to mobilize a movement. Theoretically, we want to integrate the internal processes of social movements with the analysis of the context in which they emerge. Practically, we want to know why issue-based movements occur when they do, their relationship to conventional institutional politics, and ultimately their influence on the policy process. We need to recognize both the conditions under which movements generally rise and decline and the ways in which movements can maximize their influence within a given context.

The core idea weaving together the disparate threads of political opportunity is the opening and closing of political space and its institutional and substantive location. Increased opportunity implies more space and fewer constraints. When we compare opportunities, we do so across political systems or over time. Adverse circumstances exist in one system and more favorable ones in another; or within a single system, circumstances become more or less favorable over time. This sharpens what we need to ask about the context of collective action and is a unifying dimension behind all of the specific variables under the general rubric of political opportunity.

The stability dimension

Some aspects of opportunity are deeply embedded in political institutions and culture. If they change at all, they do so very gradually over decades or centuries or through revolutionary changes in regime. From the standpoint of social movements, these aspects of opportunity are essentially fixed and given, barring dramatic and unforeseen changes beyond their control.

Other aspects are relatively volatile, shifting with events, policies, and political actors. These aspects of political opportunity are matters of contention in which movements participate although they sometimes have little or nothing to do with changes that occur. These volatile elements are at the heart of explanations of mobilization and demobilization that emphasize the interaction between movement strategy and the opening and closing of those oft cited windows of opportunity.

The stable elements are especially useful in comparisons across space, explaining differences in movement activity and relative success in different countries or other units of analysis. Kitschelt's (1986) influential article comparing the anti–nuclear power movements in France, Sweden, the United States, and West Germany is the best exemplar of this approach. Kitschelt focuses attention on the differences between the four countries in both the openness of the political system to noninstitutional challengers and the capacity of the system to produce binding outputs. He treats the emergence of antinuclear movements at a particular historical moment as a given, not his problem to explain. He seeks to discover how different state structures influence the strategies the movement employs and its overall effectiveness in influencing nuclear policy in each setting.[1]

As Rucht (1990: 196) points out, Kitschelt's structural approach emphasizes the role of "relatively inert" aspects of opportunity. Constant elements of political opportunity are not very helpful in understanding dynamic processes of mobilization and demobilization. When the focus turns to change over time, the explanatory action is in the volatile elements – for example, changes in alliances, breakdowns of social control and elite unity, shifts in public policy, and the like. Here, we must be sensitive to the interaction between structure and agency, to the ways in which opportunity and movement strategy influence each other.

Meyer (1990) addresses these issues in explaining the rise and decline of the nuclear freeze movement in the United States, a dramatic anti–nuclear weapons movement that generated widespread mobilization and attention in the early 1980s, then faded quickly from political visibility by the middle of the decade. He argues for the analytic distinction between stable and dynamic aspects of political opportunity, putting institutional structures and party systems in the stable category, contrasting them with elite alignment and public policy changes as volatile elements. Dramatically increased military spending by the Reagan administration, accompanied by bellicose and cavalier rhetoric about limited nuclear wars, undermined elite consensus on nuclear strategy and created tension with European allies in the process. Moderates and arms control advocates left the reservation and this division created both political space and resource opportunities for the nuclear freeze movement.

Subsequently, the Reagan administration responded to the movement by stabilizing military spending, reviving the arms control process, and changing its rhetoric to emphasize concern about the dangers of nuclear war. While the movement's own strategic choices affected the ultimate outcome of this challenge to U.S. nuclear policy, by the mid-1980s the window of opportunity opened by the administration almost had been closed.[2] In this more dynamic model of political opportunity, structure channels movement activities, making various choices of action appear more or less desirable, and these choices, in turn, affect the location of political space, and its relative openness inside and outside political institutions.[3]

Opportunity has a strong cultural component and we miss something important when we limit our attention to variance in political institutions and the relationships among political actors. We can underline the distinction by contrasting Nelkin and Pollack's (1981) work on anti–nuclear power movements with Kitschelt's structural approach. Nelkin and Pollack focus on two of the four countries examined by Kitschelt: Germany and France.

Nelkin and Pollack embed their analysis of social movements more deeply in the political culture and history of the countries and issue of concern. They see the conflict over nuclear power as part of a broader political challenge. Different structural constraints in France and Germany changed the way activists thought about politics. While German activists spoke in terms of morality and civic justice, "in the French context, such moral, historical, and legalistic arguments play a less important role" (1981: 74). In France, the distance between civil servants and policy-making, along with strong civil service protection, gave French scientists a degree of freedom to speak out that their German colleagues did not share. They contrast the ambivalence toward voluntary associations in France with a German cultural tradition in which freedom of association is taken very seriously. While they do not ignore differences at the institutional level, their analysis points us toward examining political discourse as a way of understanding the cultural component of opportunity.

Brand (1990a) explicitly addresses the cultural side of opportunity, reviewing a number of concepts that attempt to deal with it.[4] He focuses his attention on changes in the "prevailing cultural climate" which we so often associate with decades – for example, the "privatism and conservatism" of the 1950s, the "reformistic and cultural-revolutionary mood" of the 1960s, and the "neo-conservative, postmodern *zeitgeist*" of the 1980s (1990a: 2). He recognizes the ad hoc way in which climate is often invoked as an explanation and attempts to treat it more systematically.

Brand calls attention to the interaction between climate and movement framing strategies. In the 1970s, he argues, economic recession and the growing awareness of ecological limits to growth created a pessimistic mood which fed "a new longing for a simple and natural way of life and a widespread criticism of bureaucracy and industrialism" (1990a: 7). Movement attention shifted from state policies and political power arrangements to quality-of-life and collective identity issues. Like many other writers, Brand sees changes in cultural climate following a cyclical pattern.[5]

Brand's argument about the importance of climate is clearly about the opening and closing of political space. Basically, outside events or the maturing of internal tensions and contradictions shake up the working political consensus. This opens the door for a variety of challenges in a new cycle of protest which takes its shape from the nature of the breakdown. He acknowledges his incomplete specification of which patterns of social mood enable or discourage what particular mobilization and framing efforts, but his article represents a rare attempt to make such vague concepts as climate more useful in systematic analysis.

Using these two dimensions, we have mapped some of the many variables (Figure 12.1) included by various writers as part of political opportunity structure, so that we can see the relationships among seemingly disparate approaches. Within the "volatile" half of the figure, there are important differences in degree depending on how macro or micro the focus. The aftermath of a major war or an international economic crisis may create what Gourevitch (1986) calls an "open moment" in which actors bargain for new political arrangements. Much of what has been taken as fixed is momentarily fluid during such periods.

Such open moments reflect an analytic emphasis on "Big Opportunity," times in which the entire state system is seen to break down and to be vulnerable to political challenges. Goldstone (1980), in recoding Gamson's (1990a [1975]) data on challenging groups, argues that time is the significant variable missing from the earlier analysis. Tactics and strategies are essentially irrelevant to success, Goldstone argues, at least in comparison with the momentary openness of the system. Similarly, Piven and Cloward (1979) contend that opportunities for protest and policy change for poor people are exceptional and sporadic, suggesting that there is little poor people can do to press their claims in other times, or to make their own opportunities. Although there are certainly times when a state is more or less open, Big Opportunity approaches, by defining opportunity as global and dichotomous – either open or closed – conflate differential opportunities for various issues and constituencies; they also tend to explain away successful activist efforts to organize. Further, they suggest no potential productive activities for dissidents in "closed" periods beyond waiting.

In contrast to theorists who emphasize this opening of the whole political system, there are others who emphasize smaller, more issue-specific opportunities. This level of analysis is necessary to answer questions about why certain movements arise at certain times in the absence of a more general open moment. Why a renewed women's movement throughout most of the Western world at the end of the 1960s, anti–nuclear power movements in the 1970s, and peace movements in the early 1980s?

Like activists, policy analysts often look for narrower and more limited political opportunities. Kingdon (1984), for example, uses the concept of a "policy window"[6] which temporarily opens "an opportunity for advocates of

STABLE

myths and narratives,		strength of state institutions
values, cultural themes,	strong/weak	strength and number of
belief systems,	state	political parties
world views	tradition	judicial and legislative
		capacity and independence
		centralization of political
		institutions
		strength of social cleavages

organization and political economy
of mass media
patterns of linkage between interest
groups and government

CULTURAL--INSTITUTIONAL
(society)   (state)
   legitimacy   economic and technological
   class consciousness,   trends causing dislocations
                                   strength of indigenous organizations
   climate, <u>zeitgeist</u>
   national mood   movement infrastructure
                 mass media access

                              shifts in political alliances
          policy changes   splits among elites

issue cultures,   scope of conflict
public discourse,   capacity for social control
media frames   social control errors
 ideas in good currency   elections

VOLATILE

Figure 12.1. Political opportunity.

proposals to push their pet solutions, or to push attention to their special problems. . . . An airplane crash, for instance, opens a window for advocates of initiative in aviation safety. If they have their proposals ready, the crash provides an opportunity to urge that the proposal should be enacted" (1984: 173, 177).

In Kingdon's argument an infinite number of actors or events can cause policy windows to open or close, and he does not attempt to examine the causes. From the standpoint of the actors, open windows just appear – sometimes through unexpected events, and sometimes through scheduled and expected ones such as budget hearings. The problem, then, is how to recognize them and act appropriately, not how to bring them about or prolong them.

We have tried to capture the differences between big opportunity and small opportunity theorists on our chart by placing them differently on the stable-volatile dimension. Hence, climates are less volatile than policy windows, changing in decades or in longer cycles; policy windows may change in a matter of months. But this dimension does not fully capture that part of the difference which focuses on general opportunities cutting across a broad range of issues and those peculiar to particular policy domains.

A number of political opportunity variables seem to belong in the middle, not clearly on either the cultural or institutional side since they refer to both. Following Sewell, we can think of political opportunity structure, as other structures, as dynamic rather than static, "sets of mutually sustaining schemas and resources that empower and constrain social action and that tend to be reproduced by that social action" (Sewell 1992: 19). For Sewell, schemas refer to generalizable but often informal and unarticulated ways of doing things, as implied by our use of culture. Resources are actual capabilities or objects that can be used to enhance or maintain power, as we conceive of institutions. Clearly, there is a mutually sustaining relationship between institutions and culture. A strong or weak state tradition, for example, is reflected in political institutions that limit the authority of the executive branch, hedging it with checks and balances in different degrees. But there is also a cultural side, regarding expectations of how central a role the state should play and which areas of life are state responsibilities.

Similarly, as we move toward the more volatile end of the figure, mass media access is a matter of both organizational routines such as news beats and journalistic norms and beliefs about who the serious players are in any policy arena. Policy changes involve a new rhetoric of justification and possible reframing of issues as well as changes in organizational practice and the distribution of resources. Changes in the scope of conflict involve new definitions about who is or should be involved as well as changing the alliance possibilities and the resources involved.

Finally, we should note that for many of the political opportunity variables in this figure, there is no consensus on exactly how they affect opportunity. Some seem to open and close political space simultaneously. Do elections, for example, open opportunity for a debate and resolution of central societal conflicts? Or do they close it by suppressing debate on these conflicts and diverting attention to the personalities and characters of candidates rather than their differences on public policy? There is some evidence for both, but the precise mix of opportunity and constraint that elections provide remains an open question.

In sum, political opportunity structure is too broad to be useful by itself in helping us to understand what conditions or circumstances produce more or less space for movement action. Any explanatory power comes from the specific variables that are part of it. Many valuable ones have been suggested by different researchers and they are often helpful in understanding the strategic choices and outcomes on which they focus. While there is no agreement at this point on which variables have exclusive rights to the political opportunity label, we hope our mapping will be useful in locating where in this broad context of opportunity particular theorists have staked their claims, and in the relationships between various analytic choices.

Even the precise specification of any "objective" definition of political opportunity structure explains only a part of social movement opportunity. An opportunity unrecognized is no opportunity at all. There is a component of political opportunity involving the perception of possible change that is, above all else, a social construction. The more stable elements of political opportunity bound a field in which a variety of actors struggle to define opportunities.

MOVEMENT FRAMING OF OPPORTUNITY

A social movement is a sustained and self-conscious challenge to authorities or cultural codes by a field of actors (organizations and advocacy networks), some of whom employ extrainstitutional means of influence. Several aspects of this definition are relevant for our arguments.

A movement is a field of actors, not a unified entity. Convenience of language leads us to treat it as a single actor when distinctions are unnecessary. This is shorthand and it is often important to differentiate among the actors in the field, especially in discussing framing. The degree to which there are unified and consensual frames within a movement is variable and it is comparatively rare that we can speak sensibly of *the* movement framing. It is more useful to think of framing as an internal process of contention within movements with different actors taking different positions.

Movements often have a range of actors pursuing numerous strategies in both institutional and extrainstitutional venues. Sometimes a single organization combines institutional means of influence such as lobbying and electoral politics with extrainstitutional strategies such as demonstrations and boycotts. Greenpeace, for example, claims to walk on both legs, and derives its movement legitimacy from this dual role. Justifications for strategic choices center on definitions of *relative* opportunity, and these are recurrent issues of contention within movements. Framing consensus, then, is variable between movements and typically a contentious internal process, and the definition of opportunity is often at the center of what is most contentious. This suggests that we need to focus on this process of defining opportunity and how it works.

Classical debates within movements often concern the issue of relative opportunity for institutional versus extrainstitutional actions or campaigns.[7] "Worse is better" versus "Better is better" and working within the system versus outside the system are arguments about political opportunity. Events, of course, influence this argument. After the 1972 election in El Salvador failed to bring the winners into political power, it was easier to argue that institutional means of change were completely closed. But most events are more ambiguous and leave ample room for disagreement about where the best opportunities lie.

Sometimes there is a shared framing that an open moment exists but argument about whether institutional means will absorb, coopt, and slow the process so long that the opportunity will be gone. This is precisely what happened, Meyer (1990) and Solo (1988) argue, in the case of the nuclear freeze movement. The apparent openness of institutional opportunity suggested by the embracing of the freeze movement by various leaders of the Democratic Party tempted the movement into a cul de sac that contained it until the open moment was gone.

These debates are also about constraint and the effectiveness of social control against extrainstitutional means of influence. Can authorities effectively counter extrainstitutional actions and repress those who use them? Or is there tolerance of various actions or the inability of authorities to control them effectively? Bold actions that flaunt authorities – the propaganda of the deed – may provide arguments for those arguing the relative opportunity for extrainstitutional means of influence.

The same relative opportunity issues are reflected in scholarly debates about the impact of opening institutional space. Some scholars use an implicit hydraulic model in which opening institutional space automatically closes extrainstitutional space by redirecting the flow of movement energy. Others favor a symbiotic model in which sympathetic insiders direct resources that facilitate mobilization and extrainstitutional action by grassroots groups which in turn help to open doors for further insider efforts.

In sum, this debate about relative opportunity for institutional and extrainstitutional action is missed when we speak of opportunity for the movement as a whole. Valid statements about changes in movement opportunity as a whole may hide important changes in relative opportunity; unresolved issues in the study of social movements often concern relative opportunity rather than overall movement opportunity.

The movement framing process concentrates on the volatile end of political opportunity. The inert aspects of political opportunity are taken for granted by participants; as we move to the middle, some movement actors may challenge them while others treat them as immutable. By the time we reach the volatile end, little can be taken for granted and there is rarely consensus about whether the proper moment has arrived and how long it will last.

The process also focuses heavily on opportunity in specific issue domains and not simply on general political opportunity for movements of all sorts. The issue for the peace movement is not whether the end of the Cold War has created an open moment in general; no one would dispute this. But has it opened opportunity for action against militarism and for economic conversion? One might think so, but then how to account for the declining resources and decaying infrastructure of the movement?[8] Is this a case of opportunity opening while threat declines, or has opportunity itself closed on this issue – for example, in ease of access to mass media attention? The questions we want to answer often concern the shifting of opportunities among different issue domains rather than a change in general opportunity.

Finally, the framing of political opportunity is about one central component of collective action frames.[9] Collective action frames deny the immutability of some undesirable situation and the possibility of changing it through some form of collective action. They define people as potential agents of their own history. This necessarily implies the existence of opportunity, but does not, of course, preclude a contest over the relative opportunity for institutional versus extrainstitutional actions.

The mass media play a crucial role in defining for movement actors whether they are taken seriously as agents of possible change. When demonstrators chant, "The whole world is watching," it means they believe they matter, that they are making history. The media spotlight validates the movement as an important player. This suggests that the opening and closing of media access and attention is a crucial element in defining political opportunity for movements.

These operating assumptions about media framing of political opportunity lead us to three more specific arguments about how the process operates.

The rhetoric of change

Movement activists systematically overestimate the degree of political opportunity and if they did not, they would not be doing their job wisely. To see in what ways they do this, we contrast a rhetoric of change with what Hirschman (1991) calls a "rhetoric of reaction." Hirschman examines how those who call for inaction typically frame issues of opportunity.

He finds three central themes in the rhetoric of reaction: jeopardy, futility, and perverse effects. Jeopardy refers to the argument that by attempting some change, we risk losing achievements already won. Inaction is more prudent in this view of opportunity because the dangers of loss outweigh the possibilities of further gain. Futility refers to the argument that there is no opportunity for change, that any action is essentially a waste of time and resources, that "attempts at political or economic reform are shown to come to naught by some 'law' whose existence has allegedly been ascertained by social science" (Hirschman 1991: 70). Perverse effects refers to the argument that the very actions designed to change things will only make matters worse.[10] Inaction is better because, regardless of good intentions, the unintended negative consequences will outweigh the desired effects.

To counter the pessimism of the rhetoric of reaction, movement activists employ an optimistic rhetoric of change. Their job is to convince potential challengers that action leading to change is possible and desirable. By influencing perceptions of opportunity among potential activists, organizers can actually alter the material bases of opportunity. For each of the three themes, there is a corresponding countertheme making the opposite point about political opportunity. *Urgency, agency,* and *possibility* describe a rhetoric of change that provides alternatives to the rhetoric of reaction.

Activists counter the jeopardy argument by emphasizing the risks of inaction, and conveying a sense of urgency. If we do not act now, the situation will not remain the same but will become more and more difficult to change. Action may be risky but inaction riskier skill. One must weigh the risks of action against the risks of inaction.

Activists counter the futility argument by asserting the openness of the moment. Windows that are currently open will not stay open for long. While there is no guarantee of success, the present offers opportunity enough to keep hope alive. Action now will open the window wider and keep it open longer, allowing more room for future victories. Organizing manuals tell activists to pick some modest and winnable objectives early in a campaign as demonstrations that action can have an impact. This may be buttressed by an argument about progress and historical inevitability. As Hirschman (1991: 158) notes, "People enjoy and feel empowered by the confidence, however vague, that they *have history on their side*" (emphasis in original). Further, collective action can provoke authorities into actions that backfire, fueling mobilization efforts, drawing new allies into the movement, and creating divisions among elites that expand political opportunity. Action produces reactions that have unintended favorable consequences.

Finally, the promise of new possibilities counters the threats of perverse effects. Activists appeal to a vision of better policies, greater justice, and more human social life as alternatives which their actions can help bring about. Martin Luther King's oft-cited "I have a dream" speech is a powerful example of the mobilizing power of possibility.

These arguments serve the needs of a mobilizing frame and lead to a tendency to overestimate the existence of political opportunity – a systematic optimistic bias. It is not merely a matter of seeing the glass as half-full rather than half-empty but seeing it as half-full when it is often 90 percent empty. If activists are sometimes more pessimistic in private than in public, they also frequently succeed in convincing themselves of the existence of opportunity.

This lack of realism in assessing opportunity is generally as healthy for movement activity as it is for the economic activity of entrepreneurs.[11] Nine of ten small businesses in the United States fail within the first five years of founding, yet people continue to start them. Individuals must convince themselves they will beat the odds against success because they will work harder, have a better idea or product, or see another favorable omen. "Unrealistic" perceptions of the possible can actually alter what is possible.

Those who challenge authorities or cultural codes have similar formidable odds working against their success, and must convince others that collective action is worthwhile. There are numerous examples of past movements that demonstrated the possibilities of change that few had thought possible in advance. If movement activists interpret political space in ways that emphasize opportunity rather than constraint, they may stimulate actions that change opportunity, making their opportunity frame a self-fulfilling prophecy.

Opening media access

Mass media are another component of political opportunity structure that have both structural and dynamic elements. Ownership and consumption patterns of media, as well as their relation to the state and political parties, are relatively stable and generally beyond the scope of movement claims. At the same time, the content of news coverage and entertainment writing and programming are far more dynamic, and may dramatically influence the prospects for the mobilization of challenging claims and movements.

The media system's openness to social movements is itself an important element of political opportunity. The complicated double role of the media tends to obscure this point.[12] On one hand, the media play a central role in the construction of meaning and the reproduction of culture. Journalists choose a story line in reporting events and commentators of various sorts develop arguments and images that support particular frames. On the other hand, the media are also a site or arena in which symbolic contests are carried out among competing sponsors of meaning, including movements.

Media norms and practices and the broader political economy in which they operate affect the opportunities and constraints under which movements operate. Key organizations in the media system (in the United States, the major networks and a few national newspapers and newsmagazines) confer standing on actors. They suggest to other media organizations and to elites and issue publics who the serious players are on a given issue. Partly through a self-selecting audience, different media reach distinct publics, conveying potentially contradictory messages about urgency, issues, and efficacy. In this regard, movement organs can play an important role as an organizing resource. They convey activist frames and information, and can become part of a shared movement culture. On a more mundane level, they can provide a reliable source for organizing information, such as where and when a demonstration will take place.

Mainstream media are a potential resource as well. In the United States mainstream media follow a selectively applied balance norm. In news accounts, interpretation is provided through quotations with balance provided by quoting spokespersons with competing views. The balance norm is not automatically invoked in practice; to be applicable, journalists must define an issue as controversial.

Creating controversy, then, is a way to increase opportunity by opening media access to movement spokespersons. Once established as spokespersons, this opportunity is likely to remain open as long as the issue is salient. Nothing defines spokespersons better for journalists than having previously served in this role, particularly being quoted in one or more of the major media validators. As long as the issue is salient, journalists are likely to initiate contacts to get suitable quotes. Once media attention shifts to some other issue and the controversy has lost its salience, the open space closes again and would-be movement spokespersons no longer get their phone calls returned.

Extrainstitutional action is better than institutional action in creating controversy. The more popular and visually oriented media in particular emphasize spectacle in collective action.[13] Spectacle means drama and confrontation, emotional events with people who have fire in the belly, who are extravagant and unpredictable. This puts a high premium on novelty, on costume, and on confrontation. Violent action in particular has most of these media valued elements. Fire in the belly is fine, but fire on the ground photographs better. Burning buildings and burning tires make better television than peaceful vigils and orderly marches. The media, then, are relatively more open to extrainstitutional than to institutional action and this bias in turn structures the strategic choices of movement actors.

Of course, winning media attention requires strategies and tactics exactly opposite to those needed to win political standing within established political institutions. The media rewards novelty, polemic, and confrontation, but institutional politics prizes predictability, moderation, and compromise. Seeking both media attention and institutional influence, activists confront a difficult dilemma of balance.

Movement division of labor

Public officials and heads of large established organizations receive automatic standing from the mass media by virtue of their roles. This is not so for movement actors, who must often struggle to establish it and may require extrainstitutional collective action to do so. Members of the club enter the media through the front door, but challengers must find their way in through a window, often using some gimmick or disorderly act to do so, which may impair their effectiveness once inside. "Those who dress up in costume to be admitted to the media's party," Gamson and Wolfsfeld point out (1992), "will not be allowed to change before being photographed."

Movements can manage this dilemma in part through a division of labor among actors. Those who engage in the actions that open political opportunity do not attempt to be the main spokespersons; for this, they defer to partners who do not carry the baggage of deviance but can articulate a shared frame on the issue. In the anti–nuclear power movement, for example, the Clamshell Alliance and other direct action groups helped to define nuclear power as controversial through site occupations and other extrainstitutional actions. The space opened by such action was filled by the Union of Concerned Scientists, which better met the media definition of a respectable spokesperson.

Internal rivalries among different movement actors can undermine such convenient divisions of labor. Indeed, social movement organizers often view potential allies as liabilities, who may discredit the larger movement, or competitors who will consume needed resources. Movements frequently offer multiple frames, each identified with particular groups. Those whose actions opened media access may find their preferred frame poorly represented or may be personally jealous of those who entered through the newly opened door. They may attack and attempt to undercut their rivals. This internal movement fight can easily become the media's story. A division of labor is only likely to work if there is a consensual movement frame and a willingness to subordinate concerns about who gets credit for being the messenger.

CONCLUSION

Relatively stable elements of political opportunity are useful in comparing the incidence and success of social movements in different settings. The volatile elements, however, are more useful in understanding the process of interaction between the opening and closing of political space and the strategic choices of movements. The volatile elements help us to understand movement outcomes as involving structures which shape and channel activity while, in turn, movements act as agents that help to shape the political space in which they operate.

We have emphasized the construction of political opportunity as a struggle over meaning within movements. The issues that arise are often less about political opportunity for the movement as a whole and more about the relative opportunity for institutional and extrainstitutional action and the interaction between them. And they are more likely to focus on issue-specific opportunities rather than opportunities for movements in general.

When movements attempt to assess opportunity, they do so with a systematic optimistic bias, exaggerating opportunities and underestimating constraints. This bias is built into the functional needs of movements which need to sustain a collective action frame that includes the belief that conditions can be changed. Since movement action can sometimes create political opportunity, this lack of realism can produce a self-fulfilling prophecy.

Of course, it can also lead to misadventures and disasters in which real constraints are ignored until too late. We have done little here to suggest how one draws the line between keeping hope alive under often discouraging circumstances and pursuing some totally quixotic effort. Perhaps a healthy internal debate about the nature of political opportunity is the mechanism for maintaining the proper balance, but there are no magic formulas for success.

Finally, we emphasize the importance of the media system as both a political opportunity variable and a site of struggle about the nature of opportunity. Its role as a validator for the larger society about whose views need to be taken seriously makes it a crucial target for movement efforts to open political space. The media system operates to favor extrainstitutional actors in some ways and institutional actors in others.

Controversy makes an issue more salient and invokes a balance norm that opens the door to movement spokespersons, but the media emphasis on spectacle privileges extrainstitutional action. Those who use such means may be stigmatized as upstarts and deviants, thereby providing an opening that brands movement spokespersons from the start in ways that prevent their message from being heard.[14]

A movement united by a shared frame can overcome this problem by allowing those who open opportunity to differ from those who utilize it as spokespersons. Extrainstitutional action, however, often involves sacrifices and risks and those who undertake them must be ready to allow others to reap the benefits in the interests of broader movement goals. This kind of noble abnegation is rare enough in most areas of social life and, hence, it is a considerable achievement when it occurs.

Frame consensus, however, is usually a matter of degree within movements and we should expect internal disagreements over who speaks for the movement to be typical when media space opens up. New opportunities open the way for personal rivalries as well as contentious internal debate over the best ways of responding. The structures of political opportunity carry elements of both threat and possibility, and challengers must struggle to strike an effective balance.

13

Accessing public, media, electoral, and governmental agendas

JOHN D. McCARTHY, JACKIE SMITH, and MAYER N. ZALD

Social movements are involved in struggles over meaning as they attempt to influence public policy. An essential task in these struggles is to frame social problems and injustices in a way that convinces a wide and diverse audience of the necessity for and utility of collective attempts to redress them. Movement frames typically embody two essential components: the diagnostic element, or the definition of the problem and its source; and the prognostic element, the identification of an appropriate strategy for redressing the problem (Snow and Benford 1988). Movements usually lack the political and/or material resources necessary for routine access to political decision-makers and therefore must rely primarily on "outsider" strategies to draw the attention of publics and policymakers to the problems they wish to have resolved. Lipsky (1968) identified a fundamental logic of movement strategy as a conscious attempt to draw third parties into the conflict in order to raise the stakes in the conflict and bring favorable pressure to bear on the policy process. While movements' ultimate targets are typically policymakers, movements must mobilize people and resources within the wider society in order to influence this authoritative elite. These third parties include both the mass public and the reference elites, the people with whom the authoritative elite interacts and consults. A major tool in this process is the mass media, which can reach a much larger audience than social movement actors can reach directly.

The media are certainly a major target for social movement framing efforts, but they are not the only (or, for some, even the primary) one: Direct efforts aimed at influencing government, electoral, and the public agendas are also a major part of social movement efforts. Social movements engage in tactics that directly or indirectly target the perceptions and behaviors of diverse audiences by communicating movement frames. Social movement organizations (SMOs), for example, often have direct contact with other nongovernmental public leaders, reporters, party leaders, elected officials, and bureaucrats, but in order to enhance the political impact of their efforts, they typically must also engage in tactics that convey their message to a much broader audience. In doing so, movement agents attempt to bring their issues onto the agendas of distinct audiences: the general public, the media, political parties, and legislative and executive officials. Each of these agendas operates under its own unique logic and processes, and those attempting to shape the agendas must customize their strategies appropriately.

Scholars of social movements have increasingly recognized the central importance of the framing of issues to understanding social movement success and failure.[1] Their efforts, however, have been devoted mainly to describing the variable elements of frames and establishing the principal features of more or less widely appealing frames. While strategic framing analysts do recognize that framing efforts exist within wider institutional processes beyond movement mobilization itself, the relevant dimensions of those external processes have been left largely unspecified. This is so because their work (e.g., Snow et al. 1986; Benford 1993; Snow and Benford 1988) focuses largely on the important ideological-cognitive dimensions of framing processes. (But see Ryan 1991.)

This focus on intramovement frame processes brings the implicit assumption that all – or at least most – interpretations of reality are socially constructed and therefore amenable to movement attempts to shape or manipulate them. Movements become "sponsors" of particular frames (Gamson 1988) and their ability to successfully package these frames has been discussed largely as a function of competition within organizations (Rothenberg 1991), coalitions (Kleidman 1993), or movement industries (Benford 1993). Accepting the assumption of the manipulability of frames, we argue that these framing efforts are embedded in broader political and social contexts and that these contexts expand, limit, and shape the opportunities for movement activists to gain attention to the issues that most concern them. These background processes, moreover, interact with the strategic choices activists make in targeting their framing efforts toward gaining a place on issue agendas. Not only do the processes for getting attention differ across arenas, but the very nature of the language of frames is adapted to arenas. Although it is beyond the scope of this essay, the nature of the rhetoric, images, and argument used with a sympathetic specific public may not play well in the mass media and with other publics. And the translation from a mobilizing battle cry to a lobbyist's presentation to congressmen calls for a quite different set of frame packaging.

This chapter addresses two questions relevant to movement framing processes that have been somewhat neglected in existing research. First, we ask what specific social structures and contexts condition the opportunities for movement framing efforts. Second, we ask what repertoires of tactics emerge within these context structures. In our discussion of the contexts within which movements carry out their strategic framing efforts, we employ the concept of "arena" as discussed by Dieter Rucht in this volume (Chapter 8). We define four distinct arenas of frame competition, namely the public, media, electoral, and governmental arenas. Each of these arenas contains distinct sets of competitors, audiences, and "gatekeepers" whose interaction shapes evolving issue agendas. Second, we present an analysis of the various tactical repertoires which are available to movements seeking to compete within a given arena. By linking framing, tactics, and arenas we expose the multilayered process of spreading the social movement word.

CONTEXT STRUCTURES AND ISSUE AGENDAS

We draw on several more or less well-developed scholarly literatures, each of which aims to understand variable attention to issues, only one of which accords much significance to the strategic framing efforts of movement activists. Making the strategic framing efforts of movement activists ground and other institutional processes figure, we seek to better understand activists' variable success in achieving issue attention.[2]

Since the number of possible issues toward which any given public may address attention is vast, attention to any given issue is usefully conceived as cyclical and somewhat hierarchical. The collection of issues which are given attention at any given time constitutes an issue agenda. Over time, an issue agenda varies in what issues are on it and in the amount or hierarchy of importance of the issues on the agenda. We distinguish between the *media agenda,* the collection of issues that receive attention in the mass media, the *public agenda,* the set of issues that are accorded importance by mass and narrower publics, the *governmental agenda,* the set of issues that receive attention in one or another governmental arena, and the *electoral agenda,* the set of issues that receive attention from candidates for public office.[3] Each of these agendas, while certainly not independent, can be conceived as the result of distinctive, competitive agenda-setting processes and may bear little resemblance to any "objective" realities.

In Western democratic societies the mass media are central purveyors of information and images. Although injustices and deprivations may be directly experienced in local contexts, the larger public and reference elites learns of them mainly through the media. Similarly, although political authorities may have direct interaction with citizens and directly see local conditions, their perceptions of those conditions and their sense of citizen reaction are also shaped by media portrayals. It is easy, then, to conflate the processes which create the several issue agendas, to lapse into a media determinism in which this single agenda defines all others. It is our reading of the diverse scholarship on these several processes, however, that these four agendas are only loosely connected with one another, and that each is governed by its own incentive structures, processes, and "gatekeepers." This argument has important implications for the targeting of strategic framing endeavors by movement activists.

Activists are not the only contestants trying to bring a distinctive framing to broader attention. Western democracies have witnessed an explosion of strategic framing efforts in recent years. Analysts of each of the several agenda-setting processes we will examine recognize that of the many potential issues that could appear on the agendas, only a few actually do, and many issues that do so make only very short appearances. The narrow span of attention among mass publics, the very small newshole in the mass media, the confined range of issues raised in electoral campaigns and the restricted policy focus of officials and the bureaucratic processes within which they operate guarantee that agenda setting in any of these arenas will involve highly competitive processes.

How do strategic choices by movement activists intersect these issue agenda-setting processes thereby accentuating the likelihood that their best framed injustice packages will find a stable place on issue agendas? When and how do social movement activists – generally bit players in these agenda-setting processes – attempt to take center stage, if only for brief moments? We will explore these questions with systematic evidence that portrays the strategic targeting choices of U.S. and European movement activists. First, we examine key accounts of each of the four main targets of agenda-setting.

THE PUBLIC ARENA

In the public arena, movements compete with a range of organized interests to persuade individuals of the importance of the issues on which they work. Business, religious, charity, and other civic organizations all compete for public attention to the respective frames they actively sponsor or support. While movements attempt to communicate directly with individuals and thereby persuade them of the importance of certain issues, a more efficient strategy involves attempts to recruit blocs of people through existing organizational infrastructures (cf. Oberschall 1980). Many of these local organizations serve something of a "gatekeeper" role for the public agenda, since they typically enjoy more structured contact with individuals as well as public respect and credibility: Movements pushing issues which these organizations oppose will be far less successful than those whose issues are tolerated or especially actively embraced by local leaders and organizations.

As originally conceived, the study of public opinion, and by implication the public agenda, referred to the outcomes of processes by which members of communities, groups, or collectives came to develop shared opinions of events, objects, or issues. Thus conceived, a public agenda can develop without mediation (Blumer 1948), but the scale of modern states and the development of modern means of communication have increasingly shifted the focus of those interested in how the public agenda is set toward the role of the mass media, often measured by the results of survey research. Nevertheless, while the media may influence much of *what* people talk about, it does not determine *how* they talk about it: Issues presented in the media are further interpreted through interpersonal and social networks (cf. Gamson 1992a). Thus, of all the issue arenas targeted by social movement actors, the public one is the most decentralized and therefore most accessible. In addition to the mass media, many organizations (e.g., churches, schools, businesses, PTAs, and SMOs) as well as individuals actively compete in their attempts to shape the public agenda by communicating directly with individuals. While the size of communities has expanded, the range of technologies for efficient, low-cost communication allows even small, resource-poor operations to disseminate a message widely even without the aid of mass media through, for example, public gatherings, distributing newsletters or other literature, telemarketing, direct mail, or door-to-door canvassing. These communications help to shape individuals' knowledge of potentially significant issues. These local networks and organizations can also serve as "filters" through which information received from media, government, or other sources is interpreted.

Media and public agendas

Research on the relationship of media coverage to the public's identification of important issues yields mixed results. Following the pioneering work of McCombs and Shaw (1972), we know that awareness of an issue and its perceived importance, vis-à-vis other issues is determined by the extent to which the media focuses upon it, even if substantive opinions are not so closely tied to media messages. Recent work by Page and Shapiro (1992) found that changes in public opinion were related to the amount of national television news coverage of issues, as were the sources of the news: News commentary and reports of experts were strongly related to positive impact while protesters and groups perceived as narrow, perhaps misinformed, interest groups drew negative responses (see also Greenberg et al. 1989).

Other evidence strongly suggests that an individual's rating of a problem as *important to society* may be more related to media coverage than to personal experience. For instance, people living in communities with high unemployment are no more likely to rate unemployment as high on the public agenda than are people living in communities with low unemployment (Kiewit 1983; Kinder and Kiewit 1981). Others have shown that the mass media have a stronger impact on public opinion in areas such as foreign affairs where general knowledge of the issues are limited (cf. Larson 1984; Gamson 1988; Iyengar and Kinder 1987).

While the mass media are an important influence on the public agenda, they are not the only one, and thus the two must be viewed as distinct (cf.

Rogers and Dearing, 1988). Neuman (1990) presents a systematic comparison of media issue coverage and level of public concern about several issues over extended periods between 1945 and 1980. Correlating an index of media coverage with public ratings of "the most important problem facing this country today," he shows a vast range in the level of correspondence between the extent of media coverage and the public agenda. Dramatic events, those with clear protagonists and visible effects, and with a clear rise and fall of hard (e.g., event-oriented) news to report, show the highest correlation between media coverage and concern, while underlying issues that affect large numbers of people, like inflation and unemployment, but are not so easy to dramatize, display the highest peak public concerns but show the weakest correlations between media coverage and concern. Thus, even with minimal access to mass media or other agendas, social movements have real opportunities for bringing new issues to public agendas.

MEDIA ARENA[4]

The media arena is far more centralized than the public arena, and access to it is more difficult for social movement actors. Nevertheless, its gatekeepers – local and national reporters and editors – are typically more accessible than the gatekeepers of the governmental or electoral agendas. Getting on the media agenda, moreover, may be a common if not essential stepping stone to those more specifically policy-oriented agendas. For this reason, many movement actors consider the mass media when devising their strategies, even if they are unable to execute a deliberate media strategy (Ryan 1991).

A variety of accounts have been offered to make sense of the fact that so many events and issues could be covered by the mass media while, during any period, only a tiny proportion of them actually fit into the newshole. It is generally recognized that the size of the newshole, or the amount of space or time available in any specified source or period, is strictly limited, while the amount of potential material that might be selected to fill it is vast. Hence, analysts have crafted several general lines of explanation for the selection of, and the emphasis is given to, certain issues as media editors and producers pick and choose among events and construct the news with but few details about them. The first two perspectives we treat stem mainly from ethnographic accounts of news work; the others are developed from elaborated critiques of "news production."

News routines[5]

News gathering and reporting may look exciting from a distance, but much of the day-to-day work is accomplished according to standard procedures that routinize and regularize the tasks. "Beat" reporting, or the regular assignment of reporters to specific institutional locations, and the reliance upon customary sources, such as visible and central government officials, are examples of routines that have implications for what is considered news. Many other characteristics of typical news gathering and reporting routines have been implicated in determining what becomes news, including deadlines and their corresponding lead times. A major outcome of these operating constraints reduces social movements' possibilities for influencing media agendas: From the media perspective, government sources are generally the most ideal, since they are perceived as reliable and respected, and since their centralized location and media-friendly structure facilitates access by a centralized media industry (Kielbowicz and Scherer 1986). A reporter faces a variety of professional pressures and incentives to use government sources, and this reliance means that government officials may often enforce reporting "rules" which must be followed in order to get vital "scoop." Presidents and their media officers, for example, have not hesitated to bar a reporter's access to the White House and have directly threatened or intimidated reporters and media editors who failed to portray the news in a way that corresponded with their political intentions (Hilderbrand 1981: 52; Small 1987: 189).

News pegs: What's newsworthy

Reporters' tasks require that they gather news that is somehow "interesting."[6] Such news typically consists of events that have one or more of the following distinguishing qualities: publicly recognized (e.g., famous faces, trendy, proximate), important (e.g., current, powerful personages, wide impact), and interesting (e.g., human interest, unusual, spectacular, heart-rending, cute, culturally resonant). Events with such characteristics offer effective "news pegs" around which news reports may be constructed and are therefore more likely to become news (Ryan 1991: 96). Thus, following the reasoning of the news peg hypothesis, we would expect events or issues which are extraordinary in some way (e.g., large, long, conflictual, etc.) to be more likely to gain media attention.

Corporate hegemony[7]

News media in the United States and increasingly in other Western democracies, as in most capitalist nations, are profit-making institutions by design. In the United States they depend as much on advertisers as on consumers for these profits, if not more. As a result, it is argued, they can be expected to select and shape the news in ways that do not threaten their own or their sponsor's interests. Therefore, we expect minimal reporting of issues that might threaten those interests.[8]

Media issue attention cycles

The consensus among news gatherers about what's newsworthy, their normal routines, and the central role of ownership interests in media selection processes, however, cannot alone, or in concert, make sense of the well-known pattern of the media attention cycle – a rapidly ascending interest, indexed by the number of stories or column inches, of a previously obscure topic or issue that dominates the news for some period, followed, eventually, by decreasing interest. Some of these issue attention cycles are closely tied to dramatic policies or events like the Vietnam War and Watergate, but others are not so obviously linked to objective trends, such as attention to poverty or environmental pollution (Greenberg et al. 1989). In competitive markets, news producers compete for ratings and circulation, which ultimately affect profits. Since the consumers of the news may lose interest in a story, one part of the issue-attention cycle relates to news producers' perceptions of their audience's interests.

ELECTORAL ARENAS

The next two agendas bring us closer to the ultimate target of much social movement activity, namely, the making of public policy. Issues on the electoral and governmental agendas are ones for which some kind of official policy action is likely if not imminent. In the logic of Cobb and his colleagues, we begin to move from the public agenda (which incorporates both our public and media agendas), including "issues which have achieved a high level of public interest and attention," closer to the formal agenda, which consists of the "list of items which decision makers have formally accepted for serious consideration" (Cobb, Ross, and Ross 1976: 126). Similarly, we argue that the processes involved in bringing an issue onto one of the public agendas are quite different from those involved in raising it to the formal agenda. But even within the broader formal agenda there may be different thresholds constraining access, with electoral agendas having much lower entrance costs than governmental agendas.

The gatekeepers of these agendas are scarcer and more restricted by their official obligations, so movement access to these agendas is usually more limited than it is for the more decentralized public and media agendas. This access, however, will vary across time and place according to the structure of the electoral and legislative systems (e.g., with the number of parties and nature of party discipline affecting the amount of space available for competing issues and frames), timing (e.g., within electoral cycle or with regard to an administration's need to cultivate support for a policy), and state structures. These (and possibly other) variables help to define the broad opportunities for movements to draw attention to their issues within these policy arenas. For the most part, the various agenda-setting literatures we have reviewed do not emphasize the role of elections, but regular election cycles provide windows of opportunity to bring issues to public attention and to the attention of elites. And in the same way that hierarchies of issues get set in the media, public and governmental arenas, party platforms and campaigns themselves generate electoral issue agendas (Price 1984). Election cycles typically raise the level of public debate on policy matters as the electorate is mobilized to choose new leaders. While candidates and party leaders often seek to limit and control the range of debate, movements and others concerned with influencing the political agenda have opportunities at election time that do not exist otherwise. Electoral agendas may actually serve to bridge the public and formal agendas described by Cobb and his associates. While issues on the electoral agenda may be more likely candidates for inclusion in the formal decision-making agenda, there is no guarantee that issues raised during elections will actually be addressed once a candidate enters political office. As a result, it is theoretically easier for a movement to affect this agenda than to influence the governmental agenda.

Electoral logics often demand that candidates strive to ignore altogether or to obfuscate their stands on important issues, but party activists are known for being far more committed to particular issues than members of the general public. Getting issues on the electoral agenda and developing party stands on them, consequently, motivates much of their activism. In many highly mobilized movements, these party activists may also be, simultaneously, movement activists.[9] As a result, the activists of opposing parties tend to differ quite radically from one another on the place of issues on the electoral agenda and party stands on those issues. Miller and Jennings, for instance, in a study of Democratic and Republican party activists during the 1970s, report large differences between their issue positions on the equal rights amendment and environmental protection, but smaller differences on abortion permissiveness (1986: 164). Those same party activists differ dramatically from one another in their evaluation of activists of the antinuclear, women's liberation, moral majority, and environmentalist movements (1986: 167). Carmines and Stimson's (1989) analysis of issue competition led them to define three distinct categories of issue types which result from this competition: (1) organic extensions, or issues which fit into niches that existed previously; (2) unsuccessful adaptations; and (3) issue evolutions, which capture the public's attention and remain salient for a number of years (p. 11). They conclude that issues that succeed in sustaining long-term attention are those which are "easy," meaning that they require little cognitive skills to understand, analyze, and resolve. Issues which are not likely to succeed on the electoral agenda are the more common, "hard" issues, which "require contextual knowledge, appreciation of often subtle differences in policy options, a coherent structure of beliefs about politics, systematic reasoning to connect means to ends, and interest in and attentiveness to political life to justify the cost of extensive fact gathering and decision-making" (Carmines and Stimson 1989: 11–12). Thus, "hard" issues are seen as unlikely to sustain long-term attention and commitment and are therefore unattractive to those attempting to craft electoral agendas.

This conclusion – while true for the United States – may not be readily applicable to other national contexts. The rules of electoral competition structure public debate and largely determine what constitutes an effective electoral strategy. Electoral agenda-setting in a multiparty context, for example, may favor the inclusion of more complex issues for which a wider range of possible solutions is generated by a larger number of competing parties. In addition, American political parties have become increasingly dependent upon general audience media to reach prospective voters, and have moved away from building dense local organizational infrastructures that allow for more meaningful integration of citizens into electoral processes. Lacking routine access to social networks and infrastructures, successful candidates must produce media images capable of competing for the limited newshole of the mass media. This precludes any sophisticated and detailed analysis of issues and policy options and limits electoral strategies to the creation of "sound bites" for communicating political messages.

GOVERNMENTAL ARENAS

Changing governmental issue agendas can provide windows of political opportunity for groups seeking to bring their issue to the center of attention. Governmental arenas and agendas in democratic societies may be further broken down into legislative and executive arenas and agendas. Elected officials in the legislative arena are most concerned with selecting issues which are most likely to enhance their reelection prospects. Such issues are typically more short-term, easy issues which require low-cost or constituent-gratifying policy responses. The legislative agenda may provide greater access to some movements than does the executive agenda, given the structure of legislative debate and possibilities for the presentation of expert testimony, and so forth. Executive issue agendas are shaped by the more high-profile efforts of elected administration officials as well as by the less prominent but more omnipresent bureaucrats charged with carrying out policy. Movements that raise issues that oppose or are absent from the administration's agenda may be forced to try to affect the government agenda by raising constant opposition to administration policies, as the peace movement of the 1980s did against Reagan's nuclear weapons policy. In contrast, movements working on more consensual issues, such as the anti–drunk driving movement or some elements of the environmental movement, may find means of furthering their concerns within the executive bureaucracy. This is possible because movement organizations may provide technical or legal research or may generate public support for a policy and thereby help further bureaucrats' professional aims (cf. McCarthy 1994).[10]

MOVEMENT FRAME DISSEMINATION REPERTOIRES

Broad political and social structures influence the range of tactics available to movement actors (Tilly 1978). Movement tactics include those that directly raise the costs to authorities and publics, such as strikes, boycotts, and the use of physical coercion, as well as the dissemination of diagnostic and prognostic frames. We should also expect that agenda-setting structures and processes will influence the range of available tactics as well as the typical mixes of tactics – or repertoires – that may be used by movements attempting to situate their frames on the various agendas.

Now we explore the tactics several movements have actually employed in their attempts to influence these different agendas. A number of recent studies have gathered extensive evidence from systematic samples of SMOs about the tactics of influence they use, including tactics central to frame dissemination.[11] We compare the U.S. peace movement in the late 1980s (Pagnucco 1992), the Western European environmental movement in the mid-1980s (Dalton 1994), the U.S. anti–drunk driving movement in the mid-1980s (McCarthy 1994), local poor empowerment community organizations in the United States (McCarthy, Shields, and Hall 1994), and U.S. public interest groups in the early 1980s (Shaiko 1991).

These five studies provide a wide range of diverse movement groups, and some comparative scope. Shaiko's study reports the results of analysis of information on 250 public interest groups drawn from the files of the Foundation for Public Affairs in 1985. This sample clearly represents the largest and most influential public interest groups in the United States. The sample of peace movement organizations represents a wide array of groups from local grassroots, all volunteer ones, to national professional movement groups. The sample of European environmental organizations includes groups from ten nations. The poor-empowerment groups are quite diverse in structure but have strong membership bases and are led by professional staff. The anti–drunk driving groups are homogeneous, local, and mostly volunteer-staffed. The varying diversity of the four SMO samples and the multiple methods and motivations of the researchers suggest caution in comparing them to one another. Nevertheless, doing so allows us to begin to explore cross-movement and cross-national variation in frame dissemination repertoires. Table 13.1 provides pertinent summary information along a few dimensions for the SMOs included in each survey.

Our presentation of the frame dissemination tactics these groups used focuses on the primary targeted agenda. Clearly some tactics may not be lim-

Table 13.1. *Organizational characteristics*

	Members[a] (avg.)	Budget (avg.)
Anti–drunk driving (*n*=352)	130	$ 4,900
Poor empowerment (*n*=125)	2,225	$ 210,035
Peace (*n*=227)	18,929	$ 316,559
Environment (*n*=61)	52,000	$ 766,000
Public interest (*n*=167)	27,290	$1,356,000

[a]Includes only groups with individual members.
Sources: 1991 Survey of Poor Empowerment Groups funded by the Campaign for Human Development (McCarthy, Shields, and Hall 1994). 1988 survey of groups and organizations working for peace, summarized in Edwards (1994). 1989 survey of U.S. anti–drunk driving organizations (McCarthy 1994). For the environment, Dalton 1994; figures based on our calculations. For public interest, Shaiko 1991: 120; figures based upon our rough calculations of grouped data.

ited to a single arena. For example, demonstrations may not only (or primarily) be aimed at attracting media attention; they may also be means of communicating directly with activists or potential activists as well as with policymakers. Because the survey questions and sampling frames vary across the several studies, we cannot make a systematic comparison. Rather we wish to illustrate the range of tactics used to reach each arena and identify patterns and contrasts. Table 13.2 shows the percentages of responding groups that reported use of each tactic if it was asked about it. Each of the studies generated a distinctive list of tactics germane to the groups under study on the basis of preliminary empirical mapping of the tactical repertoires characteristic of them. Therefore, the variation in inclusion of tactics across the lists represents to some extent the real variation in frame dissemination repertoires across these movements.[12] If there is no entry in a row for a study, it means that no question about the tactic was asked in that study.

It is immediately apparent that an enormous range of particular tactics are utilized by SMOs that can serve to get their framing of injustice on an agenda and sustain it. As shown in the first panel of Table 13.2, SMOs use a variety of mechanisms to appeal directly to publics with their message ranging from contacts in an assortment of public places, through giving speeches to other groups, to approaches to citizens at their homes. Groups use many methods for attempting to get media coverage directly, including the buying of access. Public demonstrating is reported by some groups in each study, but the proclivity to demonstrate varies dramatically among the movements. Groups report using many different tactics that may indirectly affect their access to

Table 13.2 *Framing tactics of social movements by target*

Tactic	Poor empowerment ($n=125$)	Peace ($n=277$)	Anti–drunk driving ($n=352$)	Environ-ment groups ($n=65$)	Public interest ($n=167$)
Public agenda					
Distribute literature		96%			
Public lecture/meeting	26%	93			
Canvass door-to-door		20			
Build organizational coalitions	24	11			54%
Publish a newsletter			64%		
Give community awards			40		
Booths at public events			83		
Generate grassroots education	34		70	92%	83
Media agenda – direct					
Cultivate press relations		92		99	
Run advertisement		37			
Media appearances			87		
Public service announcement			37		
Public relations	29				
Media agenda – indirect					
Op-ed campaigns		76			
Public demonstration	19	72		48	11
Civil disobedience		28			
Vigils		58	72		
Electoral agenda – direct					
Electoral agenda – indirect					
Contact party leaders				55	
Electoral politics (n.s.)					8
Support candidates $, volunteer		32			
Encourage contrib./ party		7			

Table 13.2 *(cont.)*

Tactic	Poor empowerment (n=125)	Peace (n=277)	Anti-drunk driving (n=352)	Environment groups (n=65)	Public interest (n=167)
Electoral agenda – indirect					
Organize meetings for candidates		23			
Voter registration		19			
Public endorsements		11			
Initiative/referendum campaign		21			
Legislative agenda – direct					
Litigation	6	16		39	37
Legis. agenda – indirect					
Letter-writing campaign		75			
Monitor voting records		62		14	
Lobby/visit member of legislature	29	72	25		36
Testify at legislative hearing		28			58
Draft legislation		18			
Meetings with public officials	26				
Executive agenda – direct					
Executive agenda – indirect					
Work with executive agency				71	
Monitor executive agency	15				48
Lobby ministers or civil servants		14	87		

the electoral arena, such as meeting with candidates and supporting candidates, but none of the studies asked whether the groups worked directly with a political party.

Finally, groups report a wide range of ways that they directly and indirectly get their message on both the legislative and executive governmental agenda including lobbying in both venues, litigating, and testifying. There appears to be relatively less activity within this arena, and it is not too surprising that environmental and anti–drunk driving movements – those with information and constituent resources that most directly facilitate bureaucrats' aims and tasks – were those involved in executive lobbying.

Although there is extensive overlap in the report of use of many tactics across the samples of SMOs (e.g., the use of some lobbying is reported by at least some groups in each study, as is the use of demonstrating), there are also some important differences between them. These patterns conform to a pattern reported by Walker (1988) in his study of Washington interest groups – the greater the resources of groups, the more they will employ "insider" tactics (e.g., lobbying, litigating); the fewer the resources commanded by such groups the more they will use "outsider" tactics (e.g., demonstrating, attempting to get media coverage). The movement groups with fewer resources, peace groups and anti–drunk driving groups, craft repertoires with greater emphasis on the outsider tactics.[13] And while the samples of richer and more professionalized movement groups (environmental, public interest) also show evidence of the wide use of outsider tactics, their mixes include greater use of insider ones such as litigation and lobbying, with the community empowerment groups displaying a more balanced mix of insider/outsider tactics.

Though not directly addressed in these data, political opportunities and constraints may be important as resources in effecting strategies of frame dissemination. Indeed, the relative absence of high- and low-cost electoral activity by U.S. movement groups cannot be explained by internal resources: U.S. nonprofit tax laws may be the critical factor, which restricts the electoral activity of SMOs if they want to maintain their tax-exempt and charitable gift status (cf. McCarthy, Britt, and Wolfson 1991). Moreover, Pagnucco and Smith's (1993) analysis of political opportunities for the U.S. peace movement suggests that policy-making processes and accountability structures can effectively limit movements' possibilities for influencing policy – regardless of the strength of public support for the issues. Thus, although foreign policy decision-making is centralized in the Executive Branch, our evidence shows no peace movement activity within that arena. (Referent elite groups organized around the Council on Foreign Relations have a kind of access that movement groups do not.) By contrast, decision-making processes surrounding drunk-driving issues are more supportive of, and open to, movement input (McCarthy 1994).

Now that we have examined what SMOs in different movements actually do, what lessons can we draw from how movements penetrate and gain prominence on different agendas? How does the development of frame dissemination repertoires intersect with agenda-setting structures and processes?

WHAT CAN WE LEARN FROM THE REVIEW OF AGENDA-SETTING?

As we have shown there are four main issue arenas and concommitant agendas which movements may attempt to shape, and each has its own dynamic. Activists must identify the specific audience they hope to reach and tailor their framing approaches to that specific agenda. What do the agenda-setting studies imply about those possibilities?

Agenda access by the weak

Given the importance of highly organized and resource-rich groups in the competition for agenda access, it is no wonder that analysts of the processes have paid little attention to social movement activists. Most of them are weak in that they seek to empower small or poorly organized and resource-poor constituencies. As a result, Margolis and Mauser convincingly argue concerning media agendas, consistent with the research we have reviewed, that "the voices that gain access to the media predominantly belong to those groups already established" (1989: 366). And they continue: "Resource poor groups normally face considerable difficulty in getting their concerns before the public" (367). So, "For a protest group to succeed it must either solicit the support of dissident elite groups directly, or else it must use the (often unfriendly) media attention gained from outrageous behavior to attract potential allies among otherwise uninvolved elites" (369).

In contrast, the evidence developed by Page and Shapiro makes clear that, as a rule, media attention that stems primarily from protest probably can be expected to taint activists' framing efforts in the short run. This suggests that the cooptation of elites is likely to be a more effective strategy than is protest for activists trying to get sustained attention to their framing of an issue in the general audience media.

The evidence on tactic use we have reviewed, however, suggests that many resource-rich SMOs use public protest and they do so in concert with other frame dissemination tactics. Resource-rich SMOs have the luxury of using many approaches to disseminating their frames.[14] On the other hand, the resource-poor groups also display variegated repertoires for dissemination, and are certainly not restricted to protest. Certain tactics, such as litigation, are almost inherently costly. But many inside tactics are not necessarily costly as is shown by their use by the resource-poor groups.

Audiences

Each of these several agenda-setting literatures focuses upon a distinct audience that serves as the arena gatekeeper for the agenda. For the media agenda, it is the media elites and newsgatherer. Given the shrinking size of the general audience media newshole and the strong trickle-down pattern of coverage of issues, the effective audience of gatekeepers for this agenda appears to be quite small. For the public agenda the audience is the undifferentiated public, but by simple extension (Gamson 1988) it is a wide number of diverse issue publics, rather than relying exclusively upon access to the general public through the general audience media.

For the governmental agenda, it is governmental elites who keep the agenda access gates. The size of the state and its degree of centralized control should be crucial to understanding access to these audiences. Discussions (Walker 1988) of the use of insider tactics, which include lobbying and litigation, have stressed their high costs in determining which groups use them. The small number of national legislators means that access to them is highly competitive, but state and local legislators are more accessible. And the large number of policy bureaucrats who work in the far-flung offices of modern democratic states offer many points of very low-cost access for disseminating movement frames. The evidence we have assembled suggests that, in spite of the imagery of resource-poor groups being precluded from direct contact with governmental agenda setters, many of them actually do attempt to spread their interpretations of injustice in this manner.

And, for the electoral arena it is party activists, politicians, and increasingly professional consultants who are the important gatekeepers. Successful movement framing efforts will take into account the interests and aims of agenda gatekeepers, which are generally structured by the nature of interparty competition, the number of competing parties, and the extent of party discipline. These data show relatively little frame dissemination activity of social movement organizations in the electoral arena, and groups with the highest scores were those in European contexts which typically have electoral structures which allow more space for electoral debate of policy issues.[15] Of course, party activists usually want to win elections, thus the ability of social movement activists to change the public agenda, and potentially, the readiness of voters to vote for candidates and parties that support those movements has an indirect effect upon the electoral agenda. Moreover, as we argued, political activists are more in tune with the agendas of specific movements than the general public is; thus, the electoral arena is preconfigured to take up social movement issues, but actual elections may suppress them.

Agenda linkages

We began by asserting the notable independence of the various issue agenda-setting processes, and much of the work we have reviewed supports our characterization of the rather weak linkages between the several processes. This does not mean, however, that they are completely unrelated.[16] Indeed many movement tactical repertoires rely on a reverberation effect across agendas by using strategies which aim to bring issues to the public and possibly media agendas, but carry out few direct attempts to shape policy-related agendas.

Media agenda-setting is seen as important by analysts of all of the other agenda-setting processes, but is generally viewed as a mediating process rather than the object of explanation. There are convincing arguments that media agendas are affected by other agendas: (1) the public agenda, especially through the widespread application of the technology of public opinion polling by media firms which makes the agenda known in a widely credible fashion (Herbst 1993; Ginsberg 1988); (2) the governmental agenda, especially through the heavy reliance of the general audience media functionaries upon "experts" and authorities as news sources; and (3) the electoral agenda, especially through the heavy reliance of newsmakers upon the media constructionists of active candidates. This suggests that movements with diversified framing strategies that aim to influence multiple distinct audiences will be more likely to get on the media agenda. It further suggests that getting on the media agenda may sometimes be more likely if pursued indirectly through the other agenda arenas.

Agenda size and stability

Analysts of each arena emphasize the strong competition for position within its very narrow space. The media agenda appears to be the least stable of the four, because it is tied to newsworthy events. Coverage "lurches" in Baumgartner and Jones's (1990) imagery. Page and Shapiro (1992) picture the public agenda as quite stable based on their look at a wide variety of issues over long periods. This is in contrast to the picture of instability generated if one conflates media attention with public attention and concern. The governmental agenda can be characterized (e.g., Baumgartner and Jones 1990), when viewed from a longer time perspective, as quite stable – it is altered now and then by major shifts in issue attention, but incrementalism is the rule. This stability stems, importantly, from the institutional embeddedness of issues on governmental agendas, especially executive agency ones.

Dramatic events and media spectacles

Most of the analyses of agenda-setting in the various arenas downplay the role of dramatic contingent events and media spectacles (Dyan and Katz 1992), yet experience suggests that sometimes such events can be of great importance in drawing attention to issues in the general audience media, among the public, as well as among elites and governmental decision-makers. So, too, can media spectacles (e.g., the anniversary of the Normandy invasion) focus great waves of short-term attention. It is our contention that such events may provide fortuitous opportunities for short-term agenda access (e.g., Three Mile Island and Chernobyl for antinuclear activists, the O. J. Simpson case for anti–domestic violence activists, the attempted assassination of Ronald Reagan for gun control activists), but that the longer, more embedded processes we have been reviewing are probably most important for understanding sustained levels of attention to an issue, even on the media agenda. Kingdon (1984) explicitly recognizes the importance of focusing events to governmental agenda-setting processes, but he stresses what he calls the need for accompaniment. Dramatic events by themselves, he argues, cannot carry an issue to governmental policy agenda prominence. Such issues must be framed in such a way that they fit within broader agenda-setting processes. Events have enduring effects upon agendas only when they reshape and redefine social group relationships and social cleavages or set off a chain of related activities that create space on agendas.

Issue types and strategic framing

Within these more general strategic considerations of audience and agenda linkage, size and stability, movement strategic framers typically struggle to find new ways of packaging issues in order to enhance their attractiveness to these different audiences. This is, of course, the key rhetorical task of strategic framing. A number of analysts whose work we have discussed suggest that certain classes of issues – valence issues (Nelson 1984) and easy issues (Carmines and Stimson 1989) – may be inherently more effective for agenda-setting than others, particularly within the media and electoral agendas. Some of those issue dimensions are somewhat manipulable by strategic framing. This assumption, if correct, has clear implications for strategic framing projects.

Nelson defines valence issues by "their *lack of specificity* and their attempt to *reaffirm the ideals of civic life*" (1984: 28). And, recall that an "easy" issue is determined by the small amount of cognitive processing required to deal with it. Competent strategic framers typically seek to package their issues simply and in ways that are consistent with the ideals and contemporary themes of civic life. Sensitivity to this concern may aid movement activists in attracting attention to their issues. However, since movements must appeal simultaneously to a general and to an activist audience, strategic framers must be able to accommodate the varying demands of these audiences.

Evidence from research on recent strategic framing efforts by peace movement organizations demonstrates a framing shift from more general, valence issue frames during the peak of anti–nuclear weapons mobilization to more complex, multi-issue "retention" frames after the movement began to decline and as SMOs tried to sustain the interest of core activists (Marullo, Pagnucco, and Smith 1996).

Issues for which credible supporting evidence can be provided are also good for attracting attention. Kingdon's (1984) insights about the importance of crafting believable indicators of injustice trends echoes Gusfield's (1981) analysis. The widespread development of systematic indicators based upon credible research – including counts and analyses of, for example, hate crimes, human rights violations, date rape, and so forth – suggest the importance of developing apparently "scientific evidence" to both gain agenda access and to buttress frames once this has been achieved.

It remains, in our minds, an open question whether or not issues have inherent framing liabilities as suggested by several of the issue typologies we have considered here. One feature of issues, however, seems more impervious to strategic framing through the general audience media, and that is the extent to which it can be directly experienced across populations. Public agenda issues which are widely experienced directly, or indirectly through networks of personal relations like unemployment, appear to be less likely to be affected by media agendas. And issues relating to rare events less likely to be directly experienced, like rape and homicide, appear to be more affected by the media agenda, if they appear on it. Thus, Snow and Benford (1988) stress the importance of relating movement frames to common experiences, suggesting that the impact of media agenda-setting may be mitigated by movement efforts and that even the proximal dimension of personal experience is more manipulable than a view from the agenda-setting processes implies.

CONCLUSION

Our analysis has attempted to define the processes surrounding agenda-setting in different arenas and to begin to assess their implications for strategic framing possibilities. While we do not deny the common assumption in framing research that issues are malleable and subject to movement framing and reframing to improve their likely effectiveness, our review strongly suggests that movements are constrained by competitive agenda-setting logics. Within the agenda-setting environment, movements are further limited by their own capacities for developing strategic frame dissemination repertoires, or tactical combinations aimed at communicating their frames to various audiences and agenda gatekeepers.

We are now in a position to raise a general issue about the relationship of frames to forms of rhetoric and persuasion and to dissemination tactics. In their most truncated version, frames reduce complex issues into evocative phrases, metaphors, and slogans. But it is clear that these truncated frames are only part of the grievances, ideologies, and programs that movements attempt to disseminate. Moreover, the discourse in different arenas may well require more elaborated plans and programs if they are to be convincing to gatekeepers. In turn, the personnel and expertise that are required to disseminate these more elaborated proposals will vary by arena. Is it primarily the nature of dissemination tactics, or mostly framing opportunity provided by agenda-setting structures and processes, or an interaction between these several separate processes? Some of the best work on strategic framing (by, e.g., Snow and his colleagues) suggests that the rhetorical quality of frames is crucial to their success. This is a seductive position since, presumably, rhetorical manipulation and invention can be cheap.[17]

The question of the importance of rhetorical quality needs to be stated in a comparative fashion in order that it can be tested empirically. In order to develop such a test, however, the nature of what social movement activists do to disseminate their frames and the background agenda-setting processes must be included as alternative accounts of the success of agenda access. Can poorly articulated frames make it onto agendas if disseminated more effectively than superb ones? Can highly complex, cold frames get noticed because they intersect with agenda-setting structures and processes better than marvelously hot and resonant ones? Does the rhetorical quality of frames matter more in some agenda arenas than others? Are there differences across national political systems and national media structures that affect the impact of variable quality frames? Answering questions such as these empirically will help us to more adequately evaluate the *relative* importance of the quality of strategic injustice frames.

14

Media discourse, movement publicity, and the generation of collective action frames: Theoretical and empirical exercises in meaning construction

BERT KLANDERMANS and SJOERD GOSLINGA

The Netherlands has the reputation of having one of the best social security systems in the world. Part of this system is the Disability Insurance Act (WAO). It rules that everybody who is physically incapable of continuing to work on his or her own level of education and work experience is entitled to a benefit of 70 percent[1] of his or her last-earned income.

Since 1968, the year the Disability Insurance Act was implemented, work disability in the Netherlands has grown at an epidemic rate. At the time of the Act's conception it was projected that the number of people receiving a disability allowance (DA) would never exceed 200,000. But the number of people on a disability allowance (DA) rose from 160,000 in 1968 to 900,000 in the early 1990s. The "disease of worker disability" is potent only in the Netherlands. In comparable countries such as West Germany, the United States, and Sweden the number of recipients of disability benefits per 1,000 members of the labor force remained fairly stable over a 20-year period from 1970 through 1989 (oscillating around 55 in West Germany, 40 in the United States, and 70 in Sweden). In that same period figures rose in the Netherlands from 55 in 1970 to 152 in 1989 – an increase of almost 300 percent (Burk-hauser 1991).

With 900,000 persons on DA, an estimated 21 billion guilders per year, or 6 percent of the country's gross national product, is spent on disability allowances (as compared to 2.3 percent in France and 3.5 percent in West Germany). During the 1980s it became more and more clear to the experts that the number of people on DA was growing so rapidly that, in the long run, it would bring insurmountable problems to the national economy.

Indeed, the key agencies – government, employer organizations, and labor unions – agree that the growth of the number of people on DA ought to stop. Agreement on the ultimate aims, however, does not necessarily imply agreement on the way to achieve those aims. The government and employers,

The authors want to thank Bill Gamson and the editors of this volume for their comments on drafts of this essay.

on the one hand, want to change the allowance system itself in order to reduce the costs and to make it less attractive to individual workers. The unions, on the other hand, want to maintain the allowance system in its present form, but want to introduce regulations which make it more likely for an individual to continue or return to work. Profound changes in social policy do not take place overnight and are accompanied by struggles among social actors over politics and people. The disability allowance is no exception to the rule, and since 1990 unions, the government, and employers have been engaged in confrontational politics. From a generally accepted principle, DA has become a major controversy in domestic politics.

The observer of the DA controversy is intrigued by at least two questions. The first question obviously is: Why did work disability in the Netherlands grow at such a rate? In answering this question we will draw on a paper by Hooijberg and Price (1992). These authors point to the interplay of widely shared cultural values and institutional actors for an explanation. Although this may explain the difference between the Netherlands and other industrialized countries, it does not provide an answer to a second question: How did DA, despite its embeddedness in widely shared cultural values, become controversial?

Borrowing from the literature on meaning construction we will describe the DA controversy in the next few paragraphs as a collision of two different "icons." In a fascinating study of the emergence of the hazardous waste issue in the United States, Szasz (1994) introduces the concept of "political icon" to describe a specific kind of political communication, "carried by images rather than words, so that the meaning or signification takes place more through nonverbal spectacle than through narrative." In Szasz's view, claim-making rhetoric increasingly takes the form of iconography. Especially important for our discussion are his observations regarding the reception of iconic political messages and the collision of icons.

Szasz observes that the attitudinal change produced by iconic communications is shallow and evanescent. Media coverage of an issue produces an immediate, rapid increase in expressions of concerns about that issue in the polls, but the issue's importance evaporates as quickly as it forms and nothing guarantees that even widespread political discourse will have staying power. Media coverage does produce an increase in expressions of concern about an issue, but those expressions of concern fade just as quickly when coverage wanes. But in Szasz's opinion this does not mean that this kind of attitude formation is essentially hollow or politically meaningless. Attitudes and beliefs persist in some form and the right stimulus will ignite an experiential connection and vividly bring those latent attitudes alive. One of those stimuli is a collision with another icon, such as the collision between the deregulation and the hazardous waste icons under the Reagan administration that revitalized the hazardous waste issue.

We will use these ideas in our analysis of the DA controversy in the Netherlands and describe the clash of two icons: "Disability allowance as an entitlement" versus "Disability allowance as a problem."

THE DA CONTROVERSY IN THE NETHERLANDS

The disability allowance as an entitlement

In their paper on the "great Dutch work disability epidemic" Hooijberg and Price (1992: 8) refer to the important value in Dutch society "that income security is not a gift, but an entitlement, a right. . . . one does not need to be grateful when receiving some form of allowance. As a citizen of the Netherlands one is entitled to income security." This entitlement is further extended by the views concerning "suitable work." These views hold that one cannot be expected to accept work that is below one's level of education and work experience. The law states that if a disabled person cannot find "suitable" work, that person must be considered 80–100 percent work-disabled and paid a full allowance, even if the person would be capable of doing other than suitable work. The authors then continue to describe how each of the actors involved – the government, employers, and labor unions – made the DA system work to their advantage and, by pursuing their own goals and responding to their immediate demands, set the conditions for the confluence of forces that triggered the work disability epidemic. The DA system is much more favorable to the workers than the unemployment system. Therefore, individual workers prefer DA over unemployment money. This helps to explain the policy of the government and the labor unions. The government had an interest in keeping unemployment figures low and unions had an interest in allowing their members entrance to the financially more favorable DA. To employers the DA system had the advantage of making it easier to get rid of less productive workers.

The disability allowance as a problem

How, then, did DA become a problem? It seemed as if the system worked to everybody's advantage. Yet, the actors in the socioeconomic arena came to agree that the system had to be reconsidered, the main reason, of course, was the costs of DA to the nation's economy in terms of both money and loss in productivity. Van Voorden (1992) mentioned three reasons why at the end of the 1980s time was ripe for a change: (1) the extremely high proportion of people not working (in 1989 20 percent of the labor force, including unemployment), (2) the expected intensification of international competition with the opening of the European market in 1992, and (3) the necessity to reduce the national deficit. This led to an agreement between the Social Democrats and the Christian Democrats, the two political parties entering office in 1989 to drive the appeal on DA back. The intent to change the Disability Insurance Act, triggered the "DA as a problem" icon. In public discourse, the Disability Insurance Act was no longer the final piece of the country's social security system but a regulation employers, unions, and individual workers were exploiting to advance their own interests. Instead of something disabled workers are entitled to, disability allowance became a national problem.

Public opinion

This did not leave public opinion unaffected. We observe dramatic changes from 1989 through 1991. Table 14.1 summarizes some public opinion data over a ten-year period. Until 1989 there was an increasingly positive attitude toward social security payment in general and DA in specific. In the eighties the majority of the population felt that social security payment including DA could increase more than incomes in general. Moreover, not more than one third of the population thought that the Disability Insurance Act was frequently abused. Unfortunately, data are missing for 1987, 1988, and 1989 but if we assume that the same trend as in the other indicators would appear there, we may expect in 1989 even less than one third of the population being concerned about abuse of DA. Then, in 1991 a dramatic shift takes place. Admittedly, part of it is due to a general concern about the economic situation as witnessed by the changing figures regarding the desirable income development. But these changes are small in comparison to those with regard to social security payment. This is further underlined by the fact that by then 56 percent of the population believes that the Disability Insurance Act is frequently abused.

On the one hand, such changes in public opinion result from the public debate in response to the projected intervention in the DA system. On the other hand, it are these very changes in public opinion that made intervention possible.

Mayer Zald emphasizes in his essay introducing Part III of this book that social controversies almost always draw on the larger societal definitions of relationships of rights and of responsibilities. Mobilization, Zald argues, often originates from "two or more cultural themes that are potentially contradictory [that] are brought into active contradiction by the force of events." Indeed, the DA controversy resonates on a fundamental dimension Gamson (1992a) identifies in the relationship between individual and society: self-reliance versus mutuality. Self-reliance, in the sense that the individual citizen got to understand that society cannot take responsibility for everything, is an important aspect of "DA as a problem," whereas mutuality, in the sense of the responsibility society has for its less fortunate members, is a key element of "DA as an entitlement." Indeed, the DA debate seems to be part of a more fundamental debate in Dutch society about the welfare state. Mutual-

Table 14.1. *Changes in public opinion on social security*

	1980	1985	1986	1987	1988	1989	1991
Desirable development of income in view of economic situation							
increase	15	34	43	39	47	51	41
stabilize	52	58	54	56	50	48	52
decrease	29	8	4	4	3	2	7
	(1.870)	(1.833)	(1.844)	(1.800)	(1.779)	(1.716)	(1.731)
Desirable development of social security payment in view of economic situation							
increase	21	34	43	46	48	57	35
stabilize	50	53	49	45	42	36	49
decrease	30	13	8	9	10	6	17
	(1.800)	(1.829)	(1.801)	(1.817)	(1.793)	(1.744)	(7.717)
Disability Allowance insufficient	23	46	47	48	50	50	39
	(1.600)	(1.600)	(1.500)	(1.475)	(1.450)	(1.400)	(1.400)
Disability Insurance Act is abused frequently	49	34	36				56
	(1.820)	(1.745)	(1.746)				(1.624)

Source: SCP, 1992.

ity for a long time defined the rules, but it was discredited, perhaps not only for financial reasons but also as part of the more general collapse of communism and socialism as ideological frameworks. The emphasis in the debate right now is on the individual's responsibility to take care of himself and to not rely too much on society. There is no theme without a countertheme, Gamson argues, and the DA controversy only demonstrates this assertion.

Two icons in collision

From 1989 to 1993 the DA controversy has dominated Dutch national politics. The government opens the confrontation when it announces that it wants to reduce the number of people on DA and the benefits paid. In addition it wants to reduce absenteeism (seen as the first step to disability) by introducing negative incentives such as turning in holidays or no payment for the first day of absenteeism. The unions respond by indicating that they will demand compensation in contract negotiations if the government pushes that through. The government in its turn threatens to prepare a law to give the secretary of social affairs the right to cancel contracts that are detrimental to the countries economy.

Then the exchanges continue with a consent. On October 2 the so-called autumn consultations among government, employers, and unions close with an agreement. The unions agree to accept negative incentives on absenteeism on the agenda of future contract negotiations and the government withdraws the proposed law to cancel contracts. A quiet period follows until summer 1991, when the government publicizes its plans on DA. Within a few days every union official who is not on vacation is up in arms and some of those who are on vacation are called back home. The government proposes the following regulations:

1. A reduction of benefits after the first year on DA
2. A sacrifice of holidays and income in case of absenteeism
3. The first six weeks of absenteeism to be at the employer's cost
4. Employers to pay a penalty if they send an employee on DA

In the weeks that follow the unions prepare for a "hot autumn." During September and the first week of October they organize a whole array of different collective actions (short work stoppages, protest demonstrations, meetings of their members during working hours, extended luncheon meetings, short strikes, and so on). The government is not really impressed and supported by a parliamentary majority; it is determined to implement the new regulations.

Spring 1992 the next round takes place. In the context of the annual contract negotiations, the unions attempt to compensate for the governmental regulations. Occasionally, they meet resistance from employers, but on the whole they were indeed fairly successful in compensating some governmental regulation – in fact, even before regulations are implemented.

Autumn 1992 the new DA regulations are subject of debate within the Social Democratic Party and between that party and its partner in government the Christian Democratic Party, which brings the governmental coalition between the Social Democrats and the Christian Democrats near to a breakdown. January 1993 the government's proposal is approved by Parliament, but there is still a final round to go.

In the 1993 contract negotiations the unions try to compensate for the new regulations. This time employers are much more reluctant to meet the unions' wishes. Nevertheless, except for a few industries – among others engineering – agreements are reached without any strikes or other forms of industrial action. In general the unions and employers' organizations agree on some system of additional insurances workers can enter either collectively or individually, depending on the contract arrangements. Four years of intense societal debate have come to an end.

There are many different ways of studying the development of societal controversies. This chapter adopts a social cognitive approach to answer two questions: (1) How do collective action frames regarding complex socioeconomic issues such as DA develop? (2) What is the role of media discourse in this regard and to what extent are actors such as unions capable of influencing media discourse?

MEDIA DISCOURSE, MOVEMENT PUBLICITY, AND THE GENERATION OF COLLECTIVE ACTION FRAMES

The preceding section described how in public discourse DA transformed into a societal problem and how unions – forced on the defense – were confronted with the problem of generating collective action frames. In this context it was only logical for the unions to rely on the countertheme "DA as an entitlement" – the result being a collision in public discourse between the two icons. In Zald's words an active process of strategic framing by issue entrepreneurs took place. Journalists, columnists, experts, politicians, and conflict parties alike tried to define the issue. Mass media played a crucial role in this regard, but, as Zald argues and we will see in this chapter, media are not neutral. The unions faced the question of how to influence the beliefs of their constituencies in the context of public discourse as it evolved. This question concerns the impact of public discourse on individual beliefs and in this context the capability of an individual social actor to influence public discourse and the beliefs of its constituency. In this section we try to master this thorny issue conceptually by developing a theoretical framework for the study of media discourse and the generation of collective action frames. We will develop our argument in three separate steps: We will first discuss media discourse as a reflection of public discourse. We will then discuss attempts by actors to influence media discourse, and finally we will elaborate on the generation of collective action frames. Each section will provide both theoretical argumentation and empirical illustration.

Before embarking on discussion of the impact of public discourse on individual beliefs, let us briefly describe the kind of beliefs that constitute collective action frames. Gamson (1992a) defines collective action frames as consisting of three components: (1) injustice, referring to moral indignation, a so-called hot cognition laden with emotion; (2) agency, or the consciousness that it is possible to alter conditions or policies through collective action; and (3) identity, referring to a "we" in opposition to some "they" who have different interests or values.

In terms of the DA controversy a collective action frame means anger over the proposed restrictions, the belief that collective action would be effective, and the belief that it is "we" workers or "our" unions against the government and/or employers. To what extent did such a collective action frame develop among union members and to what extent were the unions capable of influencing their constituencies in that regard? In order to answer this question, let us first elaborate on media discourse and the influence unions can exert on it.

Media discourse

Social issues are debated in arenas of public discourse and action (Gamson and Modigliani 1989; Rucht 1988). Media discourse constitutes a crucial element in this process. Because we believe, like Gamson (1992), that it is a good reflection of public discourse, we will concentrate our discussion on media discourse. Although we are eventually interested in the impact of media discourse on individual beliefs, media discourse is a meaning system that can be studied in its own right and it is to this meaning system that we give our attention first.

Kielbowicz and Scherer (1986) indicate that the media are instrumental for social movements in at least three different ways: (1) Media are important means of reaching the general public, to acquire approval and to mobilize potential participants; (2) media can link movements with other political and social actors; and (3) media can provide psychological support for members. Obviously, media are not always instrumental for social movements. Van Zoonen (1992), in her study of the women's movement in the Dutch media, concludes that the media provided a biased and ridiculed picture of the movement, obstructed mobilization, and induced conflicts within the movement. In her view, this was not so much a deliberate strategy to undermine the movement as a consequence of the way media work: emphasis on events rather than issues, analysis, and background information; events reported as isolated incidents; preference for persons over issues and preference for simple issues with identifiable pros and cons.

A few years earlier, Van Dijk (1988a) concluded that in media discourse on social conflicts the dominant interpretation of the conflicts receive the most attention of the media. The views of the strikers, protestors, or contenders receive a much less prominent place. The main actors that feature in the news belong to the political elite – government officials, political parties in office, employers' organizations. Unions, oppositional organizations, and movements receive much less attention. Moreover, he demonstrates that negative, short-lived, or spectacular events receive more attention than background information.

In short, mass media do not transmit information without transforming it. Space limitations alone introduce selectivity in the production of media discourse. Mass media select and interpret available information according to principles that define news value. In so doing they produce a transformed reality which diverges from the reality as a social actor defines it.

From this characterization of the media one would expect media discourse to comprise predominantly elements that discourage the generation of collective action frames. This is, indeed, in general what Gamson (1992a) found in his study of media discourse in the United States. In terms of each of the three components of collective action frames, however, media discourse sometimes played a facilitative role. But more important, Gamson also discovered that media discourse is far from the only source individuals draw on in their conversations. His focus groups sometimes developed injustice frames, adversarial frames, or agency irrespective of whether media discourse had discouraged the generation of such beliefs or not. Gamson explains this by referring to other sources of knowledge individuals have at their disposal – experiential knowledge (direct or vicarious) and popular wisdom (shared knowledge of what everyone knows). He claims that frames based on the integrated use of all three sources of information are more robust, *and* that using an integrated resource strategy facilitates the development of collective action frames.

Analyzing news discourse. Van Dijk (1988 a, b) developed a theoretical framework and a methodology to examine news discourse. Its objective is to reveal the in-depth structure of a text based on rules that help to reduce information to a small number of so-called macropropositions. Macropropositions are different from categories in content analysis. The latter refer to a concept (a crime, an accident, social welfare); the former always consist of complete propositions (the man robbed the taxi-driver; the pedestrian was hit by a car; the government wants to cut back on social welfare). Together the propositions in a text constitute the *semantic macrostructure* of that text. Macropropositions can be put in a hierarchical order, that is from core propositions to

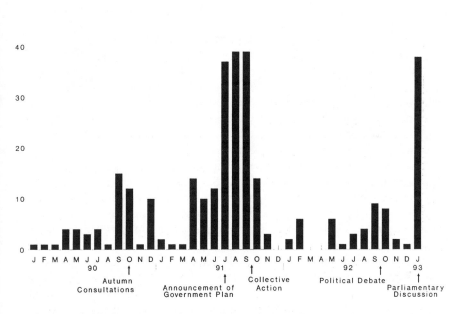

Figure 14.1. Media coverage of DA: number of articles in two national newspapers.

subpropositions and can be displayed as tree diagrams. The rules that govern hierarchical ordering are called the *syntactic macrostructures* or superstructure. The significance of the macrostructure of a newspaper article lies in the fact that there is reason to believe that it is the macrostructure that is recollected best (van Dijk 1988a).

Icons and actors: News discourse on DA

Public debate on DA peaked several times in line with the key events singled out for this study. News discourse as it took place in two national newspapers (*NRC-Handelsblad* and *Volkskrant*) reflected the intensifications of the debate by increases in coverage (Figure 14.1). In 1990 in the three-week period from September 20 through October 10, coverage of DA in these two newspapers goes up from four articles in the first week, to ten in the second, and back down to five in the third. A period of relative silence follows until an outburst of media coverage takes place in July–September 1991, when the government announces its plans and the unions stage collective actions in response to those plans. Compared to the attention of the newspapers for the DA controversy in this period, coverage of DA in the spring of 1992 with regard to the contract negotiations is rather modest. The autumn of 1992 brings the debate within the Social Democratic Party and between the Social and Christian Democrats, and in January 1993 parliamentary debate takes place.

In order to give an impression of news discourse on the issue we will present some data from the peak period – that is, July through October 1991. For this analysis we selected news articles from two national newspapers (*Volkskrant* and *NRC-Handelsblad*). Altogether 45 articles were analyzed. We applied van Dijk's (1988 a, b) method of reducing each article to a few macropropositions. We then reduced these propositions to a new set of macropropositions characterizing news discourse on DA in this period in the two newspapers. Schema 1 presents the propositions.

If we may assume that news discourse in these two newspapers is representative for news discourse in that period, Schema 1 gives us an impression of the information on the DA controversy individuals could have obtained from the newspapers. Most propositions in Schema 1 appeared over and over in the newspapers of those days. Remember also that supposedly macropropositions are the elements of news discourse that are best recollected.

The picture that emerges is relatively simple: The government has developed a plan on DA that reduces the costs of DA by limiting the duration of the allowances and the number of eligible people. There are doubts about the effectiveness of the plan and public opinion is not favorable. The political parties are divided. The employers are on the government's side. The unions are dead set against it and threaten to take any kind of action to prevent the plan from being implemented. The unions' alternative proposals have not been taken seriously. The government will hold on to the plan. The government condemns the collective actions announced by the unions.

Except for the key elements of the government's proposal little information on the content of the plan is provided in news discourse. This is even more the case regarding the union's proposals or the debates within the political parties. Of the two icons "DA as a problem" is the only one being featured. In a way the message in these newspapers in that period boils down to "The government has a plan to fix the problems with the DA system, which is supported by employers, debated by politicians, and opposed by the unions." It is clear who the actors are; it is clear that government and employers are on one side of the controversy and the unions on the other; it is much less clear what exactly the controversy is about.

Influencing media discourse

Media discourse may be but one of the tools individuals use in their attempts to make sense of an issue, for the unions it is of crucial importance to be able to influence such discourse. Admittedly, unions have their own journals, but at best these periodicals appear once a week and more usually every other

Schema 1. *News discourse in macropropositions: July–October 1991*

Government's plan
Plan implies limitation of the duration of DA.
Plan intends reducing the number of people on DA.
Plan intends reducing the costs of DA.
Plan implies punishment of employers for sending workers on DA.
Several actors express doubts on whether plan will achieve its goals.
Public opinion is opposed to plan.

Unions
Unions are against limitation of the duration of DA.
Unions will compensate via contract negotiations.
Unions threaten to mobilize for collective action.
Unions feel that their proposals have not been taken seriously.
Unions will put pressure on political parties.
Unions will explore opportunities for juridical action.

Employers
Employers are pleased with DA plan.
Employers are against punishment for employers.
Employers will resist compensation via contract negotiations.
Employers feel victimized by collective action.

Government
Government will hold on to DA plan.
Government is willing to take the edge off DA plan.
Government is not convinced by the unions' proposals.
Government condemns collective action.

Political parties
Parties in office are in favor of DA plan.
Opposition parties are against DA plan.
Social Democratic Party wants to amend DA plan.
Christian Democratic Party wants to hold on to DA plan.
Commotion within Social and Christian Democratic Party is growing.

week or every month. On many an occasion, then, mass media are the only way for a union to reach its membership, let alone those situations in which a union wants to address a general audience. Consequently, in their attempts to influence the formation and transformation of beliefs in society, unions have no choice but to rely on mass media. This is not to say that mass media are at the unions' disposal. On the contrary, unions are confronted with the same rules that apply to every social actor in its dealings with the media (Kielbowicz and Scherer 1986).

This made unions in the Netherlands not only create publicity departments within their organizations, but established elaborated arrangements with the press and radio and television networks. Indeed, publicity is among the most professionalized part of Dutch labor unions. The same holds, by the way, for the government and employers' organizations. On their part, press agencies and me ˙ ↳ have their specialists on industrial relations, who usually cover the unions. As a consequence, media discourse on the subject is to a large extent "written" by a relatively small set of people, who know each other and meet at news events such as press conferences, briefings, and the like.

Much of what Kielbowicz and Scherer (1986) mention in terms of practices that allow movement organizations to establish more effective relationships with the media is, indeed, applied by Dutch labor unions. Unions carefully adapt their news events to the rhythm and cycles of the media; they are very creative in staging events to draw the attention of the media; they have established relationships with some media or some journalists; they meticulously prepare ready-made documents that journalists can use (if they wish) in the preparation of their news item. All this is, of course, aimed at influencing media discourse.

Yet, despite all these precautions there is no guarantee that media coverage will be to the union's satisfaction. In spite of all carefully framed press releases, press conferences, interviews, and the like the union's message will not be transmitted without bias and the media's biases will not always favor the union. Even the most carefully orchestrated publicity does not assure that the union's message will come across intact.

One of the studies in our DA research program can serve to illustrate this point: A couple of weeks before the autumn consultations in 1990 took place the National Christian Union Federation (CNV) presented its policy vis-à-vis the consultations to the media at a press conference. We collected (1) written texts of all press releases issued by the CNV and observations of the press conference held by the CNV and (2) newspaper articles based on the press releases and the press conference.

The CNV had formulated a stand on each of the four issues on the agenda of the autumn consultations: (1) reduction of the number of people on DA; (2) unemployment among ethnic minorities; (3) long-term unemployment; and (4) education and labor market. As far as the DA issue was concerned, the CNV offered a number of proposals either to limit the influx of new people on DA (e.g., proposals to reduce absenteeism by improving the working circumstances and by punishing companies for high levels of absenteeism) or to encourage reentrance to the labor market for those who were already on DA (e.g., retraining, replacement, fixed quota per company of partly disabled workers). In addition to these policy items, the CNV president mentioned five major pitfalls that could easily jeopardize the consultations' chances of success.

Which of these aspects of the press conference made it into the newspapers that evening or the morning after? Schema 2 shows in the first row which

Schema 2. *Proportions of press release and newspaper articles on the five themes of the press conference*

Agenda	1	2	3	4	"Pitfalls"	Total
CNV press release	32%	9%	15%	22%	23%	100%
	553	158	248	369	387	
Newspapers						
AD	100%					100%
	240					
NRC	100%				70%	100%
	257				613	
Parool	30%					100%
	263					
Trouw	92%	8%				100%
	515	47				
Volkskrant	100%					100%
	257					

proportion of the CNV press release was devoted to each of the four issues and to the pitfalls. The remaining rows describe which proportion of the coverage of the press conference in five national newspapers was on each of these five subjects. Note that three of the five newspapers only refer to the DA issue and do not mention any other subject. Two other newspapers mention one additional item. If apparently the DA issue is so important to the newspapers, which aspect of the union's press release do they transmit?

Schema 3 presents data relevant to that question. Twelve different aspects of the DA issue were mentioned by the union president at the press conference. These aspects appeared in the press release as well. Obviously, none of the newspapers provided the complete picture. Indeed, in order to acquire a complete picture of the union viewpoint on the DA, one would have to read all five newspapers.

Use of own media

Obviously, newspapers are not unbiased transmitters of information. One strategy employed to circumvent the mass media is the use of the organization's own media. Of course, the union journals of those days attempted to persuade the union membership of the rightness of the unions' stand. We conducted content analyses on the June through November issues of the journals of the nine largest unions of the same federation.[2] Each article dealing with the DA controversy was coded on a number of dimensions related to

Schema 3. *Elements of CNV plan in DA mention in newspaper articles*

Point of view	AD	NRC	PAR	TRW	VLK
A: Prevention					
1	+				+
2	+	+	+	Headline	
3	+				
4	+	+	+	+	
5	Headline		+	+	Headline
6					+
B. Integration					
1				+	+
2				+	
3					+
4	+	Headline	+	+	Headline
5	+	+	+	+	+
6	+		+	+	+
"Union plan"	+	+	Headline	+	+

Note: Abbreviations refer to the five national newspapers that covered the press conference.

the three elements of collective action frames: injustice, identity, and agency.

As far as the identity dimension was concerned, the union journals presented a plain "us" versus "them" frame: only negative and no positive statements about the government, only positive and no negative statements about the unions, only positive and no negative statements about people on disability payment. This was in sharp contrast to the pictures drawn in the newspapers. In the union journal, a story was told about the unions taking the side of disabled workers, while government was represented as unjust authority, responsible for rank injustice to those who are on DA. Nowhere does government appear as a reasonable counterpart with whom it is possible to confer. Hardly any differentiation was found. No mention is made of possible abuse of DA, nor of budgetarian problems. Clearly, DA is defended as an entitlement of the workers offended by the government.

Moral indignation is perhaps the best typification of the union journals' accounts on DA with regard to injustice. Through interviews with and stories about people on DA the impression evolves of workers on DA as victims of unjust politics. Emotional language abounds, apparently aimed at evoking compassion for disabled workers and anger about villainous politicians.

As the events evolve, a growing proportion of the content of articles in the union journals concerns the agency dimension. This development coincides with the turn of events toward collective action. Action appeals first and enthusiastic reports on collective actions that took place later fill the columns of the journals during the last couple of months of the period under investigation.

The generation of collective action frames

Gamson demonstrated the impact of media discourse on group conversations. Such an impact is also relevant in this context of our research, because information is processed not by individuals in isolation but by people interacting with other people in informal circles, primary groups, and friendship networks. Much of what goes on within these networks concerns the formation of consensus (Klandermans 1988). People tend to validate information by comparing and discussing their interpretations with significant others (Festinger 1954), especially when the information involved is complex. People prefer to compare their opinions with those of like-minded individuals. As a rule, the set of individuals interacting in one's social networks – especially one's friendship networks – is relatively homogeneous and composed of people not too different from oneself. These processes of social comparison produce collective definitions of a situation.

The impact of media discourse on individual beliefs, then, implies an interplay of media discourse and interpersonal interactions. Although the mass media play a crucial role in framing the themes and counterthemes of public discourse, the actual formation and transformation of beliefs take place in exchange within the groups and categories with which individuals identify. Such groups may be small, composed of people whom one encounters in daily life (colleagues, friends, carpoolers), or large generic categories (e.g. whites, workers, farmers, Europeans, union members). Obviously, these informal structures of everyday life play an important role in movement mobilization as discussed in McCarthy's introductory essay to Part II of this volume. The themes and counterthemes that arise in media discourse may, to a greater or lesser degree, harmonize with the collective beliefs of these groups or categories and depending on whether they harmonize or not they have an influence on these beliefs.

Individual beliefs, according to Gergen and Semin (1990: 11) "may properly be viewed as the internalized by-products of publicly shared discourse." Gamson (1992a) concludes that media discourse is an important tool people have available in their conversations when they try to make sense of issues. Whether they make use of this tool and of other sources of information depended in his focus groups on such dispositions as proximity of consequences and engagement with the issue. Coming from an information-processing

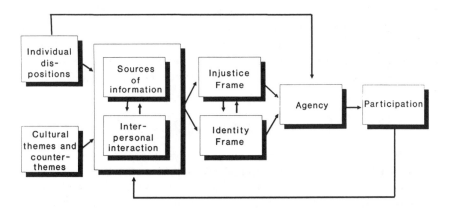

Figure 14.2. The generation of collective action frames.

angle, Petty and Cacioppo (1986) arrive at a similar conclusion: the likelihood that information will be thoroughly elaborated increases if the individual is already familiar with the subject, has an interest in the subject and is involved in the subject. This implies that any dispositional factor that increases familiarity with the issue, involvement in the issue, or commitment to social actors who are speaking out may increase the likelihood that information is elaborated. In conclusion, then, we may theorize that the key determinants of individual beliefs are (1) use of sources of information such as media discourse, experiential knowledge, and popular wisdom; (2) interpersonal interaction; and (3) individual dispositions.

In Figure 14.2 we have tried to summarize our theorizing thus far. The model comes down to the following: Participation in collective action depends on the extent to which an individual adheres to a collective action frame.

Over the years, the senior author has developed an elaborated model for the explanation of collective action participation (Klandermans 1984; Klandermans and Oegema 1987; Oegema and Klandermans 1994). This action participation model starts from the point where individuals already belong to the mobilization potential of a movement (that is, adhere to a collective action frame) and conceptualizes the process of activation. In this essay we roll theorizing further back, by elaborating the formation of mobilization potential or more precisely the formation of beliefs that define mobilization potential. We follow Gamson (1992a) in taking adherence of injustice frames, identity frames, and agency frames as crucial elements of mobilization potential. Such frames develop in interpersonal interaction in which different sources of information are employed: be it media discourse, experiential knowledge, or popular wisdom. What sources individuals use and the kind

Table 14.2. *Knowledge of government proposal on DA*

	1990[a]			1991[b]	1992[b]
	Week 1 (102)	Week 2 (99)	Week 3 (100)	(213)	(213)
Knows at least one item of government proposal	17%	40%	23%	88%	60%

[a]Three random samples in a separate sample design.
[b]One random sample in a panel design.

of information they process depends on the cultural themes and counterethemes that dominate public discourse and personal dispositions that increase the individual's engagement with those themes. In addition to their indirect influence, personal dispositions are supposed to have a direct influence on the agency component. For instance, commitment of workers to their union not only influences agency through its impact on sources of information used, information processed, interpersonal interaction, it will also have a direct impact on agency if the union mobilizes for collective action. Finally, participation in collective action will have a profound influence on interpersonal interaction and usage of sources of information.

Generating collective action frames

To what extent did the DA controversy generate a collective action frame and which factors accounted for individual variation? In the course of the four years that DA dominated domestic politics, we conducted telephone surveys at five different points in time. In the autumn of 1990 three separate random samples of 100 union members each were interviewed successively in the week before the autumn consultations, the week after the consultations, and again one week later. In the autumn of 1991 and the spring of 1992 we applied a panel design and interviewed a random sample of 213 union members at both points in time. It would exceed the space limits of this chapter to present results in great detail, but a few outcomes will be discussed to illustrate our argumentation regarding individual beliefs.

Not surprisingly, individual levels of information rise and fall with the cycles in news discourse. In response to an open question respondents were encouraged to mention as many items of the DA proposals as they could remember. Table 14.2 presents percentages of union members who are able to mention at least one item correctly. The question in 1990 concerned the DA proposals in the autumn consultations and the questions in 1991 and 1992 the DA proposals of the government.

Table 14.3. *Regression of media usage, interpersonal interaction, and dispositions of knowledge – autumn 1990: standardized regression coefficients*

	All	27-9-90	3-10-90	10-10-90
Media usage	.18*	.11	.27*	.15
Interpersonal interaction				
on socioeconomic matters	.12*	12	.09	.15
on DPA	.20*	.25*	.22*	.15
Dispositions				
level of education	.27*	.26*	.21*	.38*
interest in union affairs	.12*	.13	.10	.07
R^2	.29	.33	.26	.32
n	246	85	80	81

*Significant beta.

Autumn 1990. Obviously, the level of information in the autumn of 1990 was far below that in 1991 and 1992. Indeed, in 1990 DA as an issue is hardly salient to the average union member – a finding that reflects the limited presence of the issue in news discourse before we conducted our first measurement. The day after the consultations brought a lot of media attention and it will not come as a surprise that levels of knowledge increase – although less dramatic than one would aspect in view of the attention the agreement got in the mass media. A week later knowledge is reduced substantially. Apparently, people forget rapidly when an issue is no longer prominent.

The limited salience of DA is also witnessed by one other result from our 1990 interviews. Whereas 36 percent of the respondents reported to having talked "frequently about socioeconomic matters with colleagues," only 11 percent reported having talked with colleagues about the DA issue. Even more severely limited is the union members' knowledge of the union's standpoint on DA. Only 7.5 percent of the members know at least one element of their union's stand on DA, two-thirds of whom agree with it.

Variation in knowledge of the DA issue could reasonably well be accounted for by the relevant factors of our conceptual schema. (See Figure 14.2.) For this assessment, measures of individual disposition, sources of information and interpersonal interaction were entered in a number of regression analyses. Without going into too much detail, let us briefly summarize some of the findings that are relevant for our discussion.

Table 14.3 presents the betas for the sample as a whole and for the three points in time. For the sample as a whole each of the variables in the equation contributes significantly to the variation in knowledge about DA. Hence, media usage, interpersonal interaction, and dispositions are not only useful but necessary for the explanation of cognitions on DA (knowledge in this case). As far as the three points in time are concerned, we observe some significant differences in the pattern of determinants. There are two interesting changes to be noted: The day after the autumn consultations differences in knowledge are to a much larger extent controlled by media usage. This is, of course, what one would expect in view of the increased media attention that day. The week after the consultations knowledge is to a large extent dependent on level of education. In other words, if an issue disappears in media discourse, dispositions that are related to recollection of information gain in importance.

These results suggest that in 1990 the DA issue was still to a large extent an issue among experts and social actors involved, rather than a subject of large-scale public debate. Indeed, mass media paid attention to it, but because public opinion was not yet mobilized at that stage the issue did not yet produce any "hot" feelings. Altogether, there is little evidence that a collective action frame emerged in 1990. Knowledge of the issue is limited and nothing signifies the presence of an injustice or adversarial frame.

Autumn 1991. A year later the situation has dramatically changed. No longer is DA a dispute among experts, but an issue of mass mobilization. The persuasion machine of the actors involved operates in its highest gear and mass media coverage reaches high tide. Unlike a year before this time a collective action frame does develop at least among reasonable parts of the union membership.

As indicated in Table 14.3 the level of information in October 1991 is very high. Indeed, the key aspects of the government's plans are known by almost everybody. The little remaining variation in knowledge is related to differences in level of education and in usage of union journals as sources of information. Variation in usage of mass media as an information source did not explain any variance in knowledge at this point. Apparently, the mass media provided everybody with information on the key aspects of what the government proposed, whereas reading the union journals added some more details.

A fair proportion of the union members formed cognitions on the DA controversy which may be identified as elements of an injustice or adversarial frame. Table 14.4 presents the relevant percentages. These figures suggest the combined presence of an injustice and adversarial frame. Strong agreement with the union goes together with strong disagreement with the government; trust in the union as a source of information, with distrust in government. The government's DA plans are defined as an infringement on workers' rights, and according to one-third of the union members, not the workers but the government and the employers are to be blamed for the problems with DA. Note, however, that the majority of the union members *do* believe that the costs of DA are too high. This finding underscores our earlier assess-

Table 14.4. *Injustice and adversarial frames: percentages* (n = 213)

Positive attitude toward the union's stand	70
Negative attitude toward the government's plan	62
Costs of DA are too high	84
DA plans are an attack on workers' rights	64
Government and employers are to be blamed, not workers	36
Unions are reliable source of information	87
Government is reliable source of information	33

ment that the unions had no choice but defending "DA as a right." Denying "DA as a problem" would have been self-destructive. These beliefs are, of course, correlated, except for those about the costs of DA. Factor analysis reveals that with the exception of the beliefs about the costs of DA they load on a single factor. Empirically, it appears to be difficult to separate the injustice and adversarial frame.

Knowledge of the government's plan and commitment to the union were the two factors relevant in the explanation of these cognitive frames. The better the union members knew the plans *and* the more they were committed to the union the more likely for them to develop an injustice and adversarial frame.

To what extent did an agency frame develop? Remember that theoretically agency is not only determined by feelings of injustice and adversity, but by individual dispositions. Two such dispositions seem to be relevant: first, the belief that in case of a conflict industrial action should not be avoided; second, the preparedness to take part in various means of action. Obviously, these two cognitions are strongly correlated, but as we will see both have an independent impact on agency.

Table 14.5 presents the means on action preparedness at different points in time. In the table a distinction is made between general and specific action preparedness. The first concerns an individual's willingness to take part in collective action irrespective of the situation. General action preparedness can be defined as the point around which specific action preparedness oscillates depending on circumstances (Van der Veen 1992). In our panel study we were able to measure general action preparedness at an earlier point in time than we conducted our DA interviews. Therefore, we are able to relate specific action preparedness measured in the context of the DA controversy to independently measured general action preparedness. Theoretically, this means that we are able to distinguish the general tendency among union members to participate in industrial action from their preparedness to take action in the DA controversy, and to predict the latter from the former.

Table 14.5. *Agency frames: general and specific action preparedness (means and standard deviations)*

	General	Specific	
		October	May
Demonstrations	3.29 (1.02)	3.87[a] (1.04)	3.16 (1.03)
Work stoppages	3.54[b] (.96)	3.03 (1.15)	3.01 (1.02)
Strikes	2.36 (.97)	2.60[a] (1.14)	2.36 (1.02)

*N*s ranging from 175 to 202, means *n* = 192.
On a scale from 1 = "not prepared at all" to 5 = "very much prepared."
[a]significantly different from GAP and SAP in May.
[b]significantly different from SAP in October and May.

The figures in Table 14.5 are interesting in more than one way. They indicate a clear increase in action preparedness in October but not across the board. Whereas the preparedness to participate in demonstrations and strikes increased, that for work stoppages declined, and while the former two go down again to the level of the general action preparedness the latter stays as low as it was in October. Obviously, the fact that the government is the adversary explains the increased preparedness to take part in demonstrations. Neither work stoppages nor strikes are very useful for putting pressure on the government. Strikes at least have the advantage that they get more publicity and have more of an impact, which may explain their distinctiveness from work stoppages.

Turning back to our question of the generation of action frames, we can conclude from regression analyses with specific action preparedness as the dependent variable that the cognitive frame of the individual (that is, knowledge of the DA plan and the combination of feelings of injustice and adversity) and individual dispositions can account reasonably well for the variation in specific action preparedness (Table 14.6).

As one may expect, general action preparedness is a significant predictor of preparedness to take part in actions regarding DA as is true for the belief that in case of conflict action should not be avoided. However, knowledge about the DA plans and support of the union's standpoint contribute independently to the explained variance in action preparedness. This is the more important because support for the union's standpoint is correlated to the belief that the DA plans are an infringement on workers' rights and that employers and government rather than workers are to be blamed. These findings tell us that the more union members define collective action as a legitimate response in case of conflict and the more they are prepared to take part

Table 14.6. *Regression of cognitive frame and individual dispositions on specific action preparedness in October (standardized regression coefficients)*

Media usage	.14*
Dispositions	
In case of conflict action should not be avoided	.23**
General action preparedness	.39**
Cognitive frame	
knowledge	.23**
Union's standpoint	.23**
R^2	.55
n	213

*$p < .01$.
**$p < .001$.

in such action, the more they are prepared to take action with regard to the DA controversy, particularly when they know about that controversy and support the union's stand. Note, that media use has a direct impact on specific action preparedness. This is not how we mapped it in our model, which only accounted for an indirect impact of media use via the generation of an injustice and/or adversarial frame. This relationship holds when control variables such as level of education, political party preference, and commitment to the union are in the equation. Hence, the impact of media use is specific for the DA controversy rather than an aspect of general interest in socioeconomic or political issues. A possible explanation for this finding could be that increased action preparedness feeds back into increased media use.

Interestingly, in May 1992 when there is no mobilization taking place action preparedness is not only lower than in October, as we saw in Table 14.5, but no longer related to the DA controversy. In May action preparedness is determined by the two dispositions – the belief that action should not be avoided and general action preparedness, plus political party preference and being a union-militant or not (together these variables explain 38 percent of the variance in action preparedness). In short, in May we are indeed back to base-line action preparedness including the erasure of any connection of such preparedness with DA. As far as the union members are concerned the issue is no longer embedded in a collective action frame. This is underscored by the finding that only in the opinion of one-third of the respondents are DA-related issues the most important issues in the 1992 annual contract negotiations. The remaining two-thirds mention other issues (55 percent) or do not know what issues were at stake.

Table 14.7. *Logistic regression of individual dispositions, cognitive frame, and specific action preparedness on action participation*

	Model 1		Model 2	
Media usage	−.41	(.44)	−.81	(.48)
Dispositions				
in case of conflict action should not be avoided	.21	(.52)	−.10	(.57)
general action preparedness	.99	(.59)	.47	(.64)
Cognitive frame				
Knowledge	.40*	(.19)	.25	(.22)
Union's standpoint	.69	(.40)	.50	(.41)
Specific action preparedness			1.44**	(.56)
Constant	8.78	(2.44)	−9.05	(2.66)
2 log likelihood	95.88		96.91	
Improvement	21.80***		7.94**	

$*p < .05; **p < .01; ***p < .001; n = 141.$

The final step in our model brings us to actual participation. Altogether 14 percent of our respondents participated in some form of collective action – two-thirds in a national one-hour demonstrative break to listen to the queen's speech at the opening of the parliamentary year, which included this year the DA plans of the government,[3] one-third in the national demonstration in The Hague, and one-fifth in a strike or other work stoppage. Theoretically, action participation is a function of action preparedness. All other factors have their impact indirectly via their influence on action preparedness. Our data support this reasoning. Table 14.7 presents results from a logistic regression analysis of those variables that predicted action preparedness (see Table 14.6) on action participation. Indeed, the second model not only implies a significant improvement, but entering specific action preparedness renders all others variables insignificant.

CONCLUSION:
CONSTRUCTING A COLLECTIVE ACTION FRAME ON DA

The debate on DA is a debate on one of the four dimensions of cultural themes Gamson (1992a) distinguished in *Talking Politics:* "self-reliance" versus "mutuality." These themes are like icons – sets of latent opinions and beliefs, which can be brought alive. "DA as a problem" and "DA as an entitlement" are both latently present in Dutch society and in the minds of individual members of that society. Essentially, they are two sides of the same coin: On the one hand, DA *is* an entitlement; on the other hand, DA *is* a problem.

When, in 1990, the social actors arrived at an agreement in the autumn consultations, neither theme was very much alive. When asked, one-third of the population believed DA was abused frequently, but it wasn't a major concern. The issue drew some media attention related to the autumn consultations, but union members were not alarmed. Indeed, actors – unions, government, and employers' organizations – did very little to mobilize their constituencies. This changed dramatically in 1991 when the government publicized its proposals. Themes and counterthemes that had been latent so far moved center stage. Social actors took positions in the debate and that, of course, added enormously to the salience of the issue.

Because media discourse intensified, knowledge among the population increased, but not only did familiarity grow, engagement with the issue increased as well. Resonance with "DA as an entitlement" made for strong feelings even in the absence of detailed knowledge. Such feelings are based on the theme that is activated, rather than on factual information on the issue. This is reinforced by the way the media work: information about actors who disagree, but much less information on *what* they disagree about. Consequently, the story the average union member got from media discourse is: *My* union opposes the government and employers on the DA issue. Under these circumstances, we may expect individuals to take the side of the actor they identify with, without having detailed knowledge about the controversy and the stand of different actors. Unions naturally will appeal in their campaigns to "DA as an entitlement." Consequently, the more union members define DA as an entitlement rather than a problem, the more likely that they develop an injustice frame.

Unions have a repertoire for conflict situations. While strikes were the traditional means of action, action repertoires expanded over the last decades (Van der Veen 1992). Union members may be more or less prepared to use collective action in case of conflicts. Such general preparedness is determined by past experience and political consciousness. Union members who in general are prepared to use collective action in case of conflicts, are more likely prepared to use collective action in a specific conflict situation as, for instance, the DA controversy. This is not to say that the DA controversy did not matter as far as action preparedness was concerned. In October when the unions mobilized their constituencies, action preparedness *did* increase and this increase *was* related to beliefs about the DA controversy.

To conclude, let us return to our original questions: (1) How do collective action frames regarding complex socioeconomic issues such as DA develop? (2) What is the role of media discourse in this regard and to what extent are actors such as unions capable of influencing media discourse?

To begin with, let us conclude that our union members did develop collective action frames. Whereas in the autumn of 1990 virtually no "hot" feeling could be tapped, a year later people not only had a general idea of what the DA controversy was about, but more important, they had a clear view on where they stand: by their union! When this combined with an already existing preparedness to follow their union if it decided to stage collective action, a collective action frame was generated.

For several reasons news discourse played a limited role in this regard. In the first place, news discourse provided a limited narrative. It informed the readers about who are the actors, rather than what are the issues; about who opposes who, rather than what is it that they disagree about. In terms of the generation of a collective action frame this is not necessarily a disadvantage. As long as it is made clear – as in the case of the DA controversy – that there is a conflict, it may be enough of a signal for dedicated union members to support their union. In the second place, in October 1991, in the heat of the debate it seemingly was not so much the news media as the union journals that made the difference. Apparently, the union journals compensated for the lack of substantial information in the newspapers. For the committed union member this meant becoming converted to the union's standpoint; that is, the government is tearing down our DA system, is planning an infringement on our rights.

In a way, the limited role of the news media in the generation of collective action frames may comfort the unions, because their efforts to influence news discourse turned out to be a moderate success. Even carefully prepared press conferences do not guarantee that the union's viewpoints make it into news discourse.

This is not to say that news discourse was irrelevant. Obviously, news discourse provided information on the key elements of the government's plan, which were known indeed by almost everybody. But more important, it clearly placed the unions in opposition to the government and thus helped to generate an adversarial frame, just as Gamson (1992a) suggested in his discussion of the role of the mass media. The union journals – we may assume – added to the framing of injustice and adversity. For as it turned out, reading the union journal increased knowledge of the government's plan, and this in combination with a higher commitment to the union made the generation of an injustice and adversarial frame more likely.

15

The framing function of movement tactics: Strategic dramaturgy in the American civil rights movement

DOUG McADAM

In his essay introducing Part III, Mayer Zald seeks to refine our understanding of the concept of "framing processes" by identifying five topics that have often been confounded or otherwise blurred in previous discussions of the concept. These five topics are (1) the *cultural tool kits* available to activists for framing purposes, (2) the *strategic framing efforts* of movement groups, (3) the *frame contests* that arise between the movement and other collective actors, (4) the role of the *media* in shaping these frame contests, and (5) the *cultural impact* of the movement in modifying the available "tool kit."

In this chapter I hope to advance our understanding of topics 2–4 in this list. Specifically, I aim to do four things: (1) review the existing work on "strategic framing efforts," (2) critique what I see as the "ideational bias" in our understanding of framing processes, (3) discuss the framing function of movement tactics, and (4) conclude by using the concrete case of the American civil rights movement to illustrate the way in which tactics were consciously used to "frame" action and thereby attract media attention and shape public opinion in ways that led to a decisive victory in the movement's "frame contest" with federal officials and Southern segregationists.

FRAMING AND FRAME ALIGNMENT PROCESSES

Among the most provocative and potentially useful of the works on the cultural dimensions of social movements have been the writings of David Snow and various of his colleagues (Snow et al., 1986; Snow and Benford, 1988, 1992) on the role of "framing" or "frame alignment processes" in the emergence and development of collective action. Movements, note Snow and Benford (1988: 198), are "actively engaged in the production of meaning for participants, antagonists, and observers. . . . They *frame,* or assign meaning to

A slightly different version of this chapter appeared in *Kölner Zeitschrift für Soziologie und Sozialpsychologie* 46, 1994. I am grateful to Friedhelm Neidhardt, Dieter Rucht, and Mayer Zald for their extremely helpful comments on various drafts of the chapter.

and interpret, relevant events and conditions in ways that are intended to mobilize potential adherents and constituents, to garner bystander support, and to demobilize antagonists." By framing, then, Snow and Benford have in mind the conscious, strategic efforts of movement groups to fashion meaningful accounts of themselves and the issues at hand in order to motivate and legitimate their efforts.

The concept of framing is an important one and a necessary corrective to those broader structural theories, which often depict social movements as the inevitable by-products of expanding political opportunities (political process), emerging system-level contradictions or dislocations (some versions of new social movement theory) or newly available resources (resource mobilization). The very notion of framing reminds us that mobilization and ongoing collective action are accomplishments, even in the context of favorable environmental conditions. The point is, all that any of the facilitating circumstances noted can do is create a certain structural potential for collective action. Whether or not that potential is realized depends on the actions of insurgents. And those actions are, in turn, shaped by and reflect the understandings of the actors involved. "Mediating between opportunity and action are people and the . . . meanings they attach to their situations" (McAdam, 1982: 48).

The framing concept has also focused analytic attention on what ironically has been a neglected topic in the study of social movements, that is, the everyday activities of movement participants. Reflecting the influence of the aforementioned broad structural theories, most recent empirical work has tended to focus on the role of system-level factors in either facilitating or constraining movement activity. Consequently, we know comparatively little about the lived experience of activism and the everyday strategic concerns of movement groups. The concept of framing calls these topics to mind and invites us to theorize and ultimately study the ways in which insurgents seek – largely through various forms of "signifying work" (Snow and Benford, 1988: 198) – to manage the uncertain and typically volatile environments in which they find themselves.

Framing processes and movement-environment relations

Political movements face at least six strategic hurdles that typically must be surmounted if they are to become a force for social change. Movement groups must be able to:

1. Attract new recruits
2. Sustain the morale and commitment of current adherents
3. Generate media coverage, preferably, but not necessarily, of a favorable sort
4. Mobilize the support of various "bystander publics"

5. Constrain the social control options of its opponents
6. Ultimately shape public policy and state action

The first two goals in this list can be thought of as internal to the movement. That is, they center on the effort to maintain the movement's internal strength through the recruitment and retention of activists. Obviously, this is a critically important challenge confronting the movement. However, it is one that has been studied quite extensively by those seeking to understand the dynamics of "differential recruitment" (Gould, 1991, 1993; Marwell and Oliver, 1988; McAdam, 1986; McAdam and Paulsen, 1993; Rosenthal et al., 1985; Snow, Zurcher, and Ekland-Olson, 1980). In contrast, the last four of these goals have been the subject of very little empirical research by movement scholars. In what follows, then, I want to make them the principal focus of attention. Together they constitute the broader "environmental challenge" confronting the movement.

For all the importance attached to the question of movement emergence, it could well be argued that movements face a tougher set of challenges following initial mobilization. The emergence of collective action requires only that a relatively small number of activists seek to exploit what they see as the increased receptivity or vulnerability of whatever system they seek to change. Following initial mobilization, however, the movement and the specific social movement organizations (SMOs) that are its carriers face a very different, and arguably tougher, challenge. They now confront an established political environment composed of a number of critically important constituent publics with very different interests vis-à-vis the movement. Just how successfully the movement and its carrier SMOs negotiate the conflicting demands imposed by these established constituents will largely determine the ultimate fate of the struggle. And in seeking to manage the demands of this highly fluid and often hostile environment, the principal weapon available to the movement is its strategic use of framing processes. That is, in trying to attract and shape media coverage, win the support of bystander publics, constrain movement opponents, and influence state authorities, insurgents depend first and foremost on various forms of signifying work. In the body of this essay, I seek to show how the American civil rights movement was able, through the strategic framing efforts of Martin Luther King and his Southern Christian Leadership Conference (SCLC), to largely accomplish these four goals. But before turning to the empirical case, I want first to address what I see as the strong "ideational bias" in the prevailing conception of framing.

The ideational bias in the literature on framing

The prevailing conception of collective action frames and framing processes betrays an almost exclusive concern with ideas and their formal expression by movement actors. So empirical research on the topic tends to focus on the speeches, writings, statements, or other formal ideological pronouncements by movement actors. These conscious ideational expressions are, of course, an important component of the overall framing effort of a given social movement. But they are not the whole of that effort. Indeed, I am tempted to argue that especially during the initial stages of mobilization, the old adage is true: Actions *do* speak louder than words. That is, the actions taken by insurgents and the tactical choices they make represent a critically important contribution to the overall signifying work of the movement.

Encoded in a group's actions and tactics are a good many messages, but none more significant than the degree of threat embodied in the movement. As a good many theorists remind us, movements '∪‾ive much of their effectiveness as agents of social change from their ability ∪ ‾lisrupt public order (Lipsky, 1970; McAdam, 1982; Piven and Cloward, 1979; Tarrow, 1994). Given the critical importance of this capacity, we should likewise attach great significance to the specific types of movement framing efforts that signify this capacity. In my view, no component of a movement's overall framing work is more important in this regard than the tactical choices it makes and the actual activities in which it engages.

The practical significance of these observations stems from the conviction that the degree of perceived threat conveyed by a movement's actions and tactics is a powerful determinant of other groups responses to the movement. There are, of course, other influences as well. Perhaps the most important is the movement's stated goals. Taken together the tactics and goals of the movement largely shape the reactions of various publics to the conflict. Figure 15.1 seeks to capture this dynamic by noting the typical environmental response that a movement can expect, *within a democratic context,* given a particular mix of goals and tactics. The emphasis, in the above sentence, on "democratic context" cannot be too strongly underscored. Given the very different legitimating philosophy that underlies nondemocratic systems, the interaction between movements and other sets of actors is expected to conform to very different dynamics than those evident within ostensibly democratic systems.

To simplify the discussion, I have treated both variables – goals and tactics – as dichotomous. Goals are defined as favoring either "revolution" or "reform," depending on whether or not they require a major redistribution of wealth and/or power. As regards tactics, movement groups are differentiated on the basis of their primary reliance on either "noninstitutionalized" or "institutionalized" forms of action. When combined, these two variables largely determine the extent to which a given group is perceived as threatening by established political actors. In turn, this "perceived threat" can be expected to powerfully shape the broader environmental response to the group in question.

Tactics

	non-institutionalized	institutionalized
revolution	repression	indifference/ surveillance and harassment
reform	heightened public attention/ polarized conflict	indifference/ minimal opposition and/or support

Goals

Figure 15.1. Expected environmental responses to movements characterized by various combinations of goals and tactics.

Crossing the two dichotomous variables yields the two-by-two matrix shown in Figure 15.1. Each cell of the matrix lists the general environmental response that a group can expect given a particular mix of tactics and goals. I will touch briefly on each cell, beginning with the upper left-hand corner. As a broad category, the most threatening movement groups are those which espouse revolutionary goals and rely on noninstitutionalized tactics. Such groups signify threat through both their pronouncements and their actions. Nowhere is this more true than in regard to those groups willing and able to make use of violence in pursuit of their aims. Groups that do make use of violence should, however, be prepared for the undifferentiated opposition and extreme repression their actions invariably invite. Examples of such groups would include the Baader-Meinhof gang and the Irish Republican Army.

The upper right-hand cell would include those groups who pursue revolutionary ends primarily through institutionalized means. At first blush this might appear to be an empty cell, but, in point of fact, one can think of any number of groups whose rhetoric and substantive aims are far more radical than their tactics. The Communist Party in various West European countries affords a good case in point. Even in the United States, with its history of

Communist paranoia, the Party thrived for a period of time (during the 1930s and 1940s) as a fairly conventional organization devoted to a radical restructuring of the American political and economic system. During the late 1960s and early 1970s, the radical black power group, the Black Panthers, essayed a similar blend of rhetorical radicalism and institutionalized tactics. The ultimate fate of the latter two groups suggests the poverty of this particular blend of goals and tactics. As Gamson points out, this strategy makes little tactical sense given the social control costs that the open advocacy of revolutionary change is likely to entail. Groups that pursue this strategy "seem to pay the cost of violence without gaining the benefits of employing it. They are both threatening and weak, and their repression becomes a low-cost strategy for those whom they attempt to displace" (Gamson, 1990: 87).

I would modify Gamson's analysis only slightly. While certain groups in this category have, indeed, been repressed, many more have been greeted by a combination of indifference and low-level surveillance and harassment. In a democratic country, the espousal of revolutionary aims does not, in and of itself, legitimate violent repression on the part of authorities. It is the means by which these aims are pursued that dictates the social control response. Should the group remain within "proper channels" they are likely to remain powerless, thus affording the authorities the luxury of indifference combined on occasion with low-level efforts at surveillance and harassment. In those rare instances when tactically conventional revolutionary groups gain notoriety and a following, authorities are apt to either exaggerate the threat posed by the group – as in the "witch hunts" for Communists that took place in the United States during the early 1950s – or seek to lure the group into violent confrontations with the police as was done in the case of the Black Panthers (Marx, 1979, 1974). Either way, the intent is the same: to depict the group's *tactics* as illegitimate in order to justify overt repression. My emphasis in the preceding sentence serves to underscore the point I made above concerning the "ideational bias" evident in earlier discussions of framing. Interactive frame contests involving movement groups, the state, the media, and various bystander publics, are very likely to turn on the signifying function of action. This is especially true in nominally democratic states where freedom of speech – including the advocacy of revolutionary aims – is protected. What is *not* protected is the right of movement groups to use any *means* necessary to achieve their aims. This disparity between freedom of speech and the limits on action makes action and the battles over its interpretation the fulcrum on which many frame battles turn.

The least threatening and probably most common type of movement group would fall into the lower right-hand cell of Figure 15.1. These are SMOs who work through "proper channels" to achieve reform goals. These are the professional advocacy organizations described by McCarthy and Zald (1973) in their initial formulation of the resource-mobilization perspective.

While McCarthy and Zald may have erred in equating this specialized type of movement group with social movements in general, they were clearly prescient in describing formal movement organizations as "the trend of social movements in America." Recent work on the founding of movement groups in the United States over the past forty years confirms the increasing preponderance of the kind of professional advocacy organizations described by McCarthy and Zald (Berry, 1989; Minkoff, 1993).

Typically, such groups can expect a highly differentiated set of responses from other parties, based on the latter's perception of convergence or divergence between their interests and that of the SMO. By virtue of their narrow, reform focus, most professional SMOs stand to engender the opposition of only those few "polity members" who perceive their interests as directly threatened by the group. By the same token, such groups are likely to receive facilitative support only from those elites who see their interests as clearly aligned with those of the SMO. The vast majority of member groups can be expected to remain unaware or indifferent to the SMO. Thus having eschewed the leverage that often comes from disruptive action, the hopes of professional reform groups hinge on their ability to mobilize more allies than opponents. Should they succeed in this, they are likely to prove an effective agent of slow, piecemeal change. Failing to do so, they are apt to die a slow, unpublicized death.

When compared to the reform SMO, our final type of social movement group – located in the lower left-hand cell in Figure 15.1 – represents a considerably rarer, but arguably more effective, blend of goals and tactics. I am referring to those movement groups who pursue reform goals through non-institutionalized means. The genius of this blend derives from the cognitive ambiguities encoded in the approach. In their willingness and demonstrated ability to disrupt public order and, by extension, the realization of their opponents' interests, radical reform groups often come to be seen as powerful and threatening. Their adherence to moderate reform goals, however, bespeaks a respect for the broader system that invites support from various publics while simultaneously restraining the social control proclivities of opponents. This optimal mix of outcomes, however, is not easily achieved and must ultimately depend upon a highly developed and flexible capacity for framing. In effect, radical reform groups must master the art of simultaneously playing to a variety of publics, threatening opponents, and pressuring the state, all the while appearing nonthreatening and sympathetic to the media and other publics. It is a difficult balancing act, but when achieved it is a source of tremendous political leverage. It is the social movement equivalent of Teddy Roosevelt's "Walk softly but carry a big stick."

Martin Luther King's organization the Southern Christian Leadership Conference (SCLC) affords a perfect example of a movement group that was able, for a time, to achieve the aforementioned balancing act. The balance of this chapter is an analysis of the ways in which King and the SCLC were able, by their tactical choices and framing efforts, to surmount the four "environmental challenges" noted at the beginning of this essay, and thus to achieve a significant restructuring of race relations in the United States.

TACTICS, FRAMING, AND MOVEMENT-ENVIRONMENT INTERACTION IN THE AMERICAN CIVIL RIGHTS MOVEMENT

To fully appreciate the daunting challenge that confronted the civil rights movement, one has to understand the depths of black powerlessness on the eve of the struggle. In 1950, fully two-thirds of all blacks continued to live in the southern United States. Yet, through a combination of legal subterfuge and extralegal intimidation, blacks were effectively barred from political participation in the region. Less than 20 percent of all voting age blacks were even registered to vote in 1950 (Bullock, 1971: 227). In the states of the so-called "Deep South," the figure was several times lower. In Mississippi, for example, barely 2 percent were registered in 1950. Fear kept more from trying to register. Small wonder; as late as 1955 two blacks were killed in Mississippi for refusing to remove their names from the voting rolls (Bennett, 1966: 201).

Nor on the eve of the movement were there any signs of a crack in the "solid South" or any diminution in the will of the region's political and economic elite to maintain "the Southern way of life." On the contrary, the 1954 Supreme Court decision declaring educational segregation unconstitutional set in motion a regionwide "resistance movement" aimed at preserving white supremacy at all costs. At the heart of the movement were the local White Citizen Councils and state legislatures throughout the region. The Councils mobilized to preserve segregation locally, while the state legislatures passed statute after statute in defense of the racial status quo. Among the measures passed were bills in various states outlawing the National Association for the Advancement of Colored People (NAACP), the only civil rights organization that had been previously active in the region.

Thus, on the eve of the movement, Southern blacks remained barred from institutional politics and deprived of any real leverage within the region. If change were to come, it would have to be imposed from without. This, of course, meant intervention by the federal government. But with a moderate Republican, Dwight Eisenhower, in the White House, and Southern Democrats exercising disproportionate power in Congress, the movement faced a kind of strategic stalemate at the national level as well. To break the stalemate the movement would have to find a way of pressuring a reluctant federal government to intervene more forcefully in the South. This, in turn, meant attracting favorable media attention as a way of mobilizing popular support for the movement.

Attracting media coverage

If one were to conduct an ethnographic study of virtually any social movement organization – local or national – one would be very likely to uncover a pervasive concern with media coverage among one's subjects. The fact is, most movements spend considerable time and energy in seeking to attract and shape media coverage of their activities. Given the power of the media to influence public awareness and opinion on social issues, this concern is hardly surprising. Yet with the exception of Charlotte Ryan (1991) and Ralph Turner (1969) and his students (Altheide and Gilmore, 1972), movement scholars have granted the topic very little attention in the literature. And what little empirical work has been done has been as likely to depict the media as a detriment to the movement as an asset (cf. Gitlin, 1980). The question is, which of these views more accurately reflects the realities of social movement life? Is the media really as irrelevant in the life of most movements as the lack of scholarly attention would suggest? Or does the activist's view capture a critical dynamic too long neglected by movement scholars?

I subscribe to the latter view. Activists are neither deluded into thinking the media are important nor driven by their egos to court media attention. The simple fact is, most movements lack the conventional political resources possessed by their opponents and thus must seek to offset this power disparity by appeals to other parties. The media come to be seen – logically, in my view – as the key vehicle for such influence attempts. The civil rights movement represents a prime example of this dynamic in action. And no group in the movement mastered this dynamic and exploited its possibilities better than the SCLC and its leader, Martin Luther King, Jr.

The media's fascination with King was evident from the very beginning of the Montgomery bus boycott. Launched in December 1955, the boycott inaugurated the modern civil rights movement and catapulted King into public prominence. And from then until his death in April 1968, King never strayed far from the front page and the nightly news. What accounts for King's media staying power, and why were he and SCLC, alone among movement groups, so successful in attracting favorable media attention? In seeking to answer these questions, I will stress the role of three factors.

1. Disruptive actions as newsworthy. First, the SCLC and King mastered the art of staging *newsworthy* disruptions of public order. The first requirement of media coverage is that the event be judged newsworthy. Their experiences in Montgomery convinced King and his lieutenants of the close connection between public disruption and media coverage. It wasn't the underlying issues that drew the media to Montgomery, but the potential for violence and disruption inherent in the boycott. All of King's subsequent campaigns were efforts to stage the same kind of highly publicized disruptions of public order that had occurred in Montgomery. Sometimes King failed as in Albany, Georgia, in 1961–62, when Police Chief Laurie Pritchett responded to King's tactics with mass arrests, but without the violence and disruptions of public order so critical to sustained media attention. At other times in other places – most notably in Birmingham, Alabama, in 1963 and Selma, Alabama, in 1965 – local authorities took the bait and responded with the kind of savagery that all but guarantees media attention.

Still his mastery of the politics of disruption only explains how King and the SCLC were able to attract the media, but not the overwhelmingly sympathetic tone of that coverage. Given the openly provocative nature of the King-SCLC strategy, the generally favorable coverage accorded King's actions demands explanation. The key to the puzzle would seem to rest with King's consummate ability to frame his actions in highly resonant and sympathetic ways. The final two factors alluded to above focus on King's framing efforts, first in conventional ideational terms and secondly in terms of the signifying function of his tactics.

2. Ideational framing. As noted above, virtually all work on framing betrays an exclusive concern with ideas and their formal expression by movement actors. These conscious ideational pronouncements – speeches, writings, etc. – are, of course, an important component of a movement's overall framing effort. And in accounting for King's success in attracting sympathetic media coverage, much of the credit must go to the substantive content of his thought. Quite simply, no black leader had ever sounded like King before. In his unique blending of familiar Christian themes, conventional democratic theory, and the philosophy of nonviolence, King brought an unusually compelling, yet accessible, frame to the struggle. First and foremost, there was a deep "resonance" (Snow et al., 1986) to King's thought. Specifically, in employing Christian themes and conventional democratic theory, King succeeded in grounding the movement in two of the ideational bedrocks of American culture. Second, the theme of Christian forgiveness that runs throughout King's thought was deeply reassuring to a white America burdened (as it still is) by guilt and a near phobic fear of black anger and violence. King's emphasis on Christian charity and nonviolence promised a redemptive and peaceful healing to America's long-standing racial divide. Third, King's invocation of Gandhian philosophy added an exotic intellectual patina to his thought that many in the Northern media (and Northern intellectuals in general) found appealing. Finally, while singling out this or that theme in King's thought, it should be noted that the very variety of themes granted those in the media (and the general public) multiple points of ideological contact with the movement. So, secular liberals might be unmoved by King's reading of Christian theology, but resonate with his application of democratic theory. And so on. In short, the sheer variety of themes invoked by King combined with their substantive resonance to give his thought (and the movement he came for many to symbolize) an ideational appeal unmatched by many other movement figures.

3. The signifying function of SCLC actions. King and his SCLC lieutenants' genius as "master framers," however, extended beyond the ideational content of their formal pronouncements. In their planning and orchestration of major campaigns the SCLC braintrust displayed what can only be described as a genius for strategic dramaturgy. That is, in the staging of demonstrations, King and his lieutenants were also engaged in signifying work, mindful of the messages and potent symbols encoded in the actions they took and hoped to induce their opponents to take.

Arguably the best example of the SCLC's penchant for staging compelling and resonant dramas is their 1963 campaign in Birmingham, Alabama. Like virtually all major cities in the Deep South, Birmingham in 1963 remained a wholly segregated city, with blacks and whites confined to their own restaurants, schools, churches, and even public restrooms. In April of that year, the SCLC launched a citywide campaign of civil disobedience aimed at desegregating Birmingham's public facilities. But why, among all Southern cities, was Birmingham targeted? The answer bespeaks the SCLC's strategic and dramaturgic genius. As a major chronicler of the events in Birmingham notes, "King's Birmingham innovation was preeminently strategic. Its essence was . . . the selection of a target city which had as its Commissioner of Public Safety 'Bull' Connor, a notorious racist and hothead who could be depended on *not* to respond nonviolently" (Hubbard, 1968: 5; emphasis in original).

The view that King's choice of Birmingham was a conscious, strategic one is supported by the fact that Connor was a lame-duck official, having been defeated by a moderate in a runoff election in early April 1963. Had the SCLC waited to launch its campaign until after the moderate took office, there probably would have been considerably less violence *and* less press coverage as well. "The supposition has to be that [the] SCLC, in a shrewd . . . stratagem, knew a good enemy when they saw him . . . one who could be counted on in stupidity and natural viciousness to play into their hands, for full exploitation in the press as archfiend and villain" (Watters, 1971: 266). In the following remarkable passage taken from his 1963 book, *Why We Can't Wait,* King all but acknowledges the conscious intent of the Birmingham strategy. In describing the planning for the Birmingham campaign, King notes the "lessons" that had been learned by way of the aforementioned events (see p. 11) in Albany, Georgia:

There were weaknesses in Albany, and a share of the responsibility belongs to each of us who participated. However, none of us was so immodest as to feel himself master of the *new theory*. Each of us expected that setbacks would be a part of the ongoing effort. There is no *tactical theory* so neat that a revolutionary struggle for a share of power can be won merely by pressing a row of buttons. Human beings with all their faults and strengths constitute the mechanism of a social movement. *They must make mistakes and learn from them, make more mistakes and learn anew. They must taste defeat as well as success, and discover how to live with each. Time and action are the teachers. When we planned our strategy for Birmingham months later, we spent many hours assessing Albany and trying to learn from its errors.* (King, 1963: 34–35; emphasis added)

The implication of King's statement is that a fuller understanding of the dynamic under discussion here was born of events in Albany. Without a doubt, a part of this fuller understanding was a growing awareness of the importance of white violence as a stimulus to increased media attention, public support, and federal intervention. Needless to say, King and his lieutenants had learned their lessons well. After several days of uncharacteristic restraint, Connor trained fire hoses and unleashed attack dogs on peaceful demonstrators. The resulting scenes of demonstrators being slammed into storefronts by the force of the hoses and attacked by snarling police dogs were picked up and broadcast nationwide on the nightly news. Still pictures of the same events appeared in newspapers and magazines throughout the nation and the world. The former Soviet Union used the pictures as anti-American propaganda at home and abroad. Thus, the media's coverage of the events in Birmingham succeeded in generating enormous sympathy for the demonstrators and putting increased pressure on a reluctant federal government to intervene on behalf of the movement.

In short, by successfully courting violence while restraining violence in his followers, King and SCLC were able to frame the events in Birmingham as highly dramatic confrontations between a "good" movement and an "evil" system. Moreover, the movement's dominant religious ideology granted this interpretation all the more credibility and resonance. These were no longer demonstrators, but peaceful, Christian petitioners, being martyred by an evil, oppressive system. The stark, highly dramatic nature of this ritualized confrontation between good and evil proved irresistible to the media and, in turn, to the American public.

Mobilizing public support

While favorable media coverage was the immediate goal of King and his lieutenants, it was never conceived of as an end in itself. Instead SCLC courted the media for the role it might play in mobilizing greater public awareness of and support for the movement. That support, in turn, was seen as the key to breaking the strategic stalemate in which SCLC and the broader movement found itself. With no chance of defeating the white supremacists in a direct confrontation, the SCLC knew that its prospects for initiating change would turn on its ability to prod a reluctant federal government into more supportive action on behalf of civil rights. Ironically, the election of John F. Kennedy as president in 1960 only intensified the government's long-standing aversion to "meddling" in Southern race relations. The specific explanation for Kennedy's reluctance to intervene had to do with his narrow margin of victory in 1960 and the "strange bedfellows" who made up his electoral coalition. Not only had Kennedy garnered the so-called black vote, and the votes of Northern liberals and labor, but he was also beholden to the "solid South." In rejecting the Republican Party as the party of Abraham Lincoln, white Southerners had voted consistently Democratic since the late nineteenth century. Thus Kennedy, no less than his predecessors in the Democratic Party, counted racist Southerners *and* civil rights advocates among his constituents. The electoral challenge for Kennedy, then, was to preserve his fragile coalition by not unduly antagonizing either white Southerners or civil rights forces. More immediately, Kennedy knew that the success of his legislative agenda would depend, to a large extent, on the support of conservative southern congressmen whose long tenure granted them disproportionate power within both the House and Senate. For both electoral and legislative reasons, then, Kennedy came to office determined to assume a stance of qualified neutrality on civil rights matters.

In this context the SCLC saw its task as destroying the political calculus on which Kennedy's stance of neutrality rested. It had to make the political and especially electoral benefits of supporting civil rights appear to outweigh the costs of alienating Southern white voters and their elected officials. This meant mobilizing the support of the general public, thereby broadening the electoral basis of civil rights advocacy. The data presented in Figure 15.2 attest to the SCLC's success in this effort. Between 1962 and 1965, the salience of the civil rights issue reached such proportions that it consistently came to be identified in public opinion surveys as the "most important" problem confronting the country. In six of the eleven national polls included in Figure 15.2, it was designated as the country's most pressing problem by survey respondents. In three other polls it ranked second. Only twice did it rank as low as fourth.

Moreover the imprint of the SCLC's dramaturgic genius can be clearly seen in the figure. The two highest spikes in the figure correspond to the SCLC's highly publicized campaigns in Birmingham (April-May 1963) and Selma (March 1965). Quite simply, the SCLC's ability to lure supremacists into well-publicized outbursts of racist violence kept the issue squarely before the public and ensured the growing support necessary to pressure Kennedy and Congress into more decisive action.

Constraining the social control options of segregationists

To this point, I have said very little about the effect of SCLC tactics on Southern segregationists. But in a very real sense the success of the SCLC's politics

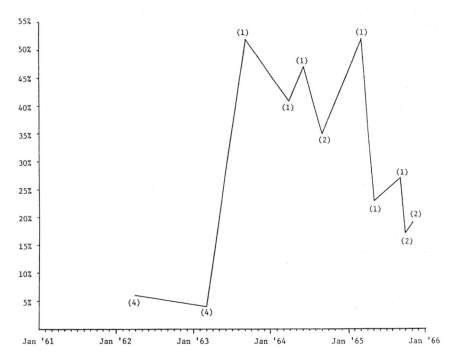

Figure 15.2. Proportion of general public identifying civil rights as the "most important problem confronting the country," 1961–65. *Source:* Gallup, 1972: 1764, 1812, 1842, 1881, 1894, 1905, 1934, 1944, 1966, 1973, 1979. "Civil rights" was the usual designation given the problem. However, in some polls it was identified as the "Racial Problem." The numbers in parentheses refer to the rank of civil rights among all the problems identified in that poll.

of disruption depended, not on the media or the general public, but the movement's opponents in the South. Had segregationists not responded to the SCLC's actions with the kind of violent disruptions of public order seen in Birmingham, the SCLC would have been denied the media coverage so critical to its overall strategy. Indeed, the SCLC's most celebrated failure turned on its inability to provoke precisely this response from segregationists. I am referring to the citywide campaign the SCLC launched in Albany, Georgia, in November 1961. In all respects the campaign was comparable to the organization's later efforts in Birmingham and Selma. But while the campaigns themselves were similar, the opponents' response to them was anything but. What was absent in Albany were the celebrated atrocities and breakdown in public order characteristic of Birmingham and Selma. This difference was due to Albany police chief Laurie Pritchett's clear understanding of the SCLC's strategy and his firm resolve to deny them the villain they so badly needed. While systematically denying demonstrators their rights,

Pritchett nonetheless did so through mass arrests rather than the kind of reactive violence that proved so productive of sympathetic media coverage in Birmingham and Selma. The data in Figure 15.2 support this conclusion. At the very height of the Albany campaign in March 1962, public concern with the issue of civil rights was at its virtual nadir.

There is, of course, a wonderful irony in all this that was not lost on the SCLC or its supremacist opponents. By framing action in the way they had, King and the SCLC had taken the supremacists' ultimate strategic weapon – violence and the threat of violence – and transformed it into a liability. In so doing they effectively broke the terror on which the system ultimately depended. In effect, any response on the part of the segregationists furthered the aims of the movement. Restraint, as in Albany, may have denied the movement its immediate need for media coverage, but it also lessened black vulnerability and fear of racist violence. On the other hand, celebrated instances of violence generated media coverage, public outrage, and increasing pressure for federal intervention on behalf of black civil rights. In his own way, President Kennedy acknowledged the dynamic under discussion here when he offered the following "tribute" to Bull Connor. In a remark to Martin Luther King, Kennedy said: "Our judgment of Bull Connor should not be too harsh. After all, in his own way, he has done a good deal for civil rights legislation this year" (in King, 1963: 144).

Shaping public policy and state action

Little remains to be said in this final section. The ultimate goal of King and the SCLC was to prod the government into action and to reshape federal civil rights policy in the process. That they were able to do so is clear from the various histories of the movement (Branch, 1988; Garrow, 1978, 1986; McAdam, 1982; Rosenberg, 1991). It is also clear that the extent and pace of their achievements were inextricably linked to their success in orchestrating the politics of disruption described here. In particular, the movement's two most significant legislative victories – the Civil Rights Act of 1964 and the Voting Rights Act of 1965 – owed, in large measure, to the Birmingham and Selma campaigns, respectively.

Birmingham, as we have seen, featured the brutality of Bull Connor and, in the waning days of the campaign, a Sunday morning bombing of a black church that claimed the lives of three little girls. As broadcast nightly into the living rooms of America, these atrocities mobilized public opinion like never before and, in turn, put enormous pressure on President Kennedy to act forcefully on behalf of civil rights. The ultimate result was administration sponsorship of the Civil Rights Act which, even in a much weaker form, had earlier been described as politically too risky by Kennedy himself. Finally, there was Selma. One last time King and the SCLC orchestrated the by now familiar politics of disruption to perfection. Initiated in January 1965, the campaign reached its peak in March with a series of widely publicized atrocities by segregationists.

On March 9, state troopers attacked and brutally beat some 525 persons who were attempting to begin a protest march to Montgomery [Alabama]. Later that same day, the Reverend James Reeb, a march participant, was beaten to death by a group of whites. Finally, on March 25, following the triumphal completion of the twice interrupted Selma-to-Montgomery march, a white volunteer, Mrs. Viola Liuzzo, was shot and killed while transporting marchers back to Selma from the state capital. (McAdam, 1982: 179)

In response to this consistent breakdown in public order and the public outrage it aroused throughout the nation, the federal government was forced once again to intervene in support of black interests. On March 17 President Johnson submitted to Congress a tough voting rights bill containing several provisions that movement leaders had earlier been told were politically too unpopular to be incorporated into legislative proposals. The bill passed by overwhelming margins in both the Senate and House and was signed into law on August 6 of the same year.

But Selma was to represent the high-water mark for King, the SCLC, and the movement as a whole. Never again was King able to successfully stage the politics of disruption at which he had become so skilled. The reason for this is simple: As the movement moved out of the American South and sought to confront the much more complicated forms of racism endemic to the North, King was deprived of the willing antagonists he had faced in the South. As King had learned, Southern segregationists could be counted on, when sufficiently provoked, to respond with the violence so critical to media attention and the increased public and governmental support sympathetic coverage inevitably produced. No such convenient foil was available to the movement outside the South. In fact, more often than not, after 1965, civil rights forces came to resemble a movement in search of an enemy. Kenneth Clark (1970: 288) captures the amorphous quality of the opposition the movement came increasingly to confront in the late 1960s:

What do you do in a situation in which you have the laws on your side, where whites smile and say to you that they are your friends, but where your white "friends" move to the suburbs leaving you confronted with segregation and inferior education in schools, ghetto housing, and a quiet and tacit discrimination in jobs? How can you demonstrate a philosophy of love in response to this? What is the appropriate form of protest?

In short, the very different character of Northern white resistance deprived King and the SCLC, in the late 1960s, of the ability to *frame* action in the dramatic and highly resonant ways they had been able to in the South. Without the dramatic instances of white racism, King and the SCLC lost the ability to attract the media, and, in turn, to mobilize the kind of public pressure productive of federal action. In no public opinion poll since 1965 has the American public ever accorded black civil rights the status of the number one problem confronting the country. Nor since then has Congress passed, with the exception of the Civil Rights Act of 1968, any significant civil rights legislation.

CONCLUSION

The veritable explosion in theory and research on social movements that has taken place in Europe and the United States over the past twenty years has profoundly altered our understanding of movement dynamics and resulted in an impressive body of knowledge regarding the phenomenon. Still, many gaping holes remain in our knowledge. In this chapter, I have sought to address two of those holes.

First, although the recent emphasis, in the literature, on the importance of "framing processes" serves as an important corrective to the somewhat mechanistic "opportunity"- or "resource"-based models proposed earlier, problems with the framing concept remain. For one, it has thus far resisted much in the way of systematic empirical application. With a few notable exceptions (e.g., Gerhards and Rucht, 1992), the literature on framing processes has been long on ringing, programmatic statements, and short on the kinds of detailed empirical applications that would allow for a real assessment of the worth of the concept. A second problem concerns what I see as the pronounced "ideational bias" inherent in our current usage of the concept. Framing has been equated with the formal ideological expressions of a movement. But, as I have tried to show, it is impossible to fully understand the "signifying work" of a movement group without close attention to its tactics and the actions in which it engages. In my view, the unique genius of Martin Luther King lay in his ability to frame action in such a way as to invoke a set of predictable responses from not one but four reference publics. The key lay in King's ability to lure segregationists into acts of extreme racist violence while maintaining his followers' commitment to nonviolence. When combined with the religious themes King invoked, the juxtaposition of peaceful black demonstrators and virulent white attackers created powerful and resonant images that triggered critically important reactions in three additional publics. The media were drawn to the drama inherent in the attacks. Through the media's sympathetic coverage, an increasingly outraged American public was moved to call for more action on behalf of the movement. Finally, as a result of the increasing public pressure, a previously reluctant federal government was prodded time and again into more decisive action. It was on the basis of this dynamic that the movement – with King as its driving wedge – was able to achieve the significant victories it did. But it was the compelling dramaturgy of King's *tactics,* rather than his formal pronouncements, that keyed the dynamic.

This recounting of the important parties – segregationists, media, general public, federal government – to the civil rights struggle underscores the second major point of the chapter. If we are ever to develop a full understanding of collective action and social conflict we must transcend the limits of the prevailing movement-centric view of social movements. Most movement scholarship focuses exclusively on a given movement or even a specific movement organization. Even those visionary scholars who have recently asserted the importance of the state to a full understanding of movement dynamics have tended to stop there (Amenta and Zylan, 1991; Duyvendak, 1992; Koopmans, 1992; Quadagno, 1992). But I would argue that virtually all instances of state–movement interaction are mediated by other publics. This was clearly the case in the American civil rights movement. Only by focusing equal attention on the actions of the movement, Southern segregationists, and the media, plus the consequent shifts in public opinion, could the analyst ever hope to make sense of federal action *and* inaction in regard to the movement. In general, as movement scholars, we need to broaden our analyses to include the full range of publics relevant to whatever movement we seek to understand.

Notes

Chapter 1: Conceptual origins, current problems, future directions

1 Though nowhere near as extensive as Layton's treatment of the subject, my own work on the American civil rights movement (Anderson-Sherman and McAdam, 1982; McAdam, 1982), focuses on two important sources of international pressure for change in America's racial politics. The first concerned the emerging cold war pressures which Layton so convincingly documents in her work. The second focused on those changes in international trade and economics that helped to undermine the critical national importance of the Southern cotton economy. These changes included the interruption of international trade during World War I, the establishment of viable cotton economies elsewhere in the world, and the transformation of the United States from a debtor to a creditor nation in the first two decades of the twentieth century (McAdam, 1982: 73–77). The net effect of these changes was to significantly reduce America's economic dependence on Southern cotton, and, by extension, the political leverage exercised by the Southern planter elite.

2 The one notable exception to this rule is Tarrow's treatment of the topic in *Power in Movement* (1994). Throughout his book, but especially in Chapter 6 and the Conclusion, Tarrow highlights the role of movements in remaking the political systems in which they first developed.

Chapter 2: States and opportunities

1 Major milestones are Skocpol's well-known book on revolutions (1979) and the theorization of her approach in Evans, Rueschemeyer, and Skocpol, 1985. On the United States, see especially Skowronek, 1982; Skocpol and Finegold, 1982; Bensel, 1991; and Vallely, 1993a, b. For a reflection and critique on the statist persuasion, see Almond, 1988, and the symposium that follows his article in the *American Political Science Review* (1988) under the title "The Return to the State."

2 Despite its striking similarity to the statist approach, Kitschelt argues that his approach is much broader "than that conveyed by 'state structure'" (p. 61, n. 11). He traces it to the concept of "dominant policy style" in comparative policy studies. Yet, like the statists, Kitschelt posits a uniform structuring impact of the state upon movements in different countries, as exemplified in Table One of his 1986 article and in his conclusions. For a useful critique and evaluation of Kitschelt's article, see Rucht, 1990.

3 Kitschelt's image of collective action around nuclear power in France as extrainsti-

tutional may be unconsciously influenced by the policy environment of nuclear energy. Nuclear power is, after all, a key arena of national policy for the French state, since it produces power for France's nuclear deterrent as well as for domestic energy needs. It is thus not surprising that the French state should "close" around it. See Lawrence Scheinman, 1965, on the links between French nuclear energy and nuclear strategy.

4 See Chapter 3 of my *Power in Movement: Social Movements, Collective Action and Politics,* for an elaboration of these points, respectively, for England, France, and the United States.

5 Readers of Charles Tilly's work will recognize that I have adopted here his definition of the national social movement. See Tilly, 1984: 305, for a logically and historically derived definition and a comparison to others' usages.

6 Tilly introduces the term "consolidated state" in his *European Revolutions, 1492– 1992* in place of the more conventional "national state," because of the implication many have drawn from the latter that it must contain a homogeneous citizenry. Tilly defines the consolidated state as "large, differentiated, ruling heterogeneous territories directly, claiming to impose a unitary fiscal, monetary, judicial, legislative, military and cultural system on its citizens" (1993b: chap. 2).

7 William Sewell (1990: 548) observes of the French Revolution that it "permanently transformed the way ordinary French men and women could conceptualize and act out their collective loyalties." Creating a new associational idiom around the idea of a state based on natural right and contract, for Sewell the Revolution forever changed the relations between civil society and the state.

8 Rucht (1989a: 79–80) estimates that the French environmental movement at its peak included about 15,000 groups with more than 2 million members and a similar degree of organizational heterogeneity to Germany's. On the heterogeneity of the Italian movement, see Diani and Lodi, 1988.

9 On political cycles, see Buerklin, 1987. For a treatment that focuses on cultural movements in particular, see Brand, 1990. On movement dynamics within cycles, see my *Power in Movement* (1994: chap. 9). On economic and political cycles, see Frank and Fuentes, 1992.

10 The study of a particular protest cycle reinforces this observation. Although many after-the-fact observers – no doubt remembering the outrages perpetrated by terrorist groups – have characterized the Italian cycle of the 1960s and early 1970s as "violent," a more detailed analysis shows that organized violence only appeared relatively late in the cycle. At its peak in the late 1960s, Italian movements were far more likely to engage in conventional or confrontational mass collective action than in violence (della Porta and Tarrow 1986).

11 Marx is worth citing in detail: "Bourgeois revolutions, like those of the eighteenth century, storm swiftly from success to success; their dramatic effects outdo each other; man and things seem set in sparkling brilliants" (1963: 19).

12 Tocqueville and many of his followers also exaggerated the subtraction of power from the local level to the benefit of the state, at least to judge from the well-documented case of Burgundy in Hilton Root's *Peasants and King in Burgundy. Agrarian Foundations of French Absolutism* (Berkeley and Los Angeles: University of California Press, 1987). The most thorough and balanced treatment of the changes in the aristocracy before the French Revolution and of its relations with the Third Estate is Simon Schama's *Citizens* (1989: chap. 3).

Chapter 3: Social movements and the state

1 In his pivotal study on political opportunities in American cities, Eisinger (1973) focused on access to the political system. Subsequent empirical studies considered

additional variables, such as electoral instability (Piven and Cloward 1977), the availability of allies, and the tolerance for protest among the elite (Jenkins and Perrow 1977), the influence of the political process (Tilly 1978; McAdam 1982). Tarrow (1983) integrated these empirical observations in the theoretical framework for his study of protest cycles in Italy. In Tarrow's framework, the components of the POS are the degree of access to political institutions, the degree of stability/instability of political alignments, the availability and strategic posture of potential allies (Tarrow 1983: 28), and – in a later work (Tarrow 1989a: 35) – the political conflicts among and within elites.

2 I refer to "behavior" as including both strategically oriented actions and unplanned events (della Porta and Rucht 1991).

3 I have collected so far information on six protest campaigns: three in Berlin and three in Rome. Those that took place in Berlin were the protest campaign of the student movement in the spring of 1967; the wave of protest surrounding the visit of President Ronald Reagan in spring 1982; and the protest sparked by a second visit by Reagan, in 1987. The protest events in Rome that I looked at were the first escalation during the student movement in 1968, the so-called "77 movement" in the spring of 1977, and Reagan's visit of 1982. For the German case basic information can be found in *Cilip* 1981; Sack and Steinert 1984; Busch et al. 1988; *Forschungsjournal Neue Soziale Bewegungen* 1988; and Katzenstein 1990; for the Italian case, in Canosa 1976 and della Porta 1990. For a comparison of the two countries, see della Porta and Rucht 1992; della Porta 1992a, 1994. A different version of this article is a chapter in my book on political violence, social movement, and the state (della Porta 1995).

4 The lack of reliable statistical data on the possible indicators of protest policing styles frustrated any attempt at controlling with quantitative measures the qualitative information coming from the case studies.

5 My information on this period is taken from Canosa 1976: chaps. 1–3.

6 As many as sixty-two demonstrators died between 1948 and 1950, thirty-three between 1951 and 1962 (Canosa 1976: chaps. 2 and 3, esp. 127–8; 134–5, 210–13, 217–24).

7 The fascist Testo Unico di Pubblica Sicurezza had in fact given the police the right to "admonish" and send individuals to "confinement" (that is restriction in a little village away from home), to enforce "compulsory repatriation" to an individual's own town of residence, to deny individuals a passport and the freedom to emigrate, to prohibit public meetings (for reasons of security), and to censor printed materials. According to article 2, the prefect – the direct deputy of the interior minister at the local level – had the authority to take all measures necessary to preserve law and order, whenever there was the threat of a generically defined "danger." A partial reform was implemented only at the end of 1956, after several interventions of the Constitutional Court – that is, the Italian Supreme Court. The new law abolished the "admonishment" and the *fermo di polizia,* but the police retained the power to assign the individuals they considered "dangerous" to territorial internment and "special surveillance" (Law 1423/56).

8 In 1950 the defense minister issued similar regulations for the use of the armed forces to maintain public order (*Vie Nuove* 1969).

9 In this period had started, indeed, the legislative process that resulted, in the early 1970s, in laws that fixed a maximum period for incarceration before judgment (Law 406/70) and increased the number of conditions under which a judge could parole a defendant even for those crimes for which arrest was compulsory (Law 773/72) (see Grevi 1984).

10 In 1964, the head of military intelligence (Sifar), Generale De Lorenzo, was accused of planning a coup d'état and had to resign. Under De Lorenzo, the security

services collected files on the public and private life of politicians from all the main parties (De Lutiis 1984). Subversive right-wing forces continued to infiltrate the intelligence services later on.

11 In particular, new regulations against criminality increased the maximum preventive detention (Law 99/74), and gave the police the right to interrogate a defendant (Law 220/74), to search without a formal warrant of suspicion, and to hold a suspect for forty-eight hours (Law 152/75).

12 Between 1969 and 1974, bombs set by right-wing terrorists killed 17 people on December 12 1969, in Milan; 6 in July 1970 on a train in Calabria; 8 during a union meeting in Brescia, in 1974; and 12 on the train Italicus, near Bologna, in 1974. On these occasions, the repression of right-wing terrorism was so ineffective that the principals and the executors of those crimes are still unknown. On right-wing radicalism in these years, see Ferraresi 1984: 57–72.

13 The participation of several leaders of the secret services in the covert "Lodge Propaganda 2" (a Masonic lodge, with subversive aims) and a series of obscure episodes during the Red Brigades' kidnapping of the president of the DC, Aldo Moro (listed in Flamigni 1988), indicate, however, that the "strategy of tension" had not lost all supporters.

14 For instance, the quest for a reform that would make the police more professional and help to defeat terrorism remained unfulfilled.

15 Police practices were not the only factor contributing to the "leaden" climate of these years: the laws changed, and in an illiberal direction (Corso 1979; Grevi 1984). The "emergency laws" authorized the arrest of anyone who violated the prohibition against disguising oneself (Law 533/77); abolished the maximum limit for preventive detention when a trial was suspended because it was impossible to form a jury or to exercise defense rights (Law 296/77); modified the rules for the formation of popular juries (Law 74/78); introduced a special prison system (Laws 1/77 and 450/77); increased sentences for terrorist crimes; and limited individual guarantees for citizens and defendants (Laws 191/78 and 15/80). In particular, the antiterrorist Law 15/80 introduced the "preventive arrest," which allowed the police to detain a person in custody when there was a suspicion that this person would commit a crime.

16 The climate of the "emergency" influenced even the judicial process itself. Several trials carried out in those years were *processi indiziari* – that is, trials based on circumstantial evidence in which the judges considered even the testimony of only one person or one's affiliation with an organization with a radical ideology as sufficient evidence of guilt. Moreover, the courts often accepted the principle of collective responsibility. This praxis, which some justified by claiming that it was difficult to find proofs, was also extended to the more radical movement organizations. After the emergency period, legal scholars expressed their concern for the often disproportionate increase in the length of sentences, a result of the vague definitions given to some crimes (for instance, subversive association; armed band; or armed insurrection against the power of the state) (see, for example, De Ruggiero 1982; Onorato 1982).

17 The "conciliatory" temper of this period is evident in the antiterrorist legislation of these years. After the "emergency" diminished, new laws were passed (particularly in 1982 and in 1986) that were designed to take advantage of the internal crisis in the terrorist organizations. Most notably, they introduced "compensations" for the members of underground organizations who collaborated with the investigations or had simply declared they had given up the "armed struggle." In addition, the implementation of prison reform created the preconditions for a reintegration of former terrorists into society.

18 In 1981, the parliament agreed on the long-discussed reform for the demilitarization and professionalization of the police forces that met some of the demands for a more professional and less militarized police expressed by a movement for democratization that had become stronger and stronger within the police itself.

19 One peace activist, for example, complained that the judge had acquitted him for "not having committed the crime," notwithstanding his "full confession" (L'Abate 1990).

20 On protest policing in this period I referred to Busch et al. 1988: 318–28.

21 Between 1951 and 1961, about 500,000 German citizens were involved in 200,000 proceedings for politically motivated crimes (*Bikini* 1981: 66).

22 For a short history of *Demonstrationsrecht* in Germany after World War II, see Blanke and Sterzel 1983.

23 By 1976, half a million persons had been investigated, and 430 excluded from the civil service because of anticonstitutional activities or participation in an anticonstitutional organization.

24 For a nationally called march in Kalkar, the police searched 122,000 persons and 68,000 cars in Northrhein-Westfalen; 147,000 persons, 75,000 cars, and a train in the rest of the Federal Republic (*Cilip* 1978: 24 ff.).

25 In Germany as in Italy, antiterrorist laws limited the opportunities for protest. In 1974 an amendment to the criminal proceedings law reduced the rights of the defendant; and in 1976 new legislation introduced the crimes of "founding a terrorist organization" (par. 129a), calling for "anticonstitutional" violence (par. 88a), and distributing of publications that encourage illegal actions (par. 130). In 1977 a law was passed prohibiting any contacts with terrorists in prison; in 1978, new laws gave the police greater power in conducting searches.

26 On protest policing and escalation in Wackersdorf, see Kretschmer 1988; on the early escalation in the campaign against the expansion of the Frankfurt airport, see Schubart 1983; and on the campaign against the conference of the IWF, see Gerhards 1993. As mentioned, in my case studies I collected information on the two visits of Ronald Reagan to Berlin, one in 1982 and one in 1987.

27 See, for instance, state reactions to the boycott of the national census at the beginning of the eighties (Appel and Hummel 1988).

28 Scharpf (1984: 57) defined this concept as "an overall understanding, among those who exercise effective power, of a set of precise premises integrating world-views, goals and means."

29 More specifically, Kriesi distinguished between integrative (facilitative, cooperative, assimilative) and exclusive (repressive, confrontational, polarizing) national strategies.

30 An incomplete list of the relevant variables would include (1) *legislation on civil rights* – in particular on citizens' rights (rights of movement, rights of expression); defendants' rights (preventive imprisonment, presence of one's attorney at interrogations, right of the police to interrogate a defendant); prisoners' rights (privacy, contacts with the external world); and (2) the *organization of the repressive apparatuses,* including primarily the police, the secret service, and the judiciary. Relevant questions about the police refer to the degree to which they are militarized (How dependent are they on the military ministry? Do they live in barracks? Are they part of the army? How great is the emphasis on "discipline"? What type of armaments do they use? Are the police unionized?); to their accountability (Are there special bodies for the control of protest? Special courts for police crimes? Do the police have the right to "shoot to kill"?); and to centralization (How much power do decentralized units have? How powerful is the central government?). The specialization of the secret services in internal versus external security and their rela-

tive dependence on the military are also relevant factors in any attempt to define the context for protest and protest policing. Characteristics relevant to the judiciary concern who has the right to initiate a trial for political crimes; the existence of special courts for political crimes; the existence of an inquisitorial legal process versus an adversarial legal process, and the body of laws on political crimes.

31 Monjardet (1990, 214–15) suggested, for instance, that – remembering the negative political consequences of the police's killing demonstrators in February 1934 – the French police are still trained to consider the demonstrator not as an enemy but as a temporary adversary, and to avoid injuring or killing people.

32 For instance, according to Zwerman (1987) the "harder" counterterrorist policies of the Reagan administration resulted from the pressure of right-wing groups (such as the Moral Majority) on the national government.

33 On escalation and unforeseen consequences of police intervention, see Monnet 1990.

34 The complex relations between repression and social movement activities can probably be explained if we take into account the fact that protest policing influences both costs and (expected) benefits of collective action. First, state repression represents one of the most relevant (potential) costs of taking part in collective behavior (Tilly 1978: 100). Even if other costs and benefits are taken into account – and even if collective behavior is not always "rational" – the weight of the cost defined by state repression would be difficult to overstate. But the form of repression influences the same grievances that spark protest in the first place, for example, by creating "injustice frames" (Gamson, Fireman, and Rytina 1982). The more "repressive" the state, therefore, the higher the potential rewards of collective action, since the "punishment" of the unfair state would become part of the expected rewards, and the need to "do something" would appear all the more urgent to some activists.

35 About 1,300 police were present at the first demonstration in Brokdorf, 6,500 at the second demonstration in Brokdorf, 5,000 at the demonstration in Grohnde, and 8,000 at the demonstration in Kalkar.

Chapter 4: Opportunities and framing in the Eastern European revolts of 1989

1 In the classic theories of revolution, such as Brinton's (1957), loss of legitimacy results from a desertion of the intellectuals who frame the political discourse in the ancien régime away from reform of taxation and other specific issues to the form of the state itself. Not all students of revolution agree. For Skocpol (1979: 31–32) "[if the state is effective] legitimacy – in the sense of moral approval or in the probably more usual sense of sheer acceptance of the status quo – will probably be accorded to the state's form and rulers by most groups in the society. . . . what matters most is always the support and acquiescence not of the popular majority of society, but of the politically powerful and mobilized groups." Conformity and revolt then boil down to whether the powerful groups remain united and whether they are able to secure the loyalty of the state's coercive apparatus. Skocpol denies that loss of legitimacy can in and of itself sap the incumbents' resolve and the police and army's willingness to execute regime repression.

2 For moral force to be effective, there has to be an asymmetry between challenger and target: on the one side power, the army, the awesome machinery of the state; on the other, dignified and courageous peaceful protesters committed to ideals and risking life and limb for their convictions. What enhanced the effectiveness of the challengers' moral force in countries like East Germany and Czechoslovakia was the lack of an equivalent moral resource of the regime. If both sides stand for principle, as in prolife confronting prochoice, moral force cancels.

3 I described a similar mobilization dynamic of how civil rights protests became the civil rights movement during the sit-ins of 1960–61 (Oberschall, 1989, 1993).

4 Of the 100 Senate seats, Solidarity and its allies took 99, and of the 161 contested Sejm seats, they took 160. Even more humiliating to the Communists was that only 5 of the 299 reserved unopposed seats received the necessary 50 percent of voter turnout necessary for filling them in the first round. Communists who failed in the first round on an unopposed national list included top Party and national figures like Prime Minister Rakowski, Interior Minister Kiszczak (who had signed the roundtable accords for the government), the defense minister, and others. In the runoff for the vacant seats – almost all of which were for the uncontested Communist slate – the voters showed their contempt by staying away from the polls: Turnout was only 25 percent compared to 63 percent in the first round.

5 Nagy's reburial had a tremendous symbolic meaning, for the Kadar regime's legitimacy was at stake. Kadar had been installed by the Soviets as the successor of the Nagy government. If the Party admitted that the execution of Nagy had been a "mistake" and that the 1956 revolution was a justified national revolt against the excesses of Stalinism, it would openly admit its questionable legitimacy.

6 The special relation of the Party to the Soviet Union was now irrelevant and the country's chances of association and membership in the European Economic Community and of getting Western economic aid and investments would be a lot better under the auspices of democratic political parties and leaders. The Soviet connection had turned from an asset to a liability in the international arena of political opportunity.

7 Hirschman's theory (1970) assumes that "exit" and "voice" are substitutes in response to unsatisfactory performance in an economic organization or the state, but in 1989 in East Germany they were complementary. Exit made protest possible, credible, and effective.

8 The Evangelical Church provided a protective umbrella for some nonconformist youth concerned with peace, social justice and environment. In early 1989, Leipzig had about twenty dissenting groups with a total of about three hundred youths, but fewer activists. Relations between the Church and the nonconformists were strained because the youth wanted bolder action than mere words. Still their regular meeting with sympathetic ministers at churches allowed a small community critical of the regime to form and for criticisms to be voiced that were off-limits and too risky elsewhere.

9 It isn't a complete record prior to September because the sources consulted (Wimmer, 1990; Sievers, 1990; Krenz, 1990; Mitter and Wolle, 1990; Opp, 1991) may not have recorded small, short-lived protests. Number of participants and arrests are estimates on which these sources differ somewhat. Arrests measure intensity of social control and cost of participation imperfectly. Some participants and bystanders were roughed up without being arrested and charged; others were released but their names recorded for later sanction. The Stasi video taped the Nikolai church events and could take reprisals later.

10 Some corroborative evidence is provided in Draper (1993).

Chapter 5: Opportunities and framing in the transition to democracy

1 Totalitarism kak istoricheski fenomen. M, 1989, p. 30.
2 A. Tyomkina and E. Zdravomyslova, "Chto Leningradtsi dumajut o neformalah." Smena, 1988.
3 *Uchredityelnoye sobranie* 6, 1989.
4 *Uchredityelnoye sobranie* 13, 1990.
5 *Svobodnoe slovo* 5, 1989.

6 *Uchredityelnoye sobranie.*
7 Resolution on tactics adopted at the 2nd congress of the DU.M., 1989.
8 *Svobodnoe slovo* 16, 1989.
9 *Svobodnoe slovo* 24, 1989.
10 *Svobodnoe slovo* 22, 26.09. 1989.
11 *Svobodnoe slovo* 6, 1989.
12 *Ogonek,* a liberal weekly sociopolitical and literary-artistic magazine which under the editorship of V. Korotich in 1988–90 was a leading force in exposing the regime and revising its history.
13 *Uchredityelnoye sobranie* 2, 12 July 1989.
14 *Kurier,* Tartu, 5, 1989.
15 *Kurier,* Tartu, 2, 1989.
16 This reformist position explains why membership in the CPSU could be combined with membership in the LPF. Even more, all the leaders of this SMO were communists.
17 *Nabat* 4, 1990.
18 *Pamyat* (Memory), a conservative national-patriotic organization which organized anti-Semitic rallies in Leningrad in August 1988.
19 The Bell has been a symbol of *Pamyat* as well as the title of the democratic journal published by A. Herzen, a Russian writer-Westernizer, who lived in London in the 1840s.
20 *Nabat* 1, 1989.
21 *Nabat* 7, 1989.
22 *Nabat* 2, 1989.
23 *Kurier,* Tartu 5, 1989, 1–15, September.

Chapter 6: Constraints and opportunities in adopting, adapting, and inventing

1 But see the vigorous dissent from that consensus by Piven and Cloward (1992).
2 Traditional liberal conceptions of the civil society (or public sphere) typically draw a strong boundary between societal institutions and the state, but also assume, as Carol Pateman (1989) has lucidly argued, that the private or household sphere is outside of the public sphere. Modern women's movements have by example and by argument succeeded in undermining the boundary between the public and the private. We follow by ignoring the boundary in our conception of mobilizing structures.
3 I mean to include all of the institutions commonly included within the boundaries of the concept "civil society" as well as institutional structures of the state and the economy that serve as relational contexts for insurgent mobilization.
4 My discussion will ignore action repertoires, for the most part, focusing primarily upon more enduring mobilizing structural forms. This emphasis is explained by a combination of space constraints and the empirical focus of the four chapters in Part II. I wish to emphasize, however, that a complete enumeration of mobilizing structural configurations must also include associated action repertoires. They can be mapped along similar dimensions of movement centeredness (e.g., public demonstration versus an illegal religious service) and formal complexity (McPhail, 1992), as well as their modular transportability across cultural settings.
5 Neil Smelser, after struggling to make sense of collective behavior almost three decades ago, says, "Although the demarcation of collective behavior is not an end in itself, and is not so intriguing as the inquiry into causes and consequences of collective behavior, it is of prime importance. Before we can pose questions of explanation, we must be aware of the character of the phenomena we wish to

explain" (Smelser, 1963: 5). Almost thirty years later both John Lofland and Clark McPhail, our most valiant demographers of collective behavior and social movement forms, echo Smelser's views. Lofland says, "I should make clear that I have no quarrel with causes and consequences foci in and of themselves. These are both proper aspects of the study of social movements. I demur, however, when analysts become so concerned with either of these questions that they neglect to develop an understanding of what they want to explain or what it is that they think has consequences. Such neglect, I think, cripples most causal and consequential accounts because their authors fail to understand their main variable, that of the characteristics of the movement itself" (1993). And, McPhail says, "Students of the crowd ... have devoted far more time to criticizing, debating, and offering alternative explanations than they have to specifying and describing the phenomena to be explained. ... In my judgement this places the cart before the horse. It is misguided to debate the pros and cons of competing explanations before the phenomena to be explained have first been examined, specified and described" (1992: xxiii).

6 This pattern was pointed out to me by Mary Anna Culleton Colwell.
7 Some movements, on the other hand, spawn collective efforts to radically change everyday social patterns. In them activists seek to lead exemplary lives based on new social principles. Earlier communal and utopian movements along with segments of the more recent movements that have come to be called identity movements display this feature, and they tend, as a result, to adopt rather distinctive mobilizing structural forms. Groups like these, however, are quite rare in contrast with the mass of groups in most movements (e.g., Lofland, 1993, for the recent U.S. peace movement). And while they draw special attention for their distinctiveness and probably require special analysis, such groups are not our central focus here.

Chapter 7: The organizational structure of new social movements in a political context

1 Morris (1984: 139) has called these organizations "movement halfway houses" – "an established group or organization that is only partially integrated into the larger society because its participants are actively involved in efforts to bring about a desired change in society."
2 Bader (1992: 219) includes "movement associations" among the SMOs.
3 Roth (1991) gives many examples of organizations which contribute to the social organization of the alternative scene, which constitutes the political potential for new social movements in Germany.
4 The distinction between self-help groups, clubs, and voluntary associations, in turn, refers to the distinction between self-help and altruism. If the constituents and the beneficiaries of the organizations are identical, we may speak of self-help groups or clubs; if this is not the case, we deal with voluntary associations engaged in altruism.
5 Following McCarthy and Zald (1977: 1218), this conceptualization of SMOs restricts the notion to complex, formal organizations, but it is more specific than theirs in that it does not include in the definition all organizations sharing the preferences of a social movement and attempting to implement those preferences.
6 Again, I follow McCarthy and Zald's basic distinctions, although I do not adopt their notion of the "social movement industry" (SMI). I prefer the notion of the SMO-infrastructure, which does not have the misleading connotations of their label, but retains the same abbreviation.

7 The following discussion has been inspired by the conceptualizations that Schmitter and Streeck (1981) have developed for the analysis of business interest associations.

8 McCarthy and Zald (1987) have pointed out that as a result of massive growth in funding, it has become possible for a larger number of professionals to earn a respectable income committing themselves full-time to activities related to social movements.

9 Gamson's (1975) well-known study of the origins of success of SMOs is probably the best example of an attempt to explain the organizational development of SMOs on the basis of internal factors. Goldstone's (1980) challenge has questioned this attempt by showing the relevance of external, political factors in this context.

10 This is an argument advanced by the institutional approach to organizations. (See Meyer and Rowan 1977; Zucker 1987.)

11 The literature on "voluntary associations" includes SMOs and interest groups undifferentiatedly under this label.

12 In my original formulation of this type, I did not take into account this possibility of selective concessions, which has been pointed out by Duyvendak (1992). Following his suggestion, I changed the label of the type from "full exclusion" to "selective exclusion."

13 Among the fifteen countries compared we find the other three of our four countries, in addition to the Anglo-Saxon countries (the United States, Canada, Australia, Ireland, Northern Ireland, and Great Britain) and Italy, Spain, Belgium, Norway, Sweden, and Japan.

14 These figures are not published. I have calculated them myself on the basis of the raw data.

15 The data were collected by a group of people: by Jan Willem Duyvendak for France; by Ruud Koopmans for Germany; by Florence Passy and Marco Giugni for Switzerland; and by Luc Wijmans, Hein-Anton van der Heijden, and a group of students under the direction of Jan Willem Duyvendak and Ruud Koopmans for the Netherlands.

16 Among the four largest SMOs, we have only included membership organizations. In other words, peak organizations; that is, SMOs of SMOs have not been included. This means that we have not counted the 850,000 nominal members of the French Federation of Associations for the Conservation of Nature (FFSPN), nor did we count the 3.3 million members of the German Association for the Protection of Nature (DNR), an umbrella organization with about a hundred associated leagues.

17 We do not have sufficient information for the urban autonomous movement, which is why it is not included in Table 7.3.

18 The distinction between traditional conservationism, pragmatic environmentalism and political ecologism has been introduced by Diani and Lodi (1988) for the study of the Italian ecology movement, and applied by Rucht (1989a) to the German and French ecology movements.

19 Greenpeace should be excluded, because it is a very exceptional case, an "outlier" in statistical terms, which distorts the overall results (see comment for Table 7.2). If Greenpeace is included, the correlations between age and resource levels are considerably lower (.12 for age with membership and .21 for age with financial resources, instead of .42 and .33 respectively); the other correlations do not change that much.

20 This discussion is based on a simple causal model which has been estimated by Lisrel on the basis of the seventy-two SMOs that have information on all these

variables (excluding Greenpeace). The model has a perfect fit. It explains about half of the variance in professionalization, almost two-thirds of the variance in the level of financial resources, but only about one-fifth of the variances of membership and formalization.

21 The Netherlands is exceptional in this regard. This exception may be more apparent than real: it could be a result of deficient data.

22 We recorded at most three external allies in our questionnaires.

23 It should be kept in mind that these data refer to the year 1989; that is they give an idea of the endpoint reached in this respect by the organizational development.

24 It should be noted that we only have information about revenue shares for the SMOs of the Swiss solidarity movement. But whether we compare the Swiss solidarity organizations to all the SMOs in the other countries or only to the SMOs of the same movement, their resource base appears to be singularly little diversified.

25 For this part of the analysis, I shall make use of data on protest events as mentioned previously. Conventional events include legal actions (such as the filing of a legal suit), conventional political actions (such as participation in a consultation procedure), conventional media-oriented actions (such as press conferences or public resolutions), and strikes as far as they are reported in the newspapers we analyzed. Unconventional events refer to any kind of public action of a demonstrative, confrontative, or violent form reported in our newspapers.

26 The smoothing allows the trends to become more visible.

27 The SMOs of the ecology movement have been involved in the protest events to a varying extent in the four countries: in France, they participated in only 15 percent of the events, whereas in other countries, their share varies between 42–45 percent (Germany and Switzerland) and 55 percent (Netherlands).

28 The newspapers often referred to the names of the organizations that were responsible for a protest event. This information has been used for the distinction between "professional SMOs" and informal "citizens' action groups." In addition to the most important SMOs that have supplied the database for the rest of this analysis, the category of the "professional SMOs" includes some other SMOs known to be organizationally developed as well.

29 There are not enough cases for such a detailed analysis of the French ecology movement.

30 I might add that the Green parties, while being a result of the mobilization of NSMs, are not products of the transformation of preexisting SMOs. Everywhere they have been newly constituted organizations. I would consider them as an external ally, rather than as part of the SMI of any of the NSMs. On the basis of their alliances with the SMI of the ecology movement, they have, of course, contributed to the institutionalization of this movement.

Chapter 8: The impact of national contexts on social movement structures

1 This essay basically summarizes two chapters of a comprehensive study (Rucht, 1994) which, based on relevant empirical literature, data on protest events, and on interviews with both movement activists and researchers, provides more detailed information on the movements under investigation.

2 Because opportunities can be seen as chances that come and go, and therefore may be missed, I would only refer to conjunctural but not stable factors as opportunities in the strict sense of the word.

3 For a conceptualization of alliance and conflict structures as part of the so-called multiorganizational field (Curtis and Zurcher, 1973), see Klandermans, 1990.

4 This is by no means a trivial assumption. Other scholars may argue that a given

social movement structure is basically the result of choices made by movement leaders or reflects a distinct stage in an inherently driven movement's life cycle.

5   The concept of "new social movements" is widely used in Europe. The term "Left-libertarian" was introduced by Kitschelt (1988) to designate a particular type of party, but can be also attributed to a type of social movement.

6   Consider, however, that environmental movements tend to be strong on the local level as well. A striking example in the United States is the *Citizens' Clearinghouse for Hazardous Wastes,* which claims to represent 7,000 grassroots groups (Freudenberg and Steinsapir, 1991: 237).

7   To be sure, in several countries in the last few decades, attempts have been made to establish women's parties; for example, in Belgium, Germany, and the United States. In Iceland, the women's party even entered parliament in 1983 and increased its share of the vote in 1987 (Kaplan, 1992: 89). As a rule, however, women's movements tended to use other structural forms and thus provided either half-hearted support, or no support at all for such parties.

Chapter 9: Organizational form as frame

1   By current standards, the case of organized labor falls outside the empirical scope of social movement studies. After all, labor is now presumed to be part of the established political regime of most industrialized nations. But the distinction between social movement and legitimate political player is necessarily relative. In the late nineteenth century, labor activists employed broad repertoires of both action and organization, many outside of regular political channels and directed toward goals much more general than economic self-interest. Thus, the debates over models of organization at the turn of the century help to explain how, and with what consequences, organized labor reconceived its own identity, moving from a variegated social movement to a politically focused, institutionalized interest group.

2   Hannan and Freeman have argued against use of the cognitive sense of "organizational form" on the grounds "that blueprints for organizations are not observable" (1986: 56). But during periods of change and innovation, debates over appropriate form do provide evidence of the basic models that constitute a group's organizational repertoire. Institutional change reflects the interplay of organizational diversity at both levels: "When efforts to implement novel forms succeed, they can result in a blurring of the boundaries among a set of forms or in the rise of a distinctly different form" (1986: 63; see Clemens 1993).

3   In drawing a contrast between *bricolage* and scientific logic, Lévi-Strauss attributes two qualities to the former that are not relevant to my discussion. He defines *bricolage* as a closed system, involving the rearrangement of a finite set of materials that are "the contingent result of all the occasions there have been to renew or enrich the stock or to maintain it with the remains of previous constructions or destructions" (1966: 17; the contrast is with raw materials that an engineer might select specifically for the task at hand). Following on this definition, *bricolage* is said to begin with events (ready-mades) which are arrayed into a structure, while science begins with structure (abstract laws or rules) and generates (explanations of) specific events. Recalling the earlier discussion of models of practical action, I argue that much of what we are interested in lies between these poles. The term *bricolage* is useful in that it recaptures an element often suppressed by the tendency of scientists to interpret the social world as rule-governed in the strong sense.

4   The contrast between rule-following and the concept of a "tool kit" echoes the

differences between Thomas Kuhn's initial analysis of scientific thought as shaped by "paradigms" (abstract sets of basic principles or laws) and his subsequent reformulation of his analysis in terms of a "disciplinary matrix" and a set of exemplars (specific classic experiments). Explaining his motives for introducing the term "paradigm," Kuhn argues: "Shared examples of successful practice could . . . provide what the group lacked in rules. Those examples were its paradigms, and as such essential to its continued research. Unfortunately, having gotten that far, I allowed the term's applications to expand, embracing all shared group commitments, all components of what I now wish to call the disciplinary matrix. Inevitably, the result was confusion, and it obscured the original reasons for introducing a special term. But those reasons still stand. Shared examples can serve cognitive functions commonly attributed to shared rules. When they do, knowledge develops differently than it does when it is governed by rules" (1977: 318–19).

5 But whereas "repertoires of collective action" structure moments of heightened activism and confrontation, the concept of an organizational repertoire is more encompassing, including the forms of solidarity and coordination evident in even the most routine aspects of social life.

6 While the concept of political opportunity structure draws on an imagery of open or closed space, the fit or resonance of organizational form reminds us that round pegs do not fit into square holes.

7 On observing an 1886 meeting of a Knights of Labor assembly in Vermont, "the reporter shrewdly noted the combination within the Knights of the 'mysticism of the masonic lodge, . . . the beneficiary elements of a mutual aid society, and the defensive and protective phases of a trade union after the old English pattern'" (Fink 1983: 76). Factional divisions among woman suffragists provide another clear instance of the *bricolage* of organizational form. In 1911, one Wisconsin woman suffrage group proclaimed its intention to "bust the suffrage trust" (the national suffrage associations) and to found an alternative organization "with a commission form of government" (Milwaukee *Evening Wisconsin,* 10/10/1911. Wisconsin Woman Suffrage Scrapbooks). Presumably, the adoption of a progressive organizational form signaled their progressive intentions, but it also potentially altered the relations of this group to others in the organizational field of reform politics.

8 Roger Friedland and Robert Alford make a similar point in their effort to develop "a nonfunctionalist conception of society as a potentially contradictory interinstitutional system." Applying this conception to the analysis of macrosocial change, they explain: "The central institutions of the contemporary capitalist West – capitalist market, bureaucratic state, democracy, nuclear family, and Christian religion – shape individual preferences and organizational interests as well as the repertoire of behaviors by which they may attain them. These institutions are potentially contradictory and hence make multiple logics available to individuals and organizations. Individuals and organizations transform the institutional relations of society by exploiting these contradictions" (1991: 232, 240).

9 William J. H. Traynor, who became president of the anti-Catholic American Protective Association in 1893, claimed membership in the Masons, Independent Order of Good Templars, Maccabees, National Union, Royal Arcanum, Order of the American Union, the Crescents, the American Patriotic League, the American Protestant Union, the Loyal Orange Institution, American Orange Knights, the Royal Black Knights of the Camp of Israel, Illustrious Order of the Knights of Malta, and the Grand Orange Lodge (Kinzer 1964: 91).

10 Conducting the war required its own *bricolage:* "As the events of 1861 showed, superiority of numbers and industrial capacity were not enough. The ability to

coordinate manpower and resources was the key to the Union's ability to prevail on the field of battle. The fact that the new organizational modes emerged through trial and error should not be taken to suggest that they were developed *ab novo.* For certain essential elements for the creation of large-scale organizations were already extant by 1860. The first and perhaps most important of these elements was the existence of a pool of men socialized to universalistic values of competence and generalized leadership ability. The second element required that this pool of men have some real experience in administering large-scale geographically extensive organizations. The third element involved the necessity that these men share an awareness of the utility of the new modes of transportation, communication, and administration that had developed since the 1820 [*sic*]. As it happened, most of these men were in civilian life when the war broke out. But the war served as a catalyst, uniting their diverse experiences and bringing them forward to the highest positions in the civil and military administration of the war effort" (Hall 1984: 229). Social movements may produce institutional change in a similar way, pushing members to apply familiar models and practices to unfamiliar problems and in innovative combinations.

11 In this case, the familiar process of deploying an existing organizational repertoire to construct a new association was evident: "Some of the founders had already had experience with veterans' societies. . . . The founders may also have received ideas from a wartime Republican society, the Strong Band. While not confined to veterans, this association was similar to the Grand Army in organization and professed purposes. It was based on a system of community, county, and state organization and used military terminology. Probably, too, the founders of the Grand Army were familiar with the Union Clubs, secret Republican societies that used rituals, passwords, and codes to impress their members and whose chief purpose was the dissemination of party propaganda" (Dearing 1952: 85). Although I have emphasized the antipartisan stance of fraternal organizations, both major parties recognized the mobilization potential of the fraternal model and attempted to adapt it for their own purposes.

12 Commenting critically on the army, the economist Thorstein Veblen explained that "These men . . . disregard the fact of local units and local relations with a facility that bespeaks their complete emancipation from the traditions of local self-government" (quoted in Schwantes 1985: 100).

13 Throughout its existence, leaders of the various armies showed considerable concern for the propriety of the marchers' behavior. The presence of women was a source of great concern, although some of the armies did allow women to join. Just as the distinction between the worthy and unworthy poor was central to the discourse of charity during this period, that between honest workmen and tramps structured debates over unemployment. As the *New York Times* observed in 1885, responding to proposed public work programs: "The honest workmen who are willing to work but can't get work will surely raise a prodigious shindy when they find reformed or unreformed tramps given work by the Government" (quoted in Leonard 1966).

14 Railroad workers, seamen, and a few other categories of employees did fall within the jurisdiction of the federal government, owing to its responsibility for interstate commerce.

15 The strong association between organized labor and the Social Democratic Party in Wisconsin is quite unusual for the United States. But while labor was able to elect its own representatives from districts in its stronghold of Milwaukee, elsewhere in the state labor representatives wore the hat of the Wisconsin State Federation of Labor and cooperated with legislators elected on the Republican, and

later Progressive, ticket. Recalling the dual organization of the Knights of Labor around official assemblies and "shadow" political committees, the arrangements in Wisconsin suggest the need to consider the determinants and consequences of the simultaneous deployment of multiple organizational models by a single movement.

Chapter 10: The collapse of a social movement

1 In the space of a single essay it is impossible to provide a theoretically satisfying account of the emergence as well as the decline of the Knights. For reasons of space, I neglect some aspects of the Knights' emergence that would be highlighted if one were to use the theoretical framework elaborated in McAdam, McCarthy, and Zald's introduction to this book. In particular, I would give greater attention to the role of political opportunities in the Knights' expansion in the 1880s, along the lines developed in Friedman, 1990.

2 Constitutionally, each local assembly had a majority of members who were manual workers.

3 The fact that district assemblies were organized territorially represented a departure from the fraternal model of organization. See Clemens (Chapter 9 of this volume) for a discussion of the fraternal model.

4 Of course, differences in workers' experience and expectations were not bridged overnight, simply by the use of a new, more universalistic vocabulary. For a discussion of the limitations of the Knights' universalism, see Voss 1993: chap. 2.

5 Stromquist (1990: 553–54) borrows Lawrence Goodwyn's notion of a "movement culture" to describe these developments in the Knights.

6 Along similar lines, Oestreicher (1986: 133) reports that by 1885 any labor leader who tried to deny the existence of class conflict was going against the current of the labor movement, at least in Detroit.

7 French socialist thinking, too, often showed the influence of producerist categories. Haupt notes that French socialists often depicted the petite bourgeoisie as being in a "precarious and poverty stricken condition," and as being the victims of large-scale capitalist exploitation. See Haupt, 1984.

8 For example, Ross (1985) argues that the Knights' ability to forge a strong sense of solidarity resulted from the decision made by Cincinnati's mayor to call out the local militia in the course of the May Day strikes. This act so outraged Cincinnati's workers, who felt that they were law-abiding while those in power were not, that they temporarily transcended their separate and often opposed identities as citizens and workers. However, because this unity was based on actions taken by those outside the working class, it did not hold, and the Knights collapsed amid increasingly bitter battles over ideology and tactics.

Since few mayors reacted to the May Day strikes by calling out the militia, it is difficult, at this juncture, to weave Ross's explanation for the Knights' failure into a more general explanation.

9 Leon Fink (1988) has recently begun to highlight the importance of employer power in the demise of the Knights. Unlike this study, however, he does not emphasize employers' associations, but focuses instead on the actions of large, dominant employers such as Andrew Carnegie. I agree that the actions of these giant employers were significant, but I believe that their actions reflected a more widespread tendency.

10 The instantaneous rate of death is the dependent variable. The rate is formally defined as

$$r(t) = \lim_{dt \to 0} \frac{Pr(\text{Death } t, \, t + dt/\text{alive at } t)}{dt}$$

where $Pr(\text{Death } t, \, t + dt/\text{alive at } t)$ is the conditional probability of a death between t and $t + dt$ given that the organization is alive at t.

Causal effects are built into the model by expressing the relation between the failure rate and the exogenous variables as follows:

$$\ln r(t) = a_0 + b_1 X_1 + b_2 X_2 + \dots c_1 Y_1(t) + c_2 Y_2(t) + \dots [2]$$

where the X's are independent variables that, although varying across local industries, do not change over time; the $Y(t)$'s are independent variables that do vary over time; and a_0, the b's, and the c's are parameters to be estimated. A loglinear specification was chosen because it ensures that all effects are expressed as proportional to the rate of failure.

Maximum likelihood estimates of this equation were obtained using RATE (Tuma 1980).

11　These dates were chosen to cover the period of greatest Knights activity and to minimize missing data. Two hundred three local assemblies were active in this period and originally included in the analysis; nine were later dropped because of missing data. In all, 97 percent of all New Jersey locals were founded between 1879 and 1895.

12　Dissolution dates were coded as follows: For locals that had their charters revoked by the national office, and for those that were formally declared "lapsed" because of failure to pay dues, the date of these events were recorded. For other locals, there is no known date of termination. In these cases, I assigned dissolution dates according to the last reference I found in either national or local sources.

13　Reduced models eliminate clearly nonsignificant variables in order to stabilize coefficient estimates for the significant factors.

14　Employers in one-industry towns frequently organized boards of trade and boards of manufactures that functioned much like employers' associations. Thus, it is likely that the one-industry town variable is partially measuring the impact of employers' organization.

15　In New Jersey the only federal intervention in this period occurred in the course of the Knights' 1887 general strike against the coal companies. The courts put the railroads into receivership and then used the receivership as a way of protecting strikebreakers. Workers saw this intervention as merely one more trick of the corrupt, monopolistic railroads; they did not view it as *state* action. Similarly, available evidence suggests that injunctions were sometimes threatened but rarely actually used.

16　In selecting the case, I began with a list of all New Jersey communities where there was both extended labor conflict and at least one employers' association. (Extended labor unrest was necessary because newspapers, my primary source, did not routinely report on labor matters when times were calm.) Since indexes for American cities in the late nineteenth century are virtually nonexistent, I next read daily reports of strikes in several communities. Most did not provide sufficient coverage of the interaction between employers' associations and the Knights. The Newark newspapers did. Newark also had the advantage of being a large, diverse town and, as such, it was the type of place where alliances between skilled and less-skilled workers most frequently took place (Voss 1988). The case was originally chosen as part of a larger project in which I also analyzed the emergence of solidarity between skilled and less-skilled workers; I therefore wanted a case where I could trace developments over time.

17 A similar pattern of small employers settling first also developed in other strikes outside the leather industry in 1886.

18 Evidence that the LMANJ was having trouble recruiting employers can be found in the *NEN* 5/9/1887. J. H. Halsey told the reporter, "The manufacturers also organized a short time ago and wanted us [Halsey and his partner] to join them. . . . We thought we had better paddle our own canoe, and declined to join."

19 As one smaller employer told a reporter, he "never entertained a thought of fighting the K. of L. when he joined the Manufacturer's Association." But now, given the highly competitive nature of the leather industry, he was trapped. He complained to a member of the Knights: "If you call out my men I can not go on with my work, and if I hold out against the order of the association, I will be ruined" (*NEN* 8/10/1887).

20 Again, the French case is instructive. In the late nineteenth century, French workers also tried to use divisions between small and large employers to win strikes. In 1901, for example, striking filemakers refused to negotiate with any employer who had not actually worked as a filemaker. As Michael Hanagan notes, workers claimed that other employers wouldn't understand the issues, but this was actually a ploy to appeal to smaller manufacturers. Similarly, Donald Reid notes that workers often sought the support of middle-class employers and shopkeepers in Decazeville. It is useful to remember Joan Scott's remark about Chartism: "political movements develop tactically, not logically, improvising appeals, incorporating and adapting various ideas to their particular cause." Hanagan 1980: 188 and personal communication; Reid 1985; Scott 1987: 8.

21 This statement is based on a reading of *John Swinton's Paper, National Labor Standard, Trenton Sunday Advertiser,* autobiographies of Terence Powderly (1968) and Joseph Buchanan (1903), and virtually every secondary source on the Knights of Labor that has ever been written.

22 Snow and Benford (1992) might argue this is an issue of empirical credibility; I have not adopted their language because I am particularly attentive to the dynamic aspect of social movements. What has empirical credibility at one point in time might not at another. The success of a collective-action frame, I would suggest, depends at least in part upon having a fortifying myth that sustains members when prognostic claims are undermined.

Another example of what I term "fortifying myths" is provided by Poland's Solidarity movement. One of Solidarity's posters is illustrated with a bright red line, indicating the pulse of the nation. It records, in jagged peaks, the years 1944, 1956, 1968, 1970, and 1976 – each date a failed national rebellion – and then, in 1980, the bright red line becomes a single word: *Solidarnosc.* Adam Michnik wrote an article about the same time this poster appeared which argued that these dates "stake out the successive stations on the Polish *via dolorosa*," the implication, of course, being that while these earlier uprisings had resulted in Crucifixion, the insurgency of 1980 represented Resurrection and Life (quoted in Weschler 1982: 36–37).

23 As with the Haymarket affair, the lessons Gompers drew about the use of militant tactics suggests that the "radical flank effect" is more varied than is often suggested.

24 The dating is adopted from Montgomery's (1979: 91–112) discussion of the strike decade that began in 1909.

Chapter 12: Framing political opportunity

1 Risse-Kappen (1991) and Gelb (1987) take a similar approach. Like Kitschelt, Risse-Kappen compares four nations, asking why domestic public opinion affects

foreign policy differently in each state. He broadens his focus beyond formal political institutions and the diffusion of state authority to include societal cleavages as well as more volatile aspects of political opportunity such as the capacity of coalitions and organizations to raise and pursue demands. Gelb, comparing the women's movements in the United States and the United Kingdom, also focuses on stable elements of political opportunity to explain the differences, but emphasizes cultural aspects of opportunity much more heavily. Eisinger (1973) and Amenta and Zylan (1991) apply the same logic, using units smaller than countries. Eisinger compared the openness of political institutions in cities to understand which ones experienced protest activity during the late 1960s. Amenta and Zylan compare states in the United States, using various measures of political opportunity, to account for the relative strength of the Townsend movement in the 1930s.

2 Meyer and Marullo (1992) argue that antinuclear activists in the West altered the political opportunities for human rights activists in the Soviet Union and in Eastern Europe. To make peace with its domestic critics, the Reagan administration offered a more conciliatory posture toward the Soviet Union, which gave Eastern reformers some room to operate. Activists in one nation thus altered the opportunities available to activists in another. Transnational relations between social movements, much less their relation to some kind of international political opportunity structure, is a potentially rich area in social movement analysis that is currently undeveloped.

3 Similarly dynamic approaches to POS are offered by a number of analysts who study particular movements or countries. McAdam's (1982) *political process* model, developed in his study of the civil rights movement in the United States, emphasized that dynamic variables were part of the structure of opportunities movements faced; he identifies, for example, the collapse of the cotton economy and federal antilynching laws as significant components of opportunity. Freeman (1975) in looking at the women's movement focuses her attention on law and public policy. Jenkins and Perrow (1977), in their study of farmworker struggles, focus on elite alignment and outside support for union campaigns. Tarrow (1989a), writing about the whole of the social movement sector in Italy over a decade, directs his attention to partisan alignment and the mechanisms of social control.

4 He also makes the distinction above between stable and volatile elements, calling the latter "conjunctural elements which vary over a shorter period of time" (Brand, 1990a: 2).

5 The most prominent examples of cyclical climate theories include Hirschman's (1982) theory of "shifting involvements" of strong commitment to the public sector followed by a phase of withdrawal into private life and Schlesinger's (1986) swings of the pendulum between conservatism and liberalism.

6 Language is yet another cultural structure that shapes the way we think about opportunity. The convenient "window" metaphor implies a stability in time and structure that is limiting. Windows are not always open or closed; sometimes they are screened, open to some actors and claims, but not others. Windows do not change in size and shape, or move from one location to another. Even when blocked, they are virtually always visible. In effect, this metaphor better serves Kingdon's purposes in analyzing institutional action than our project of assessing extrainstitutional openings. In contrast to a window, political opportunity is far more dynamic, liable to appear suddenly in a place where no architect envisioned space. Ultimately we need metaphors that illustrate without constraining. We appreciate Karen Beckwith's insight on this point.

7 Institutional means in democratic societies include the use of the electoral system, the judicial system, and the peaceful petitioning of public officials (lobbying, pre-

sentations, letters, petitions). Everything else is extrainstitutional including peaceful demonstrations, vigils, marches, strikes, boycotts, burning and looting, throwing rocks and bombs, political assassinations, and kidnappings.

8 Indeed, Meyer's (1993a) work suggests the reverse, that strong peace movements have arisen in the United States only in response to seemingly intractable and aggressive government military policies.

9 For more extended discussions of the concept of collective action frames see Gamson (1992a, b) and Snow and Benford (1992).

10 Charles Murray's *Losing Ground* (1984) provides a well-known example. Murray argued that antipoverty programs succeeded only in entrenching the poor in their poverty, actually inhibiting economic mobility.

11 Occasional tragic consequences can result from unrealistically optimistic projections about political change. American antiwar activists who bombed targets in what they thought would be an ultimately successful revolutionary campaign against the state serve as a trenchant example, one frequently invoked by critics of collective action. Optimism clearly needs to be tempered by some degree of realism.

12 For a fuller discussion of the nature of the transaction between the movement and media systems, see Gamson and Wolfsfeld (1993). This section and the one that follows draw on arguments developed in that paper.

13 Gitlin (1980) develops this argument at length in showing how the media premium on spectacle influenced the leadership and tactics of the New Left in the United States.

14 Ryan (1991) has an especially useful discussion of how this process operates and how movements can counter it in their framing strategies.

Chapter 13: Accessing public, media, electoral, and governmental agendas

1 For example, many papers appearing in several recent collections such as Morris and Mueller (1992); Klandermans, Kriesi, and Tarrow (1988); Laraña, Johnston, and Gusfield (1994) address these concerns. While most of this work focuses heavily upon injustice as the primary object of strategic framing, political opportunities may also be an important object of framing, as Gamson and Meyer argue in Chapter 12 of this volume. So, too, can movement success and failure be an object of framing, as Voss shows in Chapter 10. Framing efforts can also incorporate understandings of mobilizing potential, as we argue farther on.

2 Getting an issue on an agenda does not guarantee that one's framing of it will prevail, but it cannot prevail without getting on the agenda. We therefore emphasize a distinction between the *selection* of issues for inclusion on an agenda, the *place,* or rank, of the issue on the agenda, and the subsequent *description* or framing of issues once they are on the agenda. Because movement strategies for affecting issue selection may differ from those aimed at influencing issue framing, we concentrate our analysis primarily on the former.

3 Our terminology for the first three agendas follows closely that of Everett and Dearing (1988). The many more or less intersecting literatures which focus upon these processes do not share a common language for talking about them.

4 This section draws heavily upon McCarthy, McPhail, and Smith (1994).

5 Ryan's (1991) summary of these perspectives includes both "news routines" and "what's newsworthy" under her "gatekeeper model." Because we think these two sometimes lead us to different expectations about issue selection, we treat them separately here.

6 Cohen (1973: 205) remarked that truth is not a defining criteria for what is considered "news" by contemporary news gatherers.

7 Our statement is a truncated version of the "propaganda model" as outlined by Herman and Chomsky (1988).

8 Following this logic, we would expect that if such issues do get on the media agenda, the description of them will more likely be focused on specific events rather than on the underlying causes or dimensions of social problems (cf. Iyengar 1991).

9 This may be particularly true in countries with multiparty electoral systems (cf. Klandermans 1991).

10 Even movements whose interests conflict with administrations' aims can sometimes find bureaucratic allies. For example, Cortright (1993) shows how peace activists worked with municipal bureaucrats who opposed on logistical grounds Reagan's attempt to involve the Federal Emergency Management Agency in its attempts to develop a system for protecting urban populations from nuclear attack. Also, Dieter Rucht observed that some European authorities have sought greater cooperation with environmental organizations in their efforts to prevent regional integration from lowering national environmental standards (personal communication).

11 Many of the tactics we include here may be motivated by a variety of considerations beyond simple frame dissemination. Nevertheless, each of them can serve at least this SMO purpose, among others.

12 For presentation purposes, we have omitted some frame dissemination tactics which fit into our four arenas such as: nonviolence training, boycott, citizen exchanges (public), running a media news service or media research service (media); running for political office or working for a political party (electoral); and strategizing with or advising executive officials (governmental).

13 Peace movement organization data in Table 13.2 represent the percentages of groups with budgets above $30,000 using each tactic. Within the peace movement, we find a similar "insider-outsider" pattern as groups with budgets under $30,000 used more low-cost tactics such as letter-writing, vigils, and op-ed campaigns while they were less likely to use more costly strategies such as litigation and cultivating relations with members of the media.

14 The SMOs in the several studies we have examined tend toward the resource-rich end of the social movement sector, but there is enough range among them to allow us to speak of such variation.

15 The peace movement electoral activity may be atypically high, given that the data were collected in a presidential election year just following the mass electoral mobilization around local and national nuclear freeze issues.

16 Everett and Dearing conclude their "review of policy agenda-setting research with three generalizations: (1) The public agenda, once set, or reflected by the media agenda, influences the policy agenda of elite decision makers, and, in some cases, policy implementation; (2) the media agenda seems to have direct, sometimes strong, influence upon the policy agenda of elite decision makers, and in some cases, policy implementation; and (3) for some issues, the policy agenda seems to have direct, sometimes strong, influence upon the media agenda" (Graber 1994: 91).

17 We know that many SMOs purchase aid in crafting their messages.

Chapter 14: Media discourse, movement publicity, and the generation of collective action frames

1 Initially this percentage was 80. But in a not too successful attempt to reduce the costs of the Disability Insurance Act the percentage was cut back to 70 in 1987.

2 This section is drawn from Silvia Bunt, "The Social Construction of Protest: CNV-journals on the DA Action," Autumn 1991, unpublished master's thesis, Free University, Amsterdam.

3 The queen's speech at the opening of the parliamentary year is the official statement of the government in office's policy for the year. The speech is drafted by the prime minister and its content is the government's responsibility. That year part of the speech was devoted to the government's DA plan. The union called on their members to take a break from their work and to listen collectively to the queen's speech.

References

Abbott, Andrew
  1990 "Conceptions of Time and Events in Social Science Methods." *Historical Methods* 23 (Fall): 140–50.
Alinsky, Saul D.
  1972 *Rules for Radicals.* New York: Vintage.
Almond, Gabriel A., et al.
  1988 "The Return to the State." *American Political Science Review* 82: 853–74.
Almond, Gabriel A., and Sidney Verba
  1963 *The Civic Culture: Political Attitudes and Democracy in Five Nations.* Princeton, N.J.: Princeton University Press.
Altheide, David, and Robert Gilmore
  1972 "The Credibility of Protest." *American Sociological Review* 37: 99–108.
Amenta, Edwin, and Yvonne Zylan
  1991 "It Happened Here: Political Opportunity, the New Institutionalism, and the Townsend Movement." *American Sociological Review* 56: 250–65.
Anderson, Benedict
  1991 *Imagined Communities: Reflections on the Origin and Spread of Nationalism.* 2nd revised edition. London: Verso.
Anderson-Sherman, Arnold, and Doug McAdam
  1982 "American Black Insurgency and the World Economy: A Political Process Model." Pp. 165–88 in Edward Friedman (ed.), *Ascent and Decline in the World System.* Beverly Hills, Calif.: Sage.
Ang, Ien
  1991 *Desperately Seeking the Audience.* London: Routledge.
Appel, Roland, and Dieter Hummel
  1988 "Modellfall Volkszählung: ein Beispiel zum Umgang staatlicher Institutionen mit einer ausserparlamentarischen Bewegung." *Forschungsjournal Neue Soziale Bewegungen* 2: 34–44.
Arjomand, Said Amir
  1988 *The Turban for the Crown: The Islamic Revolution in Iran.* New York: Oxford University Press.
Ash, Timothy Garton
  1989 "The German Revolution." *New York Review of Books,* December 21.
  1990 "The Revolution of the Magic Lantern." *New York Review of Books,* January 18.

Aveling, Edward, and Eleanor Marx Aveling
1891 *The Working Class Movement in America.* London: Swan Sonnenschein (Reprint edition, Arno Press, 1969).
Bader, Veit
1992 *Kollektives Handeln.* Opladen: Leske and Budrich.
Baker, Jean H.
1983 *Affairs of Party: The Political Culture of Northern Democrats in the Mid-Nineteenth Century.* Ithaca, N.Y.: Cornell University Press.
Banac, Ivo (ed.)
1992 *Eastern Europe in Revolution.* Ithaca, N.Y.: Cornell University Press.
Barkan, Steven E.
1979 "Strategic, Tactical, and Organizational Dilemmas of the Protest Movement against Nuclear Power." *Social Problems* 27: 19–37.
Baumgartner, Frank R., and Bryan D. Jones
1993 *Agendas and Instability in American Politics.* Chicago: University of Chicago Press.
Beissinger, Mark
1991 "National Mobilization in the Former Soviet Union, 1965–1989." Unpublished paper. Department of Political Science, University of Wisconsin.
Bell, Daniel
1960 *The End of Ideology.* New York: Free Press.
Benford, Robert
1993 "Frame Disputes within the Nuclear Disarmament Movement." *Social Forces* 71: 677–701.
Bennahmias, Jean-Luc, and Agnes Roche
1992 *Des Verts de toutes les couleurs. Histoire et sociologie du mouvement écolo.* Paris: Albin Michel.
Bennett, Lerone, Jr.
1966 *Confrontation: Black and White.* Baltimore: Penguin Books.
Bensel, Richard
1991 *Yankee Leviathan: The Origins of Central State Authority in America, 1859–1877.* Cambridge: Cambridge University Press.
Berry, Jeffrey
1989 *The Interest Group Society.* 2nd edition. New York: Harper Collins.
Best, Joel (ed.)
1989 *Images of Issues: Typifying Contemporary Social Problems.* New York: Aldine de Gruyter.
Bikini
1981 *Die Funfiziger Jahren.* Berlin: Elefanten Press.
Blanke, Thomas, and Dieter Sterzel
1983 "Die Entwicklung des Demonstrationsrechts von der Studentenbewegung bis heute." Pp. 53–87 in Sebastian Cobler, Reiner Geulen, and Wolf-Dieter Narr (eds.), *Das Demonstrationsrecht.* Hamburg: Rowohlt.
Blanke, Thomas, et al.
1979 *Der Oldenburger Buback-Prozess.* Berlin: Kirshkern.
Bledstein, Burton J.
1976 *The Culture of Professionalism: The Middle Class and the Development of Higher Education in America.* New York: Norton.
1984 *Distinction: A Social Critique of the Judgment of Taste.* Cambridge, Mass.: Harvard University Press.
Blumer, Herbert
1948 "Public Opinion and Public Opinion Polling." *American Sociological Review* 13: 542–54.

1960 "Social Movements." Pp. 199–220 in A. McClung Lee (ed.), *Principles of Sociology.* New York: Barnes and Noble.

Bonnett, Clarence
1956 *Employers Associations in the United States.* New York: Vantage.

Böll, Heinrich, et al.
1976 *Die Erschießung des Georg v. Rauch.* Berlin: Wagenbach.

Bosso, Christopher
1991 "Adaptation and Change in the Environmental Movement." Pp. 151–76 in Allan J. Cigler and Burdett A. Loomis (eds.), *Interest Group Politics.* 3rd edition. Washington, D.C.: Congressional Quarterly Press.

Bourdieu, Pierre
1977 *Outline of a Theory of Practice.* Cambridge: Cambridge University Press.

Boy, Daniel
1990 "Le vote écologiste: Evolution et structures." *Cahiers du Centre d'Étude de la Vie Politique Francaise,* No. 6, Paris.

Branch, Taylor
1988 *Parting the Waters: America in the King Years 1954–1963.* New York: Simon and Schuster.

Brand, Karl-Werner
1982 *Neue soziale Bewegungen: Entstehung, Funktion und Perspektive neuer Protestpotentiale.* Opladen: Westdeutscher Verlag.
1985a *Neue soziale Bewegungen in Westeuropa und den USA: Ein internationaler Vergleich.* Frankfort: Campus.
1985b "Vergleichendes Resümee." Pp. 306–34 in Karl-Werner Brand (ed.), *Neue soziale Bewegungen in Westeuropa und den USA. Ein internationaler Vergleich.* Frankfurt: Campus.
1990a "Cyclical Aspects of New Social Movements: Waves of Cultural Criticism and Mobilization Cycles of New Middle-Class Radicalism." Pp. 23–42 in Russell J. Dalton and Manfred Kuechler (eds.), *Challenging the Political Order.* New York: Oxford University Press.
1990b "Cyclical Changes in the Cultural Climate as a Context Variable for Social Movement Development." Paper presented at workshop titled "Social Movements: Framing Processes and Opportunity Structures." Wissenschaftszentrum Berlin, July.

Brewer, John
1989 *The Sinews of Power, War, Money and the English State, 1688–1783.* New York: Knopf.

Bright, Charles
1984 "The State in the United States during the Nineteenth Century." Pp. 121–58 in Charles Bright and Susan Harding (eds.), *Statemaking and Social Movements: Essays in History and Theory.* Ann Arbor: University of Michigan Press.

Bright, Charles, and Susan Harding
1984 *Statemaking and Social Movements: Essays in History and Theory.* Ann Arbor: University of Michigan Press.

Brinton, Crane
1957 *The Anatomy of Revolution.* New York: Vintage.

Brockett, Charles D.
1991 "The Structure of Political Opportunities and Peasant Mobilization in Central America." *Comparative Politics* 253–74.

Brown, James Sayles
1897 *Partisan Politics: The Evil and the Remedy.* Philadelphia: J. B. Lippincott.

Bruszt, Lazslo, and David Stark
1992 "Remaking the Political Field in Hungary: From the Politics of Confronta-

tion to the Politics of Competition." In Ivo Banac (ed.), *Eastern Europe in Revolution*. Ithaca, N.Y.: Cornell University Press.

Bryce, James
1895 *The American Commonwealth*. Vol. 2, 3rd edition. New York: Macmillan.

Buchanan, Joseph Ray
1903 *The Story of a Labor Agitator*. New York: Outlook.

Buechler, Steven
1990 *Women's Movements in the U.S.* New Brunswick, N.J.: Rutgers University Press.

Buerklin, Wilhelm
1987 "Why Study Political Cycles? An Introduction." *European Journal of Political Research* 15: 1–15.

Bullock, Henry Allen
1971 "Urbanism and Race Relations." Pp. 207–29 in Rupert P. Vance and Nicholas J. Demerath (eds.), *The Urban South*. Freeport, N.Y.: Books for Libraries Press.

Bunce, Valerie
1990 "Rising above the Past: The Struggle for Liberal Democracy in Eastern Europe." *World Policy Journal* 7: 395–430.

Burkhauser, R. V.
1991 "The Disease of Worker Disability Is Only Potent in the Netherlands." *NRC Handelsblad,* p. 8.

Burstein, Paul
1991 "Legal Mobilization as Social Movement Tactic: The Struggle for Equal Employment Opportunity." *American Journal of Sociology* 96: 1201–25.

Busch, Heiner; Albrecht Funk; Udo Kauss; Wolf-Dieter Narr; and Falco Werkentin
1988 *Die Polizei in der Bundesrepublik*. Frankfurt on Main: Campus Verlag.

Button, James W.
1989 *Blacks and Social Change*. Princeton, N.J.: Princeton University Press.

California State Federation of Labor (CaSFL)
1901–15 *Proceedings of the Annual Convention*.

Canosa, Romano
1976 *La polizia in Italia dal 1945 ad oggi*. Bologne: Il Mulino.

Carmines, Edward G., and James A. Stimson
1986 "On the Structure and Sequence of Issue Evolution." *American Political Science Review* 80: 902–21.
1989 *Issue Evolution: Race and the Transformation of American Politics*. Princeton, N.J.: Princeton University Press.

Carnes, Mark C.
1989 *Secret Ritual and Manhood in Victorian America*. New Haven, Conn.: Yale University Press.

Cattacin, Sandro, and Florence Passy
1992 *Der Niedergang von Bewergungsorganisationen, Zur Analyse von organisatorischen Laufbahnen*. Paper presented at the Bonn-Meeting on New Social Movements, the Third Sector and the Welfare State, June 26–28.

Christie, Ian
1982 *Wilkes, Wyvill and Reform: The Parliamentary Reform Movement in British Politics, 1760–1785*. London: Macmillan.

Christmann, Gabriela B.
1992 "Selbstbilder und Weltbilder von Aktiven im Umwelt und Naturschutz." Unpublished thesis. University of Konstanz.

Cilip
1978 Numero 0.

1981 *Politik, Protest und Polizei. Eine vergleichende Untersuchung.* Special Issue 9/ 10.

Clark, Kenneth B.
1970 "The Civil Rights Movement: Momentum and Organization." Pp. 270–97 in Richard P. Young (ed.), *Roots of Rebellion.* New York: Harper and Row.

Clawson, Mary Ann
1985 "Fraternal Orders and Class Formation in the Nineteenth-Century United States." *Comparative Studies in Society and History* 27 (4): 672–95.
1989 *Constructing Brotherhood: Class, Gender, and Fraternalism.* Princeton, N.J.: Princeton University Press.

Clemens, Elisabeth S.
1990 "Secondhand Laws: Patterns of Political Learning among State Govern-ments and Interest Groups." Presented at the annual meetings of the American Political Science Association, San Francisco.
1993 "Organizational Repertoires and Institutional Change: Women's Groups and the Transformation of American Politics, 1890–1920." *American Journal of Sociology* 98 (4): 755–98.

Cobb, Roger, Jennie-Kieth Ross, and March Howard Ross.
1976 "Agenda Building as a Comparative Political Process." *American Political Science Review* 70: 126–38.

Cohen, Bernard C.
1973 *The Public's Impact on Foreign Policy.* Boston: Little, Brown.

Cohen, Jean L.
1985 "Strategy or Identity: New Theoretical Paradigms and Contemporary So-cial Movements." *Social Research* 52 (4): 663–716.

Connell, Carol, and Kim Voss
1990 "Formal Organization and the Fate of Social Movements: Craft Association and Class Alliance in the Knights of Labor." *American Sociological Review* 55 (2): 255–69.

Cook, Ezra
1886 *Knights of Labor Illustrated.* Chicago: Ezra A. Cook.

Corso, Guido
1979 *L'ordine pubblico.* Bologne: Il Mulino.

Cortright, David
1993 *Peace Works.* Boulder, Colo.: Westview.

Costain, Anne W.
1992 *Inviting Women's Rebellion: A Political Process Interpretation of the Women's Movement.* Baltimore: Johns Hopkins University Press.

Cramer, Jacqueline
1989 *De groene golf. Geschiedenis en toekomst van de millieubeweging.* Utrecht: Uit-geverij Jan van Arkel.

Cross, Whitney R.
1950 *The Burned-over District: The Social and Intellectual History of Enthusiastic Religion in Western New York, 1800–1850.* Ithaca, N.Y.: Cornell University Press.

Curtis, James E.; Edward G. Grabb; and Douglas E. Baer
1992 "Voluntary Association Membership in Fifteen Countries: A Comparative Analysis." *American Sociological Review* 57 (2): 139–52.

Curtis, Russell L., and Louis A. Zurcher
1973 "Stable Resources of Protest Movements: The Multiorganizational Field." *Social Forces* 52: 53–61.

Dalton, Russell J.
1994 *The Green Rainbow: Environmental Groups in Western Europe.* New Haven, Conn.: Yale University Press.

Dearing, Mary R.
1952 *Veterans in Politics: The Story of the G.A.R.* Baton Rouge: Louisiana State University Press.

De Goede, M. P. M., and G. H. Maassen
1980 "Meningen over werklozen en arbeidsongeschikten. *Mens en Maatschappij* 55, 245–80.

della Porta, Donatella
1990 *Il terrorismo di sinistra in Italia.* Bologne: Il Mulino.
1991 "Die Spirale der Gewalt und Gegengewalt: Lebensberichte von Links- und Rechtsradikalen in Italien." *Forschungsjournal Neue Soziale Bewegungen* 4: 53–62.
1992a "Political Socialization in Left-wing Underground Organizations. Biographies of Italian and German Militants." Pp. 259–90 in Donatella della Porta (ed.), *Social Movement and Violence: Participation in Underground Organizations.* Greenwich, Conn.: JAI Press.
1992b "Institutional Responses to Terrorism: The Italian Case." *Terrorism and Political Violence* 4: 151–170.
1994 "The Political Discourse on Protest Policing." Paper presented at the International Sociological Association, Bielefeld, July.
1995 *Social Movements, Political Violence and the State.* Cambridge: Cambridge University Press.

Della Porta, Donatella, and Dieter Rucht
1991 "Left-Libertarian Movements in Context: A Comparison of Italy and West Germany, 1965–1990." Discussion Paper FS III 91–103. Wissenschaftszentrum Berlin.

della Porta, Donatella, and Sidney Tarrow
1986 "Unwanted Children: Political Violence and the Cycle of Protest in Italy, 1966–1973." *European Journal of Political Research* 14: 607–32.

De Lutiis, Giuseppe
1984 *Storia dei servizi segreti in Italia.* Rome: Editori Riuniti.

De Ruggiero, L.
1982 "I problemi posti dai processi di terrorismo." In Magistratura democratica (ed.), *La magistratura di fronte al terrorismo e all'eversione di sinistra.* Milan: Angeli.

Diani, Mario
1992 "Analysing Social Movement Networks." Pp. 107–35 in Mario Diani and Ron Eyerman (eds.), *Studying Collective Action.* Newbury Park, Calif.: Sage.

Diani, Mario, and Giovanni Lodi
1988 "Three in One: Currents in the Milan Ecology Movement." Pp. 103–24 in B. Klandermans, H. Kriesi, and S. Tarrow (eds.), *From Structure to Action: Comparing Social Movement Research across Cultures. International Social Movement Research.* Vol. 1. Greenwich, Conn.: JAI Press.

DiMaggio, Paul, and Walter W. Powell
1991 "Introduction." In Powell and DiMaggio (eds.), *The New Institutionalism in Organizational Analysis.* Chicago: University of Chicago Press.

Downs, Anthony
1972 "Up and Down with Ecology: The Issue Attention Cycle." *Public Interest* 28: 38–50.

Draper, Theodore
1993 "A New History of the Velvet Revolution" *New York Review of Books,* January 14.
Drescher, Seymour
1987 *Capitalism and Antislavery: British Mobilization in Comparative Perspective.* New York: Oxford University Press.
1991 "British Way, French Way: Opinion Building and Revolution in the Second French Slave Emancipation." *American Historical Review* 96: 709–34.
Duchen, Claire
1986 *Feminism in France. From May '68 to Mitterrand.* London: Routledge and Kegan Paul.
Dumenil, Lynn
1984 *Freemasonry and American Culture, 1880–1939.* Princeton, N.J.: Princeton University Press.
Duyvendak, Jan Willem
1992 "The Power of Politics: New Social Movements in an Old Polity, France 1965–1989." Unpublished Ph.D. dissertation.
Dyan, Daniel, and Elihu Katz
1992 *Media Events: The Live Broadcasting of History.* Cambridge, Mass.: Harvard University Press.
Edelman, Murray
1967 *The Symbolic Uses of Politics.* Urbana: University of Illinois Press.
1971 *Politics as Symbolic Action.* Chicago: Markham.
Edwards, Bob
1994a "Organizational Style in Middle-Class and Poor People's Social Movement Organizations: An Empirical Assessment of New Social Movements Theory." Unpublished Ph.D. dissertation. Washington, D.C.: Catholic University of America.
1994b "Semi-formal Organizational Structure among Social Movement Organizations: An Analysis of the U.S. Peace Movement." *Nonprofit and Voluntary Sector Quarterly* 23:309–333.
Edwards, Bob, and John D. McCarthy
1992 "Social Movement Schools." *Sociological Forum* 7: 541–50.
Eisinger, Peter K.
1973 "The Conditions of Protest Behavior in American Cities." *American Political Science Review* 67: 11–28.
Evans, Peter B.; Dietrich Rueschemeyer; and Theda Skocpol (eds.)
1985 *Bringing the State Back In.* Cambridge: Cambridge University Press.
Evans, Sara
1980 *Personal Politics.* New York: Vintage Books.
Eyerman, Ron, and Andrew Jamison
1991 *Social Movements: A Cognitive Approach.* University Park, Pa.: Pennsylvania State University Press.
Fedeli, Franco
1981 *Da sbirro a tutore della legge.* Rome: Napoleoni.
Ferraresi, Franco
1984 *La destra in Italia.* Milan: Feltrinelli.
Ferree, Myra Marx
1987 "Feminist Politics in the U.S. and West Germany." In Mary Katzenstein and Carol Mueller (eds.), *The Women's Movements of the United States and Western Europe.* Philadelphia: Temple University Press.

Ferree, Myra Marx, and Frederick D. Miller
  1977 "Winning Hearts and Minds: Some Psychological Contributions to the Re-source Mobilization Perspective of Social Movements." Unpublished paper.
Festinger, Leon
  1954 "A Theory of Social Comparison." *Human Relations* 7: 117–40.
Fink, Leon
  1983 *Workingmen's Democracy: The Knights of Labor and American Politics.* Urbana: University of Illinois Press.
  1988 "The New Labor History and the Powers of Historical Pessimism: Consensus, Hegemony, and the Case of the Knights of Labor." *Journal of American History* 75: 115–36.
Finn, John E.
  1991 *Constitutions in Crisis: Political Violence and the Rule of Law.* Oxford: Oxford University Press.
Fischer, Claude; S. M. Baldassare; K. Gerson; R. M. Jackson; L. M. Jones; and C. A. Stueve
  1977 *Networks and Places: Social Relations in the Urban Setting.* New York: Free Press.
Flamigni, Sergio
  1988 *La tela di ragno. Il delitto Moro.* Rome: Edizioni associate.
Foner, Philip S.
  1955 *History of the Labor Movement in the United States.* Vol. 2. New York: International Publishers.
Forschungsjournal Neue Soziale Bewegungen
  1988 *Neue Soziale Bewegungen und soziale Kontrolle.* Numero Speciale 2.
Fox, Alan
  1985 *History and Heritage.* London: George Allen and Unwin.
Frank, André Gunder, and Maria Fuentes
  1992 "On Studying the Cycles in Social Movements." Unpublished paper presented to the conference on "Movimientos Cíclicos y Recurrencias en Política y Economia." Fondación Pablo Iglesias, Madrid.
Fraser, Nancy
  1990 "Struggle over Needs: Outline of a Socialist-Feminist Critical Theory of Late-Capitalist Political Culture." In Linda Gordon (ed.), *Women, the State, and Welfare.* Madison: University of Wisconsin Press.
Freeman, Jo.
  1973 "The Origins of the Women's Liberation Movement." *American Journal of Sociology* 78: 792–811.
  1975 *The Politics of Women's Liberation.* New York: David McKay.
Freudenberg, Nicholas, and Carol Steinsapir
  1991 "Not in Our Backyards: The Grassroots Environmental Movement." *Society and Natural Resources* 4 (3): 235–45.
Friedheim, Robert L.
  1964 *The Seattle General Strike.* Seattle: University of Washington Press.
Friedland, Roger, and Robert R. Alford
  1991 "Bringing Society Back In: Symbols, Practices and Institutional Contradictions." In Walter W. Powell and Paul DiMaggio (eds.), *The New Institutionalism in Organizational Analysis.* Chicago: University of Chicago Press.
Friedman, Gerald
  1985 "Politics and Unions: Government, Ideology, and the Labor Movement in the United States and France, 1880–1914." Unpublished Ph.D. dissertation. Harvard University, Cambridge, Mass.

1988 "The State and the Making of the Working Class: France and the United States, 1880–1914." *Theory and Society* 17: 403–30.

1991 "The Decline of Paternalism and the Making of the Employer Class, France, 1870–1914." Pp. 153–72 in Sanford Jacoby (ed.), *Masters to Managers: Historical and Comparative Perspectives on American Employers.* New York: Columbia University Press.

Funk, Albrecht
1990 "Innere Sicherheit: Symbolische Politik und exekutive Praxis." In *Leviathan* Special issue: 40 Jahre Bundesrepublik.

Furlong, Paul
1981 "Political Terrorism in Italy: Responses, Reactions and Immobilism." In Juliet Lodge (ed.), *Terrorism: A Challenge to the State.* Oxford: Martin Robertson.

Gallup, George
1972 *The Gallup Poll: Public Opinion, 1935–1971.* Vol. 3. New York: Random House.

Gamson, William A.
1988 "Political Discourse and Collective Action." *International Social Movement Research* 1: 219–44.

1990 *The Strategy of Social Protest.* Belmont, Calif.: Wadsworth. (First published in 1975 by Dorsey Press, Homewood, Ill.)

1992a *Talking Politics.* Cambridge: Cambridge University Press.

1992b "The Social Psychology of Collective Action." Pp. 53–76 in Aldon Morris and Carol M. Mueller (eds.), *Frontiers in Social Movement Theory.* New Haven, Conn.: Yale University Press.

Gamson, William A.; Myra Marx Ferree; Jurgen Gerhards; Monika Lindgens; Friedhelm Neidhardt; and Dieter Rucht
1993 "Abortion Discourse in Germany and the United States." Unpublished paper.

Gamson, William A.; Bruce Fireman; and Steven Rytina
1982 *Encounters with Unjust Authorities.* Homewood, Ill.: Dorsey Press.

Gamson, William A., and David Meyer
1992 "The Framing of Political Opportunity." Paper presented at the Conference on European/American Perspectives on Social Movements, Life Cycle Institute, Catholic University, Washington, D.C., August.

Gamson, William A., and Andre Modigliani
1989 "Media Discourse and Public Opinion on Nuclear Power." *American Journal of Sociology* 95: 1–38.

Gamson, William A., and Emilie Schmeidler
1984 "Organizing the Poor." *Theory and Society* 13: 567–85.

Gamson, William A., and Gadi Wolfsfeld
1993 "Movements and Media as Interacting Systems." In Russell Dalton (ed.), "Citizens, Protest, and Democracy." *Annals of the American Academy of Political and Social Science* 528: 114–25.

Gans, Herbert
1962 *The Urban Villagers.* New York: Free Press.

Garlock, Jonathan
1973 *Knights of Labor Assemblies.* ICPSR 0029. Distributed by Inter-University Consortium for Political and Social Research. Ann Arbor, Mich.

1978 "The Knights of Labor: A 19th Century American Experiment with Popular Justice." Paper presented to the Social Science History Association, Columbus, Ohio.

Garner, Roberta Ash, and Mayer N. Zald
1985 "The Political Economy of Social Movement Sectors." Pp. 119–145 in Gerald D. Suttles and Mayer N. Zald (eds.), *The Challenge of Social Control.* Norwood, N.J.: Ablex.
1987 "The Political Economy of Social Movement Sectors." Pp. 293–318 in Zald and John D. McCarthy (eds.), *Social Movements in an Organizational Society.* New Brunswick, N.J.: Transaction Books.

Garrow, David J.
1978 *Protest at Selma.* New Haven, Conn.: Yale University Press.
1986 *Bearing the Cross: Martin Luther King, Jr., and the Southern Christian Leadership Conference.* New York: Morrow.

Gavett, Thomas W.
1965 *Development of the Labor Movement in Milwaukee.* Madison: University of Wisconsin Press.

Geertz, Clifford
1973 *The Interpretation of Culture: Selected Essays.* New York: Basic Books.

Gelb, Joyce
1983 "The Professionalization of Feminism: Resources, Goals and Policy." Paper presented at a workshop on The Women's Movement in Comparative Perspective: Resource Mobilization, Cycles of Protest and Movement Success, May 6–8.
1987 "Social Movement Success: A Comparative Analysis of Feminism in the United States and the United Kingdom." Pp. 267–89 in Mary F. Katzenstein and Carol M. Mueller (eds.), *The Women's Movements of the United States and Western Europe.* Philadelphia: Temple University Press.

Gergen, Kenneth J., and Semin, Gün R.
1990 "Everyday Understanding in Science and Life." In Semin and Gergen (eds.), *Everyday Understanding: Social and Scientific Implications.* London: Sage.

Gerhards, Jürgen
1993 *Neue Konfliktlinie in der Mobilisierung öffentlicher Meinung.* Warum die IWF Tagung in Berlin 1988 zu einem öffentlichen Streitthema würde. Berlin: Sigma.

Gerhards, Jürgen, and Dieter Rucht
1992 "Mesomobilization: Organizing and Framing in Two Protest Campaigns in West Germany." *American Journal of Sociology* 98: 555–96.

Gerlach, Luther, and Virginia Hine
1970 *People, Power, Change.* Indianapolis: Bobbs-Merrill.

Ginsberg, Benjamin
1988 *The Captive Public: How Mass Opinion Promotes State Power.* New York: Basic Books.

Gitlin, Todd
1980 *The Whole World Is Watching.* Berkeley: University of California Press.

Goffman, Erving
1974 *Frame Analysis: An Essay on the Organization of Experience.* New York: Harper Colophon.

Goldfield, Michael
1982 "The Decline of Organized Labor: NLRB Union Certification Election Results." *Politics and Society* 11: 167–210.

Goldstein, Robert J.
1978 *Political Repression in America.* Cambridge, Mass.: Schenkman.
1983 *Political Repression in Nineteenth Century Europe.* London: Croom Helm.

Goldstone, Jack
1980 "The Weakness of Organization: A New Look at Gamson's *The Strategy of Social Protest.*" *American Journal of Sociology* 85: 1017–42.

1991 *Revolution and Rebellion in the Early Modern World.* Berkeley: University of California Press.

Gompers, Samuel
1925 *Seventy Years of Life and Labor.* New York: E. P. Dutton.

Goodwyn, Lawrence
1976 *Democratic Promise: The Populist Movement in America.* Oxford: Oxford University Press.

Gould, Roger
1991 "Multiple Networks and Mobilization in the Paris Commune, 1871." *American Sociological Review* 56: 716–29.
1993 "Collective Action and Network Structure." *American Sociological Review* 58: 182–96.

Gourevitch, Peter
1986 *Politics in Hard Times.* Ithaca, N.Y.: Cornell University Press.

Graber, Doris
1994 *Media Power in Politics.* 3rd edition. Washington, D.C.: Congressional Quarterly Press.

Grabner, W. J., et al.
1990 *Leipzig im Oktober.* Berlin: Wicher Verlag.

Granovetter, Mark
1973 "The Strength of Weak Ties." *American Journal of Sociology* 78: 1360–80.

Greenberg, Michael; Peter Sandman; David Sachsman; and Kandice Salmone
1989 "Network Television News Coverage of Environmental Risks." *Environment* 31: 16–20, 40–43.

Grevi, Vittorio
1984 "Sistema penale e leggi dell'emergenza: la risposta legislativa al terrorismo." In Gianfranco Pasquino (ed.), *La prova delle armi.* Bologna: Il Mulino.

Grew, Raymond
1984 "The Nineteenth-Century European State." Pp. 83–120 in Charles Bright and Susan Harding (eds.), *Statemaking and Social Movements: Essays in History and Theory.* Ann Arbor: University of Michigan Press.

Grob, Gerald N.
1969 *Workers and Utopia.* Chicago: Quadrangle.

Gundelach, Peter
1984 "Social Transformation and New Forms of Voluntary Associations." *Social Science Information* 23: 1049–81.

Gusfield, Joseph R.
1969 *Symbolic Crusade.* Urbana: University of Illinois Press.
1981 *The Culture of Public Problems: Drinking-Driving and the Symbolic Order.* Chicago: University of Chicago Press.

Habermas, Jürgen
1981 "New Social Movements." *Telos* 49: 33–37.

Haines, Herbert H.
1988 *Black Radicals and the Civil Rights Mainstream, 1954–1970.* Knoxville: University of Tennessee Press.

Hall, Peter Dobkin
1984 *The Organization of American Culture, 1700–1900: Private Institutions, Elites, and the Origins of American Nationality.* New York: New York University Press.

Hallgarth, Susan A. (ed.)
1992 *A Directory of National Women's Organizations.* National Council for Research on Women.

Hallin, Daniel C., and Paolo Mancini
1984 "Speaking of the President: Political Structure and Representational Form in U.S. and Italian Television News." *Theory and Society* 13 (6): 829–50.
Hanagan, Michael P.
1980 *The Logic of Solidarity.* Urbana: University of Illinois Press.
Hankiss, Elemer
1990 "What the Hungarians Saw First." In Gwyn Prins (ed.), *Spring in Winter: The 1989 Revolutions.* Manchester: Manchester University Press.
Hannan, Michael T., and John Freeman
1984 "Structural Inertia and Organizational Change." *American Sociological Review* 49 (2): 149–64.
1986 "Where Do Organizational Forms Come From?" *Sociological Forum* 1 (1): 50–72.
Hardin, Russell
1982 *Collective Action.* Baltimore: Johns Hopkins University Press.
Hattam, Victoria C.
1993 *Labor Visions and State Power: The Origins of Business Unionism in the United States.* Princeton, N.J.: Princeton University Press.
Haupt, Heinz-Gerhard
1984 "The Petite Bourgeoisie in France, 1850–1914: In Search of the Juste Milieu?" In Geoffrey Crossick and Heinz-Gerhard Haupt (eds.), *Shopkeepers and Master Artisans in Nineteenth Century Europe.* London: Methuen.
Havel, Vaclav
1992 "Paradise Lost." *New York Review of Books,* April 9.
Heberle, Rudolf
1951 *Social Movements: An Introduction to Political Sociology.* New York: Appleton-Century-Crofts.
Herbst, Susan
1993 *Numbered Voices: How Opinion Polling Has Shaped American Politics.* Chicago, University of Chicago Press.
Herman, Edward, and Noam Chomsky
1988 *Manufacturing Consent.* New York: Pantheon.
Hilderbrand, Robert C.
1981 *Power and the People: Executive Management of Public Opinion in Foreign Affairs 1897–1921.* Chapel Hill: University of North Carolina Press.
Hilgartner, Stephen, and Charles L. Bosk
1988 "The Rise and Fall of Social Problems: A Public Arenas Model." *American Journal of Sociology* 94: 53–78.
Hirschman, Albert
1970 *Exit, Voice, and Loyalty.* Cambridge, Mass.: Harvard University Press.
1982 *Shifting Involvements.* Princeton, N.J.: Princeton University Press.
1991 *The Rhetoric of Reaction.* Cambridge, Mass.: Harvard University Press.
Hobsbawm, Eric J.
1964 *Labouring Men.* London: Weidenfeld and Nicolson.
1974 "Peasant Land Occupations." *Past and Present* 62: 120–52.
1984 *Workers: Worlds of Labor.* New York: Pantheon.
Holt, James
1977 "Trade Unionism in the British and U.S. Steel Industries, 1880–1914: A Comparative Study." Pp. 166–96 in Daniel Leab (ed.), *The Labor History Reader.* Urbana: University of Illinois Press.
Hooijberg, Robert, and Richard H. Price
1992 The Great Dutch Work Disability Epidemic: Cultural Construction and In-

stitutional Action. Unpublished paper, Department of Psychology and Survey Research Center, Institute for Social Research, University of Michigan.

Hubbard, Howard
1968 "Five Long Hot Summers and How They Grew." *Public Interest* 12: 3–24.

Hübner, Klaus
1979 "Erfahrungen mit Einsatzkonzeptionen in Berlin." *Die Polizei* 7.

Hunt, Edward H.
1981 *British Labour History, 1815–1914*. Atlantic Highlands, N.J.: Humanities Press.

Hunt, Lynn Avery
1984 *Politics, Culture and Class in the French Revolution*. Berkeley: University of California Press.

Hunt, Scott, and Robert Benford
1992 "Social Movements and Social Construction of Reality: An Emergent Paradigm." Presented at the Workshop on Culture and Social Movements, San Diego, Calif., June.

Inglehart, Ronald
1977 *The Silent Revolution: Changing Values and Political Styles among Western Publics*. Princeton, N.J.: Princeton University Press.
1979 "Political Action: The Impact of Values, Cognitive Level, and Social Background." In Samuel Barnes, Max Kaase, et al. (eds.), *Political Action*. Beverly Hills, Calif.: Sage.

Iyengar, Shanto, and Donald Kinder
1987 *News That Matters: Television and American Opinion*. Chicago: University of Chicago Press.
1991 *Is Anyone Responsible? How Television Frames Political Issues*. Chicago: University of Chicago Press.

Jacoby, Sanford (ed.)
1991 *Masters to Managers: Historical and Comparative Perspectives on American Employers*. New York: Columbia University Press.

Jenkins, J. Craig
1977 "Radical Transformation of Organizational Goals." *Administrative Science Quarterly* 22 (4): 568–86.

Jenkins, J. Craig, and Craig M. Eckert
1986 "Channeling Black Insurgency." *American Sociological Review* 51 (6): 812–29.

Jenkins, J. Craig, and Charles Perrow
1977 "Insurgency of the Powerless: Farm Worker Movements (1946–1972)." *American Sociological Review* 42: 249–68.

Jenness, Valerie
1993 *Making It Work: The Prostitutes' Rights Movement in Perspective*. Hawthorne, N.Y.: Aldine de Gruyter.

Jepperson, Ronald L.
1991 "Institutions, Institutional Effects, and Institutionalism." In Walter W. Powell and Paul DiMaggio (eds.), *The New Institutionalism in Organizational Analysis*. Chicago: University of Chicago Press.

Johansen, Dorothy O.
1967 "A Working Hypothesis for the Study of Migrations." *Pacific Historical Review* 36 (1): 1–12.

Joppke, Christian
1991 "Social Movements during Cycles of Issue Attention: The Decline of the Anti-nuclear Energy Movements in West Germany and the USA." *British Journal of Sociology* 42: 43–60.

1992 "The Social Struggle over Nuclear Energy: A Comparison of West Germany and the United States." Unpublished Ph.D. dissertation. University of Berkeley.

1993 *Mobilizing against Nuclear Energy: A Comparison of West Germany and the United States.* Berkeley: University of California Press.

Joyce, Patrick

1991 *Visions of the People: Industrial England and the Question of Class, 1848–1914.* Cambridge: Cambridge University Press.

Judt, Tony

1992 "Metamorphosis: the Democratic Revolution in Czechoslovakia." In Ivo Banac (ed.), *Eastern Europe in Revolution.* Ithaca, N.Y.: Cornell University Press.

Kanter, Rosabeth Moss

1972 *Commitment and Community.* Cambridge, Mass.: Harvard University Press.

Kaplan, Gisela

1992 *Contemporary Western European Feminism.* London: Allen and Unwin.

Kaplan, Steven L.

1984 *Provisioning Paris: Merchants and Millers in the Grain and Flour Trade during the Eighteenth Century.* Ithaca, N.Y.: Cornell University Press.

1992 *Contemporary Western European Feminism.* London: Allen and Unwin.

Kaster, Gregory L.

1990 "'We Will Not Be Slaves to Avarice': The American Labor Jeremiad, 1827–1877." Unpublished Ph.D. dissertation. Boston University.

Katzenstein, Peter

1990 *West Germany's Internal Security Policy: State and Violence in the 1970s and 1980s.* Western Societies Program. Ithaca, N.Y.: Cornell University.

Kellerman, Kathy

1991 "The Conversation MOP: II: Progression through Scenes in Discourse." *Human Communication Research* 17 (3): 385–414.

Kennan, George

1990 "Witness" *New York Review of Books,* March 1.

Kielbowicz, Richard B., and Clifford Scherer

1986 "The Role of the Press in the Dynamics of Social Movements." *Research in Social Movements, Conflicts and Change.* Vol. 9, Greenwich, Conn.: JAI Press, pp. 71–96.

Kiewiet, D. Roderick

1983 *Macropolitics and Micropolitics: The Electoral Effects of Economic Issues.* Chicago: University of Chicago Press.

Kinder, Donald, and D. Roderick Kiewiet

1981 "Sociotropic Politics: The American Case." *British Journal of Political Science* 11: 129–61.

King, Martin Luther, Jr.

1963 *Why We Can't Wait.* New York: Harper and Row.

Kingdon, John

1984 *Agendas, Alternatives, and Public Policies.* Boston: Little Brown.

Kinzer, Donald L.

1964 *An Episode in Anti-Catholicism: The American Protective Association.* Seattle: University of Washington Press.

Kitschelt, Herbert P.

1985 "New Social Movements in West Germany and the United States." *Political Power and Social Theory* 5: 273–324.

1986 "Political Opportunity Structures and Political Protest: Anti-Nuclear Movements in Four Democracies." *British Journal of Political Science* 16: 57–85.

1988 "Left-Libertarian Parties: Explaining Innovation in Competitive Party Systems." *World Politics* 40 (2): 194–234.

Klandermans, Bert

1984 "Mobilization and Participation: Social Psychological Expansions of Resource Mobilization Theory." *American Sociological Review* 49: 583–600.

1988 "The Formation and Mobilization of Consensus." Pp. 173–97 in Bert Klandermans; Hanspeter Kriesi; and Sidney Tarrow (eds.), *International Social Movement Research*, Vol. 1, *From Structure to Action: Comparing Movement Participation across Cultures*. Greenwich, Conn.: JAI Press.

1990 "Linking the 'Old' and 'New': Movement Networks in the Netherlands." Pp. 122–36 in Russell J. Dalton and Manfred Kuechler (eds.), *Challenging the Political Order: New Social and Political Movements in Western Democracies*. New York: Oxford University Press.

1993 "A Theoretical Framework for Comparisons of Social Movement Participation." *Sociological Forum* 8: 383–402.

Klandermans, Bert; Hanspeter Kriesi; and Sidney Tarrow

1988 *From Structure to Action: Comparing Movement Participation across Cultures*. Greenwich, Conn.: JAI Press.

Klandermans, Bert, and Dirk Oegema

1987 "Potentials, Networks, Motivations and Barriers: Steps toward Participation in Social Movements." *American Sociological Review* 52: 519–31.

Klandermans, Bert, and Sidney Tarrow

1988 "Mobilization into Social Movements: Synthesizing European and American Approaches." *International Social Movement Research* 1: 1–38.

Kleidman, Robert

1993 *Organizing for Peace: Neutrality, the Test Ban and the Freeze*. Syracuse, N.Y.: Syracuse University Press.

Kleinert, Hubert

1991 "Die Grünen 1990/91. Vom Wahldebakel zum Neuanfang." *Aus Politik und Zeitgeschichte* B44/91: 27–37.

Kluger, Richard

1976 *Simple Justice*. New York: Knopf.

Koopmans, Ruud

1990a "Patterns of Unruliness: The Interactive Dynamics of Protest Waves." Unpublished manuscript. University of Amsterdam: PdIS.

1990b "Bridging the Gap: The Missing Link between Political Opportunity Structure and Movement Action." Paper presented at ISA World Congress, Madrid, July.

1992 "Democracy from Below: New Social Movements and the Political System in West Germany." Unpublished Ph.D. dissertation.

Koopmans, Ruud, and Jan Willem Duyvendak

1991 "Protest in een pacificatie-democratie De Nederlandse nieuwe sociale bewegingen in internationaal vergelijkend perspectief." *Mens en Maatschappij* 66 (3): 233–56.

Krenz, Egon

1990 *Wenn Mauern fallen*, Vienna: Paul Neff.

Kretschmer, Winfried

1988 "Modellfall Wackersdorf: Protest, Controlle und Eskalation." *Forschungsjournal Neue Soziale Bewegungen* 2: 23–33.

Kriesi, Hanspeter

1980 *Entscheidungsstrukturen und Entscheidungsprozesse in der Schweizer Politik*. Frankfurt am Main: Campus.

1988 "Local Mobilization for the People's Petition of the Dutch Peace Movement." Pp. 41–81 in Bert Klandermans, Hanspeter Kriesi, and Sidney Tarrow (eds.), *From Structure to Action: Comparing Social Movement Research Across Cultures.* Greenwich, Conn.: JAI Press.

1989a "New Social Movements and the New Class in the Netherlands." *American Journal of Sociology* 94 (5): 1078–1116.

1989b "The Political Opportunity Structure of the Dutch Peace Movement." *West European Politics* 12: 295–312.

1990 "Federalism and Pillarization: The Netherlands and Switzerland Compared." *Acta politica* 25 (4): 433–50.

1991 "The Political Opportunity Structure of New Social Movements: Its Impact on Their Mobilization." Paper presented at a conference on Social Movements: Framing Processes and Opportunity Structures" held at Wissenschaftszentrum Berlin, July 1991. FS III 91/103.

Kriesi, Hanspeter, and Marco G. Giugni
1990 "Nouveau Mouvements Sociaux dans les Années '80: Evolution et Perspectives." Pp. 79–100 in *Avenire d'État (Annuaire Suisse de Science Politique).* Bern and Stuttgart: Verlag Paul Haupt.

Kriesi, Hanspeter; Ruud Koopmans; Jan Willem Duyvendak; and Marco G. Giugni
1992 "New Social Movements and Political Opportunities in Western Europe." *European Journal of Political Research* 22: 219–44.
1995 *The Politics of New Social Movements in Western Europe. A Comparative Analysis.* Minneapolis and St. Paul: University of Minnesota Press.

Kriesi, Hanspeter; René Levy; Gilbert Ganguillet; and Heinz Zwicky
1981 *Politische Aktivierung in der Schweiz, 1945–78.* Grüsch: Rüegger.

Kuhn, Thomas
1977 *The Essential Tension: Selected Studies in Scientific Tradition and Change.* Chicago: University of Chicago Press.

Kursbuch
1968 *Der nicht arklärte Notstand 12.*

Kusin, Vladimir
1990 "The Elections Compared and Assessed." *Report on Eastern Europe* July 13: 38–46.

Laba, Roman
1991 *The Roots of Solidarity.* Princeton, N.J.: Princeton University Press.

L'Abate, Alberto
1990 "Storia tragi-comica di un processo per Comiso." *Linea d'ombra* 7: 71–76.

Laber, Jiri
1989 "Fighting Back in Prague." *New York Review of Books,* April 27.

Laraña, Enrique, Hank Johnston, and Joseph R. Gusfield (eds.)
1994 New Social Movements: From Ideology to Identity. Philadelphia: Temple University Press.

Larson, James
1984 *Television's Window on the World: International Affairs Coverage on the U.S. Networks.* New York: Ablex.

Layton, Azza Salama
1995 "The International Context of the U.S. Civil Rights Movement: The Dynamics between Racial Policies and International Politics, 1941–1960." Unpublished Ph.D. dissertation, University of Texas, Austin.

Lefebvre, Georges
1947 *The Coming of the French Revolution.* Princeton, N.J.: Princeton University Press.

Leikin, Steve
  1992 "The Practical Utopians: Cooperation and the American Labor Movement, 1860–1890." Unpublished Ph.D. dissertation. University of California, Berkeley.
Leonard, Frank
  1966 "'Helping' the Unemployed in the Nineteenth Century: The Case of the American Tramp." *Social Service Review* 40 (December): 429–34.
Levine, Susan
  1983 "Labor's True Women: Domesticity and Equal Rights in the Knights of Labor." *Journal of American History* 70: 323–33.
Lévi-Strauss, Claude
  1966 *The Savage Mind.* Chicago: University of Chicago Press.
Linebaugh, Peter, and Marcus Reidiker
  1990 "The Many-Headed Hydra: Sailors, Slaves, and the Atlantic Working Class in the Eighteenth Century." *Journal of Historical Sociology* 3: 225–52.
Lipset, Seymour M.
  1963 *Political Man.* Garden City, N.Y.: Doubleday Anchor.
Lipsky, Michael
  1968 "Protest as a Political Resource." *American Political Science Review* 62: 1144–58.
  1970 *Protest in City Politics.* Chicago: Rand McNally.
  1971 "Case Study of a Harlem Rent Strike." Pp. 326–35 in Gary T. Marx (ed.), *Racial Conflict.* Boston: Little, Brown.
Lofland, John
  1985 *Protest: Studies of Collective Behavior and Social Movements.* New Brunswick, N.J.: Transaction Books.
  1993 *Polite Protesters: The American Peace Movement of the 1980s.* Syracuse, N.Y.: Syracuse University Press.
Lorwin, Val R.
  1952 "France." Pp. 313–409 in Walter Galenson (ed.), *Comparative Labor Movements.* New York: Prentice-Hall.
Maier, Pauline
  1972 *From Resistance to Revolution: Colonial Radicals and the Development of American Opposition to Britain, 1765–1776.* New York: Knopf.
Malpricht, Günter
  1984 *Interaktionsprozesse bei Demonstranten. Interaktionsprozesse zwischen Teilnehmern an Massenaktionen mit Tendenz zu unfriedlichen Verlauf und der Polizei.* Heidelberg: Kriminalistak Verlag.
Margolis, Michael, and Gary A. Mauser (eds.)
  1989 *Manipulating Public Opinion: Essays on Public Opinion as a Dependent Variable.* Pacific Grove, Calif.: Brooks/Cole.
Marks, Gary
  1989 *Unions in Politics: Britain, Germany, and the United States in the Nineteenth and Early Twentieth Centuries.* Princeton, N.J.: Princeton University Press.
Marks, Gary, and Doug McAdam
  1993 "Social Movements and the Changing Structure of Political Opportunity in the European Community." Paper presented at the Annual Meeting of the American Political Science Association in Washington, D.C., September 1993.
Marullo, Sam; Ron Pagnucco; and Jackie Smith
  1996 "Frame Dynamics and Movement Contraction: U.S. Peace Movement Framing after the Cold War." *Sociological Inquiry* 66 (1).

Marwell, Gerald, and Pamela E. Oliver
   1988 "Social Networks and Collective Action: A Theory of the Critical Mass
   III." *American Journal of Sociology* 94: 502–34.
Marx, Gary T.
   1974 "Thoughts on a Neglected Category of Social Movement Participant: The
   Agent Provocateur and the Informant." *American Journal of Sociology* 80:
   402–42.
   1979 "External Efforts to Damage or Facilitate Social Movements: Some Patterns, Explanations, Outcomes, and Complications." Pp. 94–125 in Mayer N.
   Zald and John D. McCarthy (eds.), *The Dynamics of Social Movements.* Cambridge, Mass.: Winthrop.
Marx, Karl
   1963 *The Eighteenth Brumaire of Louis Bonaparte.* New York: International Publishers.
Mayer, Margit
   1991 "Social Movement Research and Social Movement Practice: The U.S. Pattern." Pp. 47–120 in Dieter Rucht (ed.), *Research on Social Movements: The
   State of the Art in Western Europe and the USA.* Frankfurt am Main: Campus
   Verlag; and Boulder, Colo.: Westview Press.
McAdam, Doug
   1982 *Political Process and the Development of Black Insurgency, 1930–1970.* Chicago: University of Chicago Press.
   1983a "The Decline of the Civil Rights Movement." Pp. 298–319 in Jo Freeman
   (ed.), *Social Movements of the Sixties and Seventies.* White Plains, N.Y.:
   Longman.
   1983b "Tactical Innovation and the Pace of Insurgency." *American Sociological
   Review* 48: 735–54.
   1986 "Recruitment to High-Risk Activism: The Case of Freedom Summer." *American Journal of Sociology* 92: 64–90.
   1988a *Freedom Summer.* New York: Oxford University Press.
   1988b "Micromobilization Contexts and Recruitment to Activism." *International
   Social Movement Research* 1: 125–54.
   1994 "Culture and Social Movements." In Joseph R. Gusfield, Hank Johnston,
   and Enrique Laraña (eds.), *Ideology and Identity in Contemporary Social Movements.* Philadelphia: Temple University Press.
   1995 "'Initiator' and 'Spinoff' Movements: Diffusion Processes in Protest
   Cycles." In Mark Traugott (ed.), *Repertoires and Cycles of Collective Action.*
   Durham, N.C.: Duke University Press.
McAdam, Doug; John D. McCarthy; and Mayer N. Zald
   1988 "Social Movements." Pp. 695–738 in Neil J. Smelser (ed.), *Handbook of Soci-
   ology.* Newbury Park, Calif.: Sage.
McAdam, Doug, and Ronnelle Paulsen
   1993 "Specifying the Relationship between Social Ties and Activism." *American
   Journal of Sociology* 98: 640–67.
McAdam, Doug, and Dieter Rucht
   1993 "The Cross-national Diffusion of Movement Ideas." *Annals of the American
   Academy of Political and Social Science* 528: 56–87.
McCarthy, John D.
   1987 "Pro-Life and Pro-Choice Mobilization: Infrastructure Deficits and New
   Technologies." Pp. 49–66 in Mayer N. Zald and John D. McCarthy (eds.), *So-
   cial Movements in an Organizational Society.* New Brunswick, N.J.: Transaction
   Books.

1994 "The Interaction of Grass-roots Activists and State Actors in the Production of an Anti-Drunk Driving Media Attention Cycle." In Joseph R. Gusfield, Hank Johnston, and Enrique Laraña (Eds.), *From Ideology to Identity in Contemporary Social Movements.* Philadelphia: Temple University Press.

McCarthy, John D.; David W. Britt; and Mark Wolfson
1991 "The Institutional Channeling of Social Movements in the Modern State." *Research in Social Movements: Conflict and Change* 13: 45–76.

McCarthy, John D.; Clark McPhail; and Jackie Smith
1994 "Images of Protest: Dimensions of Selection Bias in Media Coverage of Washington Demonstrations, 1982, 1991." Unpublished paper, Life Cycle Institute, Catholic University, Washington, D.C.

McCarthy, John D., Joseph J. Shields, and Melvin F. Hall
1994 "The American Catholic Bishops and the Empowerment of the Poor through Community Development." In John H. Stansfield, II (ed.), *The Nonprofit Sector and Social Justice.* Indianapolis: Indianapolis University Press.

McCarthy, John D., and Mark Wolfson
1988 "Understanding Rapid Social Movement Growth: The Role of Organizational Form, Consensus Support, and Elements of the American State." Paper presented at Social Movements Conference, Ann Arbor, Mich.
1992 "Consensus Movements, Conflict Movements and the Cooptation of Civic and State Infrastructures." Pp. 273–98 in Aldon D. Morris and Carol McClurg Mueller (eds.), *Frontiers in Social Movement Theory.* New Haven, Conn.: Yale University Press.

McCarthy, John D., and Mayer N. Zald
1973 *The Trend of Social Movements in America: Professionalization and Resource Mobilization.* Morristown, N.J.: General Learning Press.
1977 "Resource Mobilization and Social Movements: A Partial Theory." *American Journal of Sociology* 82 (6): 1212–41.
1987 "Appendix: The Trend of Social Movements in America: Professionalization and Resource Mobilization." Pp. 337–92 in Zald and McCarthy (eds.), *Social Movements in an Organizational Society.* New Brunswick, N.J.: Transaction Books.

McCombs, Maxwell E., and Donald L. Shaw
1972 "The Agenda Setting Function of the Mass Media." *Public Opinion Quarterly* 36: 176–87.

McGerr, Michael E.
1986 *The Decline of Popular Politics: The American North, 1865–1928.* New York: Oxford University Press.

McNeill, George E.
1887 *The Labor Movement: The Problem of Today.* Boston: A. M. Bridgman.

McPhail, Clark
1992 *The Myth of the Madding Crowd.* New York: Aldine de Gruyter.

Medici, Sandro
1979 *Vite di poliziotti.* Turin: Einaudi.

Melich, Anna (ed.)
1992 *Les valeurs des Suisses.* Berne: Lang.

Melucci, Alberto
1976 "L'azione ribelle. Formazione e struttura dei movimenti sociali." Pp. 3–68 in Alberto Melucci (ed.), *Movimenti di rivolta.* Milan: Etas.
1980 "The New Social Movements: A Theoretical Approach." *Social Science Information* 19: 199–226.

1985 "The Symbolic Challenge of Contemporary Movements." *Social Research* 52: 789–815.

1988 "Getting Involved: Identity and Mobilization in Social Movements." Pp. 329–48 in Bert Klandermans, Hanspeter Kriesi, and Sidney Tarrow (eds.), *From Structure to Action: Comparing Social Movement Research across Cultures.* Greenwich, Conn.: JAI Press.

1989 *Nomads of the Present.* Philadelphia: Temple University Press.

Meyer, David S.

1990 *A Winter of Discontent: The Nuclear Freeze and American Politics.* New York: Praeger.

1993a "Peace Protest and Policy: Explaining the Rise and Decline of Antinuclear Movements in Postwar America." *Policy Studies Journal* 21: 29–51.

1993b "Protest Cycles and Political Process: American Peace Movements in the Nuclear Age." *Political Research Quarterly* 47: 451–79.

Meyer, David S., and Sam Marullo

1992 "Grassroots Mobilization and International Change." *Research in Social Movements, Conflict, and Change* 14: 99–147.

Meyer, David S., and Suzanne Staggenborg

1994 "Movements, Countermovements, and the Structure of Political Opportunities." Unpublished paper.

Meyer, John W., and Brian Rowan

1977 "Institutionalized Organizations: Formal Structure as Myth and Ceremony." *American Journal of Sociology* 83 (2): 364–85.

Mihály, Andor

1991 *Rendszerváltás Dimbesdombon* Budapest: Vita.

Miller, Sally M.

1973 *Victor Berger and the Promise of Constructive Socialism, 1900–1920.* Westport, Conn.: Greenwood Press.

Miller, Warren E., and M. Kent Jennings

1986 *Parties in Transition: A Longitudinal Study of Party Elites and Party Supporters.* New York: Russell Sage Foundation.

Minkoff, Debra

1993 "Shaping Contemporary Organizational Action: Women's and Minority Social Change Strategies, 1955–85." Paper presented at the Annual Meetings of the American Sociological Association, Miami.

Mitchell, Robert C.

1981 "From Elite Quarrel to Mass Movement." *Transaction/Society* 18 (5): 76–84.

1985 "From Conservation to Environmental Movement: The Development of the Modern Environmental Lobbies." Discussion Paper QE 85-12. Resources for the Future, Washington, D.C.

Mitchell, Robert C.; Angela G. Mertig; and Riley E. Dunlap

1991 "Twenty Years of Environmental Mobilization: Trends among National Environmental Organizations." *Society and Natural Resources* 4 (3): 219–34.

Mitter, Armin, and Stefan Wolle

1990 *Ich Liebe euch doch alle!* Berlin: Basisdruck.

Monicelli, Mino

1978 *L'ultrasinistra in Italia. 1968–1978.* Bari: La Terza.

Monjardet, Dominique

1990 "La manifestation du coté du maintien de l'ordre." In Pierre Favre (ed.), *La Manifestation.* Paris: Presses de la Fondation Nationale des Sciences Politiques.

Monnet, Jean-Claude
1990 "Maintien de l'ordre ou création du désordre? La conclusion de l'enquête administrative sur la manifestation du 23 mars 1979." Pp. 229–44 in Pierre Favre (ed.), *La Manifestation*. Paris: Presses de la Fondation Nationale des Sciences Politiques.
Montgomery, David
1979 *Workers' Control in America*. Cambridge: Cambridge University Press.
Moore, Kelly
1993 "Doing Good While Doing Science: The Origins and Consequences of Public Interest Science Organizations in America, 1945–1990." Unpublished Ph.D. dissertation. Department of Sociology, University of Arizona.
Morris, Aldon
1981 "The Black Southern Sit-in Movement: An Analysis of Internal Organization." *American Sociological Review* 46: 744–67.
1984 *The Origins of the Civil Rights Movement: Black Communities Organizing for Change*. New York: Free Press.
Morris, Aldon D., and Carol McClurg Mueller (eds.)
1992 *Frontiers in Social Movement Theory*. New Haven, Conn.: Yale University Press.
Moss, Bernard H.
1976 *The Origins of the French Labor Movement: The Socialism of Skilled Workers, 1830–1914*. Berkeley: University of California Press.
Mueller, Carol McClurg (ed.)
1987 *The Politics of the Gender Gap: The Social Construction of Political Influence*. Beverly Hills, Calif.: Sage.
Murray, Charles
1984 *Losing Ground*. New York: Basic Books.
Naimark, Norman
1992 "Ich will hier raus: Emigration and the Collapse of the German Democratic Republic." In Ivo Banac (ed.), *Eastern Europe in Revolution*. Ithaca, N.Y.: Cornell University Press.
Neidhardt, Friedhelm
1989 "Gewalt und Gegengewalt. Steigt die Bereitschaft zu Gewaltaktionen mit zunehmender staatlicher Kontrolle und Repression." Pp. 233–43 in Wilhelm Heitmeyer, Kurt Möller, and Heinz Sünker (eds.), *Jugend-Staat-Gewalt*. Weinheim and Munich: Juventa.
1992a "Comments on Movement Mobilizing Structures." Conference on European/American Perspectives on Social Movements. Life Cycle Institute, Catholic University of America, Washington, D.C., August.
1992b "Social Movements: Framing Processes and Opportunity Structures – Some Questions and Perspectives for Further Research." Paper prepared for Conference on European/American Perspectives on Social Movements. Life Cycle Institute, Catholic University, Washington, D.C., August.
Nelkin, Dorothy, and Michael Pollak
1981 *The Atom Besieged: Extraparliamentary Dissent in France and Germany*. Cambridge, Mass.: MIT Press.
Nelson, Barbara J.
1984 *Making an Issue of Child Abuse: Political Agenda Setting for Social Problems*. Chicago: University of Chicago Press.
Neuman, W. Russell
1990 "The Threshold of Public Attention." *Public Opinion Quarterly* 54: 159–76.

New Jersey Bureau of Statistics of Labor and Industries
  1888 *Tenth Annual Report of the Bureau of Statistics of Labor and Industries for the Year Ending October 31, 1887.* Somerville: State of New Jersey.
  1901 *Twenty-third Annual Report of the Bureau of Statistics of Labor and Industries for the Year Ending October 31, 1900.* Camden: State of New Jersey.
Nolan, Joseph T.
  1985 "Political Surfing When Issues Break." *Harvard Business Review* 63 (January/February): 72–81.
Oberschall, Anthony
  1973 *Social Conflict and Social Movements,* Englewood Cliffs, N.J., Prentice-Hall.
  1978 "The Decline of the 1960s Social Movements." Pp. 257–90 in L. Kriesberg (ed.), *Research in Social Movements, Conflict and Change,* Vol. III. Greenwich, Conn.: JAI Press.
  1980 "Loosely Structured Collective Conflict: A Theory and an Application." In *Research in Social Movements, Conflict and Change* 3: 45–68.
  1989 "The 1960's Sit-Ins: Protest Diffusion and Movement Takeoff." *Research in Social Movements, Conflict and Change* 11: 31–53.
  1992 "Moral Force, Legitimacy and Mobilization in the East European Revolution of 1989." Paper presented at the Conference on European/American Perspectives on Social Movements. Life Cycle Institute, Catholic University, Washington, D.C., August.
  1993 *Social Movements.* New Brunswick, N.J.: Transaction Books.
Oegema, Dirk, and Bert Klandermans
  1994 "Non-conversion and Erosion: Two Unwanted Effects of Mobilization." *American Sociological Review* 59, 703–22.
Oestreicher, Richard
  1984 "Urban Working-Class Political Behavior and Theories of American Electoral Politics, 1870–1940." *Journal of American History,* no. 74: 1257–86.
  1986 *Solidarity and Fragmentation: Working People and Class Consciousness in Detroit, 1875–1900.* Urbana: University of Illinois Press.
  1987 "Terrence V. Powderly, the Knights of Labor, and Artisanal Republicanism." Pp. 30–61 in Melvyn Dubofsky and Warren Van Tine (eds.), *Labor Leaders in America.* Urbana: University of Illinois Press.
Offe, Claus, and Helmut Wiesenthal
  1985 "Two Logics of Collective Action." In John Keane (ed.), *Disorganized Capitalism.* Cambridge, Mass.: MIT Press.
Oliver, Pamela
  1989 "Bringing the Crowd Back In." *Research in Social Movements. Conflict and Change* 11: 1–30.
Olson, Mancur
  1965 *The Logic of Collective Action.* Cambridge, Mass.: Harvard University Press.
Onorato, Piervincenzo
  1982 "Processi di terrorismo e inquinamento della giurisdizione." In Magistratura democratica (ed.), *La magistratura di fronte al terrorismo e all'eversione di sinistra.* Milan: Franco Angeli.
Opp, Karl-Dieter
  1991 "DDR '89. zu den Ursachen einer Spontanen Revolution." *Kölner Zeitschrift für Soziologie und Sozialpsychologie:* 302–19.
Orren, Karen
  1991 *Belated Feudalism: Labor, the Law, and Liberal Development in the United States.* Cambridge: Cambridge University Press.

Ost, David
1990 *Solidarity and the Politics of Antipolitics.* Philadelphia: Temple University Press.
Page, Benjamin I., and Robert Y. Shapiro
1989 "Educating and Manipulating the Public." Pp. 294–320 in Michael Margolis and Gary A. Mauser (eds.), *Manipulating Public Opinion: Essays on Public Opinion as a Dependent Variable.* Pacific Grove, Calif.: Brooks/Cole.
Pagnucco, Ron
1992 "Tactical Choice by Groups Working for Peace in the Contemporary U.S.: The Ruly/Unruly Divide." Unpublished Ph.D. dissertation, Department of Sociology, Catholic University of America, Washington, D.C.
Pagnucco, Ron, and Jackie Smith
1993 "The Peace Movement and the Formulation of U.S. Foreign Policy." *Peace and Change* 18: 157–81.
Paley, Vivian Gussin
1984 *Boys and Girls: Superheroes in the Doll Corner.* Chicago: University of Chicago Press.
Pappi, Franz Urban
1989 Neue soziale Bewegungen und Wahlverhalten in der Bundesrepublik. Forschungsbericht des DFW-Projekts "Nachwahlstudie 1987. Sociale Bewegungen und Wahlverhalten." Institut für Soziologie der Christian-Albrechts-Universität zu Kiel.
Pasquino, Gianfranco
1990 "I soliti ignoti: Gli opposti estremismi nelle analisi dei presidenti del consiglio." Pp. 93–117 in Raimondo Catanzaro (ed.), *Ideologie, movimenti, terrorismi.* Bologna: Il Mulino.
Pateman, Carol
1989 *The Disorder of Women: Democracy, Feminism and Political Theory.* Stanford, Calif.: Stanford University Press.
Pehe, Jiri
1990 "Czechoslovakia." *Report on Eastern Europe* 1 (1), January 5.
Pekonen, Kyosti
1986 "Symbols and Political Cycles." A paper presented at the ECPR-Workshop Cycles of Politics, March 25–30, 1985. Barcelona: Jyvaskyla Publications.
Perlman, Selig
1918 "Upheaval and Reorganization (since 1876)." Pp. 195–387, vol. 2, in John R. Commons (ed.), *History of Labor in the United States.* New York: Macmillan.
1928 *A Theory of the Labor Movement.* New York: Macmillan.
Perrot, Michelle
1987 *Workers on Strike.* Leamington Spa: Berg.
Petty, Richard E., and John T. Cacioppo
1986 "The Elaboration Likelihood Model of Persuasion." *Advances in Experimental Social Psychology* 19: 124–205.
Piven, Frances Fox, and Richard A. Cloward
1979 *Poor People's Movements.* New York: Vintage.
1992 "Normalizing Collective Protest." Pp. 301–25 in Aldon D. Morris and Carol McClurg Mueller (eds.), *Frontiers in Social Movement Theory.* New Haven, Conn.: Yale University Press.
Popper, Samuel H.
1951 "Newark N.J., 1870–1910: Chapters in the Evolution of an American Metropolis." Unpublished Ph.D. dissertation. New York University, New York.

Powderly, Terence V.
  1968 In Harry J. Carman, Henry David, and Paul N. Gutherie (eds.), *The Path I Trod: The Autobiography of Terence V. Powderly.* New York: AMS Press.
Powell, Walter W., and Paul J. DiMaggio
  1991 *The New Institutionalism in Organizational Analysis.* Chicago: University of Chicago Press.
Praag, Philip van, Jr.
  1992 "De smalle marges van een brede beweging. Vredesprotest in Nederland." Pp. 99–120 in J. W. Duyvendak et al. (eds.), *Tussen verbeelding en macht, 25 jaar nieuwe sociale bewegingen in Nederland.* Amsterdam: SUA.
Price, David E.
  1984 *Bringing Back the Parties.* Washington, D.C.: Congressional Quarterly Press.
Prins, Gwyn (ed.)
  1990 *Spring in Winter: The 1989 Revolutions.* Manchester: Manchester University Press.
Przeworski, Adam
  1991 "The 'East' Becomes the 'South'? The 'Autumn of the People' and the Future of Eastern Europe." *PS: Political Science and Politics* 24: 20–24.
Putnam, Robert
  1992 *Making Democracy Work.* Cambridge: Cambridge University Press.
Quadagno, Jill
  1992 "Labor Unions and Racial Conflict in the War on Poverty." *American Sociological Review* 57: 616–34.
Raines, Howell
  1977 *My Soul Is Rested.* New York: Bantam.
Raschke, Joachim
  1991 *Krise der Grünen. Bilanz und Neubeginn.* Marburg: Schüren Presseverlag.
  1993 *Die Grünen. Wie sie sind, was sie wurden.* Cologne: Bund.
Reich, Jens
  1990 "Reflections on Becoming an East German Dissident." In Gwyn Prins (ed.), *Spring in Winter: The 1989 Revolutions.* Manchester; Manchester University Press.
Reid, Donald
  1985 *The Miners of Decazeville.* Cambridge, Mass.: Harvard University Press.
Rice, C. Duncan
  1982 "The Missionary Context of the British Anti-Slavery Movement." In James Walvin (ed.), *Slavery and British Society, 1776–1846.* Baton Rouge: Louisiana State University Press.
Risse-Kappen, Thomas
  1991 "Public Opinion, Domestic Structure, and Foreign Policy in Liberal Democracies." *World Politics* 43: 479–512.
Roach, John, and Jürgen Thomanek (eds.)
  1985 *Police and Public Order in Europe.* London: Croom Helm.
Rogers, Everett M., and James W. Dearing
  1988 "Agenda-Setting Research: Where Has It Been and Where Is It Going?" Pp. 555–94 in James A. Anderson (ed.), *Communications Yearbook.* Vol. 11.
Root, Hilton
  1987 *Peasants and King in Burgundy. Agrarian Foundations of French Absolutism.* Berkeley and Los Angeles: University of California Press.
Rosanvallon, Pierre
  1988 *La question syndicale.* Paris: Calmann-Lévy.

Rosenau, James
1990 *Turbulence in World Politics: A Theory of Change and Continuity.* Princeton, N.J.: Princeton University Press.
Rosenberg, Gerald N.
1991 *The Hollow Hope.* Chicago: University of Chicago Press.
Rosenthal, Naomi; Meryl Fingrutd; Michele Ethier; Roberta Karant; and David McDonald
1985 "Social Movements and Network Analysis: A Case Study of Nineteenth Century Women's Reform in New York State." *American Journal of Sociology* 90: 1022–55.
Ross, Steven J.
1985 *Workers on the Edge: Work, Leisure, and Politics in Industrializing Cincinnati, 1788–1890.* New York: Columbia University Press.
Roth, Roland
1991 "Herausforderung demokratischer Institutionen durch neue Formen politischer Mobilisierung. Zur Situation in der Bundesrepublik." *Schweiz Jahrbuch für Politische Wissenschaft* 31: 209–34.
Rothenberg, Lawrence S.
1991 "Agenda Setting at Common Cause." Pp. 131–50 in Allan J. Cigler and Burdett A. Loomis (eds.), *Interest Group Politics.* 3rd edition. Washington, D.C.: Congressional Quarterly Press.
Rucht, Dieter
1988 "Themes, Logics, and Arenas of Social Movements: A Structural Approach." Pp. 305–29 in Bert Klandermans, Hanspeter Kriesi, and Sidney Tarrow (eds.), *From Structure to Action: Comparing Movement Participation across Cultures. International Social Movement Research.* Vol. 1. Greenwich, Conn.: JAI Press.
1989a "Environmental Movement Organizations in West Germany and France: Structure and Interorganizational Relations." Pp. 61–94 in B. Klandermans (ed.), *Organizing for Change: Social Movement Organizations across Cultures. International Social Movement Research.* Vol. 2. Greenwich, Conn: JAI Press.
1989b "Vorschläge zur Konzeptualisierung von Kontextstrukturen sozialer Bewegungen." Paper presented at the conference "Vergleichende Analysen sozialer Bewegungen." October, Berlin.
1990 "Campaigns, Skirmishes, and Battles: Anti-Nuclear Movements in the USA, France, and West Germany." *Industrial Crisis Quarterly* 4: 193–222.
1992a "Parteien, Verbände und Bewegungen als Systeme politischer Interessenvermittlung." Discussion Paper FS III 91–107. Wissenschaftszentrum Berlin.
1992b "The Impact of National Contexts on Social Movement Structures: A Cross-Movement and Cross-National Comparison." Paper presented at the Conference on European/American Perspectives on the Dynamics of Social Movements. Life Cycle Institute, Catholic University, Washington, D.C., August.
1993 "New Social Movements in France and West Germany: Explaining Differences in Their Overall Strength and Dynamics." In Margit Mayer (ed.), *New Social Movements: European and American Interpretations.* London: Routledge (in press).
1994 *Modernisierung und neue soziale Bewegungen. Deutschland, Frankreich und USA im Vergleich.* Frankfurt am Main: Campus.
1995 "New Social Movements in France and West Germany: Explaining Differ-

ences in their Overall Strength and Dynamics." In Margit Mayer (ed.), *New Social Movements: European and American Interpretations*. London: Hutchinson.

Rudzio, Wolfgang
1987 *Das politische System der Bundesrepublik Deutschland*. 2nd revised edition. Leverkusen: UTB.

Ryan, Charlotte
1991 *Prime Time Activism*. Boston: South End Press.

Sack, Fritz
1984 "Die Reaktion von Gesellschaft, Politik und Staat auf die Studentedbewegung." Pp. 107–227 in Fritz Sack and Heinz Steiner (eds.), *Protest und Reaktion*. Opladen: Westdeutscher Verlag.

Sack, Fritz, and Heinz Steinert
1984 *Protest und Reaktion*. Opladen: Westdeutscher Verlag.

Sainteny, Guillaume
1991 *Les Verts*. Paris: Presses Universitaires de France.

Salvatore, Nick
1982 *Eugene V. Debs: Citizen and Socialist*. Urbana: University of Illinois Press.

Schama, Simon
1989 *Citizens: A Chronicle of the French Revolution*. New York: Knopf.

Scharpf, Fritz W.
1984 "Economic and Institutional Constraints of Full-Employment Strategies: Sweden, Austria, and West Germany." Pp. 257–90 in John H. Goldthorpe (ed.), *Order and Conflict in Contemporary Capitalism*. Oxford: Clarendon Press.

Scheinman, Lawrence
1965 *Atomic Energy Policy in France under the Fourth Republic*. Princeton, N.J.: Princeton University Press.

Schlesinger, Arthur
1986 *The Cycles of American History*. Boston: Houghton-Mifflin.

Schlozman, Kay Lehmann
1990 "Representing Women in Washington: Sisterhood and Pressure Politics." Pp. 339–82 in Louise A. Tilly and Patricia Gurin (eds.), *Women, Politics, and Change*. New York: Russell Sage Foundation.

Schmitter, Philippe C., and Wolfgang Streeck
1981 "The Organization of Business Interests. A Research Design to Study the Associative Action of Business in the Advanced Industrial Societies of Western Europe." Berlin: Wissenschaftszentrum IIM/LMP 81-13.

Schneider, Joseph W.
1985 "Social Problems Theory: The Constructionist View." *Annual Review of Sociology* 11: 209–29.

Schubart, Alexander (ed.)
1983 *Der Starke Staat. Dokumente zum Prozeß*. Hamburg: Buntbuch Verlag.

Schwantes, Carlos A.
1985 *Coxey's Army: An American Odyssey*. Lincoln: University of Nebraska Press.

Scott, Joan Wallach
1987 "On Language, Gender, and Working-Class History." *International Labor and Working-Class History* 21: 1–13.

Sereditch, John (ed.)
1991 *Your Resource Guide to Environmental Organizations*. Irvine, Calif.: Smiling Dolphins Press.

Sewell, William H.
1980 *Work and Revolution in France: The Language of Labor from the Old Regime to 1948.* Cambridge: Cambridge University Press.
1985 "Ideologies and Social Revolutions: Reflections on the French Case." *Journal of Modern History* 57 (1): 57–85.
1990 "Collective Violence and Collective Loyalties in France: Why the French Revolution Made a Difference." *Politics and Society* 18: 481–526.
1992 "A Theory of Structure: Duality, Agency, and Transformation." *American Journal of Sociology* 98: 1–29.
Shaiko, Ronald G.
"More Bang for the Buck: The New Era of Full Service Public Interest Groups." Pp. 81–109 in Allan J. Cigler and Burdett A. Loomis (eds.), *Interest Group Politics.* 3rd edition. Washington, D.C.: Congressional Quarterly Press.
Shorter, Edward, and Charles Tilly
1974 *Strikes in France 1830–1968.* Cambridge: Cambridge University Press.
Sievers, H. J.
1990 *Studenbuch Einer Deutschen Revolution,* Zollikon: GZW Verlag.
Silbey, Joel H.
1991 *The American Political Nation, 1838–1893.* Stanford, Calif.: Stanford University Press.
Skocpol, Theda
1979 *States and Social Revolution.* Cambridge: Cambridge University Press.
1985 "Cultural Ideology and Political Ideologies in the Revolutionary Reconstruction of State Power." *Journal of Modern History* 57 (1): 86–96.
1992 *Protecting Soldiers and Mothers: The Politics of Social Provision in the United States, 1870s–1920s.* Cambridge, Mass.: Harvard University Press.
Skocpol, Theda, and Kenneth Finegold
1982 "State Capacity and Economic Intervention in the New Deal." *Political Science Quarterly* 97: 255–78.
Skowronek, Stephen
1982 *Building a New American State: The Expansion of National Administrative Capacities, 1877–1920.* Cambridge: Cambridge University Press.
Small, Melvin
1987 "Influencing Decision Makers: The Vietnam Experience." *Journal of Peace Research* 24: 185–98.
Smelser, Neil J.
1963 *Theory of Collective Behavior.* New York: Free Press.
Smith, Christian
1991 *The Emergence of Liberation Theology.* Chicago: University of Chicago Press.
Smith, Jackie; Ron Pagnucco; and Winnie Romeril
1994 "Transnational Social Movement Organizations in the Global Political Arena." *Voluntas* 5: 121–54.
Snow, David A., and Robert D. Benford
1988 "Ideology, Frame Resonance, and Participant Mobilization." Pp. 197–217 in Bert Klandermans, Hanspeter Kriesi, and Sidney Tarrow (eds.), *From Structure to Action: Social Movement Participation Across Cultures.* Greenwich, Conn.: JAI Press.
1992 "Master Frames and Cycles of Protest." Pp. 133–55 in Aldon Morris and Carol M. Mueller (eds.), *Frontiers in Social Movement Theory.* New Haven, Conn.: Yale University Press.

Snow, David A.; E. Burke Rochford, Jr.; Steven K. Worden; and Robert D. Benford
1986 "Frame Alignment Processes, Micromobilization, and Movement Participation." *American Sociological Review* 51: 464–81.

Snow, David A.; Louis A. Zurcher, Jr.; and Sheldon Ekland-Olson
1980 "Social Networks and Social Movements: A Microstructural Approach to Differential Recruitment." *American Sociological Review* 45: 787–801.

Soldani, Simonetta
1973 "Contadini, operai e 'popolo' nella rivoluzione del 1848 in Italia." *Studi storici* 14: 557–613.

Solo, Pam
1988 *From Protest to Policy.* Cambridge, Mass.: Ballinger.

Sontheimer, Kurt
1989 *Grundzüge des politischen Systems der Bundesrepublik Deutschland.* 12th revised edition. Munich: Piper.

Spector, Malcolm, and John I. Kitsuse
1977 *Constructing Social Problems.* Menlo Park, Calif.: Cummings.

Staggenborg, Suzanne
1988 "The Consequences of Professionalism and Formalization in the Pro-Choice Movement." *American Sociological Review* 53 (4): 585–605.
1991 *The Pro-Choice Movement.* New York: Oxford University Press.

Starr, Kevin
1981 *Americans and the California Dream, 1850–1915.* Santa Barbara, Calif.: Peregrine Smith.

Stearns, Peter N.
1968 "Against the Strike Threat: Employer Policy toward Labor Agitation in France, 1900–1914." *Journal of Modern History* 40: 474–500.

Stimson, Grace Heilman
1955 *Rise of the Labor Movement in Los Angeles.* Berkeley and Los Angeles: University of California Press.

Stromquist, Sheldon
1990 "United States of America." Pp. 543–577 in Marcel Van Der Linden and Jurgen Rojahn (eds.), *The Formation of Labour Movements, 1870–1914: An International Perspective.* Vol. 2. Leiden, Netherlands: E. J. Brill.

Swidler, Ann
1986 "Culture in Action: Symbols and Strategies." *American Sociological Review* 51 (2): 273–86.

Szabo, Mate
1990 "Legitimationsprobleme des Institutionellen Wandels: der Fall Ungarn." *Sudosteuropa* 39 (3–4): 222–240.

Szasz, Andrew
1994 *Ecopopulism: Toxic Waste and the Movement for Environmental Justice.* Minneapolis: University of Minnesota Press.

Tarrow, Sidney
1983 *Struggling to Reform: Social Movements and Policy Change During Cycles of Protest.* Western Societies Program Occasional Paper No. 15. New York Center for International Studies, Cornell University, Ithaca, N.Y.
1988 "National Politics and Collective Action: Recent Theory and Research in Western Europe and the United States." *Annual Review of Sociology* 14: 421–40.
1989a *Democracy and Disorder: Protest and Politics in Italy, 1965–1975.* Oxford: Oxford University Press.
1989b "Struggle, Politics, and Reform: Collective Action, Social Movements, and

Cycles of Protest." Western Societies Program Occasional Paper No. 21. Cornell University, Ithaca, N.Y.

1991a "Comparing Social Movement Participation in Western Europe and the United States: Problems, Uses, and a Proposal for Synthesis." Pp. 392–420 in Dieter Rucht (ed.), *Research on Social Movements. The State of the Art in Western Europe and the USA.* Frankfurt on Main: Campus Verlag; and Boulder, Colo.: Westview.

1991b "Kollektives Handeln und Politische Gelegenheitsstruktur in Mobilisierungswellen: Theoretische Perspectiven." *Kölner Zeitschrift für Soziologie und Sozialpsychologie* 43: 647–70.

1991c "Struggle, Politics and Reform: Collective Action, Social Movements and Cycles of Protest." Cornell Studies in International Affairs. Western Societies Paper, No. 21.

1991d "Understanding Political Change in Eastern Europe." *PS: Political Science and Politics,* March: 12–20.

1992a "Mentalities, Political Cultures and Collective Action Frames: Constructing Meanings through Action." In Aldon Morris and Carole Mueller (eds.), *Frontiers of Social Movement Research.* New Haven, Conn.: Yale University Press.

1992b "Social Protest and Policy Reform: May 1968 and the *Loi d'Orientation.*" *Comparative Political Studies* 25: 579–607.

1993 "Modular Collective Action and the Rise of the Social Movement: Why the French Revolution Was Not Enough." *Politics and Society* 21: 69–90.

1994 *Power in Movement: Social Movements, Collective Action and Mass Politics in the Modern State.* Cambridge: Cambridge University Press.

Taylor, Verta
1989 "Social Movement Continuity: The Women's Movement in Abeyance." *American Sociological Review* 54 (5): 761–75.

Tilly, Charles
1978 *From Mobilization to Revolution.* Reading, Mass.: Addison-Wesley.

1984 "Social Movements and National Politics." Pp. 297–317 in Charles Bright and Susan Harding (eds.), *Statemaking and Social Movements.* Ann Arbor: University of Michigan Press.

1992 "War and the International System, 1900–1992." CSSC Working Paper No. 134.

1993a "Contentious Repertoires in Great Britain, 1758–1834." *Social Science History* 17: 253–80.

1993b *European Revolutions, 1492–1992.* Oxford: Blackwell's.

Tilly, Charles; Louise Tilly; and Richard Tilly
1975 *The Rebellious Century 1830–1930.* Cambridge, Mass.: Harvard University Press.

Tocqueville, Alexis de
1954 *Democracy in America.* Vol. 1. New York: Vintage.

1955 *The Old Regime and the French Revolution.* Trans. Gilbert. Garden City, N.Y.: Doubleday Anchor.

Touraine, Alain
1969 *La société postindustrielle.* Paris: Denoel.

1981 *The Voice and the Eye: An Analysis of Social Movements.* Cambridge: Cambridge University Press.

Troyer, Ronald J., and Gerald E. Markle
1983 *Cigarettes.* New Brunswick, N.J.: Rutgers University Press.

Tsebelis, George, and John Sprague
   1989 "Coercion and Revolution: Variations on a Predator-Prey Model." *Mathematical Computer Modelling* 12: 547–59.
Tuma, Nancy
   1980 "Invoking Rate." Menlo Park, Calif.: SRI International.
Tuma, Nancy, and Michael T. Hannan
   1984 *Social Dynamics: Models and Methods.* Orlando, Fla.: Academic Press.
Turner, Ralph
   1969 "The Public Perception of Protest." *American Sociological Review* 34: 815–31.
Turner, Ralph, and Lewis Killian
   1957 *Collective Behavior.* 3rd edition. Englewood Cliffs, N.J.: Prentice-Hall.
Ulman, Lloyd
   1955 *The Rise of the National Trade Union.* Cambridge, Mass.: Harvard University Press.
U.S. Senate
   1885 *Testimony Taken by the Committee upon the Relations between Labor and Capital.* Vol. 1. Washington, D.C.: GPO.
Urban, Jan
   1990 "Czechoslovakia: The Power and Politics of Humiliation." In Gwyn Prins (ed.), *Spring in Winter: The 1989 Revolutions.* Manchester: Manchester University Press.
Useem, Bert, and Mayer N. Zald
   1982 "From Pressure Group to Social Movement: Efforts to Promote Use of Nuclear Power." *Social Problems* 30: 144–56.
Vallely, Richard
   1993a "Party, Coercion and Inclusion: The Two Reconstructions of the South's Electoral Politics." *Politics and Society* 21: 37–68.
   1993b "The Puzzle of Disenfranchisement. Party Struggle and African-American Suffrage in the South, 1867–1894." Presented to the Workshop on Race, Ethnicity, Representation and Governance, Harvard University, January.
Van der Veen, Gerrita
   1992 *Principes in praktijk.* Kampen: Kok.
Van Dijk, Teun A.
   1988a *News Analysis: Case Studies of International and National News in the Press.* Hillsdale, N.J.: Lawrence Erlbaum.
   1988b *News as Discourse.* Hillsdale, N.J.: Lawrence Erlbaum.
Van Voorden, W. Het
   1992 Arbeidsvoorwaardenbeleid onder invloed van de volumebeheersingsmaatregelen zw/wao. *Sociaal Maandblad Arbeid* 47: 6–11.
Van Zoonen, Elisabeth A.
   1992 "The Women's Movement and the Media: Constructing a Public Identity." *European Journal of Communication* 7: 453–76.
Vie Nuove
   1969 Numero speciale 14.
Visser, Jelle
   1987 "In Search of Inclusive Unionism. A Comparative Analysis." Unpublished Ph.D. dissertation. University of Amsterdam.
Voss, Kim
   1988 "Labor Organization and Class Alliance: Industries, Communities, and the Knights of Labor." *Theory and Society* 17: 329–64.
   1992 "Disposition Is Not Action: The Rise and Demise of the Knights of Labor." *Studies in American Political Development* 6: 272–321.

1993 *The Making of American Exceptionalism: The Knights of Labor and Class Formation in the Nineteenth Century.* Ithaca, N.Y.: Cornell University Press.
Walker, Jack L., Jr.
1991 *Mobilizing Interest Groups in America: Patrons, Professions and Social Movements.* Ann Arbor: University of Michigan Press.
1977 "Setting the Agenda in the U.S. Senate." *British Journal of Political Science* 7: 423–45.
Wang Fu-chang
1989 "The Unexpected Resurgence: Ethnic Assimilation and Competition in Taiwan." Unpublished Ph.D. dissertation. Sociology Department, University of Arizona.
Ware, Norman J.
1929 *The Labor Movement in the United States 1860–1895: A Study in Democracy.* New York: D. Appleton.
Washington State Federation of Labor (WaSFL)
1913 *Proceedings of the Annual Convention.*
Watters, Pat
1971 *Down to Now: Reflections on the Southern Civil Rights Movement.* New York: Pantheon Books.
Weber, Max
1958 *From Max Weber: Essays in Sociology.* New York: Oxford University Press.
Weiss, Robert
1990 *Chronik Eines Zusammenbruchs.* Berlin: Dietz.
Wellman, Barry, and S. D. Berkowitz
1988 *Social Structures: A Network Approach.* Cambridge: Cambridge University Press.
Weschler, Lawrence
1982 *Solidarity: Poland in the Season of Its Passion.* New York: Simon and Schuster.
1989 "Reporter at Large." *New Yorker,* November 11.
Wilson, John
1976 "Social Protest and Social Control." *Social Problems* 24: 469–81.
Wimmer, M., et al.
1990 *Wir Sind Das Volk. Die DDR im Aufbruch.* Munich: Wilhelm Heyne Verlag.
Wisconsin State Federation of Labor (WiSFL)
1896–97 *Official Directory.*
1905–15 *Proceedings of the Annual Convention.*
Woliver, Laura R.
1993 *From Outrage to Action: The Politics of Grass-Roots Dissent.* Urbana: University of Illinois.
Wright, Carroll D.
1887 "Historical Sketch of the Knights of Labor." *Quarterly Journal of Economics* 1: 137–68.
Zald, Mayer N., and Roberta Ash
1966 "Social Movement Organizations: Growth, Decay and Change." *Social Forces* 44: 327–41.
Zald, Mayer, and John McCarthy
1980 "Social Movement Industries: Competition and Cooperation among Movement Organizations." Pp. 1–20 in Louis Kriesberg (ed.), *Research in Social Movements: Conflicts and Change.* Vol. 3.
1987a "Social Movement Industries: Competition and Conflict among SMOs." Pp. 161–180 in Mayer N. Zald and John D. McCarthy (eds.), *Social Move-*

ments in an Organizational Society, New Brunswick, N.J.: Transaction Books.

1987b *Social Movements in an Organizational Society.* New Brunswick N.J.: Transaction Books.

Zald, Mayer N., and Bert Useem

1987 "Movement and Countermovement Interaction: Mobilization, Tactics, and State Involvement." In Mayer N. Zald and John D. McCarthy (eds.), *Social Movements in an Organizational Society: Collected Essays.* New Brunswick, N.J.: Transaction Books.

Zaller, John R.

1992 *The Nature and Organization of Mass Opinion.* Cambridge: Cambridge University Press.

Zeitlin, Jonathan

1987 "From Labor History to the History of Industrial Relations." *Economic History Review* 40, no. 2, 2nd series: 159–84.

Ziolkowski, Janusz

1990 "The Roots, Branches and Blossoms of Solidarnosc." In Gwyn Prins (ed.), *Spring in Winter: The 1989 Revolutions.* Manchester: Manchester University Press.

Zucker, Lynne G.

1987 "Institutional Theories of Organization." *Annual Review of Sociology* 13: 443–64.

Zwerman, Gilda

1987 "Domestic Counterterrorism: United States Government Responses to Political Violence and Terrorism." *Social Justice* 16: 31–63.

Index